1980

Basic
Philosophical
Analysis

Charles L. Reid

YOUNGSTOWN STATE UNIVERSITY

DICKENSON PUBLISHING COMPANY, INC.

Encino, California, and Belmont, California

To Frances, Jeff And Sylvia

Library of Congress Catalog
Card Number: 70–140173
Printed in the United States
of America
1 2 3 4 5 6 7 8 9 10—73 72 71

Contents

Preface   vii

Part One
Tools and Methods of Analysis

1 **Philosophy**   2
   General Assumptions and General Conclusions   2
   Speculative Philosophy as General Conclusions   4
   Analytic Philosophy: Clarification of Assumptions and
   Concepts   8
   Motives for Philosophical Analysis   11
   Analytic Philosophy Examines Ideas, Not Things   14
   Language As an Instrument   18
   The Nature and Types of Philosophical Analysis   24
   Suggestions for Further Reading   29

2 **Meaning and Truth**   31
   Descriptive Meaning   32
   Traditional Theories of Truth: Correspondence,
   Coherence, and Pragmatic   36
   "True for Me and False for You"   40
   Connotation, Denotation, and Definition   43
   Meaning and Use: Nondescriptive or Noncognitive
   Uses of Language   48
   Meaning as Use and Traditional Theories of
   Truth: Redundancy Theory   53
   Suggestions for Further Reading   55

3 **Logic**   58
   Inference: Deductive and Inductive   59

The Logic of Terms: The Traditional Calculus of
Classes 66
The Logic of Sentences: The Sentential Calculus 79
The Functional Calculus 91
Informal Fallacies 91
Suggestions for Further Reading 95

4 Explanation 97
Understanding: Psychological and Logical Factors 98
Description, Discovery, and Demonstration 100
Theories, Laws, Hypotheses, and Facts: Some
Problems of Usage 102
The Covering-law Account of Explanation 105
Historical Explanation and Explanation in the Social
Sciences 109
Philosophical Explanation 113
Suggestions For Further Reading 115

**Part Two
Readings**

5 The Nature of Philosophy 118
Bertrand Russell: Speculative Philosophy Paves the
Way for Science 120
Moritz Schlick: Critical Philosophy Paves the Way
for Science 125
John Wilson: Philosophy As Insight Into the Games
of Life 140

6 Freedom, Determinism, and Responsibility 150
Paul H. D. Holbach: Free Will Is an Illusion 152
Moritz Schlick: Soft Determinism 163
Charles Arthur Campbell: Errors of Soft Deter-
minism 174
R. S. Peters: Causes, Reasons, and Human Actions 197

7   Causality and the "Problem of Induction"   **214**
David Hume: Cause Is Expected Sequence   216
A. C. Ewing: Causes Are Reasons   219
Bertrand Russell: The Risks of Induction   229
Paul Edwards: Russell's Needless Doubts About
Induction   236

---

8   Religious Language and the Existence of God   **253**
Paul Tillich: The Religious Attitude in an Age of
Science   255
Huston Smith: The Religious Significance of Drugs   263
F. C. Copleston and Bertrand Russell: The Existence
of God—A Debate   278
Richard Taylor: God Has Left Proof of Himself   299
Antony Flew: God's Existence Not an Empirically
Meaningful Question   307
John Hick: Talk About God Is Empirically
Meaningful   311

---

9   The Nature of Ethical Judgments and Concepts   **331**
Plato: The Acid Test of Morality   333
Lucius Garvin: Why Egoism Is an Untenable Theory   336
W. T. Stace: Cultural Relativism: Pros and Cons   353
G. E. Moore: "Good" Indefinable but Meaningful   367
Charles L. Stevenson: Ethical Disagreements Con-
cern Attitudes More Than Facts   378
Richard M. Hare: "Good" Commends and Informs   386

---

10 Political Philosophy   **405**
Thomas Hobbes: Civil Society Based on Self-
Interest   407
John Locke: Property and Government   422
Friedrich Engels: Theory of Socialism   434
Sidney Hook: Civil Disobedience and Protest   453
B. F. Skinner: Utopia Reaffirmed   464

Index   482

Preface

This book offers two things to the beginner in philosophy: selected writings by professional philosophers who advocate the views they present and are not mere reporters of others' ideas, and most of the analytic tools with which to evaluate these writings and come to one's own conclusions about them. All too few textbooks do this within the covers of one volume. Instructors should find this a flexible instrument for teaching; some will want to stress the analytic tools more, others less, but the materials are there for the student to refer to as need and interest dictate.

I wish to thank Professors Edmund Abegg and Hubert Morrow for comments on the earlier drafts of the introductory chapters and Profesors Romane Clark and Edward Schuh for very valuable help on later drafts. To those readers for Dickenson Publishing Company who remain anonymous, I owe a special debt for detailed, frank, and nearly always constructive criticism of the manuscript, and to Mr. Richard Trudgen, Editor-in-Chief, for his enthusiastic and helpful encouragement. Elaine Linden and Wanda Conger, of Dickenson Publishing Company, did a superb job of editing. Needless to say, these people are not to blame for any errors. To my wife, Frances, my daughter, Sylvia, and Mrs. Lois Holcomb I am indebted for substantial secretarial assistance. Youngstown State University contributed reduction in teaching load during the Winter Quarter, 1969, and help in reproducing the material in the readings.

C.L.R.

Part One

Tools and Methods of Analysis

1

Philosophy

A college or university student who opens his first textbook in calculus or organic chemistry already has some idea of what they are about. After all, it is not his first acquaintance with mathematics or science. But when he signs up for a course in some branch of philosophy, chances are that he will soon feel a lack of familiarity with the field. A general, dictionary definition of philosophy will not help such a beginner to find his way around in a particular area of the field, for no single description can do justice to all the different ways in which recognized philosophers have gone about their business. Any definition that reduces all the traditional goals of philosophical inquiry to a single formula will be either neutral and uninformative or one-sided and misleading.

General Assumptions
and General Conclusions

Since philosophy is what philosophers with very different aims have done, it is no one thing. "Philosophy" is an ambiguous word.

It might mean either examining the general assumptions with which you *approach* things, or the activity of drawing extremely general conclusions *from* a study of things. The two are not easily distinguished, for today's conclusions become tomorrow's assumptions, and today's assumptions, tomorrow's conclusions. The lack of finality in philosophy is often lamented, but such uncertainty is, after all, a feature of all areas of inquiry. No conclusion in science is sacrosanct; every scientist stands ready to revise or scrap any conclusion if sufficient facts are presented against it, facts that any competent observer can check for himself. However, after a decent amount of evidence has been found in favor of his hypotheses, he and his colleagues do treat them as conclusions until respectable counterevidence is found, and nonscientists often mistake this policy for certainty and finality.

You can see the interaction of assumptions and conclusions if you imagine that you have decided to write your autobiography. You have done this for a more or less scientific purpose: to find out what kind of person you are now, and why. Presumably you will not want to bore, confuse, or embarrass any reader with every detail of your life, so your first task is to decide: What am I about to do? Just what is my autobiography? Which events deserve a place in it? Perhaps some apparently trivial ones were very important to you—like the morning when, as you were brushing your teeth, you looked in the mirror and decided that you were an ugly duckling. You decide to include this, but to omit descriptions of brushing your teeth on other mornings. You have thus made use of an assumption: that only important events should be included in your life story. But deciding which events are important and which are not involves still another assumption. Suppose that you then decide to define "important event" as one that influences all subsequent events. (In the case of death and many other *expected* events, the expectation will influence events that occur beforehand.) That may be nothing more than a truism, but it is a concept that guides your efforts. Presumably you will have to make another decision from time to time: To what extent can you trust your own memory of what has happened, and how much must you depend on the memories of other people? This brings you to the problem area where facts end and interpretation of facts begins.

As you progress, you will stop occasionally and read what you have written. Perhaps you will be surprised and say, "What a prig I was then!" or, "I'm not really as introverted as I thought I was." Are these reflections conclusions about yourself? They are tentative ones, at least. The important point is that they will probably enter into the way you go about writing the rest of your life history. You may tend to select or omit facts that bear out or that disprove these self-estimates. You may even go back and rewrite some pages because of them. And when you have finished your history, although you may or may not have arrived at some clearer image of yourself, one thing is almost certain: That image will be different from the self-image you held when you started, and so, also, will be your ideas about autobiographies, human beings in general, and many other things. These conclusions in turn will become a part of your approach to yourself and other people in the future.

It is an analogy at least partly valid to say that mankind, too, both makes and interprets his own history. Much of that history is the story of his changing ideas, beliefs about things, and attitudes toward them. His conclusions in one realm often become starting points for his approach to other matters. The theory of evolution was arrived at in biology, but it furnished sometimes revolutionary assumptions for fields far removed: religion, psychology, politics, and economics. Many people think that application of the theory of evolution to several of these fields was misguided. To say that is to make a judgment that is decidedly philosophical, for it is a judgment *about* these fields and not *in* them.

Speculative Philosophy as General Conclusions

Contemporary British and American philosophers often say that philosophical questions are always *about*, but never *in*, any other discipline. Scientific questions, on the other hand, are *in* science and *about* the world, but not *about* another field of human inquiry. These distinctions solve at a stroke the problem of whether philosophy has any subject matter all its own, for a discipline that is about all other disciplines must be distinct from them. But as we have seen from a brief consideration of the interrelations of assumptions and conclusions, the relations between problems in one field of specialized inquiry and between separate fields of inquiry are very complex. It is difficult to get a clear idea of just how philosophy is always *about*, but never *in*, other disciplines, most of which are in turn *about* the world.

This is especially true in regard to what C. D. Broad has called "speculative philosophy" as distinguished from "critical" or "analytic philosophy." The chief preoccupation of this book is with critical philosophy. But, since the popular conception of philosophy is the traditional one—that philosophy is speculation about life and the universe—it will be necessary to clear the ground by showing that science has removed from the realm of legitimate speculation more and more questions about life and the universe, and that it has, accordingly, become more and more important for philosophy to help people to assimilate these findings of science into a balanced world-perspective.

In Broad's description, speculative philosophy is roughly equivalent to speculative metaphysics, the study of the nature of reality. As Broad describes the work of the speculative philosopher, it consists of taking over the results of the sciences, adding the insights of ethics and religion, and drawing general conclusions about the nature and prospects of man in the universe. We can see that this task consists of drawing the most general conclusions possible, not of examining general assumptions. We might say, rather simplistically, that as thus described speculative philosophy uses the general conclusions of all other disciplines as subtotals from which it arrives at a grand total, what all human knowledge adds up to, or that it takes the scientific and other pictures of separate aspects of the universe and arranges them in a montage, giving us the "big picture." It appears then that the question, What is the nature of all reality? is not *in* any other specific discipline but *in all* of them, in some interdisciplinary way, and that it is not so much *about* other disciplines as it is *about* the world, that is, all real things. There are awesome obstacles to such a program. It involves some very unclear and questionable assumptions, the main one of which is the concept of "reality as a whole."

In the West, philosophy began as speculative (nonexperimental) physics, with the question first, What stuff is everything made of? and later, How does the stuff of which everything is made come to take on so many different forms? Recall that in the ancient world there were no lines of specialization between different sciences and subject matters. A person could ask questions about the whole of things without having to take into consideration today's glut of information about all the special aspects of the whole.

In the Renaissance, physics separated from speculative philosophy by employing mathematics to state its problems and conclusions and by finding ways to test its hypotheses by experiment and observation. One by one, chemistry, biology, and other specialized sciences declared their independence in similar ways: "mental philosophy" (speculative psychology) began to give way to experimental psychology in the late nineteenth century. Like the social sciences, it is still refining its methods.

Today, looking through the catalogue of courses in a large university, one might well ask whether there is any significant aspect of the universe that is not now being investigated by some special science, and what part of reality then is left for philosophy to study. Speculative philosophers have some very prompt and outspoken replies, such as "universals," "being," and other things that have occupied philosophers for centuries. But as Broad described it, speculative philosophy actually tries to study the whole of reality, to put together some complete picture of which the sciences, religion, and ethics can give us only parts. Plausible and important as this kind of work may at first seem, it is difficult if not impossible to spell out any sense in which philosophy does study the whole of reality. If anyone were literally to try to take over the results of all the sciences, religion, and ethics, and from them to construct an interpretation of all reality, it would be a very ambitious undertaking. Could any physicist put into one formula or even a long essay a summary of all that physics has learned about the universe? But, for speculative philosophy, this task or something like it would have to be accomplished for each of the sciences and then a summary made of all these summaries. And, as to the insights of ethics and religion and their role in the interpretation of all reality, we must ask, *Which* insights of which ethics and of which religions? Some standards for choosing these insights rather than others would have to be invoked, and the justification of those standards would be a long and arduous preliminary to speculative philosophy proper.

The different sciences that have developed since philosophers first asked about the whole universe tell us about many similarities and many differences between things. If we try to describe all real things with one formula we are trying to reduce a gigantic collection, comprising myriads of different kinds of things, to one. Granted that this is often possible on a surprisingly sweeping scale: Physics has always been impressive in the generality of its laws, covering everything from galaxies to particles. But the speculative question, What do all real things have in common by virtue of which they are called real? calls for something far more vast. There is, in fact, no reason why all real things should have anything in common, except the assumption that everything called by the same name has some common feature or features. This assumption works well in most instances, but not in all. All colts have something in common: They are young and they are horses. But what do all works of art have in common? All good things? All true statements? If you stubbornly insist that all real things *must* have something in common, you have gone at it backwards: First find that common trait, then talk about it.

There remains one telling reply that the speculative philosopher can make to critics of his preoccupation with the whole of things, or with wholes rather than parts. From the beginning of this chapter there has been constant reference to the interaction of assumptions and conclusions. A philosopher of speculative bent can argue that the frame of reference in which anyone makes an assumption or draws a conclusion is a complex of interrelated parts. He can point out, with some justification, that the twentieth-century philosopher's attempt to deal with specific, isolated issues "critically" or "analytically" itself uncritically assumes many things or simply tries to ignore relevant issues. The thrust of this criticism is simply that in the world of thinking the whole body of our thoughts has more influence on each part than the part has on the whole. The implication of this is that everyone *does* have a speculative philosophy, an overall view of the world, a *Weltanschauung*, whether he knows it or not.

As sound as this reply is, it still does little to show how any clear sense can be given to the expression "the whole of reality" so that it refers to something that is more than a collection of miscellaneous things. The speculative philosopher does not, by saying "You're another," give his critics any standards for what would constitute a better overall view of the world than a worse one.

But if all these objections to speculative philosophy seem strained or directed at straw men, it might be argued that speculative philosophy can be carried on as a more modest venture: not as an attempt to draw conclusions about the whole of reality, but as an effort to go beyond present knowledge in more limited realms. Bertrand Russell points out that many of the guesses of earlier philosophers have been proven correct. For instance, the theory that the earth goes around the sun and the atomic theory of matter were propounded centuries before experimental instruments and procedures were developed for testing them. If speculation means seeing beyond what is presently visible, all sorts of theorists in and out of science have engaged in it. So the defense of speculation might continue.

This can be granted without admitting that speculation as such is likely to be a fruitful source of true theories. It does not matter whether an experimenter gets his hypotheses from an opium pipe, random words fed into a computer, or a blow on the head: If the theory proves out well in a test, it is a good one; if it does not, it is not. So any source of hypotheses, including pure speculation, is valid, and no artificial curb should be put on creativity. But this does not mean that all other sources of hypotheses will be as fruitful as careful examination of the puzzling phenomenon that one is trying to explain. In this respect also the increase in specialization has made speculative philosophy much more difficult. Unless the speculative philosopher first makes a fairly comprehensive study of science he may find himself "discovering" all sorts of things that have already been discovered. Scientists themselves find it difficult to avoid duplicating achievements of previous researchers, simply because there have been so many successful researches that it is hard to keep up with all of them. So far as the larger problems of science are concerned, anyone who could develop a meaningful, much less true, hypothesis on one of those issues would probably be more scientist than philosopher, in fact if not name.

Analytic Philosophy: Clarification of Assumptions and Concepts

It is sometimes said that philosophy seeks the limits of human knowledge. Roughly, man's knowledge is limited at one end *by* the assumptions and data with which his inquiries begin, and at the other end *to* the general conclusions in which his investigations result. We have seen how some philosophers try to expand the boundaries of present knowledge, filling in the very considerable gaps with speculation and arriving at the most general conclusions possible. In the same context C. D. Broad described another kind of activity, which he called "critical philosophy." Since he made the distinction in 1923, English-speaking philosophers have largely replaced the label "critical" with the name "analytic." As Broad described it, this kind of philosophizing is concerned with the opposite limit of science, religion, and ethics: If speculative philosophy *synthesizes the conclusions* of science, religion, and ethics, critical philosophy *analyzes the assumptions* of these fields. Analytic philosophy seeks to extend the limits of human knowledge by making its assumptions clearer. In looking at this kind of philosophical activity we can see plainly that it has a subject matter all its own and in no way competes with science, that the questions with which critical philosophy deals are not *in* other fields but *about* them.

According to Broad, "critical [analytic] philosophy" is the clear statement and searching examination of the concepts and assumptions that are basic to science, religion, and ethics. He cited only a few of these, but we can flesh out his account with a list of those concepts and beliefs that philosophers have debated about for centuries: cause and effect, right and wrong, appearance and reality, true and false, valid and invalid, mind and matter, political justice, God, law, history, art, the state, immortality, time and space, and others. Among basic assumptions that philosophers of all kinds have puzzled over are "Every event has a cause," "Like cause, like effect," "God exists," "Man is a free moral agent," "The soul is immortal," "Life (or history) has a meaning," and "Art for art's sake." Speculative philosophers have discussed these, too, but more for the purpose of using conclusions about them in a system of philosophy than for describing how they function for specialists or in common sense.

According to Broad, science and common sense *use* such concepts as cause and effect and *assume* such beliefs as "Every event has a cause." To say that all inquiry rests on assumptions is not to say that all inquiry is carelessly conducted or fails to arrive at genuine knowledge. It is just to say that we must mark off the starting point of an inquiry more or less arbitrarily and say "With this, science begins." No inquiry can begin without several assumptions. If you ask, Can anything be known at all? this question presupposes that words like "know" and "knowledge" are intelligible—to you, if to no one else. Further, you are presupposing that there is a difference between knowing and not knowing. Thus your question presupposes some concept of knowledge. You arrived at your concept somehow. The analytic philosopher is interested in learning how one concept is better than another, and how one belief is better than another—as conceptual tools *for specific purposes*.

Finding the causes of an earthquake is the job of a geologist. He assumes that all earthquakes have causes. But it is not part of science to determine just what in general a cause is, or how well founded is the assumption that all earthquakes have causes on the basis that all events have causes.

The Moona Moomoo earthquake was caused by volcanic shock

is a conclusion in science, but

The cause (or effect) of a phenomenon is a set of conditions invariably connected with it in time and space

is a (fairly inexact) conclusion in philosophy of science and an assumption of science. As Broad pointed out, no amount of experimenting will enable a scientist to arrive at a definition of cause and effect. Rather, his practice will be guided by the definition of cause and effect that he takes to his experiments. Unless he knows what he means by his words, he will not be able to decide whether the hypotheses in which these words occur are true or false. Experiment and observation will be useless to him unless he knows what he is looking for when he is looking for a cause. Collecting facts will be useless to him unless he knows which facts are relevant to his problem. He will not know whether he has solved his problem about the earthquake if he does not know what would count as a solution to it.

Usually a concept is an answer to the question, What is——? We can soon see that concepts are pivotal for assumptions. Take the common assumption "Every event has a cause." Is this true or false? It is not true by definition, and we could never prove it true without observing every event and showing that it had a cause. We could prove it false, however, very quickly, *if* we could find just one event that did *not* have a cause. But what would it be like to do that? When one says

This event has no cause,

what does this mean? Presumably it means, at least,

There is no set of conditions invariably connected with this event in time and space.

Because of obvious difficulties in proving that a certain set of conditions does not exist and because of our habitual use of the *concept* of cause and effect, we will not be likely to get general acceptance of "This event has no cause." The natural reaction to this statement is, "There *must* be a cause; we just haven't *found* it."

But isn't the basic belief "Every event has a cause" either true or false regardless of what people insist on believing? The point is that we are not likely to agree on what "cause" means if we do not agree on what it is like to find an event that does not have a cause. In the debate on the existence of God reprinted in the readings in this volume, Bertrand Russell's conception of what it is like to find a causeless event seems to be very different from the notion held by Father Copleston.

Then what is the status of "Every event has a cause"? If we think of it as a belief, it is a strange one. Every discovery of causes counts in the assumption's favor, but few people allow repeated failures to find causes to count against it. Analytic philosophers nowadays are more inclined to treat it as a rule of inquiry than as a belief. A belief is either true or false; a rule is neither true nor false, but something that you do or do not follow. Science and common sense generally prefer to follow this rule and to *act as if* every event has a cause.

In the readings in this volume on causation and induction, several writers discuss the concept of cause and the basic assumption "Like cause, like effect," or "the problem of induction."

Exercises

Classify the following disputes as to whether they are *in* or *about* science or geometry.

1. Mr. Stone: "Water boils at sea level at one hundred degrees centigrade."
   Mr. Wood: "I beg your pardon, it's Fahrenheit."
2. Professor Gold: "As you know, Steel, the axioms, postulates and definitions of Euclidean geometry are all true."
   Professor Steel: "Oh, no. Those are simply rules, and rules are neither true nor false."
3. Miss Snow: "Did you know that on the sun it's now four P.M.?"
   Miss Frost: "Don't be ridiculous; there's no time on the sun."

Motives for
Philosophical Analysis

At this point one might well ask what value or interest there is in trying to clear up common assumptions and concepts. There is little interest in the activity for its own sake. When an occasion does arise to ask, Is there a God? or, Will I live on somewhere else after I die? people are so baffled by these questions that they either adopt a skeptical or agnostic attitude toward them or accept the authority of someone else, often without much enthusiasm, as providing the answer they want. As Broad suggests, people are geared to *using* concepts and assumptions, not to *examining* them. Analytic philosophy is the only discipline that makes a serious and systematic attempt to develop techniques by which people can reach some defensible conclusions about the concepts and beliefs that are basic to science, religion, and ethics.

It is only natural and right that people should be more interested in using concepts and beliefs than in examining them. They are, after all, intellectual tools, and the worker who spends all his time improving his tools never gets his work started. Usually there is no great need to examine basic assumptions and basic concepts, just as usually most tools function well. But occasionally in all work, whether it is manufacturing or thinking, something goes wrong with the tools, and work on the job has to stop and work on the tools begin. In all industrialized and technologically sophisticated countries a very large industry is devoted to nothing but the servicing and repair of machinery of all kinds, from dynamos to ladies' watches.

It does not often occur to us that numerous as are man's mechanical inventions, what Bacon called "the instruments of the mind" are much more widely distributed and more sophisticated. And just as machines and instruments extend man's powers, being extensions of his hands, eyes, ears, and other sense organs, so do the instruments of the mind extend the powers of his naked brain. Imagine a brain without tools and you have less than an animal brain. The human brain is large but at birth it is more empty of instincts than that of any other known animal in the universe. The instruments of the mind that extend the powers of the brain are images, scientific laws, rules, schemas, experiments, predictions, questions, commands, explanations, signals, assertions, axioms, postulates, definitions, fictions, myths, theories, concepts, words, symbols, formulae, proofs, metaphors, and analogies. Several of these are ingredients in logic. These instruments break down, too, and there are often problems about their use and function. Sometimes they simply wear out or become ill adapted to new jobs and have to be discarded, like many other tools.

But when something goes awry with our thinking we may not even be aware of it, for we cannot see and hear the symptoms as we can when a machine strips a gear, short-circuits, or flashes a red warning light. There may be no early warning signals or signs of "clear and present danger" except that something seems a bit odd. But more of that under "Language As an Instrument," pp. 18–24.

Let us look now at one of the very practical motives for examining basic assumptions and basic concepts: Some of our basic assumptions seem to conflict with others. We have seen that "Every event has a cause" and "Like cause, like effect" are commonly assumed by scientists and by the man in the street. But the man in the street, if not the scientist, also accepts another basic assumption: "Man has free will," or "Man is a free moral agent." This is supposedly one of the presuppositions of legal responsibility and morality: "I ought, therefore I can." But does acceptance of the two basic beliefs about cause and effect leave any room in human actions for free will? For, after all, human actions are events. Surely they are not uncaused? And if under identical conditions identical events occur, could I have done any differently than I did, given the condition of my brain, nervous system, heredity, and environment? Can any credence be given to the notion that there is some nonphysical cause called "myself" that enters into all my actions? If all my thoughts and decisions are definitely correlated with certain conditions of my brain and nervous system, how can I attribute any of my actions to anything but heredity and environment? This is the perennial problem of free will.

Apparent conflicts between two beliefs are a fertile source of philosophical reflection. The relation between scientific beliefs and those of religion, morality, and art have furnished a prolific source of philosophical problems in the West: "Matter is neither created nor destroyed—except by God." "Everything has a cause—except God."

Exercises

Which of the two kinds of philosophizing, critical or speculative, is going on in these statements?

1. "The accumulated weight of evidence for immortality that is offered by what we know in science is very strong."

2. "It will not do to say that the cause of a certain event is the set of circumstances that is next to it in space and immediately precedes it in time, for the cause of some events is simultaneous with them."

3. "All of human history shows that the triumph of stupidity over intelligence is inevitable."

4. "Many assume that one test of a good scientific theory is

whether it enables us to predict certain events under certain circumstances, but this is not the case with the theory of evolution."

Analytic Philosophy
Examines Ideas, Not Things

If we accept the notion that philosophical questions are about but not in any other discipline, we have committed ourselves to the position that philosophy examines ideas about the world, not the world itself. Analytic philosophers today usually regard the study of the world as preempted by the sciences. But from the statement that philosophers study ideas one should not infer that they study all ideas or all aspects of ideas with the same emphasis. Some types of analytic philosophy, as we shall see, are much less selective than others as to which ideas they study. All types of analytic philosophy are primarily concerned with *the logical relations of ideas.*

Ideas have different kinds of relations to each other and to things and people. The most familiar is association, in which one idea leads to another by reminding us of it. One person's associations will be different from another's, depending on his experience. Study of the relations of association and the patterns they exhibit is a matter for psychology, not philosophy. Broadly interpreted, the relations of ideas that the analytic philosopher examines are *logical relations.* Everyone is familiar with the logical relation called contradiction, but many are likely to have only a vague notion of it, that is, to be unable to draw the line between contradiction and other kinds of logical relations. The logician's concept of contradiction is that two statements *contradict* if when one is true the other must be false. Another more or less familiar logical relation is entailment: One statement *entails* another if the second follows from the first. These two relations are between *ideas.* Ideas also have relations to things and to people who hold them and who use them as instruments for many purposes. Study of some of these relations is still in its infancy. The least controversial interpretation of logical relations is this: When a person asserts anything, he commits himself to asserting certain other things and denying still others.

You can illustrate this by imagining that you are the person who coined the English word "red." You have detected a color that has no name. Since your surname is "Red," you decide to name the color for yourself. You point out the color to your friends and teach them the rules for using the new word. It catches on and becomes part of the language, and in so doing it enters a set of logical relationships. Its users commit themselves to saying some things and denying others when they say "red." They will not apply "red," for instance, to anything to which they would not apply the word "colored," or say "Red is two feet square," "Red things are green all over," or "Red is invisible."

This is not to say that the word "red" will not undergo changes in usage. Years later it may come to be applied figuratively to certain political beliefs and practices, for example. But rules for the new figurative and other uses will emerge with the uses themselves, just as the rules of a game emerge with the game itself, not later.

Study of logical relations of ideas is inextricably bound up with study of language, the use of words as a human instrument. This is so much so that analytic philosophy these days is sometimes called simply *linguistic analysis*. What people are primarily interested in about assumptions is whether they are true or false, reliable or unreliable, and what are their implications. In other words, What does this assumption mean? What logical relations does it have to other assumptions, beliefs, and concepts? When we speak of assumptions and conclusions we are talking about *validity*, a concept that both the logician and the man in the street use, though it is a much more restricted concept for the logician. We cannot talk about the truth, validity, and clarity of ideas, or about confusion in thinking, without considering language as the central focus. Logical relations *always* involve words (or other symbols), whatever else they may involve—people and things, for instance. What you can *assert* is true or false. The *relation* between the things that you assert is valid or invalid. It is your use of *symbols* that is confused when you are confused.

If all this is no exaggeration, analytic philosophy as the examination of ideas through the study of our use of language is a study of words not just for their own sake but as tools that we cannot do without. It is what we can and cannot do with these tools that is of primary interest to all of us, not the intrinsic oddity, beauty, or intricacy of the tools. Disappointment that philosophy is concerned with the importance of words is like the disillusionment of a little girl when she first learns that boys, of all things, have something to do with the making of babies.

If words are public but ideas are not, then analysis of language is not really an examination of ideas, and analytic philosophy is a wild-goose chase. Many people believe that words and ideas have only a casual sort of relationship and that words are a necessary evil, a poor inadequate instrument for communication or expression of ideas. Ideas, so the story goes, are private and subjective. If so, of course, they are open to study by no one but their possessors, by introspection, and neither philosophers nor psychologists these days have courses in techniques of introspection. Yet everyone claims that it is possible to examine not only your own ideas but to some extent those of others as well.

Analytic philosophers themselves disagree on the relation of ideas to language. Some do not think there are any identifiable entities called ideas or meanings. The historic debate about ideas continues. If we ask ourselves whether the color red (as distinct from instances of the color) or the number two is a real thing, we can begin to see some of the reason for the puzzlement. Since all our experience is of particular things, how do we get the idea of red as something applicable to all red things? Answers vary widely. Plato's was an insistence that ideas are purely objective entities that do not depend on any mind or material objects for their existence, that the subjective concept of red comes from "seeing" The Idea Red in "the heaven above the heavens" in another life, and "learning" red is really just remembering Red.

Plato's was a doctrine of innate ideas. Aristotle claimed that ideas are somehow built into our experience of objects, and abstracted from experience by reason. Locke, like Aristotle, rejected innate ideas and claimed that we get all our ideas from experience, but thought that ideas have much less objectivity than Aristotle said. Ideas are *images,* Locke said. Since the experience of each individual is a unique pattern and since Locke held that words stand for images in the mind, one could then never be sure that two persons mean the same thing by their words because no one can see the images for which another's words stand. By and large, the average layman today accepts this as an accurate account of the relation of ideas to words. But many recent linguistic studies indicate that words and ideas are much more intimately connected than that, and that our language *is* our ideas. If this is the case, ideas are as public as words are, and as open to examination.

One of the facts of linguistic life that has been stressed over and over by recent analytic philosophy is that one learns the use of words by apprenticeship to other users. In this on-the-job training, the child has very strong incentives to use words in standard ways that will get him what he wants—attention, toys from other children or his parents, the fun of pretending he is doing adult things (which requires faithful imitation of adult use of words), postponement of bedtime by lying about thirst, and so on. When we think of it, there is seldom any motive for anyone to be whimsical in his use of words. The price is failure to communicate and to accomplish the desired effects for which we use words. We might as well assign some nonstandard value to the coins in our pockets as to assign our own meanings to words. I might assign the value of thirty-seven cents to a nickel, but could I get someone else to give it to me? Coins can have sentimental value, of course, but this does not affect their exchange value: My lucky penny is worth exactly one cent as a medium of exchange. Even if collectors value a certain kind of nickel at five thousand dollars, it is still a standard value of sorts—standard for that group of people. If everyone agrees to call telephone poles "horses," that is their business. And if I decide on my own that I will call telephone poles "horses" while everyone else is still calling those things "telephone poles," that is my business, but then I cannot expect to use the word "horse" to communicate.

Where the average person's version of Locke's theory of language is false is in the assumption that the meaning of a word is made up of all the associations the word has in the mind of an individual. The associations of a word will vary greatly between different individuals, because of their different experiences in relation to it, but only a few of these associations are essential for communication. As we have seen, these few essentials are standardized, transmitted by cooperation of the users and learners of language as a trade is passed on from father to son in European countries. *It is in agreement on these rules for usage that the objectivity of ideas lies.*

Analysis as a method of doing philosophy is controversial, as virtually all things in philosophy are. But the justification for primary attention to language as a way of getting at ideas can be put as a matter of emphasis or strategy. Just as critical examination of problems is a necessary preliminary to solving them, finding the clearest statement of these problems in words is a necessary preliminary. Critics of analytic philosophy are irked by the fact that its practitioners seldom get beyond analysis of the language in which traditional philosophical questions and answers have been phrased. Critical philosophers themselves do not agree on whether analysis of language is the end-all or merely the begin-all of philosophy. In any case it seems to have a perfectly good place in today's world as the begin-all, if not the end-all, of the study of ideas and other instruments of the human mind.

Language As an Instrument

For purposes of showing the relations of ideas to language we can divide ideas into two kinds, beliefs and concepts, corresponding to two basic units of meaning in language, sentences and terms.

Declarative sentences are used ordinarily to assert a belief. For example, the belief that God exists is usually asserted by using the marks or sounds "God exists." But declarative sentences have many other uses, such as the one on this page in which the writer is not *asserting* the belief that God exists but *mentioning* it. The declarative sentence "We don't do that here" could be used either to *state a fact about* customs or simply to *encourage* someone to *observe* the customs. In the latter use the sentence is still grammatically declarative but is functionally imperative, and has the same use as is standard for the grammatically imperative "Don't do that here!"

Believing is the state of mind of accepting or assuming that something is true; we have used "assumptions" as a very rough approximation for "beliefs." The thing that is accepted is called a belief. The same thing can also be the object of other states of mind: disbelief, knowledge, and so on. Calling "God exists" a belief, then, serves only to remind us that the question of whether we should accept it as true is the main interest we have in what is asserted by "God exists." It is a belief not literally but only figuratively if nobody has yet accepted it as true. Any declarative sentence can be used to set forth something that *may* be a plausible candidate for acceptance to various people under various circumstances.

Belief is often contrasted with knowledge, but the distinction will not hold up if believing means accepting: We do accept everything we know, therefore we also believe it. However, mere belief is distinct from knowledge. If you are an astronomer and tell me "Saturn has rings," and I am ignorant of astronomy but believe your statement, you *know* "Saturn has rings" is true, while I *merely believe* "Saturn has rings" is true. The difference is the evidence on which our two different states of mind are based. What constitutes sufficient evidence for knowledge as opposed to mere belief is determined by the present state of the science in which the belief is classified. Although trying to find one general standard for applying the word "knowledge" has been a favorite occupation of philosophers through the ages, such efforts are usually based on a mistaken idea about the use of words. One formula that has gained fairly wide acceptance is this: For you to *know* that X is true: (1) X must first be true, since you cannot know something that is false; (2) you need sufficient evidence that X is true; (3) you must believe that X is true. This is only a rule of thumb, and there are some unsettled problems about accepting these criteria.

As beliefs are correlated with declarative sentences, so concepts are correlated with terms or expressions other than sentences. (A term can consist of several words; for example, "first President of the United States" is a term.) Beliefs are true or false; concepts are accurate or inaccurate. Both are about the way things are, but they are about two different kinds of things. Suppose we say, "Santa is a fat, jolly old man with a white beard who delivers gifts by sleigh each Christmas Eve." When we say "Santa is" we are committing ourselves not to the belief "Santa exists" but only to a certain definition of "Santa" or a certain use of the word "Santa."

Traditionally, one's concept of anything was thought to be his definition of the word for it. Recently it has become clearer that some nouns and adjectives are indefinable. This means that these words do not convey a *descriptive* meaning, such as was constituted by the definition of "Santa" (things called "Santa" have the characteristics a, b, c, d). It has been widely suggested that "good," "art," "true," and "games" are such words, since English-speaking people do not commonly agree on what all good things have in common, or all works of art, or all true statements, or even all games. Then what is your *concept* of these things? Your concept of good is your set of rules for using the word "good," and the same applies for the other words. Some analytic philosophers maintain that this conception of concepts applies not only to indefinable terms but to all terms: Wittgenstein said that the public decides what is and what is not a cow. Good things are what people call "good" and the concept of good is the set of linguistic conventions they observe in calling things "good." But even from this conventionalism we cannot conclude "Well, then, good is whatever an *individual* chooses to call good." No. He can call it what he likes, but that does not mean that his language then will serve the purposes for him that language usually serves. Language is inescapably public, and the public character of the words in it affects their meaning.

Many people refuse to believe that some words are indefinable. To such people one can only say, "Very well, keep on trying if you like, and let me know how it goes!" An experiment with the word "table," however, will illustrate the plausibility of the suggestion that words can be indefinable. If you are trying to teach the word "table" to a foreigner whose language does not have a corresponding word (such as the Spanish *mesa*), you will find yourself unable to teach him quickly how to apply the word correctly to all that vast range of furniture that in English we call tables, for these may have virtually nothing in common except that they are furniture, and that does not help much at all. But a child in our culture gradually learns to use the word as he sees more and more tables, and his usage comes to conform fairly well with that of other English-speaking people. We would not say that he has no concept of table just because he cannot tell us succinctly how he recognizes a table when he sees one.

We have seen how beliefs and concepts (under the general heading "assumptions") function for the individual and the group as a means of orientation to the environment. They enter into the formulation of every problem we face, and thus they affect every solution we arrive at, for the way we conceive of the problem, the frame of reference in which we set it, is to our intellectual orientation what maps, charts, soundings, or sonar and radar readings are to the navigator. John Dewey used to say that once you have formulated the problem you have arrived at some vague suggestions for its solution. The problem is somewhat like a jigsaw puzzle with a piece or pieces missing: Only a blank shape is there, the shape of the solution. Formulating the problem tells us what solutions will fit and what solutions will not. Analytic philosophy stresses again and again: If you are not sure what the problem is, you will never be sure whether you have the solution. To the extent that people disagree on what problems are, they are likely to disagree on their solutions. Language as an instrument for formulating problems provides some common focus; therefore, if people disagree on the use of words in formulating problems, they also will probably disagree about the solutions. Human disagreement exists in spite of a common language, not because of it.

Since Freud, we in the West have been constantly reminded of how little objectivity and rationality there is in man, although Freud himself (consciously, at any rate!) intended not to fan the flames of irrationality, but to nurture and preserve the element of reason that is in us. Language is a powerful tool of reason. The lower animals have their knowledge built in, for the most part. What the individual dog learns is so much a matter of conditioning that it often seems almost as much a part of him as his instincts. He does not pass on to his unsuspecting offspring the lessons of a close brush with a speeding automobile. But to the extent that knowledge is literally a part of us, it is not so much a tool for us as we are a tool for it: A dog's knowledge "uses" him as much as he uses it. He has little control over the images or whatever that pass before him as he listens intently to a distant sound and wonders what it is and what to do about it; we cannot suppose that he methodically calls up any mental pictures and arrives at a hypothesis, which he then proceeds to test by bounding off to investigate. But man does—when not in the grip of his own conditioning, neuroses, or defense mechanisms. And language is there as an ever present tool to help him objectify his ideas, to stand off from them and look at them, to rearrange them in new, creative ways. If necessary, he can arrest them, put them in writing. Language is available; but that does not mean that he will use it, or use it well, by any means.

While instruments of the mind are like instruments of the hand in many ways, there are important differences, some of which may even make it difficult to conceive of these intellectual tools as instruments at all. This is especially true of language, by which our ideas are expressed. First, language is peculiar in that, as a tool, a word or sentence can be in several places at once. That could not be said of a screwdriver or a vacuum cleaner, the use of which is restricted to one place at one time. Second, linguistic tools are acquired and used in a different way from physical instruments; a person has acquired the tool of language when he has learned how to use it. As we have seen, learning the language is largely by apprenticeship to other speakers. In other kinds of on-the-job training we can become skilled in using the tools without acquiring the tools themselves, but you have got the language when you have got the skill to use it; it's yours. Third, although we do not in any sense make or create a socket wrench or can opener each time we use it, something like this does happen with language: We form a word when we speak or write it.

Up to a point there is a similarity between a word and a paring knife. The knife was designed and made according to a drawing and a set of specifications. In a sense the blueprints and the specifications *are* the knife. Thousands of paring knives are made according to the same blueprints and specifications. Words have a similar duality. In one sense the word "red" is just one thing: the standards or criteria for using the word "red." But each use of it in a context, each time it is spoken or written, we have a repetition of the word "red." The nineteenth-century American philosopher C. S. Peirce called these two senses of "the word red" the *type* red and the *token* red, respectively. You token a word of a certain type each time you utter or write it. Coining a word is creating a type and is somewhat like designing a new kind of paring knife.

The use of words differs from the use of physical instruments in still other ways. Hearers and readers are using our words (tokens) when they listen to or read what we say or write. They may be using them, however, for a very different purpose than we are. I may be using words to describe the sports car I own. My listener, on the other hand, may be using my words to learn about me as a person who likes sports cars. In this case it is not so much the relation of my words to the car that he is interested in as the relation of my words to myself. He is inferring something not so much from what I say as from the fact that I say it.

The concerns of analytic philosophy with language are many. The philosopher is concerned not with mere words but with the work that people do with them, communicating information and expressing feelings, proving, warning, threatening, commanding, and so on. Surprisingly often, people are not doing with their words what they think they are doing or are trying to do. For instance, they may think they are stating facts, describing, when they are really commanding and prescribing. Then, too, we can scarcely talk about whether an idea is true or false without identifying it, being sure just which idea it is. This requires stating it in words on which we can agree, which in turn requires careful attention to the meanings and uses of words. In those larger contexts in which the problem is whether an idea is true or false, we have to know what is the evidence for and against the idea. That requires clear statement in language, too.

Analytic philosophers have other concerns with intellectual tools (of which "language" is the general term for the most important, for it is by language that all the other tools are brought to bear). We have already discussed how beliefs and concepts (general assumptions, we have called them), as intellectual tools, furnish us with our orientation to any problem that faces us. They are like radar, sonar, altimeters, compasses, chronometers, and maps of the territory of knowledge and intellect. It is important that the instruments be accurate, but just as important that we be able to read them in standard ways, to understand what they are saying, and, especially, to use the right instrument for each job. We must, then, fully understand our concepts and beliefs at the outset, for we literally will not know what we are looking for until we clearly understand what we have already found, or think we have.

Like hand tools, intellectual tools often are put to uses for which they were not originally designed. A wrench may not make an efficient hammer or punch, and a hammer, although it can to some extent function as a wrench on a large nut or bolt head, will be wasteful of time and effort when so used. Ones of the penalties of paying too little attention to the nature of ideas as tools is that we often fail to see that intellectual tools designed for one job are being used, and not very well, for another. This is especially the case because metaphors, analogies, and comparisons can be so fruitful in approaching problems: "This is like that." We have mentioned that years ago the theory of evolution was applied to problems in religion, society, politics, and economics by enthusiastic scientists and philosophers who evidently believed that entities in those fields are like animal species in the environment. Early modern psychology was so impressed with the success of physics that it looked at the mind as if it were a kind of ghostly matter, or counterpart of matter, made up of little atoms called ideas that could be put together and taken apart. But these were foolish and capricious misuses of good intellectual tools. We *can* speak of groups as if they were simply collections of individuals, or as if they were like individuals in their behavior, but it is risky; the concepts that function well when applied to the individual do not work so well for understanding groups. We *can* speak of the laws of science or of nature as if they were like the laws passed by kings or legislatures, or think about wholes the way we think about parts, but it is inviting stupid mistakes. If every part of the universe had a beginning, does that prove that the universe as a whole had a beginning?

If "philosophy" is, etymologically, "the love of wisdom," surely that emphasis in philosophy today that we call "analytic philosophy" is a love of wisdom. It is a desire to know what you are doing, and not to let tools that you have made for one good purpose trip you up in trying to accomplish another. In our physical technology we have seen how miracle drugs can have unexpected, even fatal, side effects. So with our intellectual technology. The landscape of the mind has its own ecology, and it is easy to upset the balance of nature in it.

Describing logic as an aid to clear thinking, Aristotle called it an instrument. Trying to put science on a firmer and more productive basis, Bacon took up the metaphor and gave a ringing call for the fashioning of new and better instruments for discovering and applying truths about man and the universe. But the physical results of applied science have proved to be a mixed blessing, creating staggering economic and social dislocations, making wars ghastly in their destructiveness, and polluting the land, air, and water on which man depends for survival. We are not always so forcefully reminded of it, but the staggering advances in human knowledge that modern intellectual instruments such as science, mathematics, and logic have implemented, and the inevitable penumbra of speculation and pseudoscience that has accompanied them, have created an intellectual and spiritual atmosphere that teems with ideas, old and new; and the mass media have filled the very air our minds breathe with ideas. Which are true? Which false? Which fruitful? Which nonsense? What are their implications and interrelations? Analytic philosophers try to provide means for coming to terms with this complex and baffling ecology of human beliefs and attitudes. Surely if by its means a person can keep his sanity, he will have acquired something called wisdom, and in so doing will have acquired analytic tools for choosing and using other intellectual tools to the best human advantage.

The Nature and Types
of Philosophical Analysis

Most of our problems are real in the sense that something we legitimately desire is lacking, and we have at least an inkling of what it is that we want. Some of our problems, however, are unreal. This in itself is a very big problem. The man who keeps trying to get his hands clean by constant washing with soap and water has a problem, but it is not dirty hands. It is that nothing will satisfy his standards for clean hands, and it is up to a psychiatrist to show him that the problem lies elsewhere than in his hands.

The same is true with intellectual puzzles and problems that people pose to themselves and to others. Some of them have no answer and must be regarded as pseudoproblems, for nothing would count as an answer. An example of a pseudoproblem is: What happens when an irresistible force meets an immovable object? This is a complex question, puzzling because it is really two questions demanding one answer. Does or can an irresistible force meet an immovable object? No. Anything in the universe that will win from us the championship title "Irresistible Force" will be such that no object can be immovable in the face of it. For anything to win from us the championship title "Immovable Object," it will have to be such that against it no force can be called irresistible. So no such historic encounter as this can take place.

Unless we change the basic rules for using these words, there is no way we can say, "An irresistible force has just met an immovable object." Nothing will count as an answer to, What happens when——? A similar question would be, Are there round squares on Mars? We have only to ask what would qualify. If anything on Mars or anywhere else meets the tests for "round," it will fail the tests for "square," and vice versa. Anything of which we could say "This is a round square" would be described thus: "An object with all points on its circumference equidistant from its center, and having four equal sides and four equal angles." Telling an astronaut to look for a round square would be like telling him to issue a secret proclamation. There are analytic philosophers who believe that there are no genuine philosophical problems, that they are all pseudoproblems.

The point in looking at these two puzzles is that, unless we know what we are looking for, we are not sure what our problem is, and we do not even know whether it *is* a problem. It may, like these, resemble a problem only in the sense of the puzzlement, wonder, or confusion that a problem generates.

Philosophical analysis is always an attempt at clarification. In the classical, first type of philosophical analysis there is an attempt to analyze sentences or expressions that are puzzling to someone, and to do this by restating these in clearer language. How this deserves the name "philosophy" rather than "lexicography" may not be easy to say. But to the extent that the analyst tries to get a feel for the logical relations and the rules, standards, or criteria of usage involved, it tends to be philosophical rather than lexicographical study. Such an analysis tries to give an exact equivalent, one that will be true wherever the other was true and false wherever the other was false. If in teaching the following proverb to a foreigner, I replace

All that glitters is not gold

with

Not everything that glitters is gold,

I have done so to avoid the possibility of his thinking that nothing that glitters is gold.

More often, philosophers who have engaged in philosophical

analysis have done something slightly different. When asking "What do you mean by 'I see a star'?" many have been prompted by what they know about physics to suppose that there is a genuine unclarity in "I see a star." After all, the star is not yellow as it looks, it is not small as it looks, and certainly I cannot be said to see the star as it is now, because it takes the light so long to reach my eyes. So various philosophers have analyzed such statements as "I see a star" to be more accurately stated as, "I have a star-like sense-datum," that is, some sort of visual representation. This second kind of analysis is *reductive*, in that it reduces one kind of thing to another: *X* is really *Y*. When Plato said that nothing could count as knowledge unless it was certain, he was doing this. When Tolstoy said that nothing could count as a work of art unless it caused a feeling of unity between viewer and artist, and indeed all mankind, he was performing a reductive analysis of the term "work of art." When John Stuart Mill said that material objects are "permanent possibilities of sensation," he did a similar thing.

Since this type of analysis promises to tell us what things are really like, or the true meaning of words we think important, it has always had a great deal of appeal. But it performs the reductive task by means of a linguistic recommendation, not a discovery of meanings. It invents new meanings and tries to get people to accept them; it does not discover meanings that are there. Occasionally this technique of simply *stipulating* meanings may be a necessary cure for vagueness, that is, for a word or term having little meaning that registers. For instance, "age of consent" has to be stipulated by law, for there is no obvious place at which to draw a line and say, "Beyond this is the age of consent." But more often the problem with words is not too little meaning but too much, not vagueness but ambiguity.

A third type of analysis has been practiced in the twentieth century. It goes back to a feeling we all may have had sometimes— that words are treacherously inexact. A lawyer must resort to certain highly artificial expressions such as "party of the first part" and "party of the second part" to correct the possible ambiguity of such pronouns as "he" and "she" in legal contracts. The seventeenth-century philosopher and mathematician Leibniz conceived of a type of mathematical notation that could be substituted for words, by means of which there would be a separate symbol for each different possible thing, event, relation, and so on. This was, of course, the idea of a symbolic logic, which was developed in the nineteenth and twentieth centuries. One thing, one symbol; one relation, one symbol, to analyze all ideas into their elements and express any meaningful combination. That group of philosophers called *logical positivists* or *logical empiricists* adopted the ideal of an artificial language by means of which all ideas could be analyzed. Ideas that could not be so analyzed were regarded as meaningless, or literal nonsense. The main criterion for meaningfulness was "the verifiability theory," according to which a statement was not meaningful if it was not possible to show that it was a tautology, a self-contradiction, or something that could be at least theoretically shown to be true by sense experience.

Such a program ruled out such statements as "God exists" and value statements such as "Murder is wrong," declaring that they were not even false, just nonsense, like "Jabberwock," and thus automatically alienated many people regardless of its merits. Many criticisms were advanced against positivist analysis on its merits, too, however. It failed to produce a rigorous artificial language that could do justice to the richness of ordinary language, though some American analysts still seem to be working at this program. Again, it was argued that the criterion of meaningfulness was meaningless when applied to itself, since it was not verifiable by sense experience, not a tautology, and not a self-contradiction. But a recognizable version of the verifiability theory of meaning has remained as a test for empirical meaningfulness: the falsifiability criterion, according to which if one cannot tell what it would be like for a statement to be false, the statement is not an empirically meaningful statement. This criterion is enshrined in J. O. Wisdom's essay "Gods" and in Antony Flew's application of part of that essay in a piece reprinted in the present volume. A third criticism of positivist analysis is that it gets the cart before the horse: You should not decide what the meaning of a statement is by asking how to verify it; you should ask how to verify it by asking its meaning. In spite of these criticisms and in spite of its loss of cohesion and identity as a movement, many of the emphases and ideals of positivist analysis have a place in philosophy that is probably permanent, for they represent a tradition going back to David Hume in the eighteenth century.

What were positivists to do with statements that people had thought made literal sense but that by positivist standards did not? People thought "Murder is wrong" says something. If it does not, what status does it have? The positivists had argued that it is simply an expression of emotion disguised as a statement of fact. This was a type of analysis that had important suggestions for those who rejected the severity of positivist analysis yet insisted on knowing what our sentences and expressions mean. From Ludwig Wittgenstein, a philosopher who had previously been oriented toward positivist analysis, came the slogan "Don't ask for the meaning, ask for the use." This typified a fourth kind of analysis: *ordinary language analysis.* If you looked for the meaning of "wrong" as you did for "murder," you would be disappointed, for there is nothing in an act discoverable by inspection that can be identified and isolated called the act's wrongness. But about certain acts there is something, which can be identified by legal experts or even a jury of twelve good men and true, that makes those acts murder rather than killing in self-defense, legal execution, killing in war, or accidental killing. The positivists had claimed that "Murder is wrong" is not a description of an act but a condemnation of it. Ordinary language analysis agreed in large measure and said that a declarative sentence does not necessarily declare but, depending on its use in a specific context, can also do such jobs as prescribe or commend. However, as the selection from R. M. Hare in this volume claims, "This is a good cricket-bat," if not "Murder is wrong," may indeed give *some* descriptive information. Such value words as "good" may do two jobs at once: evaluating and describing.

Ordinary language analysis argues that ordinary language is correct language, that departures from it for special purposes such as science are all right, but that other departures from it are generally confused and confusing. Wittgenstein argued that all philosophical problems arise from a departure from ordinary language, an attempt to make words do something they cannot do. He claimed that when the philosopher discovers the error of language in a philosophical problem, he has *dissolved* the problem and need no longer worry about it. This kind of analysis is generally called the *therapeutic* type of ordinary language analysis, because it sees traditional philosophy as "the disease of which it should be the cure," that is, the disease of pathological uses of language. Wittgenstein seemed to say that anyone might mistake diseased language for healthy, but that a professional philosopher should know the difference; that, instead, philosophers often spread the disease instead of curing it, like doctors ignorant of antiseptic techniques. Some advocates of this kind of analysis, however, believe that some points in philosophical questions are genuine problems, and that at least some of the things traditional philosophers have said are true.

The fifth type of analysis is an outgrowth of ordinary language analysis, as the therapeutic kind is. This kind stresses the dangers of imposing some ready-made scheme upon the examination of the meaning of words. Each statement, each expression is seen as having its own logic or logical behavior, that is, its own set of relations to other sentences and expressions. This kind of philosophy goes in for *linguistic analysis* as a study that is valuable in its own right, not just as an analysis of basic concepts and basic beliefs, as C. D. Broad and other analytical-minded philosophers have said.

Critics of this kind of analysis—of whom Broad is one—maintain that it is trivial and that it is not philosophy at all but lexicography. Indeed, the practice of one of its adherents, the recent Oxford philosopher J. L. Austin, seems to bear this out: He would devote an entire course to the meticulous study of one word, or two, like "if" and "can." In defense of such detailed study of a single word, it can be pointed out that many books of respectable prestige have been devoted to the analysis of a single concept. If we call it a concept instead of a word it sounds more impressive, but surely Austin thought he was clarifying the concept of free will by examining in detail the use of "if" and "can" in our talk about actions.

The introductory remarks in this book are based squarely on the assumption that whatever else philosophers may do, their first job is to be clear about what they are doing. This necessarily includes a thorough examination of the questions with which they wrestle, so that they are sure they know what they are looking for. This is inevitably the task of philosophical analysis.

Suggestions for Further Reading

Adler, Mortimer, *The Conditions of Philosophy*. New York, Atheneum Publishers, 1965. The author argues that analytical philosophy is mostly trivialization and evasion of philosophers' historic responsibilities.

Broad, Charlie Dunbar, *Scientific Thought*. London, Routledge and Kegan Paul, Ltd., 1923. The Introduction contains the classic critical-speculative distinction. See Lewis, below, for Broad's later thoughts on what philosophy is.

Danto, Arthur C., *What Philosophy Is*. New York, Harper & Row, Publishers, 1968. Paperback. This contains some significant, up-to-date views on analytical philosophy.

Feigl, Herbert, "De Principis Non Disputandum . . ." Reprinted in Max Black, ed., *Philosophical Analysis*. Englewood Cliffs, N.J.,

Prentice-Hall, Inc., 1950. This is a rather technical discussion of the status of basic beliefs.

Feuer, Lewis, "American Philosophy is Dead." *New York Times Magazine*, April 24, 1966. Feuer says analytic philosophy is decadent and uncreative in this stimulating polemic.

Hospers, John, *An Introduction to Philosophical Analysis*, 2d ed. Englewood Cliffs, N.J., Prentice-Hall, Inc., 1967. This is a sound classic introduction. A separate volume of readings edited by Hospers and published by Prentice-Hall accompanies it.

James, William, "The Sentiment of Rationality." This essay has various editions. James notes how synthesis and analysis in philosophy contrast and complement each other.

Johnstone, Henry W., ed., *What Is Philosophy?* New York, The Macmillan Company, 1965. Paperback. This is a collection of representative readings on the nature of philosophy, with a significant contribution in the editor's introduction.

Lewis, H. D., ed., *Clarity Is Not Enough*. New York, Humanities Press, 1963. Thoughtful arguments pro and con analytical philosophy are presented. Two lectures by C. D. Broad update his views on philosophy, some of which are sharply critical of linguistic analysis as a type of philosophy.

Nagel, Ernest, "The Mission of Philosophy," in Lyman Bryson, ed., *An Outline of Man's Knowledge of the Modern World*. New York, McGraw-Hill, Inc., 1960. This is an erudite, technical discussion of the role of general principles or basic beliefs.

Sellars, Wilfrid, "Philosophy and the Scientific Image of Man," in his *Science, Perception and Reality*. London, Routledge and Kegan Paul, Ltd., 1963. This is rather technical for a beginner. In it the author develops the concept of philosophy as "conceptual cartography."

"What, if Anything, to Expect from the Philosophers." *Time Magazine*, January 7, 1966. This summarizes main orientations in contemporary philosophy. It bemoans the lack of direct contribution by philosophers to the solution of contemporary social and spiritual ills, taking much inspiration from Adler, above. Broad in Lewis, above, is an excellent reply to this editorial.

Wisdom, J. O., *Philosophy and Psychoanalysis*. Oxford, Basil Blackwell and Mott, 1964. The title essay says natural psychological and linguistic temptations team up to produce philosophical puzzles.

Wittgenstein, Ludwig, *Philosophical Investigations*. Oxford, Basil Blackwell and Mott, 1953. The later thought, published posthumously, of the most influential analytical philosopher of this century. He sees philosophical problems as due to "the bewitchment of our intelligence by means of language."

2

Meaning and Truth

Americans are required by law to study their language longer than any other people. Not even the English study English as long as Americans do. Yet in the public schools we are brought only superficially into contact with problems of meaning, truth, and validity as these arise with regard to what people say or try to say. For purposes of philosophical analysis, the public schools furnish little in the way of a vocabulary for talking about ideas. True, the average American's working vocabulary includes many words that refer to various kinds and characteristics of ideas; one can find at least a hundred of these, perhaps twice as many if he wants to split the categories up more finely. Everyone can use, in some context, words like "abstract," "concrete," "logical," "theory," "thought," "belief," "statement," "vague," "ambiguous," "true," "fallacy," "equivocation," "original," and "concept." But as working parts of one's vocabulary they usually are very inexact, blunt instruments. Philosophy sharpens these tools by giving a precise and restricted use to them in criticism—the opposite of what often happens in speculation. It develops techniques of using them to identify, classify, evaluate, and relate ideas to each other.

Descriptive Meaning

In Chapter 1 it was argued that the meaning of words and the truth of statements are interrelated, and it was suggested how this is so; now let us spell this out in more detail.

Since there are different uses of words, even of the same sentence, there are also different kinds of meaning. The *descriptive* (or *literal*, or *cognitive*) meaning of words and sentences is distinguished by its role in knowledge, especially in conveying what we call information or facts. When we know the cognitive meaning of a sentence, we know what would make true or false the statement made by asserting that sentence.

It must be recalled here that a sentence, even a declarative sentence, may not be a statement. We can use sentences, written or spoken, simply as examples, for instance, and not state anything with them. The sentence "Your house is on fire," printed here, does not alarm you, for you know that it is not a statement about danger to your house. The question of the truth or falsity of this sentence never arises in this context, or in a novel, or in a game that requires the players at a certain point to shout, "Your house is on fire!" But you know what conditions would have to exist in order for the sentence to make a true statement.

Let us look at three kinds of declarative sentence in relation to their truth conditions, that is, what makes them true or false.

Tautologies or *analytic* statements are made by those sentences that say the same thing twice, or have their predicate contained in their subject. The truth of such a statement can be determined merely by analyzing its meaning:

A locomotive is a machine

is a tautology, for "locomotive" contains as part of its meaning "machine." We do not have to examine any particular locomotives or machines of other kinds to know that the statement is true, for that is simply the way that people use these words. *A tautology is always true.* Every tokening of it yields a true statement because its type is true.

But suppose we have

A locomotive is not a locomotive.

This is a *self-contradiction,* the second kind of statement, and it is false. There is no imaginable set of conditions under which a locomotive would not be a locomotive if we are using the word in its standard way. *A self-contradiction is always false,* for one part of it cancels the other.

But most of the assertions we make are by means of *empirical statements,* which are *contingent* upon something in the world, not upon the meaning of words. When we use

There is a locomotive in the roundhouse

to make a statement, its truth or falsity can be decided only by looking, or otherwise observing, to see if there is indeed a locomotive in the roundhouse referred to. Yet merely looking will not tell us whether the statement is true: We must know what to look for, and in order to do that we must know what the *descriptive meaning* of the sentence is. Only then do we know those conditions under which it will be true. The descriptive meaning of a term is its *logical connotation;* the descriptive meaning of a sentence is its *intension.*

It is not always easy to recognize when a sentence is usable for empirical purposes and when it is not. Take the familiar puzzle:

What happens when an irresistible force meets an immovable object?

This turns out to be a question not about the world or facts but about the use of words, for

An irresistible force has met an immovable object

is a self-contradiction, and false, and

An irresistible force cannot meet an immovable object

is a tautology, and true. If this seems trivial, it should be noted that some philosophical problems are like this one. Philosophers have talked wistfully about material things, wondering what they are *really* like. They have argued that we see things only as they look to us, and that surely that is not the way they really are; they have puzzled over how things would look if no one were looking at them! This is much like wondering what would happen to an irresistible force if it were resisted by an immovable object: Both questions have a fascination for a certain type of mind, but they are questions about words.

The empirical, contingent statement "This rose is red" is found to be true or false by applying the criteria specified in its *connotative* meanings. Connotation for logical and philosophical purposes must not be confused with the broader notion of connotation in general use, in which the connotations of a word are simply its associations, as, for example, "foul smell" is associated with "Limburger." The cheesemaker uses not "foul smell" as a criterion for distinguishing Limburger from, say, Cheddar, but the differences in the processes by which the two cheeses are made. So, while all that is associated with roses in people's minds may include the logical connotation of "rose," only those associations that enable us to distinguish roses from other flowers and nonflowers are parts of the connotation of "rose" in the logician's sense. We might even have to consult a botanist on whether a particular flower is a rose, and a physicist on whether the rose reflects light in the red or some other range. For most purposes, however, we are able to tell whether "This rose is red" is true or false without going to these lengths, for just as we recognize a word spoken in an accent or high or low pitch as being the same word, so we recognize meanings as the same despite the associations.

When "This rose is red" fulfills the criteria specified in the meaning of the sentence, it is the connotative meanings of the crucial *terms* "rose" and "red" that have been of most concern. But there is a parallel kind of meaning for a *sentence,* called *intension.* A sentence is usable to make true or false statements. A term is neither true nor false; it is applicable or inapplicable to a thing, event, or situation. Since terms and sentences constitute two different kinds of *meaning units,* the words for their descriptive meaning are different: *connotation* and *intension,* respectively. Just as a term's connotation is the set of criteria, or necessary and sufficient conditions, for its application, so a statement (made by using a declarative sentence) has for its intension the set of conditions necessary and sufficient for its truth. A necessary condition for anything is any condition without which that thing would not exist. The sufficient conditions for anything are all the necessary conditions or prerequisites. When the sufficient conditions exist, the thing exists. For instance, in "This rose is red" they would be that something, referred to by "This," meets the criteria for being a rose and meets the tests for being red. Then the necessary and sufficient truth conditions for "This rose is red" are seen to be fulfilled, and the statement is declared true.

If any of the necessary conditions, the *sine qua non's*, are missing, then the *sufficient* conditions for calling the statement true have not been met. Thus

Jones is alive

would have as one necessary condition that Jones is using oxygen. (We discount the fact that one can live briefly without oxygen.) But oxygen alone will not keep Jones alive. Then what are the sufficient conditions constituting the descriptive meaning of "Jones is alive"? All the necessary ones, yes, but what are they? A physiologist might smile at the question. It is easier to show the statement false than to show it true, though with such developments as heart transplants, physicians have even had to revise their connotation for "dead": With the advent of the removal of the heart from a patient to be replaced by another heart, it would not do to say that absence of a heartbeat is proof of death! Currently the main criterion is this: A person is dead if there is no electrical activity in his brain. If brain transplants in turn become feasible, that criterion will have to be altered, of course, since there will be at least a brief interval when the person does not have a brain, or at least when it is sensible to ask, Electrical activity in which brain?

The discussion of the necessary conditions for human life is designed to show what booby traps await us when we begin to talk about knowing when a statement is true and when it is false. A physician tries to make certain that a person is dead before signing a legal certificate saying that he is, and is now to be treated as a dead body and disposed of by burial or otherwise. But what if a distraught wife says, "Doctor, you should have waited longer, much longer, to be sure that he was dead"? How long? How many observations must he make? The poor woman can cite many tales from the nineteenth century of people who were buried alive after just such legal and medical certification. And the main thing about being dead is that you do *not* revive. Most of us shrug at these considerations, of course: "—well, all sorts of things *might* happen, a miracle worker might revive him, he might revive if he were frozen and kept until medical technology had advanced much further in its powers, but, after all, we've got to draw the line *somewhere,* so we let the medical profession decide what is a reasonable doubt and let it go at that." If the man does rise from the dead several days or weeks later, the doctor will be legally protected if he has observed all the precautions required by law, professional ethics, hospital rules, and so on.

All of this reflects a long debate by philosophers about *verification.* Literally to verify a statement is to show that it is true, but, as we have seen, we often have to be satisfied with a very high degree of probability. Later observations *might* show false the statement that we had confidently declared true on excellent evidence. But when we say "might" we mean that it is *logically possible,* that is, there is no contradiction in saying,

Jones showed all the symptoms we now accept for "dead"

and saying,

Jones later showed all the vital signs,

or between

It seemed to all the experts that Jones was dead

and

Jones was not dead.

Traditional Theories of Truth: Correspondence, Coherence, and Pragmatic

---

Much use has been made of the words "true" and "truth" in the discussions we have carried on about meaning. But what is it for a statement to be *true?* It is, of course, "for the conditions specified in its intensional meaning to be fulfilled," yet that answer seems peculiarly unsatisfying to philosophers and to philosophical laymen. It has always been an enterprise of much importance to "seek truth" and a virtue to "tell the truth," and that triumvirate "the good, the true, and the beautiful" has often captured the human imagination.

Traditionally it has been assumed that the adjective "true" refers to a property of things or a relation between things. Let us suppose that the thing that has the property, or that stands as one term in the relation, is a statement or a belief, since these are the kinds of things that philosophers have said are true or false (though people sometimes speak of "true believers," or of things that have a "true foot" as opposed to things that have pseudopods, and so on). What we are occupied with in the problem of truth is a question in the theory of knowledge, a cognitive problem, and philosophers have usually approached the problem of truth in this way: What do all true statements have in common that makes them different from false statements? In short, they have looked for a connotative definition of "true." What they usually have settled on is that it is some sort of relation that statements or beliefs have to something else that makes them true rather than false. Now it is not always easy to distinguish a relation from a property: "to the left of" is a relation and "red" names a property, but when philosophers speak of truth and falsity, they will often speak as if they meant a property of statements rather than a relation that statements have to something else. But in the strictest sense, they have been discussing a relation, not a property.

So the question, What is truth? came down to this: What is the other thing to which a true statement is related and what is the nature of that relation? For centuries philosophers and laymen alike thought of truth as some sort of *correspondence* between statements and that which statements are about, for example, facts or the world. Thus the statement "There is a house on the lot" is true if and only if there *is* a house on the lot referred to by "the lot." Aristotle said that we tell the truth when we say of what is that it is. Following Hobbes, Locke remarked that "true" and "false" apply only to propositions, strictly speaking; but, since he was interested more in the psychology of knowledge than in language, he applied these adjectives to "ideas"—in his sense of the word, sensations and introspective data, especially mental images. According to Locke, your idea is true if something exists that is like it. Thus Locke's theory of truth came to be called the "copy" theory: Ideas copy reality.

This account, especially cruder, more popular versions of it, was so unsatisfactory that Bertrand Russell gave it a more sophisticated formulation in *The Problems of Philosophy* by introducing into it the notion of "facts," rather strange entities, neither material nor mental things but nevertheless real. Russell asserted that a statement is true when its structure accurately reflects the structure of what it refers to. Thus if the relation of loving really did exist between Desdemona and Cassio as it was asserted to exist in Othello's (unspoken) belief "Desdemona loves Cassio," his belief was true and not otherwise. But Russell says Othello incorrectly "knitted together" the terms "Desdemona" and "Cassio" and "loving" and arrived at the wrong conclusion as to how they were related to each other; his belief did not accurately reflect reality.

Later, Alfred Tarski developed a linguistic version of the theory that truth is a correspondence between what we say or think and the way things are. His theory tried to do justice to all that had been learned about the relations of words to things—semantics—since Aristotle, and was called the semantic theory of truth. The theory was more subtle and complex than any other theory of truth, but it shared the chief difficulty of all correspondence theories of truth—the crucial notion of correspondence itself.

Precisely *how* does the thought or the sentence correspond with what the thought or sentence is about? By copying it? By having within itself relationships between items, analogous to relationships in the world? Correspondence theories, like many or all other theories of truth, fail because no single theory can cover all instances of true statements. We cannot discern any such uniform, specific relation as "truth" between words and the world as we can discern the relation "to the left of" between two objects in space.

The second theory of truth, the *coherence* theory, declares that those things that are related to each other when one says that a statement is true are statements themselves, or, to use the language of Brand Blanshard, the coherence theory's most noted recent exponent, are "judgments." Recognizing that the progress of human knowledge (whether in the individual or the race of men) is cumulative and that there is a fantastically complex network of relations among all the things that we know, Blanshard argued that truth is coherence among our judgments. For him, "coherence" meant primarily lack of contradiction but also mutual entailment and coherence with experience. "Mutual entailment" is used to mean that two true judgments logically require the truth of one another; that if you know one is true you can somehow learn that the other is true by looking at the interrelations of the judgments alone. Granted, this would require knowing not just that one judgment is true but also knowing all other judgments that can be made and knowing which of them are true and which false. Thus, if you know all true judgments but one, you can deduce the truth of that one from the others. Such a theory dictates that we cannot be sure of the truth of a statement until we are sure of its relation to all other statements. That, of course, we cannot do until all is known—and knowing all is impossible. The coherence theory, however, has always had advocates who believe that there is nothing that is *not* known by *some* mind, somewhere; that everything real is either a mind or something in a mind. This position is called idealism.

Surely, if truth is a relation, and if there is nothing real but minds and their contents, the coherence theory is the best theory of truth. But people who hold other notions about reality and ideas quickly point out that you cannot go on forever saying that one thing is true because another thing is true, that you cannot derive the truth of every statement from *other* statements. They argue that, although the statements in a novel are coherent, no one supposes that their coherence makes the statements true. Blanshard tried to clarify this point by arguing that coherence includes "coherence with experience"; in this case, since no one but the novelist has ever thought of the people and events in the novel, much less met or talked to the people or witnessed the events, there has been no coherence with experience. But this "coherence" looks like "correspondence" in disguise.

The third theory of truth, the *pragmatic* theory, was given its most famous development by William James and was elaborated upon by John Dewey. James said that truth is not a relation between words and world, or between ideas alone, but a relation between an expectation and a fulfilling experience. If I believe the statement, "This is the key to my door," then I expect to have a certain experience when I try the key: I expect the key to open the lock. If it does, then my belief is true; if it does not, my belief is false. More than this, James and Dewey went on to say that a belief is not true before it is acted upon. Dewey is generally thought to have claimed that we are "warranted" to assert only beliefs that have been so verified, and this futurism repelled many from the pragmatic theory of truth.

It is not so much the specific holdings of traditional theories of truth as the assumption underlying all of them that has made it so difficult to give them whole-hearted acceptance. That assumption is simply that "true" is an adjective that describes, and that there is some property or relation to which it refers; that something is the same in all true statements, and is lacking in all false statements. As we shall see later, the advocates of the redundancy theory of truth point out that this assumption is of a piece with the assumption that all good things, or all works of art, have something in common. Whether or not this criticism is just, each theory's difficulty in accounting for *all* true statements has caused many to hesitate in accepting it. The pragmatic theory works well for scientific hypotheses; the coherence theory works well for statements in geometry and other branches of mathematics; the correspondence theory appeals to the man in the street, who thinks that there is some sort of relation between the way we think things are and the way they really are. But none of the theories does justice to the enormous variety of statements that people quite properly call true.

"True for Me and False for You"

Many people believe that a statement can be true for one person and false for another—that is, they think they believe this. A brief examination shows the muddy thinking responsible for this "belief." Do they mean that a statement is both true and false at the same time? This is a self-contradiction: They are asserting and denying something at the same time. Whatever "true" means, if you say,

S is true and S is false,

you are both asserting and denying "S is true," and that is self-canceling. Another analysis of "S is true for me and false for you" seems more plausible initially. Take

I am a female.

That would be "true for" slightly more than half the people in the United States and "false for" the rest, according to this analysis. But as a *type*, "I am a female" is neither a true nor a false statement, and once we have specified what "I" refers to in each *tokening* (occurrence) of the sentence, the supposed relativity of truth retreats. When each female person substitutes her own name for "I," the more precise statement

Jane Doe is a female

is just as true for every male as it is for her.

Another possible analysis of "*S* is true for me and false for you" is

To me the room is hot, and to you the room is cool.

As usual, an ambiguity is involved. When we find that I mean by "hot" anything over 67 degrees Fahrenheit and you mean by "cool" anything under 90 degrees Fahrenheit, we see that there is no problem of relative truth here. It would, of course, be even clearer if we could analyze "hot" and "cool" in terms of "comfortable" and "uncomfortable," so that "is hot" would mean "causes uncomfortable sensations of warmth" and "is cool" would mean "causes uncomfortable sensations of cold."

But surely there is some basis for such a widespread impression as the notion that a statement can be true for me and false for you? Surely such a champion of relativity as William James might be cited in its defense? Suppose we take an oversimplification of James's doctrine that if a belief works it is true. Let us assume that

Somebody up there likes me

works for Smith and does not work for Jones; that is, Smith gets completely satisfactory results from believing it, and Jones gets no satisfactory results from believing it. Then is the statement true for Smith and false for Jones? Again, if this means that it is true *and* false, it is a self-contradiction. What makes it plausible to believe that "It works" means the same as "It's true" is the ambiguity of "works." Jones's standards for what works are different from Smith's, if the same thing that satisfies Smith does not satisfy Jones. But in that case it is less misleading all around to say

S meets Smith's standards and S does not meet Jones's standards.

As applies to "true" it would also be less confusing to say

S is true according to Smith's definition of "true" and false according to Jones's definition of "true."

   The widespread belief that truth is relative to the individual,
then, is due to the same sort of problem that makes people conclude that morals are relative to the individual: the difficulty of
finding a definition of "true" that everyone or at most everyone
can accept and that will apply to all true statements. Advocates
of the redundancy theory of truth discussed later in this chapter
say that "true" does not describe and therefore has no definition
and needs none.
   The notion that a statement can be true for me and false for
you, then, soon begins to become a puzzle. No obvious analysis
seems to come forward of "for me" and "for you" in the case of
"true for me" as it might in "good for me."

Strawberries are good for me and are bad for you,

for instance, has a perfectly good usage if "are good for me" means
"produce good health in me" and "are bad for you" means "make
you break out in hives." What people presumably mean by the confusing "true for me and false for you" is:

I believe S and you do not believe S.

That is, as we saw in Chapter 1, simply this:

I think S is true and you think S is not true.

This is a much more modest statement than "S is true for me and
false for you." At least we know what it means.

Connotation,
Denotation, and Definition

While we have warned repeatedly against the assumption that all problems of meaning are problems of definition, it is true that many are. At any rate, we will see more clearly that problems of definition are not all there is to problems of meaning if we examine some techniques of definition and learn how traditional techniques of argument work.

Definition applies only to signs and symbols, not to the things for which we use signs and symbols. One cannot define a rock, but he can define "rock." "Rock" is a word, while a rock is not. Unless we use "ostensive" definition, which consists simply of pointing to something and saying the word that applies to that thing, for example, pointing to a rock and saying "rock," definition is a process of finding verbal equivalents. A definition is a kind of equation, in which the word being defined is on one side of an equals sign and the definition on the other; if genuine equality of usage does not exist then the definition is a bad one. We may mean two main things when we say that a definition is a kind of verbal equivalence.

The first is that what is on the right-hand side of the equals sign is an accurate set of criteria for applying the word on the left: the necessary and sufficient conditions for applying the word, which we have called its (logical) connotation. *Connotative definitions* of that kind are the most familiar in dictionaries. The most generally used technique for such connotative definitions is *definition by genus and difference*. This consists of putting the class of things—say, "colts"—into two other classes—say, "young things" and "horses." Thus a fair definition of "colt" is "young horse," and being in both these classes constitutes criteria for use of the word "colt." If we are told that Prince is a colt and we ask how old he is, there is something linguistically improper if we are told that he will be thirty-seven years old next April. Farmers and racing enthusiasts might disagree about the further meaning of "young," but neither they nor anyone else would recognize this as standard usage: A presidential candidate at thirty-seven would be young, but a horse would not. Being young is the *difference* between colts and other things in the *genus* "horse." ("Genus" here is a relative term, of course, since it is not a genus in the zoological sense, but simply more general than different kinds of horses within the class "horse.")

The second thing we may mean in saying that a definition is a verbal equivalent is that the words on the right-hand side are equated to the word on the left if they constitute a list of all the members of the word's class, or at least enough members of the class to provide a good set of examples. We might, for instance, define "furniture" as "chairs, tables, desks, beds, cabinets, and so on." A connotative definition of "furniture" would list all the membership requirements for the class "furniture," but a list of members of the class would constitute its *denotation* and would make up a *denotative definition* of the word that names the class. The denotation of a term is simply all those things to which a word properly applies; the connotation is the criteria for application.

Obviously a denotative definition has some advantages and some disadvantages over a connotative one. With the word "furniture," for instance, it might be better to list a set of things called furniture than to try to find precisely that set of criteria that will distinguish furniture from nonfurniture. Would we, for instance, include appliances, such as stoves, room air conditioners, and television sets? If so, we would have to have more inclusive criteria than if we did not. To avoid this problem we might simply give some examples of furniture and end by saying "et cetera" or "things like that." The disadvantage of denotative definitions can be seen here, too: What do all our examples have in common? It may not be easy to say. What is worse, of course, is that a denotative definition often leaves us wondering whether we should apply the word to something that was *not* mentioned. This is especially bothersome with new things, like newly invented or newly developed products of technology. A denotative definition does not, like a good connotative definition, tell us exactly and explicitly what kinds of things to apply the word to.

One technique of arriving at connotative definitions is to examine the usage of the word and to ask what all of the things in the denotation *do* have in common. This is to infer the connotation from the denotation, inductively. One book on tragedy, for instance, arrives at a definition of "tragedy" in this way: Look at all the plays, especially the more famous ones, that have commonly been called tragedies, and then ask what all of them have in common; those common properties will constitute the defining characteristics of tragedy. It is a torturous process in this particular case, and one with a dubious conclusion. As with many other words it makes a questionable assumption: that people have some fairly definite criteria in mind when they agree to call a new thing by an old name, and that these criteria are the same that people before them had in mind when *they* applied the word to old things. Wittgenstein's famous remarks about games remind us of this: What does anything have to have or be in order to be called a game? Don't assume that it *must* have something in common with everything else that is called a game; rather, look and see how people do, in fact, use the word "game." Don't ask for the meaning [that is, definition], ask for the use," Wittgenstein said, and told us that instead of some tidy set of necessary and sufficient conditions for the use of the word "game" we would find only "family resemblances" among games. Wittgenstein's remarks are controversial but have given new life to the subject; his procedure would make of the philosopher not a lexicographical pedant but a canny connoisseur of the ways of words, a person with a feel for language, not a man who goes around saying, "What is life? Life is *A, B,* and *C* because——" when life is really far more complex and subtle than that and when people's use of the word "life" is more rich and varied than the philosopher has ever dreamt.

But while there is a surprisingly large number of words that cannot be defined except misleadingly, there are many that can, and there are some serviceable rules for good definitions. They center around the fact that a definition is supposed to be an equivalence.

The first rule of definition is called the *rule of substitution.* According to it, if the definition cannot be substituted in a sentence for the word being defined, it is not equivalent and is a bad definition. G. E. Moore pointed this out with his famous remarks about definitions of "good." One definition of "good" that has been fairly popular equates "good" with "pleasant" or "pleasure-producing." But a sentence may not mean the same thing at all if we strike out "good" and substitute "pleasant" or "pleasure-producing." For instance:

Adultery is pleasant

and

Adultery is good

do not mean the same thing, since they have different truth conditions. It will be recalled that the descriptive meaning of a declarative sentence consists of the criteria for deciding its truth. The criteria for these two sentences are not the same. The suggestion that "good" means nothing more than "pleasant" may be tempting, but usage does not countenance it, and it turns out to be a "linguistic recommendation" like Tolstoy's theory of art. Our society has refused to accept the use of "pleasant" for "good," in spite of pressures to do so, for at least one excellent reason: The things that some people find pleasant and good, others find pleasant and bad. Plato long ago pointed out that good varies independently of pleasure, bad independently of pain, and that they thus cannot be identical.

The *rule of inference*, on the other hand, asserts that if a definition is equivalent in meaning to the word being defined, we can, after we have substituted the definition for the word in a sentence, draw all the inferences from the new sentence that we could from the old. Thus, from

Prince is a colt

we could infer

Prince is a horse.

Now, "ought to be done" is part of the meaning of "right" as truly as being a horse is part of being a colt. It is false, according to the general usage of the word "right," to say that adultery is right, or at least is an exaggeration to say without qualification that it ought to be done. That would be a very good argument that "right" cannot be defined as, say, "pleasant," for, as with our previous example of "good,"

Adultery is right

is not equivalent to

Adultery is pleasant,

and the reason is simply that we could not infer from the second statement what we could from the first, namely, that adultery ought to be done.

There are other tests of a good definition. One is that it ought not to be circular: Above all, it ought not to include as part of the definition the word being defined or its cognates. Defining "dream" as "what a person has when he's dreaming" tells us nothing; if we understood "dreaming" we would probably understand "dream."

Another rule is that a definition should not be too broad or too narrow. The denotation of the definition should be equivalent to the denotation of the word. To define "abode" as "dwelling house" would be to eliminate mobile homes and tents, and give us a definition that is too narrow. But to define "abode" as "building" would be to include tool sheds, stores, and factories and would make the definition too broad.

All in all, definitions should not attempt to change the usage of a word, although such changes are sometimes necessary. There are times when ordinary usage helps little, as when scientists must use words that they take from ordinary language. A word such as "law" may be useful to the scientist only after he has sharpened it for his purposes, or at least honed some of its many edges: Law is surely a fundamental concept in science, but the scientist cannot retain in his definition of "law" that part of ordinary usage in which laws are statutes or decrees. He does not claim that only *his* meaning of "law" is right, but that his definition of "law" is an instrument used in his work.

Exercises

1. Give a definition by genus and difference for: astronaut, aquanaut; carpet, bedspread; analgesic, antiseptic; wife, husband; mayor, governor.

2. Think of the different kinds of tables that are classified as articles of furniture (not such things as multiplication tables and water tables). Now look up "table" in a dictionary. How has the word fared? Is the definition good by all the standards we have examined? Is "table," like "games," one of those words that have a use but not a definition? Could you tell from the dictionary definition the difference between a table and a stool? A desk? A stand? Now if you think Wittgenstein has exaggerated about "games," look it up. Can you tell from the dictionary definition the difference between games and other things that people do?

3. Which of the following definitions are too narrow?
   a. *Letter:* a sealed, typewritten message sent by mail.
   b. *Closet:* a small room in a hallway where coats are hung.
   c. *Mammal:* a land animal that reproduces without laying eggs, and suckles its young.
   d. *The president of a country:* the man who is the country's chief executive.
4. Which of the following definitions are too broad?
   a. *Chair:* something you sit on.
   b. *Milk:* a digestible liquid.
   c. *Timepiece:* a watch.
   d. *Train:* several wheeled vehicles, not self-propelled, linked together, on rails, to carry freight.

Meaning and Use: Nondescriptive or Noncognitive Uses of Language

---

Debate in early twentieth-century British and American philosophy about the main concepts in ethics centered on whether these convey any information. Am I telling you anything at all about stealing when I say, "Stealing is wrong"? A. J. Ayer and C. L. Stevenson maintained that "Stealing is wrong" gives us no more information than "Stealing is stealing," that wrongness is not any property of things or actions and "wrongness" is not a word that describes. "Postemotivists" like R. M. Hare helped to set them right—so most analytic philosophers would say—but not in a way that would vindicate older or common-sense ideas about right and wrong. The main significance of the debate for our purposes here is that it highlighted a virtually unexplored realm in talking about meaning, and that is *use.*

Just as tradition supposed that art was the imitation of nature and truth was correspondence between ideas and reality, so traditional ideas on language assumed that the basic if not exclusive function of language was the communication of information. This would include, of course, not only description but such activities as argumentation as well. Now surely that is probably the most important function that language serves—telling how things are. But to assume that any particular piece of discourse one comes upon is such is courting disaster. The course by which such a disaster might come about could be charted thus:

> Since "good" is an adjective that describes good things, everything that people agree in applying it to has something in it called goodness, just as everything people agree to call red has redness. But there is something funny here. I can teach you to recognize redness but not goodness, for I cannot point out the goodness in things as I could the redness in things. So "good" does not describe in the same way that "red" does. If not, how does it describe? Does it refer to some mysterious property of things that we cannot see, hear, or smell, but that is there nevertheless? Or perhaps it does not describe anything at all (remember "Stealing is wrong," above?). But if it does not describe, isn't it a bogus notion, a sham, a piece of outworn dogma?

Such skepticism is the inevitable result of the mistaken idea of language that if an adjective like "good" or "wrong" does not describe, it must be a fake. (In the case above, of course, it is going too far to say that "good" does not describe at all: If I say to you, "I have lost a hat," and you ask, "what kind?" and I say, "Oh, a *good* one," I have given you *some* information, unless I have peculiar ideas about what constitutes a good hat.) The train of thought in the foregoing example is the result of a wrong expectation caused by our looking at how we think words *ought* to behave rather than at how they *do*. Observing Wittgenstein's dictum "Don't ask for the meaning [definition], ask for the use" would have spared us this pain. In the case of "good," the use is complex; not merely to describe but to *commend* as well. G. E. Moore saw that there is no general definition of "good" but argued that it is nevertheless descriptive, saying that it refers to some unobservable property of things. Ayer and Stevenson could not accept his "unobservable property" and declared that "good" does not refer at all, but simply is used to express approval under the guise of describing. Radical as such theories were, they helped to show that describing is hardly the only use that certain adjectives have; in the case of "good," it seems to be a rather minor use.

Another development that focused attention on use at the expense of traditional assumptions about language was Bertrand Russell's harsh words on grammar and logic. Working with the apparently innocuous word "the," Russell pointed out that grammar sometimes holds no clue to meaning. Take "The present king of France is bald," he said; it almost seems that we are referring to someone or something that exists, although we all know that there has been no king of France for many decades. Russell's point was that philosophers may make all sorts of nonsensical statements and get away with them, and even be thought profound, because their statements are grammatically correct. Rudolf Carnap snorted at such a statement by Martin Heidegger, the German existentialist: "The Nothing nothings." The collection of words is grammatically impeccable, but Carnap examined it and found no sense in it. We have seen how questions especially can be misleading because they are grammatically in order. "What time is it on the sun?" is superficially like "What time is it in Denver?" but grammar is about all the two questions have in common. It is not the words or their arrangement but their use that is all wrong. One cannot literally ask "What time is it on the sun?" although he can arrange the words and put a question mark after them.

Sentences, whether interrogative or declarative, may have more than one use and even several uses at the same time. Just as an adjective might fail to describe, a noun fail to name, or an interrogative sentence fail to express a question, so a declarative sentence might fail to "declare" (that is, state or assert) or describe. Declarative sentences are very versatile. It has come to be said that sentences of all sorts can do three standard things, three very general uses of language. (1) They can *inform*, including describing and arguing. These uses are the staple of what we have called the descriptive or cognitive uses of language. (2) They can *express*, including "letting off steam" or otherwise expressing emotion. The same function can be performed nonverbally by, for instance, kicking something or pounding one's fist on a table. The expressive function is also served when one person uses words to arouse emotions in others. (3) They can *direct*, influencing behavior, for instance, getting someone to stop or start an action. Commands are examples, but asking a question is also an instance.

As an example of how mistaken it is to speak of "the meaning" of a sentence as if it had only one, take three uses that might be carried out simultaneously with the sentence

It's almost midnight.

Let us suppose that a boy and his girl are dealing with a somewhat old-fashioned father who has threatened never to let her go out with the boy again if he does not get her home before twelve o'clock. If she thinks the boy has lost track of the time, she *in-*

forms him by saying, "It's almost midnight." She might at the same time give the sentence such an inflection as to *express* her regret that it is almost time to part. And, as a dutiful daughter or from a determination not to do anything that will keep her from seeing the boy again, she might at the same time clearly use "It's almost midnight" to mean "Please take me home now"—a *directive* use. Now we, as users of the language, know that it has all these subtleties. Why we ignore them when we start to philosophize is a good question, but there is scarcely any context other than philosophy in which we would accept "It's almost midnight" as a simple declarative sentence the only purpose of which is to convey information.

Considerations such as these have led some to state that we should say not

X means the same as Y

but

X has the same *use* as Y

just as in the case above

It's almost midnight

had the same use as

Please take me home now.

But, of course, the two sentences would seldom be interchangeable. At any rate, it is the *speaker's* meaning that we are most concerned with here; what he intends to do by uttering these words in this way in this situation. Reference to the *standard* or *conventional* usage of "It's almost midnight" would only mislead us. And, after all, what uses do words have except "here" and "now" and "in this situation"? The standard or conventional uses are simply a long list of particular occasions repeated many times over. Words do not mean anything independently of their use.

The late Oxford philosopher J. L. Austin has given us many insights into usage through studies carried out in meticulous detail. His most famous is "the performative." When a judge pronounces the sentence "Thirty days in the workhouse," it is just that—pronouncing a sentence. Quite possibly the accused's lawyer has already told the prisoner that this sentence is mandatory, so the sentence uttered by the judge is not informative, nor is it necessarily meant to be so; perhaps there is no one in the courtroom who does not know that the sentence is mandatory. We could not say that it is expressive, either, particularly if the judge utters it matter-of-factly. Nor would we say that it is intended to cause anyone to do anything, as "Bailiff, put that man in irons" might do. Surely, when the sentence has been uttered, they will take the prisoner away, as the law requires. No, Austin says, such uses of language as "I sentence you to thirty days in the workhouse," or "I now pronounce you man and wife," or "I christen thee Buttercup" when performed in ceremonies do not so much have the purpose of informing, expressing, or directing as simply of *performing* the ceremony. These are words that do things. The ceremony is not legally complete, or socially acceptable, until this form of words has been uttered. Performatives have a place not only in ceremonies but also in private contexts. Take promising, for example. "I promise" is much more a doing of something called promising than it is of informing, directing, or expressing. Threatening would be similar: "I'll get you yet, you scoundrel!" is integral to this particular act of threatening. It can be uttered in such a way as to sound like a warning or an expression of emotion or a notice, but basically it is simply a threat, for all its obvious complexity.

The importance of context becomes apparent when we consider what would happen if a judge, clergyman, threatener, or promiser said of his utterance later, "Of course I *said* it, but I didn't really *mean* it." If the threatener or promiser has been taken to court for his words or his words and deeds, the judge and jury are not going to be swayed by such protests. How *could* a judge be joking when he sentences you in a court of law to thirty days in the workhouse? How *could* a clergyman be jesting when he pronounces you man and wife at a marriage ceremony? Depending on the circumstances, the same can be asked about promises and threats: How could you be joking when you angrily threaten someone who has wronged you? How could you be joking when you borrow five dollars and promise to pay it back? *Res ipsa loquitur* (the thing speaks for itself) is a principle not only of law but of language and human relationships.

Exercises

1. Tell whether the use of the declarative sentence "My cigarettes are on the mantel, dear" is primarily informative, expressive, or directive in the following contexts: (a) Uttered by a wife to her husband as he lights a cigar and she feels an urge to smoke also; (b) uttered by a husband in response to his wife's request for a cigarette on a jet airplane after the plane becomes airborne and the "No smoking" sign goes off; (c) uttered by a wife to her husband as she leaves for a bridge party and in response to his complaint, "I'm out of cigarettes."
2. Identify the performative utterances:
   Mickey Mantle hit .528 this season.
   I christen thee Janie Doe Smith.
   I now declare this session of the Jolly Girls Club adjourned.
   Great scott, the sink's stopped up again!

Meaning as Use
and Traditional Theories
of Truth: Redundancy Theory

The newer emphases on use and the discovery of such uses as the performative one have given impetus to a radical reassessment of traditional theories of truth. These theories were under attack long before Austin. Ironically, Austin held a version of one of them, the correspondence theory. But "performatives" gave to P. F. Strawson, an Oxford colleague of Austin, just the push he needed toward an ingenious version of a theory of truth to end theories of truth.

It can be noticed that

I did not kill the victim

is a denial of

I killed the victim.

It is the same as if we said

"I killed the victim" *is false.*

But suppose we say

"I killed the victim" *is true.*

What does the adjective "true" refer to? Does it describe any-thing? We might assume that it refers to or describes some prop-erty or relation, such as the traditional theories of truth have said. But what about our experience with the adjective "good" and the noun "art"? "Good" does not behave like a typical adjective. "Art" does not behave like a typical noun. Perhaps "true" is in the same case? Taking a cue from the nineteenth-century German mathematician Gottlob Frege, several philosophers have argued that "true" does not describe at all. When you say

"I killed the victim" is *true,*

you are not *describing* the statement "I killed the victim," you are *asserting* it. Far from describing, "true" is redundant. When you say

"I killed the victim" is *false,*

you are not describing "I killed the victim," you are *denying* it. It would be foolish to say that you are describing its *falseness* when you say, " 'I killed the victim' is false," but traditional theories of truth assume that you are talking about its trueness when you say it is true. Why should the one case be different from the other? P. F. Strawson has urged that saying "It's true" is like saying "Ditto" or "The same goes for me." It is, he says, a way of admit-ting, confirming, or conceding the statement without quoting the statement. So, although "true" is redundant taken as a description of a statement, it has good uses. The assumption that "true," being an adjective, describes, or names a property or relation, has led us to suppose that there is something called truth that all true statements have in common. Nothing but a dubious theory about words leads us to that assumption. In light of our discussion of "the meaning" of a sentence as its truth conditions, it seems the height of folly to suppose that all statements whose truth conditions are fulfilled would have the same truth conditions!—or, to put it otherwise, that all statements whose truth conditions were fulfilled would have the same criteria for that fulfillment, that is, the same descriptive meaning.

Strawson's theory of truth is relatively new, as such things go, despite its antecedents in Frege, Ramsey, Ayer, and Carnap. It may have undiscovered, fatal flaws. But the importance of use gives it a plausibility that even its opponents recognize. It is simpler than Tarski's cumbersome semantic theory, which Strawson criticizes. And Strawson's and Waismann's theories about "true" (see Bibliography) are altogether too closely paralleled by "art" and "good" to be ignored.

Suggestions for Further Reading

Ambrose, Alice, "The Problem of Linguistic Inadequacy." Reprinted in Max Black, ed., *Philosophical Analysis*. Englewood Cliffs, N.J., Prentice-Hall, Inc., 1950.

Austin, John Langshaw, *How to Do Things with Words*. New York, Oxford University Press, Inc., 1965. Paperback. Austin is second only to Wittgenstein as an influence on analytic philosophy.

———, *Philosophical Papers*. New York, Oxford University Press, Inc., 1961.

Ayer, Alfred Jules, *Language, Truth and Logic*, revised (copyright 1936). This classic of logical positivism is available from Dover Press in paperback.

———, ed., *Logical Positivism*. New York, Free Press of Glencoe, Inc., 1959. Classics of the movement are reprinted; Ayer's valuable and authoritative "Editor's Introduction" gives a survey of the movement's development.

Black, Max, *The Labyrinth of Language*. New York, Frederick A. Praeger, Inc., 1968. This includes both philosophical and linguistic approaches to the nature and function of language on a level comprehensible to a beginner.

Danto, Arthur, *Analytical Philosophy of Knowledge*. New York, Cambridge University Press, 1968. Chapter 11 is an up-to-date discussion; see also his *What Philosophy Is*. New York, Harper & Row, Publishers, 1968.

Feigl, Herbert and Wilfred Sellars, eds., *Readings in Philosophical Analysis*. New York, Appleton-Century-Crofts, 1949.

Flew, Antony, ed., *Logic and Language*, 1st and 2d series. Oxford, Basil Blackwell and Mott, 1951, 1953. Paperback. This contains essays in ordinary language analysis.

————, ed., *Essays in Conceptual Analysis*. New York, St. Martin's Press, Inc., 1956.

Gorovitz, Samuel, Ron G. Williams, et al., *Philosophical Analysis: An Introduction to Its Language and Techniques*. New York, Random House, Inc., 1963. Paperback. This is an elementary introduction to all areas of philosophical analysis with much emphasis on the use of logic.

Hempel, Carl, "Problems and Changes in the Empirical Criterion of Meaning." Reprinted in Nagel and Brandt. The author follows the fortunes and misfortunes of the verifiability theory of meaning.

Hill, Thomas E., *Contemporary Theories of Knowledge*. New York, The Ronald Press Company, 1961. This is a valuable exposition for the beginner.

Hospers, John, *An Introduction to Philosophical Analysis*, 2d ed. Englewood Cliffs, N.J., Prentice-Hall, Inc., 1967. Standard text.

James, William, "Pragmatism's Theory of Truth." Reprinted in various James collections and introductory anthologies.

Locke, John, *Essay Concerning Human Understanding*. Book III, containing his theory of language, is excerpted in Nagel and Brandt.

Nagel, Ernest and Richard B. Brandt, eds., *Meaning and Knowledge*. New York, Harcourt, Brace & World, Inc., 1965. This is an authoritative collection of readings, many of which will be difficult for beginners.

Nowell-Smith, Patrick, *Ethics*. Baltimore, Md., Penguin Books, Inc., 1954. Paperback. Chapters 5 and 6 analyze ethical adjectives and their relations to other words.

Pitcher, George, ed., *Truth*. Englewood Cliffs, N.J., Prentice-Hall, Inc., 1964. Paperback. This contains selected essays, primarily on the redundancy theory of truth, and an excellent bibliography.

Quine, W. V. O., "Two Dogmas of Empiricism." Reprinted, in part, in Nagel and Brandt, above.

Rorty, Richard, ed., *The Linguistic Turn*. Chicago, Ill., University of Chicago Press, 1967. This is a representative anthology on the importance of language in philosophy, with a thorough bibliography.

Russell, Bertrand, *The Problems of Philosophy*. New York, Oxford University Press, Inc., 1912. This has a durable introduction; the chapter on truth is reprinted in Nagel and Brandt.

Ryle, Gilbert, *Dilemmas*. New York, Cambridge University Press, 1954. Paperback. Ryle argues that typical philosophical problems arise from linguistic misconceptions.

Schlick, Moritz, "Meaning and Verification." Reprinted in Feigl and Sellars. Schlick replies to C. I. Lewis's article "Experience and Meaning," reprinted in the same volume.

Strawson, Peter F., "Truth." Reprinted in Pitcher and in Nagel and Brandt.

Tarski, Alfred, "The Semantic Conception of Truth." Reprinted in Feigl and Sellars.

Toulmin, Stephen, *The Uses of Argument*. New York, Cambridge University Press, 1958. This shows how the context and use affect the deployment of formal arguments.

Waismann, Friedrich, "How I See Philosophy." Reprinted in Ayer, *Logical Positivism* and various anthologies.

————, *Principles of Linguistic Philosophy*. New York, The Macmillan Company, 1965. Waismann tries to develop a logic of questions, and presents points on truth in preceding article in more detail.

————, "Verifiability." Reprinted in Flew, *Logic and Language* and in Nagel and Brandt. This is a searching criticism of the notion that verification of a statement is an open-and-shut enterprise.

Wilson, John, *Language and the Pursuit of Truth*. New York, Cambridge University Press, 1967. Paperback. This is an elementary conceptual analysis of a nondoctrinaire kind.

Wittgenstein, Ludwig, *Philosophical Investigations*, 2d ed. Oxford, Basil Blackwell and Mott, 1958.

3

Logic

To have knowledge that can be expressed in words is to know that a statement is true or false. The importance of logic is that in knowing that one statement is true a person knows more. He knows that its contradictory is false, that those statements implied by it are true, and that their contradictories, in turn, are false. Just how one knows all this is the main interest of this chapter.

The preceding discussion of theories of truth need cause no confusion in discussing logic. Whatever the definition of "true" and "false," they are opposite values and mutually exclusive except in some very special and advanced branches of logic that cannot concern us here. Thus to assert that "It is raining" is true is to assert that the conditions specified in its intensional meaning are fulfilled. To deny "It is raining," whether by asserting that it is false or simply by saying "It is not raining," is to deny that those conditions are fulfilled.

If my dinner host shouts, "It's raining!" from the doorway, I know his descriptive meaning. I do not know whether this empirical statement is true, but from the context I am inclined to believe that it is raining; that is simply to say that the truth conditions, I believe, are fulfilled. I can test his statement only by seeing for myself the meteorological conditions. If he yells, "Rain is water falling from the sky!" his statement is analytic, a tautology, and I know that it is true as soon as I know its descriptive meaning; this sentence is true by virtue of its type, true each time it is tokened. I do not have to examine rain or anything else to know this. He could be joking if he shouted, "It's raining!" but there is no comparable sense in which an analytic statement might be intended to deceive me. (Of course, it might *remind* me of something and mislead me because of its nonliteral associations.) But if he shouted, "Rain really isn't rain!" it would be a very strange utterance. It might be a joke, a kind of riddle or puzzle, and philosophy abounds with such. Literally and descriptively, however, I should have to take it as a self-contradiction and as false, and that, again, I know simply from knowing "the meaning."

Inference: Deductive and Inductive

The reason for reviewing these three kinds of statement is to point out that I *can* know in various ways whether they are true or false; two of them simply by knowing their descriptive meaning, one by checking it against the facts, by observation. Now all three *can* be known to be true or false without the kind of reasoning that consists of saying something like

A is true, therefore B is true.

If I were in a favorable position to observe the weather I would not need to do any reasoning like that. But how much of my knowledge is gained in this way? How much of it is based on direct observation or the simple apprehension of the descriptive meaning of a statement? Even though my waking hours are flooded with data from my senses, even though I spend most of them hearing people talk, talking myself, or reading, if I live for seventy-five years I am awake during only fifty of those. There are billions of other years, billions of other events, billions of other people; these I know only indirectly, though often with very high probability that my beliefs about them are correct. This knowledge constitutes a much larger percentage of my total knowledge than do my direct experience and the things I know from the analytic or self-contradictory statements that happen to come to my attention. Most of my knowledge comes through some kind of *inferential reasoning*, conscious or unconscious, about what I *do* know through my senses and read and hear.

Let us take the example "It is raining." If, instead of hearing my host, I hear the sound of thunder and automobile tires swishing on wet pavement, see flares of brightness that seem to be lightning flashes, and remember that it was cloudy when I came in, then I probably will conclude that it is raining. If I cannot see out from my place at the dinner table, I probably will ask someone, "Is that rain?" The reasoning from the evidence above was done *inductively*, and I do not know that "It is raining" is true as certainly as I know that "Rain is water falling from the sky" is true or that "Rain is not really rain" is false. I could not be mistaken about the latter two, but I could be mistaken about the first statement even on very good evidence. Whereas there would be inconsistency in saying

Rain really never is rain

or

Rain isn't water falling from the sky

there is no inconsistency in saying

All the sights and sounds associated with rain are present

and

It is not raining.

These issues are clarified in the readings on induction. The point here is that in inductive reasoning there is always the possibility that, however good the quality or however large the quantity of the evidence, the conclusion reached from it *may* be false, in that it is not inconsistent to admit the evidence and yet deny the conclusion drawn from it. With good *deductive* reasoning, on the other hand, this cannot happen. This chapter is almost wholly concerned with deductive logic.

Generally we may define "logic" as the principles of correct reasoning. We cannot even discuss the subject without doing so in terms of the relations between ideas that are formulated by declarative sentences as assertions. Those assertions that are used as evidence are called *premises;* those the truth of which is derived from the premises are called *conclusions.* The classification of a statement as premise or conclusion depends on which position it occupies in a particular argument; for instance, the conclusion of one argument can be a premise in another argument. The whole collection of statements in which one statement (the conclusion) is derived from others (the premises) is called an *argument* (not to be confused with a quarrel). The process of drawing a conclusion from evidence is called *inference,* which should not be confused with implication, as is often done. Drawing a conclusion is inferring; trying to get someone *else* to draw a conclusion from what you indirectly point out to him is implying. For example:

> When George said, "I see Ted is sober today," he implied that Ted is usually drunk; at least, that is what I inferred from what he said.

Here, we must notice, "imply" is not used in the more technical sense of the logician but more in the sense of "insinuate." As we shall see, insinuation is too imprecise a notion for the logician, but it helps distinguish "imply" from "infer."

In the best of deductive reasoning, if the argument is such that we cannot admit the premises and at the same time deny the conclusion without contradicting ourselves, the argument is called *valid.* Logicians usually reserve "valid" as a term for *deductive* arguments only. It is easy to be confused about the relationship between the notion of validity and the notion of truth: Can an argument be valid if its premises are false? Surely, just as a mathematical problem can be worked out correctly even though the figures in it represent nothing real, factual, or true. For instance, if I say,

I have four million dollars in the Chase Manhattan Bank.
I have three million dollars in my mattress.
Therefore I have at least seven million dollars,

my arithmetic is faultless and my argument is valid. Could you admit my premises, yet deny my conclusion? No. Naturally you are most interested in whether my premises are true, but to determine that you will have to look outside the argument, examine my mattress and bank account, not my words. Validity is a matter of *if: If* the argument is such that the premises cannot be admitted while the conclusion is denied, the argument is valid. *If* I have the first two sums mentioned, there is literally no denying that I have the third. "Valid" is not in logic, as in ordinary language, a term of blanket praise. It is appraisal of only one aspect of an argument: its *form*, the way it is put together. Everyone will rightly demand *true* premises in any argument that is presented to him as proof that a conclusion is true. An argument that both is correct in its reasoning (valid) and has true premises is called *sound*. But in a mathematics book we do not ask whether the statements in the problems are true or false; the principle is the same. Even hard-headed businessmen do not always demand true premises, but may reason thus: "Suppose we invest a hundred thousand for the plant, have a first year's gross of thirty thousand, . . ." But many people are flabbergasted when they pick up a logic book and read "An argument can be valid even if there is not a true statement in it." Truth and validity are two different things. Validity is purely a matter of syntax, of relations between statements. Truth is a more vexing notion, but unless the coherence theory of truth is correct, we cannot know the truth of all statements by relating them to other statements.

To clarify further the notion of validity and the difference between induction and deduction, take two arguments that seem similar. Take:

All colts are young horses.
Zap is a colt.
Therefore, Zap is a young horse.

You cannot admit the premises without being forced to admit the conclusion. But then take:

All cases of botulism have been fatal.
Ricky has botulism.
Therefore, Ricky will not recover.

The upward path of medicine is strewn with arguments like this that have been smashed, which means that people have successfully admitted the premises of those arguments and denied the conclusions. To do so with this argument one need only produce a cure for botulism and apply it to Ricky so that he *does* recover. The second argument is properly inductive, the first is deductive. If a person insists that the second argument makes it impossible to deny the conclusion once one has admitted the premises, he is *claiming* it is deductive, and valid as well. But such a position places an impossible burden on his argument, which properly can claim the highest *probability* for the conclusion, but not theoretical *necessity*. The difference between them that makes it possible to deny the conclusion of the second while admitting apparently overwhelming evidence for it, that is, admitting the premises, is that the premises in the botulism argument contain two different classes of case, past and present cases of botulism. Ricky's has not yet been fatal, since he is still alive. Only if botulism were defined as fatal, which it is not, would the argument give us a deductive relationship between the premises and the conclusion. And that kind of relationship is the one we do have in the Zap argument: It will be recalled from the discussion of definition by genus and difference that anything classified as a colt is automatically classed as a young thing and as a horse.

Not all valid deductive arguments depend on the kind of meaning relationships in the Zap argument. Consider:

All soldiers who died in the Spanish-American War were over sixteen.
Tony was a soldier who died in the Spanish-American War.
Therefore, Tony was over sixteen.

Whether any of these statements is true does not concern us, only what relations exist between them if all the premises were true. The point is that the class of soldiers who died in the Spanish-American War is closed; there will be no more of them, as there will or might be cases of botulism and fatalities. Since the class of soldiers who died in the Spanish-American War is included in the class of people who are over sixteen and Tony is included in the first class, Tony is also included in the second class. There is no denying the conclusion once we admit the premises; thus this is a valid deductive argument. The botulism argument is inductive, though one might mistakenly try to present it as deductive.

Another issue may confuse us here: how the *premises* are arrived at. Surely there is nothing wrong and much right in saying that we know *inductively* both the premise of the inductive argument, "All cases of botulism have been fatal," and the premise of the deductive argument, "All soldiers who died in the Spanish-American War were over sixteen." However, we classify an argument as inductive or deductive not on the basis of how its premises are arrived at but on the basis of how its conclusion is arrived at. In the Spanish-American War argument, the conclusion is necessarily true if the premises are true. In the botulism argument, the conclusion is very highly probable, it is one that in light of the premises is very reasonable, but it is *not necessarily* true, even if the premises are true.

This is not to say that invalid deductive arguments are simply inductive, either! It is clearly to say that an argument that is such that if its premises are true its conclusion cannot possibly be false is both deductive and valid. The difference between invalid deductive arguments and inductive arguments is this: If an argument is *presented* as one whose conclusion cannot possibly be false if its premises are true, it is presented as a deductive argument, and must be judged accordingly; if its conclusion can be false, then the argument is invalid deductive. If an argument is presented as one whose conclusion is *probably* true (this always has *degrees*) if its premises are true, it is presented as an inductive argument. Obviously there are obscurities here about the nature of induction. Bertrand Russell, regarded as one of the greatest English-speaking logicians, denied that there is anything properly called inductive logic, though he admitted there is inductive reasoning. Some who say that there is inductive logic claim that it argues that, because one case is similar to another case in respects X and Y, it is therefore probably similar in respect Z. With deduction, it is claimed that the conclusion is true simply because of the relation of its *meaning* to the meaning of the premises.

There is in general circulation a popular definition of the difference between induction and deduction, which says that induction argues from the particular to the general and that deduction argues from the general to the particular. As a rule of thumb that is not bad. But consider the following:

Washington is north of Atlanta.
Atlanta is north of Miami.
Therefore, Washington is north of Miami.

That is a deductive argument of a type familiar to logicians, but it is about nothing but particulars. The fact that in this deductive argument each of these cities can be treated as a class of one does not throw any light on the subject; they are nevertheless particulars from beginning to end. That is, if Washington is "all cities located at longitude L and latitude I," it is nevertheless a particular city, and so are Atlanta and Miami. So the popular rule of thumb does not enable us to tell whether this argument is deductive or inductive. A clearer way has already been indicated.

Before we get into the fundamental particulars of formal logic, one more thing should be said. In all our examples of reasoning so far, nothing has been said to indicate that in logical reasoning we are "thinking," in terms of having thoughts go through our head. Nothing indeed has suggested that logic is even remotely concerned with the psychological processes of our minds while we are reasoning. And that is as it should be. It took centuries for logic to get free from its association with speculative psychology. (Up until about the same time, speculative psychology had been a part of philosophy, but then with empirical methods in the study of mental and neural phenomena it became an independent subject, psychology proper.) When logic finally did separate from psychology with such men as Gottlob Frege, it was under the inspiration of mathematics that it did so. Mathematicians were trying to straighten out the foundations of their own discipline when more or less as a by-product they established mathematical and symbolic logic on a firm foundation.

Reasoning is relating things to each other. Logical reasoning is the process of relating signs or symbols to each other—somewhat complicated ones, such as symbols for classes of statements or symbols for statements.

Professor Gilbert Ryle has compared the difference between eating and digesting to that between acquiring and processing knowledge. As the digestive mechanism of the stomach may be in perfect working order even when there is nothing in the stomach to digest, so logic is a purely formal set of machinery that can grind on even though there is no content. It works as well on a dry run as with real flesh and blood content.

Exercises

1. Which of the following arguments are inductive and which are deductive?
   a. All *A* is *B*; All *B* is *C*; Therefore, all *A* is *C*.
   b. If the sponge is saturated with water then the sponge is wet.
   c. A man resembling the suspect was noticed leaving the murder scene a few minutes after the murder. Therefore, the suspect is guilty.
   d. The sun will rise tomorrow because it always has risen in the past.
2. Which of the following deductive arguments are valid and which invalid?
   a. All chickens are rats; All rats are cobras; Therefore, all chickens are cobras.
   b. Anyone with a quarter can buy a cup of coffee at Joe's; Slim has a Harvard degree and a quarter; Therefore, Slim can buy a cup of coffee at Joe's.
   c. If you eat that you'll die within ten minutes, so if you want to be sure of living for at least ten more minutes, all you have to do is keep from eating that.
3. According to the definition of "valid deductive argument" an argument can be valid even though all its statements are false. What does the following "argument" show about the relation between true statements and valid arguments?

   The Pentagon in Washington, D.C. is one of the smallest public buildings in the world, having a floor space totaling six square inches. Since there are a total of twelve government employees on duty at the Pentagon, this is one half of a square inch floor space for each employee.

The Logic of Terms:
The Traditional Calculus of Classes

We know without possibility of denial that if anything is a colt it is a young horse, for that is what all colts are, by definition. The inference here is absolutely solid, and when we are told that Zap is a colt, we infer immediately that he is a young horse. If someone tells us, "Ha, I fooled you. Zap is like that 'young' woman in *Lost Horizon;* he only looks young, actually Zap is fifty-six years old!" we would simply say, "Then Zap is not a colt, since he is not young." That's logic and there is nothing that can be replied to it, if "colt" is going to have the meaning it usually has.

Classical or traditional logic furnishes us with several ways of seeing relationships between statements that provide the basis for inference, and it also warns us against trying to draw tempting but unwarranted inferences—*fallacies.* Traditional logic as begun by Aristotle and developed considerably by later logicians provided us with four kinds of *categorical proposition;* that is, propositions asserting a relation of *class inclusion* or *class exclusion.* The basic characteristic of each was that it related two *terms,* or *classes,* to each other by class inclusion and class exclusion; hence the name "calculus of classes." This way of deduction is based on the relation of classes *within* sentences, not simply the relation of sentences (which will be discussed in the next section). For example:

A. All men are egotists. All S is P.
E. No men are egotists. No S is P.
I. Some men are egotists. Some S is P.
O. Some men are not egotists. Some S is not P.

(The labels A, E, I, O have an uncertain origin. It has been suggested that the affirmative propositions are labeled "A" and "I" because those are the first two vowels in the Latin word for "affirm," while "E" and "O" occupy a comparable position in the word for "negate.") The first term, "men," is the subject class, hence the abbreviation S. The second term, "egotists," is the predicate term, hence the abbreviation P. It should be noted here that symbols are important in logic for two reasons. First, they shorten the welter of details so that we can get to the skeletal framework of the argument, which is its *form.* Second, symbols are neutral, and instead of talking about women, sex, race, religion, politics, and so on, we can by using symbols in an argument concentrate attention away from emotional reactions and on the form of the argument, which is the basis of the argument's validity.

Given that an A-form of categorical proposition is true, what follows from it? If

All men are egotists,

what follows? We are inclined to think, "Well, it follows that the world is a pretty bad place in which to live." Perhaps that is one consequence, but logically it is a fairly remote one. We need other "suppressed" (unstated) premises to derive

The world is a pretty bad place in which to live,

premises that will include the terms "world" and "pretty bad place in which to live." The question that we are asking is much more literal and simple-minded: What do we know about egotists and men if we know that all men are egotists? We know one thing:

Some men are not egotists

is false if "All men are egotists" is true. And *vice versa*. The two propositions A and O are *contradictories*, which is to say that wherever one is true the other must be false. The same sort of relation exists between E,

No men are egotists,

and I,

Some men are egotists;

that is, wherever we know that the one is true, we know that the other is false.

If A, "All men are egotists," is true *and* there are any men, then I, "Some men are egotists" is true. Here we must be careful to remember how literal-minded the logician is: What would be the point in saying that some men are egotists if all men are egotists? Granted we would think of few situations in which it would be appropriate to utter or write I when A is true. But we have to grant the logician this: If there are any men, and if all of them are egotists, it follows that at least one man is an egotist! "At least one" is the meaning that is conventionally assigned to "some." At least one, perhaps more, perhaps even all, but no less than one, is covered under "some."

Another point we have to attend to about "all" is this: "all" and "no" are treacherous words. Consider:

All unicorns have one horn.
No unicorns have one horn.

Are we saying that there are any unicorns when we utter these propositions? Logicians puzzled over this for several years, and most decided this: We are not saying that there are any unicorns at all when we say "All unicorns . . ." We are saying something like "If there are any unicorns, all unicorns . . ." or "All the unicorns there are . . ." When this is realized, a strange thing happens: A and E can both be true at the same time; all the unicorns there are have one horn and none of the unicorns there are have one horn. Both these statements are true for a very simple reason: There are no unicorns, the subject class is empty, has no members.

Thus the two *universal* propositions, "All S is P" and "No S is P," are best taken as denials of the existence of members in certain classes, and the two *particular* propositions, "Some S is P" and "Some S is not P," must in all cases be taken as asserting that certain classes do have at least one member. To see how this works it is important to introduce the concept of a *complement*. For instance, relative to the class "egotists," everything in the universe falls into just two classes: egotists and non-egotists. "Non-egotists" in the complement are simply those things that are other than egotists; they are not necessarily anti-egotists. A rock is, presumably, a non-egotist, but not, we suppose, anti-egotist. To assert the A-form

All men are egotists

is to assert

No men are non-egotists,

that is,

The class of non-egotistical men is empty.

Or in terms of S and P,

S non-$P = 0$

We can show the complement of a term by putting a bar across the top of the term: Thus non-S would be $\overline{S}$, non-P, $\overline{P}$:

$S\overline{P} = 0$

The E-form turns out to be fairly noncomplex, not using a complement:

No men are egotists; No S is P; $SP = 0$

The I-form uses no complement too:

Some men are egotists; Some S is P; $SP \neq 0$

The "$\neq 0$" means "is not empty," that is, has members; there is at least one SP. The O-form is more complex:

Some men are not egotists; Some S is non-P; $S\overline{P} \neq 0$

Now we are in a position to see some of the other relations that traditional logic has discerned between the various terms and their complements in the four standard form categorical propositions—the relations of *obversion, conversion,* and *contraposition.* The process of drawing such conclusions is called *immediate inference.*

Conversion is the simplest of the operations by which immediate inferences are drawn. It is simply the reversal of the terms:

A: All *S* is *P. Converse:* All *P* is *S.* INVALID.
E: No *S* is *P. Converse:* No *P* is *S.* VALID.
 I: Some *S* is *P. Converse:* Some *P* is *S.* VALID.
O: Some *S* is not *P. Converse:* Some *P* is not *S.* INVALID.

A and O do not yield valid converses; E and I do. If one is tempted to think that the converse of O is the same as O, he should remember that "There is at least one thing that is in class *S* but *outside* class *P*" does not say or imply that "There is at least one thing that is *in* class *P,*" and so on. It is also sometimes tempting in an argument to convert an A-form, but it is fallacious to do so.

Obversion is a process of changing the affirmative or negative quality of the proposition (from "all" to "no"; from "is" to "is not") and of replacing the predicate term with its complement. The overall effect is a double negative that puts the proposition right back where it was, and thus all obverses of the four forms are valid immediate inferences:

A: All *S* is *P. Obverse:* No *S* is non-*P.* VALID.
E: No *S* is *P. Obverse:* All *S* is non-*P.* VALID.
 I: Some *S* is *P. Obverse:* Some *S* is not non-*P;* Some *S* is *P.* VALID.
O: Some *S* is not *P. Obverse:* Some *S* is non-*P;* Some *S* is not *P.*
   VALID.

Note that on the O-form when the quality of the proposition is changed from "is not" to "is" this does not change *P* to its complement. That is performed by "non-*P,*" which has the effect of undoing what the change in quality from negative to affirmative accomplished.

Contraposition is accomplished by replacing subject *and* predicate with their complements and reversing them thus:

A: All *S* is *P. Contrapositive:* All non-*P* is non-*S.* VALID.
E: No *S* is *P. Contrapositive:* No non-*P* is non-*S.* INVALID.
 I: Some *S* is *P. Contrapositive:* Some non-*P* is non-*S.* INVALID.
O: Some *S* is not *P. Contrapositive:* Some non-*P* is not non-*S.*
   VALID.

These devices may seem a pedant's delight, but they are useful in doing the legitimate tinkering with syllogisms that is necessary to get them into valid form. This, as we shall see more fully later, is one of the main problems in the practical application of formal logic—getting everyday language into the forms in which the machinery of logical proofs and disproofs and tests of ideas can be brought to bear.

The *syllogism* is the form of argument used in traditional logic to prove and disprove assertions and to test ideas. For more than two thousand years it was the only generally recognized method of proof and disproof using words as distinct from mathematical symbols. It is a rigidly defined form in which there are three classes, of which the subject and predicate of the conclusion are only two, and are designated by the *S* and *P* already made familiar above. There are two premises, consisting of categorical propositions, and a conclusion, also a categorical proposition. The third term, abbreviated *M* for "middle," occurs in each premise but does not appear in the conclusion. Take the following syllogism, made up of three universal propositions.

All men are egotists.
No egotists are happy people.
Therefore, no men are happy people.

The term "men" in the conclusion is the subject term for the whole syllogism, being abbreviated *S* wherever it occurs. "Happy people" is the predicate term of the conclusion and is indicated by *P*. The third term is "egotists," and is labeled *M*. That it is the middle term can be seen by drawing a tiny circle and labeling it *S* for "men," a slightly larger circle enclosing it labeled *M* for "egotists," and a still larger circle enclosing both the others and labeled *P* for "happy people." The circle *M* is, as you see, in the middle, being a larger class than *S* but a smaller class than *P*. In any case, *S* and *P* are the *S* and *P* of the conclusion and *M* is the term not included in the conclusion.

A device for testing the validity of this syllogism can be constructed by remembering the remarks made about terms and their complements in the preceding discussion of immediate inference. The principles involved are: (1) Relations between two of the classes affect the other class as well, and (2) the definition of validity is that, in a valid argument, if the premises are true then the conclusion must also be true, on pain of self-contradiction.

In the universe of discourse in which men, egotists, and happy people are the three classes, these three classes and their three complements make *eight*, and *only* eight, possible permutations of classes to which any individual thing might belong. We list these in a table, which we will use in testing the validity of the syllogism:

1. Happy man egotist
2. Happy man non-egotist
3. Happy non-man non-egotist
4. Non-happy non-man non-egotist
5. Non-happy non-man egotist
6. Non-happy man egotist
7. Non-happy man non-egotist
8. Happy non-man egotist

We test the validity of the argument by marking the table in relation to both premises and asking whether, having marked what we say when we assert the premises, we have also marked what we say when we assert the conclusion. In this case, the first premise asserts

All men are egotists.

This says there are no men who are non-egotists, or that 2 and 7 have no members. We can indicate this in various ways; a good way is to draw a line through the number, not the terms in it. (In this way we mark that entire combination but do not make it illegible on the table; if pencil is used, the table can be corrected or reused.) The second premise is

No egotists are happy people.

This declares that there are no happy egotists, that 1 and 8 have no members, so we can draw a line through the numbers 1 and 8. This completes the depicting of what the premises are asserting about the three classes. The completed table is marked thus:

1̶. Happy man egotist
2̶. Happy man non-egotist
3. Happy non-man non-egotist

    4. Non-happy non-man non-egotist
    5. Non-happy non-man egotist
    6. Non-happy man egotist
    7. Non-happy man non-egotist
    8. Happy non-man egotist

Next we check the conclusion to see whether in asserting the premises we have also asserted the conclusion. Recall that the definition of a valid argument is this: If the premises of an argument are such that if they are true then the conclusion cannot be false without self-contradiction, the argument is valid. Look now at the conclusion:

    No men are happy people.

It asserts that there are no happy men. Then "happy" and "man" should not now occur together anywhere in the diagram, if the argument is valid. They were originally listed together only twice: in 1 and 2. Both of these have been declared empty by the premises. Therefore, in asserting the premises, we have asserted the conclusion, and the argument is *valid*.

    It is easy to see from this that when we say something about two of the terms we say something by implication about the other term, and that when the final reckoning comes, that is, in asking what we are saying when we assert the conclusion, we find in a valid argument that we have already said in the premises what the conclusion is saying. The table as marked shows what it is like for the premises to be true, and at the same time shows that it is impossible for the conclusion to be false.

    Using the same table, without the ordinary language terms, let us test a second argument, one containing a mixture of particular and universal propositions.

    No egotists are happy people.
    Some men are not egotists.
    Therefore, some men are happy people.

"Men" in the conclusion is *S*, "happy people" is *P*, and "egotists" is *M*. This time, instead of writing the table with the equivalents or values of S, P, and M, we shall simply use S, P, and M and their complements (note: the *order* is "man," "happy," "egotist," etc.):

1. SPM
2. $SP\overline{M}$
3. $S\overline{PM}$
4. $\overline{SPM}$
5. $\overline{S}PM$
6. $\overline{S}PM$
7. $\overline{S}P\overline{M}$
8. $S\overline{P}M$

The first premise is

No egotists are happy people: $MP = 0$

This says that the combination MP is empty whenever it occurs, which is in 1 and 6; these numbers we can draw a line through. The second premise is

Some men are not egotists: $S\overline{M} \neq 0$

which asserts that $S\overline{M}$ has at least one member. But a problem arises here. The table shows two combinations of $S\overline{M}$, numbers 2 and 3: "man happy non-egotist" and "man non-happy non-egotist." To say that a class has at least one member we shall have to mark the table differently than in the previous instances, which have all involved universal categorical propositions ("all" and "no"). We can show that a class has members by marking a small x *before* it (remembering that x does not mean crossed out). But, if there is at least one man who is not an egotist, is he a happy or non-happy person? He cannot be both at once. Yet 2 is happy and 3 is non-happy. What are we to do? We can solve the problem by putting a question mark before 2 and 3, to show that the second premise is asserting that *one* but not *both* of these classes has at least one member.

The indicating of the premises is thus complete. The completed table is marked thus:

$\cancel{1}$. *SPM*
? 2. *SPM*
? 3. *SPM*
4. *SPM*
5. *SPM*
$\cancel{6}$. *SPM*
7. *SPM*
8. *SPM*

It remains now to ask if in asserting the premises we have asserted the conclusion:

Some men are happy people: $SP \neq 0$

SP should have at least one member, according to the conclusion; 2 is the only place in the table where this might be asserted, and our premises have not definitely asserted it. The premises have said there is *at least* one $S\overline{M}$; whether it is an $SP\overline{M}$ or an $S\overline{PM}$, they have *not* said. So the conclusion *can* be false, while the premises are true: If there should be *only* one $S\overline{M}$ (which possibility has not been ruled out by the premises), and should it happen to be $S\overline{PM}$, then $SP \neq 0$, the conclusion, would be false. Thus the diagram shows that this syllogism is invalid.

A happier situation occurs with the following argument:

No egotists are happy.
Some men are happy.
Therefore, some men are not egotists.

The conclusion has "men" in the *S* position and "egotists" in the *P* class. "Happy people" constitutes the *M* term. The table for checking the validity of this argument is marked thus:

$\cancel{1}$. *SPM*
2. $SP\overline{M}$
3. $S\overline{P}M$
4. $\overline{S}PM$
5. $\overline{S}PM$

6. $\overline{S}PM$

7. $\overline{S}P\overline{M}$

x8. $S\overline{P}M$

The first premise,

No egotists are happy: $PM = 0$,

asserts that there are no happy egotists and eliminates PM wherever it occurs (in 1 and 6). The second premise,

Some men are happy: $SM \neq 0$,

declares that there is at least one happy man, so we place an x by 8; SM occurred in 1 also, but the arguer has already declared that 1 is empty. (This shows, by the way, that when we have one universal and one particular premise in a syllogism, we should diagram the universal premise *first*, for it will eliminate something.) The fact that 1 has been eliminated by the first premise leaves no possibility that there are happy men anywhere except in 8. The conclusion,

Some men are not egotists: $S\overline{P} \neq 0$,

declares that there is at least one non-egotist man. Have the premises already said that? Yes, in 8 the second premise said it, after the first premise had eliminated 1. So it would be impossible for the conclusion to be false while the premises are true.

This survey gives us the essentials of the traditional logic of terms. One can see its limitations, for though there are 256 possible combinations of the four standard categorical propositions into syllogisms (that is, permutations of S, P, and M and "all," "no," and "some"), only a few of these combinations yield valid syllogisms. But of more importance is the fact that with a syllogism you can prove or disprove only those statements that declare that some class has members or does not have members. (This includes, by the way, asserting that things do or do not have a certain predicate, as in "All roses are red," and that something performs or does not perform a certain action, as in "Some cars don't run," and so on.) This limitation is a point that critics of the syllogism have been making, in one way or another, since the Renaissance. A much more versatile logic, using sentences rather than terms as the things to be related to each other, was developed in the late nineteenth and early twentieth century. The *sentential calculus* will be the subject of the next section.

Exercises

1. The following syllogism is not valid but also it is not in correct syllogistic order. Find the conclusion. Identify *S* and *P*. The other term in the syllogism will be *M*. Then place the statements in the syllogism in the proper syllogistic order.

> Some on-duty policemen are not armed because some on-duty policemen are undercover agents and some undercover agents are not armed.

2. On the following table show the invalidity of the following syllogism.

> No albinos are brown-eyed.
> No Kibkus are brown-eyed.
> Therefore, all Kibkus are albinos.

> 1. SPM
> 2. $SP\overline{M}$
> 3. $S\overline{PM}$
> 4. $\overline{SPM}$
> 5. $\overline{S}PM$
> 6. $\overline{S}PM$
> 7. $\overline{SP}\overline{M}$
> 8. $S\overline{P}M$

3. Check the following for validity on the preceding table.

> All *M* is *P*.
> Some *S* is *M*.
> Therefore, some *S* is *P*.

4. Check the following syllogism for validity on the preceding table.

> All Communists support Brown for dogcatcher.
> Alf Klotchmer supports Brown for dogcatcher.
> Therefore, Alf Klotchmer is a Communist.

The Logic of Sentences: The
Sentential or Propositional Calculus

If we assert that all men are egotists, we are relating two classes and their members to each other in one sentence: we are saying that all members of the class "man" are also members of the class "egotist." In advancing a syllogism in argument we are, of course, relating the sentences in the argument to each other in a very definite way. But this is only a means of relating the *classes* to each other. Now suppose that we take two sentences and form a compound sentence with them, such as

Napoleon was emperor of France and Bismarck was king of Siam.

On a true-false examination in a class on world civilization, the whole statement would be marked "false," since one statement within it is false while both statements within it are asserted to be true—or, rather, are simply asserted. On such a true-false examination it is a cardinal principle that if one sentence in a compound sentence that is a conjunction (two sentences joined by "and") is false, the whole compound sentence is false.

Sentence logic as represented by the calculus of propositions (as distinguished from the calculus of terms) relates *sentences* to each other, not classes, and has four kinds of *compound proposition*: the *conjunction*, the *negation*, the *disjunction*, and the *conditional*. They are based on the same principle as the example from the true-false examination: The truth or falsity of the compound is determined by (is a function of) the truth or falsity of the noncompound propositions within the compound. Thus if one or both of the propositions in a conjunction is false, the conjunction itself is false. We can show this by a device called a *truth table*, which we will use for the other three kinds of compound proposition also. Let us represent

Napoleon was emperor of France

by *p,* and

Bismarck was king of Siam

by *q*. For "and," the all-important word by which we relate these two sentences, we use simply a centered dot, and the conjunction is symbolized thus:

$p \cdot q$

Just as the little table that we used to check the validity of syllogisms showed all the possible permutations of the three classes in a syllogism, the following table shows all the possible permutations of truth and falsity of two statements in a compound. The columns *p* and *q* are the *reference columns*. Line 1 shows that when *p* is true and *q* is true, *p* · *q* is true. Lines 2, 3, and 4 show that when one or both of the constituents *p* and *q* are false, the compound *p* · *q* is false.

	p	*q*	~*q*	*p* · *q*	~*p*	*p* ∨ *q*	*p* ⊃ *q*
1.	*T*	*T*	*F*	*T*	*F*	*T*	*T*
2.	*T*	*F*	*T*	*F*	*F*	*T*	*F*
3.	*F*	*T*	*F*	*F*	*T*	*T*	*T*
4.	*F*	*F*	*T*	*F*	*T*	*F*	*T*

Besides the connective "and" used in a conjunction to relate propositions together, the connectives "not," "either . . . or," and "if . . . then" are generally used to relate propositions in the other compound propositions, that is, in negations, disjunctions, and conditionals, respectively.

It might seem at first that

Bismarck was not king of Siam

is not a compound at all, for there is only *one* statement inside the whole. Yet that very fact does make it truth-functional: The truth or falsity of

Bismarck was not king of Siam

is determined by the truth or falsity of the statement contained in it,

Bismarck was king of Siam.

If that statement within the negative compound is false, the compound is true; if it is true, the compound is false. The denial of my statement is thus a truth-functional compound. The symbol used to deny the truth of a statement is the tilde: Bismarck was king of Siam is symbolized thus:

$\sim p$

"Either . . . or" is a relation we often assert between statements: that either one is true or the other is true. In the logic of propositions this is the disjunction, and it means that at least one and possibly both are true.

Either Napoleon was emperor of France or Bismarck was king of Siam.

This is symbolized thus, letting *p* represent the first statement and *q* the second:

$p \vee q$

("v" is for the Latin *vel*, a very inclusive sense of "or"). Like $p \cdot q$, this compound has four possible permutations in the reference columns of the truth table. It is true under all conditions except one, that in which *p* is false and *q* is false. If it seems strange that the table shows $p \vee q$ true under the condition that *both p* and *q* are true, remember that this is the *inclusive* sense of "either . . . or," not the *exclusive* sense used most often in ordinary language and in which not both the alternatives can be true at the same time.

    The last of the four truth-functional compound propositions is called the conditional:

If Napoleon was emperor of France then all men are egotists.

The two compounds are *p,* "Napoleon was emperor of France," and *q,* "All men are egotists." The "if . . . then" relationship asserted to hold between these two statements is symbolized by a horseshoe, and the compound is symbolized thus:

p ⊃ q

As you notice on the truth table, *p ⊃ q* is false under only one condition, when *p* is true while *q* is false. This requires some explanation.

The meanings of "if . . . then" in ordinary language are several: (1) A causal connection is asserted by "if . . . then," in which we assert that if a cause is present then its effect will follow ("If you mix blue paint with yellow, then you will have green paint"). (2) There is a meaning of "if . . . then" that applies purely to matters of definition; for example, "If Zap is a colt then Zap is a young horse." (3) There are such things as *promises* made in terms of "if . . . then," in which we take two propositions that are not necessarily otherwise related and connect them; for example, a gangster says, "If you hit Fink then I give you the bread."

The logician's horseshoe symbol means only what all of these relations have in common, and that is simply this: Wherever the first statement is true, the second statement is true. The horseshoe asserts that *p* is the *sufficient* condition for *q.* If this *relation* does not hold—if *p* is true and *q* is false—then of course the assertion —*p ⊃ q*—that it does hold is false, and that is what is noted in line 2 of the truth table.

The odd—or seemingly odd—feature of the conditional relationship is that according to the definition spelled out by the truth table, "If Napoleon was emperor of France then all men are egotists" is true even if it is *false* that Napoleon was emperor of France (lines 3 and 4). The simplest explanation of this is that "If *p* is true then *q* is true" does *not* say what will "happen" if *p* is false, only what will "happen" if *p* is true. Take this piece of belligerent talk:

"If you had moved another inch then I'd have clobbered you."

The person called "you" did *not* move another inch in the situation described. The only way the remark could be shown false would be if "you" *had* moved the inch in question and the threatener had *not* clobbered "you" or, if the threat were made about the *future* ("If you move another inch, then I'll clobber you"), for "you" to move the other inch in question and the threatener not clobber "you." In the conditional statement, the first statement, *p* (called the *antecedent*), is related to the second statement, *q* (the *consequent*), in exactly the same manner that the premises of a valid argument are related to its conclusion. That is, if wherever the premises are true the conclusion is true, the argument is valid; if wherever the antecedent is true the consequent is true, the conditional statement is true. This does not resolve all the difficulties in understanding the oddities of the conditional, but for that purpose one should consult a book in logic or logical theory such as those that are listed in the bibliography at the end of this chapter.

The truth table above has been used to *define* the four basic kinds of relations asserted in truth-functional compounds. It did this by telling the conditions under which those four compounds would be true and the conditions under which they would be false. As we saw in Chapters 1 and 2, this is a very vital part of knowing what a statement means. But the truth table can also be used to test the validity of arguments composed of these truth-functional compounds.

Let us examine a very common type of reasoning that is casually carried out so rapidly and automatically that it may seem pedantic to formalize it. (It is easy enough to fall into a fallacy in the use of "if . . . then" that it is worth noticing the differences between valid and fallacious forms of argument using the conditional.) Take this situation: You are driving down a New York street and you meet a car that looks like your best friend George's car. It is being driven by a man who looks like a thug. You wonder, Has someone stolen George's car and perhaps done harm to him in the bargain? As you watch the car in your rear-view mirror, you see that it bears an out-of-state license plate. You drop the subject from your mind. Your lightning-fast reasoning process has gone something like this:

If that had been George's car then it would have had a New York plate.
It did *not* have a New York plate.
Therefore, it was not George's car.

Or, in the symbols we have used for the conditional:

$$p \supset q$$
$$\sim q$$
$$\therefore \sim p$$

This form of argument is called *modus tollens*.

To use a truth table to test the validity of an argument in the propositional calculus, one must remember first the meaning of "valid": that it is impossible for a valid argument to have all true premises and a false conclusion. Since a truth table shows *all* the possible combinations of truth and falsity of the statements listed in its columns, it is a perfect test of the validity of an argument. To test the argument about the car and the license plate above, look at the truth table, and look for one thing: the combination of all the premises *T* and the conclusion *F*, for if you find it, the argument is invalid. First simply check those lines on the truth table that show *F* for the conclusion ~ *p*—lines 1 and 2. But you find that line 1 shows *F* for one premise and line 2 shows *F* for the other. Thus, since the truth table shows *all* possible combinations of truth and falsity for the premises and conclusion of this argument, and shows *no* combination of all premises *T* and conclusion *F*, it is impossible for that combination to exist, and the argument is valid.

Valid, yes. But something *can* go wrong with the argument, and it can happen to any argument: One or more of the premises might be false, that is, the argument might be *unsound*. But that does not affect its validity. Suppose that you had a thousand dollars in your mattress when you left home this morning, and that on the way to the bus stop you saw a used car priced for a thousand dollars, tax included. You would certainly conclude that you had enough money to buy the car for cash. But should the dealer have raised the price by the time you got the money and returned to the lot to buy the car, or should a thief have stolen the money from the mattress while you were gone, your conclusion would be wrong even though there was nothing at all wrong with your reasoning.

A second type of valid argument, called *modus ponens*, using the conditional is "illustrated by a similar situation." You and a friend are debating whether George is over twenty-one. You say "No." Your friend says "Yes." Then your friend says, "He voted in the last November election." That reasoning goes thus:

If he voted in the November election then he's over twenty-one.
He voted in the November election.
Therefore, he's over twenty-one.

It is formalized as:

$$p \supset q$$
$$\underline{p}$$
$$\therefore q$$

A quick look at the truth table shows no line in which the premises are all true and the conclusion false: You lose. The friend's argument is valid. Whether it is sound is a different matter, of course. If George somehow falsified his age, if he did not in fact vote in the November election, or if he lives in a state in which one does not have to be over twenty-one to vote, then the argument is unsound because at least one of its premises is false. But even if all the statements in it are false it is as solid a piece of reasoning as $2 + 2 = 4$.

There are two fallacious forms of argument using the conditional in ways that look very similar to these two valid arguments. Consider:

If it's George's car, then it has a New York license.
It has a New York license.
Therefore, it's George's car.

A look at the truth table shows that

$$p \supset q$$
$$\underline{q}$$
$$\therefore p$$

which is the form of this argument, is invalid, because line 3 contains the combination all premises T and conclusion F. We can easily spot this fallacy (in *other* people's arguments, anyway!), and often pinpoint it by such remarks as, "Just because it has a New York license doesn't mean it's George's car." Apparently what the arguer has done is to reinterpret his first premise and confusedly think of it as:

If it has a New York license then it's George's car,

which is far from what he stated. The fallacy is called the *fallacy of affirming the consequent.*
A similar fallacy is this:

If it's George's car, then it has a New York license.
It is not George's car.
Therefore, it does not have a New York license.

The form is:

$p \supset q$
$\sim p$
$\therefore \sim q$

The truth table shows in line 3 the combination of all the premises true and the conclusion false. The fallacy is that of *denying the antecedent.*
Disjunctives also offer two valid and two invalid forms of importance. Remembering that a disjunctive is false only under one condition, when both disjuncts are false, it is easy to see that an argument of the following form is valid:

Either George voted illegally or George is over twenty-one.
George is not over twenty-one.
Therefore, George voted illegally.

$p \vee q$
$\sim q$
$\therefore p$

A glance at the truth table shows no line in which both premises are true and the conclusion false, so the argument is valid. It would be the same for either disjunct:

Either George voted illegally or George is over twenty-one.
George did not vote illegally.
Therefore, George is over twenty-one.

$$p \vee q$$
$$\sim p$$
$$\therefore q$$

Again there is no line on the truth table that shows both of these premises true and the conclusion false at the same time. This form is called *disjunctive syllogism*.

It is quite another story if we argue interpreting "either . . . or" in an exclusive rather than an inclusive sense:

Either George voted illegally or George is over twenty-one.
George voted illegally.
Therefore, George is not over twenty-one.

$$p \vee q$$
$$p$$
$$\therefore \sim q$$

Line 1 on the truth table shows all the premises of the above argument true but the conclusion false. The argument is invalid. The same is true if we affirm q and deny p:

$$p \vee q$$
$$q$$
$$\therefore \sim p$$

Line 1 again shows all premises true and the conclusion false, making the argument invalid.

These are simple arguments, but valid arguments of any length can be made with the apparatus of the sentential calculus. One of its advantages over the categorical syllogism is its greater flexibility and versatility. By punctuating as in mathematics, longer, more complex propositions can be formulated in the sentential calculus:

$$[(p \vee q) \supset (r \cdot s)] \vee \{[(p \supset q) \cdot r] \supset s\}$$

Arguments involving a *mixture* of the different kinds of truth-functional compounds, whether it be in terms of very complex premises or simple premises using the different compounds, require larger truth tables with more lines, since more constituent statements and more possible combinations of truth and falsity are involved than in the ones illustrated thus far.

Although truth tables furnish a sure-fire test of validity for any and all arguments, of whatever complexity, in the sentential calculus, there is a method of *formal proofs*, like that of proving theorems in geometry, that is used for longer arguments. It involves two principles. First, it makes use of the valid inference patterns already checked out on the truth table, as a carpenter or dressmaker who uses many pieces of the same kind need not measure each new piece but can cut one piece and use it as a pattern for all others of the same kind. Once we know that a certain inference pattern, like *modus ponens, modus tollens,* or disjunctive syllogism, is a valid form of argument, we know that any argument having that form will be valid, for form is the basis of validity. Logicians refer to valid inference patterns as *inference rules*. Second, the method of formal proofs of validity makes use of these valid inference patterns in *steps*, just as a geometrical proof does. It uses the conclusion validly yielded in one step as a premise for another step, until, if the argument is valid, the conclusion of the last step in the proof is the same as the conclusion of the whole argument. Let us look at an example using the inference rules tested thus far.

1. If there was a struggle then there would be signs of a struggle.
2. There are no signs of a struggle.
3. Either there was a struggle or the victim knew the killer.
4. If the victim knew the killer then the accused is the most likely suspect.

Therefore, the accused is the most likely suspect.

We have to assign an abbreviation for each proposition; we will begin with *p* and use later letters in the alphabet as needed:

$p =$ There was a struggle.
$q =$ There are signs of a struggle.
$r =$ The victim knew the killer.
$s =$ The accused is the most likely suspect.

Each premise must be numbered for reference (the conclusion is not numbered). The argument formalizes thus:

1. $p \supset q$ *Proof:* 5. $\sim p$ (MT 1, 2)
2. $\sim q$ 6. r (DS 5, 3)
3. $p \lor r$ 7. s (MP 6, 4)
4. $r \supset s /\therefore s$

In the formal proof we look for something that is definitely asserted, something about which there are no *if*'s, *and*'s, or *but*'s
(in logic, "but" is the equivalent of "and"). Such a loose thread to
grasp for the purposes of unraveling is furnished by premise 2: We
can see that together premises 1 and 2 constitute a *modus tollens*,
and will validly yield $\sim p$ as the conclusion of the first step. We
number this step 5, as if it were another premise. Then we can see
that premise 3 and $\sim p$ constitute a disjunctive syllogism, a valid
inference pattern tested above on the truth table. A disjunctive
syllogism of these two yields r, which is listed as step 6. Then r,
validly arrived at, can function in a *modus ponens* form with
premise 4 to yield the conclusion of the original argument, which
is s. *Quod erat demonstrandum.* The argument is valid.

A list of about twenty inference rules is usually furnished by
elementary symbolic logic books, and in advanced symbolic logic
texts a proof consisting of twenty or thirty steps is not unusual.
The preceding discussion, however, must suffice in this volume for
purposes of illustrating the methods available for proof.

But the old standby is the truth table, for it is by this that the
simple inference patterns are tested and the most complex can be
tested also. There is a one-line truth table that furnishes a short
cut; the following introduction to it is something of a brain teaser.
Take the argument we have just shown valid by a formal proof.
The labels for all the columns for a complete truth table to test it
will read thus:

p	q	$\sim q$	r	s	$p \supset q$	$p \lor r$	$r \supset s$

Remember that the meaning of validity is this: If an argument is
valid, it is impossible for all the premises to be true while the conclusion is false. A complete truth table with reference columns for
$p, q, r,$ and s would have twelve lines, but if the argument were
invalid one of those lines would read T for all the premises and F
for the conclusion. What we do in a one-line truth table is attempt
to construct a line that shows the fatal combination. We first

arbitrarily label the conclusion F; then we *try* to label all the premises T. If the conclusion, s, is false, will it be logically possible for the premises to be true? The first ramification of false under s is that when we label the premise $r \supset s$ true we must label r false (*modus tollens*). Then if we are to label the premise $p \lor r$ true, we must label p true, since r is false (disjunctive syllogism). But when we have done that, the logical chickens come home to roost and end abruptly our attempts to label all the premises true while the conclusion is false: If we are to label the premise $p \supset q$ true we must label q true by *modus ponens*, but if q is true, then we cannot label the premise $\sim q$ true, but must label it false. In so doing we have demonstrated that there would *not* be a line on the complete twelve-line truth table in which all the premises were true and the conclusion false. In short, it is impossible for the premises of this argument to be true while its conclusion is false, and the argument is therefore shown to be valid.

Exercises

p	q	$\sim p$	$\sim q$	$p \cdot q$	$p \lor q$	$p \supset q$	$\sim p \supset q$
1. T	T	F	F	T	T	T	T
2. T	F	F	T	F	T	F	T
3. F	T	T	F	F	T	T	T
4. F	F	T	T	F	F	T	F

1. Formalize (put into p, q, and so on, symbols) the following sentences.

   a. (Conjunction) He was fat but now he is slim.

   b. (Conditional) You move an inch and I'll let you have it!

   c. Either you leave or I call the cops.

   d. I did not invite you.

2. On the preceding truth table check these arguments for validity.

   a. $p \supset q$ b. $p \lor q$ c. $\sim p \supset q$

      $\dfrac{q}{\therefore p}$ $\dfrac{q}{\therefore p}$ $\dfrac{\sim q}{\therefore p}$

3. Formalize and construct a formal proof using the inference rules listed below: Use p, $\sim p$, q, and r to formalize the argument.

   a. Either Ed keeps his job or he loses his girl.

   b. If Ed loses his girl then he'll leave town.

   c. Ed won't keep his job. / Therefore, Ed will leave town.

Disjunctive syllogism:
$p \lor q$
$\sim p$
$\overline{\therefore q}$
Modus ponens:
$q \supset r$
q
$\overline{\therefore \quad r}$

The Functional Calculus

There is still a more sophisticated kind of notation, and it is the ultimate in flexibility and versatility for stating precisely and showing the logical relations between all sorts of statements. It is too complex to present in any detail here. It is the functional calculus. It will state both the arguments in the sentential calculus and the categorical syllogisms in the calculus of classes: It will handle both propositions and classes. What more could anyone want? The basic principle is this: We can state that an individual (or any number of individuals) exists, belongs to a certain class or has a certain predicate, has a certain relation to other things or classes (this includes performs a certain action). Also, any statement that an individual or a certain quantity of individuals is in this class, has this predicate or relation, can then be placed into the conjunctive, conditional disjunctive, or other relations to other statements as in the sentential calculus, and a formal proof can be constructed using the inference rules of the sentential calculus plus a few other special rules for the functional calculus.

Informal Fallacies

A fallacy is an error in argument. We have seen some of the formal fallacies, that is, fallacies of the arrangement of things, whether of terms or sentences, included in an argument: the fallacy of converting an A-form categorical proposition, affirming the consequent, denying the antecedent, and so on. But few philosophers commit formal fallacies in their arguments in print. That does not mean that people who are untrained in logic do not commit formal fallacies in their arguments about philosophical issues, of course. But since philosophical analysis is primarily concerned with the analysis of philosophical talk, and since most philosophical talk that is preserved and comes to people's attention is in the writings of philosophers themselves, formal fallacies are of passing interest primarily.

It is much more likely that a philosopher will commit an informal fallacy. No rearrangement of the material in an argument will cure an informal fallacy. It is an argument that must either be scrapped or have an analysis so thoroughly emphatic and warning that it might as well be scrapped and a fresh start made. An informal fallacy is due not to the arrangement of the material but to the content of the argument, the material itself. There are two basic types of informal fallacy: fallacies based on the treachery of the language used, called *fallacies of ambiguity*, and fallacies based on the use of "evidence" that is persuasive but irrelevant, the persuasiveness being based not on logical relations but on logically irrelevant considerations such as hopes, fears, and prejudices, called *fallacies of relevance*. It is the surface deceptiveness of fallacious arguments that has led one writer to subtitle his book on fallacy "the counterfeit of argument."

There is literally no end to the number of fallacies that might be tabulated, for, though there is a limited number of ways of doing things right, there is no limit to the number of ways in which they can be done wrong—since "being done wrong" includes not being done at all, but only claiming to be done, and so on. The following discussion of informal fallacies is a tabulation of some of the more tempting and more common fallacies, some of which are purportedly illustrated in the writings included in this anthology. Like formal logic generally, these are only some of the more serious blunders to be on guard against.

Fallacies of Relevance

Genetic fallacy "I know where you came from; you're not so hot, after all. I knew you when." The origin of a thing or person is here assumed to stamp some indelible character on it.

Ad hominem (to the man) "Nietzsche had syphilis; you can't believe a word he said." This fallacy discredits a man's ideas by discrediting his character, morals, and so on.

Appeal to authority   "If Gappo Blades are good enough to shave Slugger Southpaw, they're good enough for you." It is not always easy to distinguish this fallacy from one that appeals to the "authority" of the public or public opinion, called *ad populum*. In our society a celebrity carries weight from one field to another.

Hasty generalization   "All Kambelonnians are stupid. My uncle once knew one who tried to peep through the keyhole in a revolving door." This fallacy is similar to *false cause:* "There's CO_2 in your breath; that's what makes a match go out when you breathe hard at it." Also it resembles *Post hoc, ergo propter hoc (after this, therefore because of this)*: "Don't go to that hospital. Right after Ned's grandpa went there, he died." It takes some logical subtlety to see the technical differences between these, but keeping the name in mind helps.

***Petitio principi* (begging the question)**   "I know Smith wouldn't lie. He told me himself he was a truthful man." The argument *assumes* that its conclusion is true, it does not show it.

Appeal to ignorance   "President Jones is a cannibal. His enemies have repeatedly made the charge and he has never denied it." This assumes that something is true because it has not been shown to be false.

Accident   "It's never right to run the red light; why, yesterday a policeman directing traffic *insisted* that I run it, and I reported him to the captain." This fallacy forgets that there are exceptions to many, if not all, rules. It is the opposite of hasty generalization above, which would say that it is all right to run a red light at all times because a traffic officer once told you to do so.

Complex question   "Why did you murder the victim, Mr. Jones? Surely you knew this jury would convict you, as it will when it votes." This is the have-you-stopped-beating-your-wife technique of high pressure. It asks two questions but demands one answer for both.

***Ignoratio elenchi* (pure and simple irrelevance)**   "Join our fanatics. The world is in a desperate condition, and it's time for desperate action." Which kind?

Fallacies of Ambiguity

In contrast to fallacies of relevance, *fallacies of ambiguity* are found in arguments that may seem formally correct and seem to have premises that are relevant to their conclusion. These are particularly tricky errors and more than one well-known philosopher has fallen into them.

Reification "The state," "the masses," and the like are entities made by abstraction. A mere collection or some aspect of a thing or situation is made into a thing in its own right or personified.

Equivocation This ambiguity is present when a word is used to refer to two different things, thus it may not mean the same in the conclusion as in the premises. "This action is desirable, for there are people who have actually desired it." "Desirable" means "ought to be desired," not "actually desired." John Stuart Mill's *Utilitarianism* is often accused of this use of "desirable" and "desired."

Amphiboly This is a syntactic error, getting the relationship of one word to others wrong, instead of the relationship of words to things. "My doctor turned out to be a fine one. He threatened to kill me! He did! I told him my heartbeat was erratic and he said he'd put a stop to *that!*" The reference of "that" is ambiguous: Was it the erratic heartbeat or all heartbeats? The doctor (let us hope) meant the former, the patient took it to mean the latter.

Composition "You can tear a Manhattan phone book in half easily. After all, it's only thin sheets of paper." This fallacy thinks the whole is like its parts, using "phone book" ambiguously here. Many accuse some arguments for the existence of God of this.

Division "The battalion marching in step broke the bridge down. Man, those soldiers must have been stamping!" The opposite of the composition fallacy is going on here, and the assumption is that the parts are like the whole. A few men stamping might not have collapsed the bridge. Many soldiers marching in step and not stamping, might.

Exercises

Name the fallacy in each case, paying close attention to the literal significance of the names of the fallacies where two fallacies seem alike.

1. "You ought to let your fellow student copy from your paper during exams because everyone should be neighborly."
2. "If each thing has a cause then the whole world and all human history has a cause."
3. "Astrology is true. My astrologer told me so."
4. "Good morning, madam. Thank you for answering my knock on your door. Allow me to introduce myself: I'm Al Kooper; I'm selling vacuum cleaners. What kind of accessories do you want with the one you're going to buy?"
5. "The armaments makers started the war. It's never been shown they didn't."

Suggestions for Further Reading

Cohen, Morris and Ernest Nagel, *An Introduction to Logic and Scientific Method.* New York, Harcourt, Brace & World, Inc., 1934.

Copi, Irving M., *Introduction to Logic*, 3rd ed. New York, The Macmillan Company, 1968.

———— and James A. Gould, eds., *Contemporary Readings in Logical Theory.* New York, The Macmillan Company, 1967. Advanced.

————, eds., *Readings on Logic.* New York, The Macmillan Company, 1964. Paperback. Classics comprehensible to the ambitious beginner are presented.

Kneale, William, *Probability and Induction.* New York, Oxford University Press, Inc., 1949.

Lewis, Clarence I., *The Analysis of Knowledge and Valuation.* La Salle, Ill., The Open Court Publishing Company, 1946. Good chapter on probability theory. Advanced.

Mill, John Stuart, *A System of Logic.* Classic. Several editions available.

Quine, W. V. O., *The Methods of Logic*, rev. ed. New York, Holt,

Rinehart and Winston, Inc., 1959. Authoritative; for beginners but not easy.

Russell, Bertrand and A. N. Whitehead, *Principia Mathematica,* 2nd ed. New York, Cambridge University Press, 1927, 3 vols. First volume, or a part thereof, is available in paper. "Reduces" mathematics to logic.

Skyrms, Brian, *Choice and Chance: An Introduction to Inductive Logic.* Belmont, Calif., Dickenson Publishing Company, Inc., 1966. Paperback.

Strawson, Peter F., *Introduction to Logical Theory.* New York, John Wiley & Sons, Inc., 1952. Shows influence of "ordinary language" orientation.

Toulmin, Stephen E., *The Uses of Argument.* New York, Cambridge University Press, 1958.

4

Explanation

Karl Marx complained that philosophers before him had tried to interpret the world when they should have been trying to change it. He evidently was sure that he had accomplished the first task and was ready for the second. Today speculative philosophers, Marxist and non-Marxist, bemoan the analytic philosopher's disavowal of both aims. Granted that if analytic philosophy does not *indirectly* do both, it is hard to keep from calling it a waste of time; but we should not do a very good job of understanding the world or changing it if everyone were engaged directly in doing so and never stopped to ask themselves what they were doing. This chapter is concerned with one of the concepts basic to the sciences and everyday talk—*explanation*—and is directed toward some of the most important things we are doing when we seek or give an explanation.

It was noted in Chapter 1 that basic concepts sometimes seem to conflict with one another. Several writers have pointed out that a psychiatrist would be ill advised to try to apply the therapeutic techniques he uses on his patients to his own domestic problems. In saying that, are they holding that the psychiatrist must be somewhat schizoid to get along well in this world? This is a question about the functioning of different kinds of intellectual tools and their relation to science and common sense. Any answer to it would have to touch upon the concept of explanation.

Understanding:
Psychological and Logical Factors

The occasions on which we demand from others or seek for ourselves an explanation are those times when we feel that we do not understand something that we know or believe. A demand for an explanation does not arise from blank ignorance. When we seek an explanation it is because we wonder not *whether* something is true but *why* it is true. The blonde sprawled on the drawing-room carpet is all too obviously dead; the groom is already two hours late for the wedding, "long overdue and presumed lost"; what the detective and the bride respectively wonder is not whether something is amiss but why it is, for the facts stand out from their background and call attention to themselves. It is especially such unexpected facts for which we seek explanations, in cases in which the facts do not fit well with what we already know or believe. There is a gap, a chasm, and we try to fill it, to link the strange facts up with the main body of our knowledge so that they no longer stand out in tantalizing isolation.

We want to understand. But "understanding" is an ambiguous word. Leaving aside such important near-synonyms as "empathize" and "sympathize" and restricting ourselves to a more or less scientific frame of reference, we still find more than one meaning. Let us suppose that a person asks for an explanation and we give him one. Still not satisfied, he asks, "Yes, but why?" Either he is raising a new question requiring a separate explanation, or else he is falling under the spell of a puzzle posing as a problem. After Newton had given the formula for gravitation he said he still did not *understand* that mysterious force. It was, of course, his conception of it as a kind of thing or entity that created the puzzle. If a physicist explains the difference between high C and middle C as a difference in frequencies, someone is almost certain to say, "Yes, but why should our ears detect one as high C and the other as middle C?" Is such a person asking for a further explanation, or is he in the grips of a puzzle that has no answer? If he can give some sense to his question, some account of what would count as an answer, then at least one might have some idea of where and how to look for an answer to it. But to these puzzles about gravitation and sounds no such specification seems to be forthcoming.

It is apparent that one person, for whatever reason, might not be satisfied by an explanation that satisfies everyone else. The difference may well be between *psychological* and *logical* criteria. One is psychologically satisfied by an explanation when he feels no irritation of dissatisfaction, logically satisfied when the specifications that he has laid down are met. The two vary independently, and one may be wildly out of line with the other. The man who has a hand-washing compulsion is never satisfied with the cleanliness of his hands, while a person who literally never washes never feels dissatisfied. Neither has a clear criterion for an answer to the question, When are your hands dirty and when are they clean? Most people have some sort of rule of thumb for this: Their hands are dirty when dirt is visible on them, when they have an unpleasant odor or feel sticky, when there is reason to believe that there may be danger of getting many germs from them, and so on. People would usually suppose that it is unreasonable to demand more than the absence of those conditions. If what satisfies the usual criteria does not satisfy someone, it is incumbent upon him to state his criteria. The main criterion of a person with a wash-compulsion is that he must *feel* clean, and he is obviously unable to give further criteria for what it would take to bring that about. Until he can produce these criteria, however, no one is obligated to share his dissatisfaction. Analysis of the concept of explanation must focus on the *logical criteria* to be satisfied by an explanation, what people *ought* to be satisfied with, rather than what various individuals might demand. It will, however, be important to avoid the assumption that there must be some *one* set of criteria for all types of explanation.

Another question faces anyone who tries to explain explanation: What is the difference between explaining and explaining away? Opponents of reductive theories claim they explain away rather than explain a thing when they say "*X* is *really* just *Y*." The issue here is about the correct description of the thing to be explained. Suppose someone asks, "How do you explain the existence of so many concentration camps in the United States today where political prisoners are incarcerated?" If his respondent objects that there are no concentration camps in the United States, and no political prisoners, he may call this reply a "white-wash"; he may label any attempt to explain the federal prison system and the administration of federal statutes an explanation of a different kind of thing. Obviously no resolution of the dispute will be forthcoming until these two people agree on just what facts constitute the explanandum or thing explained.

Description, Discovery and Demonstration

Description

A persistent popular conception of science declares that scientists tell us *how* things happen, not *why*, but the how-why dichotomy is not very strict. A metallurgist tells you why a bridge falls, as truly as a theologian does. Why? is not necessarily a more profound question than How? Perhaps a persistent speculative tendency in our thinking forces us to look for something in events above and beyond regular connections to previous events of certain kinds, and particularly to look for some conscious purpose. But even if we granted that science always answers questions like, How did it happen? we would not be saying that scientific explanation is simply description. There is, after all, quite a bit of difference between science and bird-watching.

As a reconstruction, a detective's explanation of a murder might seem to be a description: "Chief, the killer stood here, raised his gun, and fired. The victim pitched forward on the carpet there, face down. Then the killer turned and went out the open window, there. The chambermaid heard the shot but by the time she got downstairs the killer had gotten away." We can call this a description, but it is a highly selective one. It does not tell us that the canary in the cage was singing off key or that the victim had a hole in the toe of his left size-twelve sock. It does not give a description of the victim, much less the killer. Yet it tells how the shooting took place. Murders have probably been solved by attention to such minute details as a hole in a sock or a canary's song, but in this particular case the details are not relevant to an explanation of why the blonde was found sprawled on the drawing-room carpet with a bullet in her back soon after a shot was heard.

Discovery

Rightly or wrongly, we associate the notions of explanation and proof with the notion of discovery. What are their actual relationships? Since discovery is intimately connected with originality and creativity, it is often remarked that no one can *teach* the rules of discovery, since they are, as it were, discovered along with the thing for which they *are* rules. Though scientific methods are the same everywhere, the scientific imagination is not. Like politicians or novelists, different researchers have different styles. Paul De Kruif's *Microbe Hunters* pictures Pasteur as somewhat flashy and flamboyant; Metchnikoff as impetuous and erratic, almost a comic mad-scientist type, though he made some important discoveries about phagocytes and immunology; and Koch as plodding and careful, though he occasionally made premature pronouncements.

Discovery requires imagination, for the metallurgist as for the artist or inventor. It requires the ability not only to see things the way they are but also to see them the way they *might* be, with a few major or minor changes here and there. The scientific method is no magic substitute for this ability. The scientific method is as much concerned with the destruction of hypotheses as with building them up from scratch. Knowing that your hypothesis is going to have to meet some scientific tests may help you in formulating it, but not much. Knowing *what* tests it will have to meet may be half the battle. It requires some imagination to come up with a list of things that *meet* the specifications. These are, as it were, the specifications for the explanation. Some discoveries in science have been the product of something like a vision—for example, Kekulé's discovery of chemical ring formulae. Kekulé reports that he had wrestled with the structure of the benzene molecule without success until one day, as he sat dozing before the fire, he "saw" atoms dancing in the flames, then suddenly form themselves into a snake that seized its own tail in its mouth like the "hoopsnakes" of American folklore—and he had his benzene ring. But for most researchers, the answer does not come so dramatically, and some do their work well, some badly. Each has his own style of working.

One place at which knowledge helps imagination most in research is in the stock of images, the background of experience from which to draw hypotheses that might be relevant. Suppose that Kekulé had had no encounters with snakes? Had never even seen a picture of a snake? He could hardly have come upon the ring formula in the way that he did. The "manifest content" of his dream would have come from some other source. Another place where knowledge helps imagination is in knowing what you are looking for, a slippery expression that is meant to include such things as the "shape" of the piece of the puzzle that is missing, what criteria it will have to meet. Dewey's account of problem-solving (which by no means covers all thinking) asserts that often the solution to the problem is suggested by the problem itself; that is, one who knows the shape and size of the blank in his knowledge is well on the way to filling it, for he has a good idea of what he is looking for. If a person is puzzled but unsure what he is puzzled about, his feeling of having a knowledge gap may be due to a philosophical obscurity rather like Newton's, when he, of all people, said that he didn't understand gravity. Then the puzzler would do well to ask what it would take to fill his knowledge gap, when he would be and when he would not be satisfied that it was filled. If he cannot answer those questions, he does not know what he is looking for and his search is foredoomed.

From the foregoing, one might conclude that explanation and discovery are the same. Not exactly. Like hypotheses, explanations are *constructed*, and that is a creative process. Laws are discovered. Now, although laws can be used to explain *other* laws, and are often part of the explanation of a phenomenon, an explanation comprises more than a law.

Demonstration

Explanation is not the same as demonstration in the sense of proof, either. According to the most widely accepted theory of explanation (discussed later), an explanation has the form of a deductive argument, with the explanandum as the conclusion. Even if we concur in that theory, it does not give an explanation the same function as an *argument*. An argument is meant to show *that* a statement is true. In seeking an explanation we already know that the statement in question is true; we seek to know *why*.

Theories, Laws, Hypotheses, and Facts: Some Problems of Usage

Usage of the terms "hypothesis," "theory," "law," and even "fact" is often rather loose. One of these terms may be used by one author in a way that another of them would be used by another author, so that they seem to be synonymous or interchangeable. To some extent it is obvious that they can be used interchangeably; for example, a law or even a hypothesis may attain such stature for practical purposes of research that it can be taken as a fact.

Here it must be made clear that there are disadvantages in identifying a *statement of fact* with *the fact* that is stated. If they were the same, we would be speaking redundantly when we talk about "stating facts." A law-statement is not the same as the data that the law summarizes or generalizes about. Once we have reminded ourselves that we are using a kind of abbreviation when we equate facts to the statement of them, laws to the statement of them, we can continue to speak as if the facts and their statement were the same. The status of facts in the world is a confusing problem, but most philosophers today probably regard them as "states of affairs" or "whatever is the case." They are what makes statements of fact true, and are not statements themselves. A statement of fact never makes *itself* true. If we talk about "true facts" as if we were talking about true statements, we would seem to commit ourselves to the existence of false facts, too, an even stranger entity. Facts either exist or do not exist; they are neither true nor false.

Much could be said about the relative corrigibility of laws and theories, but the important thing distinguishing laws, theories, and hypotheses is not so much the tentativeness of these things as another feature they have. A law, as we have said, is an empirical generalization of a rather special kind. Examples of laws are Boyle's and Charles's laws of gases—their pressure and contraction, their reaction to heat and cold; Snell's law of the passage of light through transparent media—how the light is refracted and leaves and enters a medium at an angle from the path that it travels while it is in the medium; Galileo's law of the acceleration of free-falling bodies. These laws state quantitative relationships. "Calling their shots" as they do, they can be confirmed or disconfirmed by experiment. But one peculiar feature of the empirical generalizations that we call laws is that they are not invalidated by just any kind of counterinstance. An example cited by Toulmin is Snell's law about refraction of light: A piece of high-grade Iceland spar looks like glass, but light does not behave in this transparent substance as it does in glass or in water. This fact does not invalidate Snell's law; physics simply makes an exception here and says that Snell's law applies to such things as water and glass, but not to Iceland spar.

Laws are peculiar empirical generalizations in another way: They are not just accidental generalizations. That is, you could not formulate just any universal proposition about matters of fact and call it a law. For instance, "All the chairs in this building are Chippendales" is an accidental generalization, not a law. Laws are not just what happens to be the case, but what *would* be the case if such and such conditions were met, even though they are *not* met at this particular time. Such statements are called contra-factual conditionals, which are of the form, "If X were true (which it is not), then Y would be true," while an accidental universal asserts that certain things happen to be true.

A scientific theory (sometimes called a general hypothesis), in contrast to a law, contains at least one term that refers to an unobservable entity. Unlike laws, then, theories are not subject to direct testing. Experiments measuring the angle at which a ray of light is deflected or the increase in pressure of a gas corresponding to the increase in temperature of the gas are capable of testing Snell's law or the Boyle's-Charles's gas laws. But how would you test whether there are atoms? Not directly, until observational instruments are devised (and much clarification would be needed to say what would count as "observing" an atom of hydrogen—one might "observe" them indirectly, for example, making tracks in a cloud chamber).

Theories are a step higher in the hierarchy of scientific statements than are laws. It is often said that laws can be deduced from theories, as many laws have been from the atomic theory itself. Though theories can be embraced and abandoned as the history of science unfolds, the giving up of a theory has more sweeping consequences for the other statements in science than the wrecking of a law. In this sense, it should be said that theories are more basic than laws, though "higher" in the hierarchy. For instance, if we should abandon the atomic theory, or at least the theory that matter is composed of irreducible particles, many other scientific beliefs would have to be scrapped or revised substantially.

In explanation, *hypotheses* are popularly thought to be the main, or even sole, constituent of explanation. If we define "hypothesis" broadly, this is true; if narrowly, it is not. One can compare hypotheses with theories better than with laws. Hypotheses are tentative statements. So is a theory, in its way. A law has the least amount of tentativeness of the three kinds of statement. We would not find in a hypothesis the rather exact ratios stated in some laws, unless the hypothesis were a law in the making. (It is difficult to imagine a scientist formulating such a mathematically exact hypothesis until he has accumulated a great deal of data tending to confirm a law. But in the case of the law about vacuum pumps "lifting" a substance to a height no greater than the atmospheric pressure will push it at that altitude, we can see that it would not be wise to be dogmatic on this point.) Also, a hypothesis is generally different from a law in what it refers to: Usually it refers to individual things, not to a class; usually it refers to particular events, such as the ascent of a balloon or the assassination of a premier.

Though swapping of terminology occurs in the history of science ("gravitational theory" *versus* "law of gravity," "planetary hypotheses" *versus* "law of planetary motions"), hypotheses usually have less generality in their reference to unobservables (that is, entities that are in principle, not merely in fact, unobservable). They are more like pawns than bishops, castles, kings, and queens, but they are valuable, as a pawn is valuable in chess.

There are other terms in the philosophy of science that are likely to be confusing, such as "principles" and "postulates." One may hear the assumption that matter and energy are neither created nor destroyed referred to either as the "principle" of the conservation of matter and energy or as the "law" of the conservation of matter and energy. Certainly it is not, and cannot be, an *empirical* law. This fact coupled with the basic nature of the assumption argues for calling it a principle rather than a law.

In Chapter 1 we saw that many basic beliefs are methodological policies or commitments. Whether it is proper to call such things beliefs, that is, to imply that they are the kinds of things that *could* be either true *or* false, is part of the philosophy of science. Take, for instance, Mill's "principle of induction," and beliefs about causal relationships; these are notorious examples. It is even said that determinism (the doctrine that every event—except, perhaps, those studied by quantum physics—is determined by previous events) is a scientifically basic methodological assumption, and thus a principle or a postulate.

What is a postulate? The name itself suggests that it is a working assumption, a methodological assumption. A postulated *entity*, if the postulate in question is about such a thing, is, of course, a theoretical entity, and thus unobservable. One does not postulate that which he *knows*, by observation or otherwise.

The Covering-law Account of Explanation

It is usually *events* that we are interested in getting the explanation of—something that happens, such as the devaluation of a nation's currency or the sinking of a supposedly unsinkable ocean liner. Also, it may be a *class* of events for which we want an explanation; for example, Why is light always deflected (with a few well-known exceptions) at just this angle when it passes through a transparent substance? The question is a demand for an explanation of the *law* that light is so deflected, a demand for explanation not of one event but of the class of events covered by the law. *Theories*, in the sense discussed above, are invoked to explain laws.

The most widely held, but widely disputed also, theory of scientific explanation is one that was formulated by Carl Hempel and Paul Oppenheim in 1948. It is usually credited to Hempel, who has spent much time and effort in defending and extending it. According to Hempel, an explanation accounts for an event by making a sentence describing the event (the *explanandum* sentence) the *conclusion of a deductive argument*. For premises, the explanation has (1) a statement or statements that formulate a law (hence William Dray's name, "the covering law theory") and (2) a statement or statements describing the *conditions* under which the event occurred, conditions that place the event under the law's coverage. The covering-law theory is not as difficult in principle as it looks. If we ask, Why does X have characteristic c? it is explained that X is a member of class m, and all members of class m have characteristic c. The form of a scientific explanation, Hempel says, is this:

Conditions statement:	This straight stick is partly in and partly out of the water.
Law statement(s):	Light rays leaving water and entering the air are deflected.
	Straight objects partly in and partly out of water appear bent.
Explanandum:	(Therefore) This straight stick, which is partly in and partly out of the water, appears bent.

We can see that without much alteration this can be made to be a *valid* deductive argument. The point of it, however, is not to prove but to explain the conclusion, which is already known to be true independently of the other statements. Hempel insists that the explanandum be deducible from the explanatory premises, which constitute the *explanans*, or explanation proper.

Another point Hempel makes about this model of explanation is that it is of exactly the same form as a prediction. The law statements, being universal statements, are timeless: Whenever the conditions are met, the event will occur. Hempel argues that *prediction* of what will occur and *retro*diction of what has occurred are of the same form.

Now the form of the explanation given above is almost too neat. Would all events that we manage to explain satisfactorily fit into this tidy little mold? No, Hempel says, remembering that not all laws that are the key to the explanation are as neat and tidy as Kepler's, Newton's, Boyle's, Charles's, and Snell's. Some laws are more obviously statistical generalizations than these are. For the use of these in the premises of explanations Hempel has made a distinction. The former model of explanation using the "bent" stick as an example Hempel calls the "deductive-nomological" (*nomos*, Greek for "law") model. On the other hand, those laws that are stated statistically figure as the premises of scientific explanations that he calls "statistical-probabilistic" or "inductive-statistical" explanations. These laws and the form of the explanation in which they are ingredient are inductive through and through, not deductive. For example, we do not know with the assurance we have in the case of Newton's laws what will happen to a patient who, to use Hempel's example, has a certain set of symptoms and to whom a certain drug is administered in a certain dosage, but from past cases we may be able to arrive at a high degree of probability: In percentage p of previous cases of the same kind, administration of drug d in amount a has produced result r. As retrodiction or prediction, Hempel argues, connecting this law with result r will give us an argument whose reliability is as good as the probability of the law. Any explanations that include such probabilistic laws, however, must have this lack of deductive certainty written into them. The probability will not be *that* the event has happened, for that is known independently of the explanation of *why* the event happened. The probability will be that the circumstances were the *cause* of the event. As is often remarked, Hempel's theory of explanation is a *causal* theory.

Most of the objections to the covering-law theory have centered around the *form* that Hempel says an explanation should have. He has argued strongly that the *ideal* explanation is in the form of a deductive argument that is valid and that has true premises. But he has also found more and more subforms of explanations, making the model more and more flexible. If there are those who are horrified at the suggestion that a scientific explanation is somehow associated with deductive logic, they should set their minds at ease. There is no law against the use of deduction in science; indeed, every time a scientific researcher tests a hypothesis he uses deduction. He says something like this:

If my hypothesis, *h*, is true, a certain observation, *o*, should occur in circumstance *c*. (For example, if there was a violent struggle, there should be signs of it if the scene of the crime has been left as is.)

If the expected observation does *not* occur in those circumstances, by a use of *modus tollens* the researcher counts that fact very heavily against his hypothesis; it may even be fatal to it. Or if he is shown that his hypothesis, *h*, entails (by any kind of logic one wants to call it) a *false* statement, *s*, then he must in all consistency call the hypothesis false by that application of *modus tollens* that is traditionally known as *reductio ad absurdum*—reduction to the absurd. Such reason is deductive from beginning to end.

Far from being a drawback, the deductive model of explanation is one with definite *psychological* advantages. It gives us what we want when we are led to ask for an explanation, completeness in our knowledge, since it supplies sufficient conditions for the occurrence of the event specified in the explanandum.

However, there are other objections, more specific, brought against the theory of Hempel as a general account of explanation, for instance in explaining why certain events did *not* happen: Suppose a dish, an heirloom, has remained unbroken for two hundred years. To explain why it is not broken one might use a Hempel-type explanation:

All chinaware dropped from a height of 5,000 feet unto a slab of marble is something that is broken.

This chinaware is not chinaware dropped from a height of 5,000 feet onto a slab of marble.

(Therefore) This chinaware is not something that is broken.

Hempel can very quickly reply that (1) this is an invalid argument (the conclusion says something about all things that break; the first premise does not) and (2) the first statement in the explanans is not a genuine law statement, being rather one of those accidental universals of which we spoke earlier, so that we have doubly failed to deduce the explanandum from a covering law and a conditions statement.

But it is not so simple for the theory to avoid the criticism of which the example above is illustrative. We can cure both problems:

All water expands when frozen.
This water did not expand.
(Therefore) This water was not frozen.

This example is valid, not having one of the fallacies of the syllo-gism as the first one did, but rather being a valid form. It also does indeed feature a bona fide statement of a law about water. But against Hempel it can be argued that the example ought to explain *why* this water was not frozen, since it meets his require-ments for an explanation but nevertheless is silly and is *not* an explanation of why this water was not frozen. It appears at any rate that Hempel needs to tighten up the "conditions of adequacy" cited as criteria for a good explanation.

Historical Explanation and
Explanation in the Social Sciences

The English philosopher Thomas Hobbes spoke of the "body politic" as being quite literally like a physical body; its units, in-dividual people, he compared to the atoms in a physical body. Such a theory, which explains *one* kind of phenomenon in terms of another (social behavior—physiology), is called *reductive* or *reductionist*. Hobbes would have reduced social science to physics and explained the actions of individuals and of groups by refer-ence to the laws of physics. Now, almost four hundred years after Hobbes, a program for this reduction still seems far in the future. If it is ever achieved, the line between the natural sciences and the social sciences will have been eliminated. The reasons that it has not yet been done help to throw further light on the nature of explanation.

There are many more variables in explaining and predicting *people's* actions than in explaining events in physics. Moreover, these variables are often inaccessible to examination. It is pointed out (perhaps too often) that the fact that people *interpret* situa-tions makes it very difficult to generalize about an individual's be-havior, what he will or will not do, and why he did or did not do a certain thing: One individual's interpretation of a situation will vary markedly from another's, influencing his behavior accord-ingly. It is at any rate easier to generalize about *groups* of people, as the insurance actuaries remind us, than about an individual. When the average American of a certain race, age, occupation, and so on, will die can be computed well enough that insurance companies do not lose any significant amount of money betting, as it were, that this *average individual* will die then. Betting that a *particular individual* will die then is much more risky: The old saying is "Death is certain, the hour uncertain."

Thus Hempel's statistical-probabilistic model of explanation may work quite well in the social sciences, in which generalizations that may count as laws or law-like statements about *groups* of people or about people over the long range are formulated in sociological studies. In such explanations, the laws or law-like statements, which are crucial to Hempel's theory, will yield an explanation that is probable to the degree that those covering laws are probable. But with history it is a very different thing. In history we have to explain what has happened only *once—this* revolution, not just the "average" revolution (if there is any such thing); *this* commanding general's decision, not just the "average" general's; the outcome of *this* disarmament conference, not just the "average" one of its kind, and so on. In the history of a student who drops out of college, it may be a rather pale substitute for an explanation of *his* action if someone generalizes about the "average" college dropout or the "younger generation" today. The student himself might not be sure why he quit: whether his reason was grades, money, or simply a general frustration that reached such a level that one day he walked away and never came back. It may seem very audacious indeed, then, for an outsider, a century or a millennium later, to pick up the few fragments of records that remain of even a famous man's life and times and piece them together into that coherent whole that we expect an explanation to be, telling us why these events and not some others occurred at this particular time.

It is notorious among historical scholars that general laws "governing" the course of history, for example, economic or evolutionary laws, are hard to come by, if any exist at all. In this connection it has often been remarked that historical explanation is in a realm all by itself. Someone has made a distinction between those studies that are "nomothetic" and those that are "ideographic." The former, as Ernest Nagel describes them, deal with events that are repetitive and operate according to patterns called laws: the seasons of the year, the phenomenon of orbiting, the water cycle, the life cycle of plants and animals, and so on, including not only cyclical phenomena but any events that are repeated whenever certain circumstances are present. As opposed to these, "ideographic" phenomena are *unique:* Caesar crosses the Rubicon only once; Washington crosses the Delaware only once, and so on. On the same subject, the Spanish philosopher Ortega y Gasset said that man does not have a *nature* but only a *history.* A law that would follow the pattern of physical laws might yield a historical explanation like this: "Caesar crossed the Rubicon because that's what anybody like Caesar would do in circumstances such as Caesar found himself in." That fails to be enlightening as an explanation, since no one else is exactly like Caesar, or ever encounters exactly those circumstances that Caesar encountered. It is said that if there are any laws in history they have to be so watered down that they are *trivial,* and that if anyone does come up with world-shaking historical laws they are almost certain to be *false.* Thus Hempel's covering-law theory of explanation as he himself has applied it to the explanation of events in history has met widespread skepticism.

Hempel has been aware that historical explanations will be rather different in detail from those in the natural sciences or in the social sciences generally. To provide for the logical form of explanation of historical events he has made a distinction between "partial explanations" and "explanation sketches." As an example of a partial explanation he cites Freud's explanation of a slip of the pen that Freud once discovered he himself had made: Freud had set down an appointment on his calendar an entire month earlier than the day on which he should have written it. His explanation was that he was impatient about this delay and setting the appointment a month ahead was symbolic wish-fulfillment. As an explanation of the covering-law kind, this is rather incomplete. The explanation goes well in the early stage: "All strong, unfulfilled desires receive some sort of symbolic fulfillment no matter how seemingly insignificant." But as it goes along and gets to the slip of the pen, what is that law going to be: "All slips of the pen are symbolic wish-fulfillments"? Not even the founder of psychoanalysis claimed that *all* slips are Freudian; obviously, some slips of the pen are caused by such things as having one's elbow jogged by an earthquake or nervousness. That statement would simply be false. But to weaken it by saying "*Some* slips of the pen are symbolic wish-fulfillments" would make the argument (which Hempel insists that an explanation must have the form of) invalid. Clearly, some sentence is needed distinguishing Freudian from non-Freudian slips. No point will be served by detailed examination of Hempel's partial explanations, but this example shows that they need quite a bit of care in filling in to yield a valid argument.

The main kind of incomplete explanation that Hempel stresses is historical explanations. He gives to these the name *explanation sketches*. According to Hempel, when the historian explains why a certain action was taken by a general or an emperor, he is offering an explanation so incomplete that it is really only a sketch. In his article "The Function of General Laws in History," he says that such an explanation is "a more or less vague indication of the laws and initial conditions considered as relevant, and it needs 'filling out' in order to turn into a full-fledged explanation." However, in his collected essays on explanation, *Aspects of Scientific Explanation and other Essays in the Philosophy of Science* (1965), Hempel's own explanation of explanation sketches is sketchy. It appears from those essays that what is incomplete is the precise formulation of hypotheses and laws and more evidence giving us a more detailed or precise statement of the conditions under which the explanandum-event happened. We may suppose that it is the familiar problem of the historian—too little data extant—that is at the root of this incompleteness.

In assessing Hempel's application of the covering-law theory of explanation to the explanation of historical events, one finds a fundamental ambiguity in the expression "general laws." Hempel himself did not claim that he was discussing the role of *historical* laws, as distinguished from economic, sociological, or physical laws, and we have seen that many historians are very skeptical about the existence of specifically historical laws. It might well be a case of the fallacy of composition to think that history should display laws; after all, the peculiarity of history as a set of events is that the events are *past*, and the peculiarity of history as a discipline of historiography is that of digging up that past and presenting it in as complete and ordered a manner as possible (without boring the reader with trivia). What laws should be displayed by events merely by virtue of their "pastness"? Why should there be a law that history does or that history does not repeat itself, apart from that branch of learning that we call probability theory? That can be seen as a problem that is purely mathematical, the problem of whether, say, historical events display the characteristic of being nonrepeatable.

There is another meaning of "general laws," and it is the one with which Hempel was primarily concerned in his famous paper on the subject of general laws in history: general laws of *any* kind, of physics, sociology, economics, and so on. The paper undertook to deny and refute the very widespread, even predominant notion that history does not repeat itself, and does not because the deeds done by men are not subject to the laws of science. One is struck by the grotesqueness of the notion as he looks back on it, for it is a denial of the very possibility of a social science, of the past or of the present. Hempel has done the service of reminding us that if we can explain people's behavior while they are living, their being dead changes nothing essentially except to make it harder to gather data about them. If we explain people's behavior in the present by reference to general statements about people, statements the truth or probability of which is open to empirical examination, then surely there is nothing about the past as past that, in principle, makes any different the task of explaining the behavior of people who have died since they did their deeds. The difficulties of historical explanation (aside from the inaccessibility of data about the past) are the same as the difficulties of *generalizing about human behavior* in the present. The problems of history, except for pastness, are exactly those of the other social sciences and the behavioral sciences generally. This seems to be in part, why there are few, if any, *historical* laws—because there are few laws in the other social sciences.

The question about historical explanation that *may* be raised about the covering-law theory of Hempel concerns laws as they apply to the deeds of men. One might object that there are no laws that apply purely to history as history—to events qua past. That is a line with which Hempel seems to agree; at least he seems very skeptical about the possibility of finding such laws because of the unempirical nature of the entities or forces—destiny, God, and so forth—involved in such laws. One may object then that laws covering human behavior, whether that behavior is present or past, are not applicable to human events as physical laws are to physical events like water freezing or chinaware breaking, but this seems to be a denial of the possibility of *any* behavioral science, *any* large body of safe predictions about what people will do in given conditions. As we have said, the social sciences (rather like physical sciences) are on risky ground predicting just what *this* individual will do in *this* situation, but are much safer predicting what most people will do in this situation, or what most people with a similar background will do.

Philosophical Explanation

Ordinary-language philosophers point out many uses of the word "explanation." At the outset of this book we said that philosophy has long been thought to explain something, for example, "life" or "the universe," but that modern developments in and out of philosophy have cast a shadow on that assumption. To try to explain "life" is to develop a theory to put alongside many previous theories. That is speculative. To try to decide as between different theories requires tests of theories. Development of such tests is doing critical or analytic philosophy. Ordinary-language philosophers themselves have certainly repudiated the task of explaining events, reality, life, and other such traditionally discussed philosophical topics. What, then? Does philosophy explain anything or not? Before we can answer that question we must remember the two main divisions of philosophy mentioned at the opening of Chapter 1—speculative, and critical or analytic. Speculative philosophers who are also non-Marxists (and Marxists, despite Marx's gibe that philosophy should have as its main task changing the world and not explaining it, do indeed try to explain the world in providing a philosophical foundation for Communist ideology) would certainly think it a useless or unworthy task to philosophize if one did *not* arrive at explanations of *something* important.

Critical or analytic philosophy does explain something. When someone demands an explanation of what we mean, he is asking for an explication (a making explicit) of our meaning. When he asks for an explanation of what kind of theory we are working on or trying to establish, he is asking not for something exactly similar to the explication of meanings, but for an explanation that certainly gives to basic concepts and basic beliefs a prominent role in the discussion. Critical philosophy as the explication of concepts and criticism of basic beliefs is very much involved in the business of explaining. As the different branches of philosophy such as philosophy of science, philosophy of religion, and theory of knowledge illustrate, "philosophy" is *explaining what people are doing when they are doing science, when they are engaged in philosophical debate about religion, when they make ethical judgments, when they make knowledge claims, and what speculative philosophers are doing when they try to explain "life" or "the universe."*

But it is one thing to engage in the philosophy of science and quite another to engage in science itself. When a scientist tells you what he's doing, that's different from doing the thing he's doing. The first is philosophy of science; the second is science. Thus the philosopher is not in competition with *any* branch of learning or research. What the philosopher explains is not anything that the other specialist *in* his specialty explains. What the philosopher may do is something that people in other specialties also do with reference to the philosopher's specialty: As a scientist may philosophize about science when he examines its basic concepts and basic assumptions, so the philosopher may become a psychologist of sorts when he introspects and asks what kind of images are in his mind, whether he can introspect anything called "himself" or not, and so on. Each of these persons entering the other's field will be an amateur to the extent that he is ignorant of how to do the other's job, and will be competent to the extent that he knows how to do it. But neither can expect to jump headlong into the other's domain without learning quite a little of what the other one knows, especially about the pitfalls that await him.

Suggestions for Further Reading

Brodbeck, May, ed., *Readings in the Philosophy of the Social Sciences*. New York, Appleton-Century-Crofts, 1968.

Campbell, Norman, *What Is Science?* New York, Dover Publications, Inc., 1921 original copyright. Paperback.

Danto, Arthur, *Analytical Philosophy of History*. New York, Cambridge University Press, 1965.

―――― and Sidney Morgenbesser, eds., *Philosophy of Science*. New York, Meridian, 1960. Paperback.

Dray, William: *Laws and Explanation in History*. New York, Oxford University Press, Inc., 1960.

Feigl, Herbert and May Brodbeck, eds., *Readings in the Philosophy of Science*. New York, Appleton-Century-Crofts, 1953.

―――― and Grover Maxwell, eds., *Current Issues in the Philosophy of Science*. New York, Holt, Rinehart & Winston, Inc., 1961.

―――――――, eds., *Minnesota Studies in Philosophy of Science*, Vol. 3. Minneapolis, Minn., University of Minnesota, 1962.

―――― and Wilfred Sellars, eds., *Readings in Philosophical Analysis*. New York, Appleton-Century-Crofts, 1949.

Feyerabend, Paul K., "Explanation, Reduction and Empiricism." Reprinted in Feigl and Maxwell, *Minnesota Studies*, Vol. 3.

Fodor, Jerry A., "Explanation in Psychology." In Max Black, ed., *Philosophy in America*. Cornell, 1965.

Gardiner, Patrick: *The Nature of Historical Explanation*. New York, Oxford University Press, Inc., 1952.

———— ed., *Theories of History*. New York, Free Press of Glencoe, Inc., 1959.

Hanson, Norwood R., *Patterns of Discovery*. New York, Cambridge University Press, 1958.

Hempel, Carl G., *Aspects of Scientific Explanation*. New York, Free Press of Glencoe, Inc., 1966.

————, *Philosophy of Natural Science*. Englewood Cliffs, N. J., Prentice-Hall, Inc., 1966. Paperback.

Hospers, John, "What Is Explanation?" In Antony Flew, ed., *Essays in Conceptual Analysis*. New York, St. Martin's Press, Inc., 1956.

Kuhn, Thomas, *The Structure of Scientific Revolutions*. Chicago, Ill., The University of Chicago Press, 1962.

Nagel, Ernest, *The Structure of Science*. New York, Harcourt, Brace & World, Inc., 1961.

Popper, Karl, *The Logic of Scientific Discovery*. New York, Basic Books, Inc., 1959. Original copyright, 1935.

Rudner, Richard S., *Philosophy of Social Science*. Englewood Cliffs, N. J., Prentice-Hall, Inc., 1966. Paperback.

Scriven, Michael, "Explanations, Predictions and Laws." In Feigl and Maxwell, *Minnesota Studies*, Vol. 3.

————, "The Limits of Physical Explanation." In Bernard Baumrin, ed., *Philosophy of Science: The Delaware Seminar*, Vol. 2. Interscience Publishers, 1963.

Shapere, Dudley, ed., *Philosophical Problems of Natural Science*. New York, The Macmillan Company, 1965. Paperback.

Smartt, J. J. C., *Between Science and Philosophy*. New York, Random House, Inc., 1968.

Toulmin, Stephen, *The Philosophy of Science*. New York, Harper & Row, Publishers, 1953.

Winch, Peter, *The Idea of a Social Science*. London, Routledge and Kegan Paul, Ltd., 1958.

Part Two

Readings

5

The Nature
of Philosophy

Any definition of philosophy is likely to mislead or be uninformative. John Wilson, contemporary British philosopher, tries to get the beginner to avoid a familiar frustration: agreeing with every philosopher he reads even though each contradicts the one before. The belief that philosophy is a collection of opinions which one can take or leave denies that philosophers, collectively or individually, add to knowledge. The opposite extreme is regarding philosophy as a science. Moritz Schlick, trained as a physicist, was a leading philosopher of the logical positivist movement in Vienna who argued that philosophy does not seek truth about the world but clarifies the questions which science can then answer. Bertrand Russell, on the other hand, points out that traditionally philosophy has made a contribution to the content of science by propounding speculative theories which ran far ahead of available evidence but which could be tested by science later.

In contemporary linguistic philosophy there is much that could be taken as "science" of a sort: the science of usage. John Wilson is sympathetic with this view but declares that it is too restricted a view of philosophy. Without going on to argue that the philosopher is a sort of superscientist, Wilson presents a picture of him similar to the one that describes him as a kind of mapmaker who sketches the boundaries of the different fields of knowledge and human interest. Only, Wilson depicts this activity in terms of describing the "games"—most of them quite serious—which constitute the greater part of human activity.

Speculative Philosophy
Paves the Way for Science

Bertrand Russell

Bertrand Russell (1872–1970), with Moore, pioneered in twentieth-century realism and analysis. He is best known for his Principia Mathematica *(with A. N. Whitehead), arguing that mathematics is derived from logic. His popular reputation was based on his image as an advocate of controversial and colorful causes in ethics, politics, and education. A master of style, his many books show him to be a man who never feared to change his mind as time went on. He taught in Cambridge University.*

Philosophy has had from its earliest days two different objects which were believed to be closely interrelated. On the one hand, it aimed at a theoretical understanding of the structure of the world; on the other hand, it tried to discover and inculcate the best possible way of life. From Heraclitus to Hegel, or even to Marx, it consistently kept both ends in view; it was neither purely theoretical nor purely practical, but sought a theory of the universe upon which to base a practical ethic.

Philosophy has thus been closely related to science on the one hand, and to religion on the other. Let us consider first the relation to science. Until the eighteenth century, science was included in what was commonly called "philosophy," but since that time the word "philosophy" has been confined, on its theoretical side, to what is most speculative and general in the topics with which science deals. It is often said that philosophy is unprogressive, but this is largely a verbal matter: as soon as a way is found of arriving at definite knowledge on some ancient question, the new knowledge is counted as belonging to "science," and "philosophy" is deprived of the credit. In Greek times, and down to the time of Newton, planetary theory belonged to "philosophy," because it was uncertain and speculative, but Newton took the subject out of the realm of the free play of hypothesis, and made it one requiring a different type of skill from that which it had required when it was still open to fundamental doubts. Anaximander, in the sixth century B.C., had a theory of evolution, and maintained that men descended from fishes. This was philosophy because it was a speculation unsupported by detailed evidence, but Darwin's theory of evolution was science, because it was based on the succession of forms of life as found in fossils, and upon the distribution of animals and plants in many parts of the world. A man might say, with enough truth to justify a joke: "Science is what we know, and philosophy is what we don't know." But it should be added that philosophical speculation as to what we do not yet know has shown itself a valuable preliminary to exact scientific knowledge. The guesses of the Pythagoreans in astronomy, of Anaximander and Empedocles in biological evolution, and of Democritus as to the atomic constitution of matter, provided the men of science in later times with hypotheses which, but for the philosophers, might never have entered their heads. We may say that, on its theoretical side, philosophy consists, at least in part, in the framing of large general hypotheses which science is not yet in a position to test; but when it becomes possible to test the hypotheses, they become, if verified, a part of science, and cease to count as "philosophy."

The utility of philosophy, on the theoretical side, is not confined to speculations which we may hope to see confirmed or confuted by science within a measurable time. Some men are so impressed by what science knows that they forget what it does not know; others are so much more interested in what it does not know than in what it does that they belittle its achievements. Those who think that science is everything become complacent and cocksure, and decry all interest in problems not having the circumscribed definiteness that is necessary for scientific treatment. In practical matters they tend to think that skill can take the place of wisdom, and that to kill each other by means of the latest technique is more "progressive," and therefore better, than to keep each other alive by old-fashioned methods. On the other hand, those who pooh-pooh science revert, as a rule, to some ancient and pernicious superstition, and refuse to admit the immense increase of human happiness which scientific technique, if wisely used, would make possible. Both these attitudes are to be deplored, and it is philosophy that shows the right attitude, by making clear at once the scope and the limitations of scientific knowledge.

Leaving aside, for the moment, all questions that have to do with ethics or with values, there are a number of purely theoretical questions, of perennial and passionate interest, which science is unable to answer, at any rate at present. Do we survive death in any sense, and if so, do we survive for a time or forever? Can mind dominate matter, or does matter completely dominate mind, or has each, perhaps, a certain limited independence? Has the universe a purpose? Or is it driven by blind necessity? Or is it a mere chaos and jumble, in which the natural laws that we think we find are only a fantasy generated by our own love of order? If there is a cosmic scheme, has life more importance in it than astronomy would lead us to suppose, or is our emphasis upon life mere parochialism and self-importance? I do not know the answer to these questions, and I do not believe that anybody else does, but I think human life would be impoverished if they were forgotten, or if definite answers were accepted without adequate evidence. To keep alive the interest in such questions, and to scrutinize suggested answers, is one of the functions of philosophy.

Those who have a passion for quick returns and for an exact balance sheet of effort and reward may feel impatient of a study which cannot, in the present state of our knowledge, arrive at certainties, and which encourages what may be thought the time-wasting occupation of inconclusive meditation on insoluble problems. To this view I cannot in any degree subscribe. Some kind of philosophy is a necessity to all but the most thoughtless, and in the absence of knowledge it is almost sure to be a silly philosophy. The result of this is that the human race becomes divided into rival groups of fanatics, each group firmly persuaded that its own brand of nonsense is sacred truth, while the other side's is damnable heresy. Arians and Catholics, Crusaders and Moslems, Protestants and adherents of the Pope, Communists and Fascists, have filled large parts of the last 1,600 years with futile strife, when a little philosophy would have shown both sides in all these disputes that neither had any good reason to believe itself in the right. Dogmatism is an enemy to peace, and an insuperable barrier to democracy. In the present age, at least as much as in former times, it is the greatest of the mental obstacles to human happiness.

The demand for certainty is one which is natural to man, but is nevertheless an intellectual vice. If you take your children for a picnic on a doubtful day, they will demand a dogmatic answer as to whether it will be fine or wet, and be disappointed in you when you cannot be sure. The same sort of assurance is demanded, in later life, of those who undertake to lead populations into the Promised Land. "Liquidate the capitalists and the survivors will enjoy eternal bliss." "Exterminate the Jews and everyone will be virtuous." "Kill the Croats and let the Serbs reign." "Kill the Serbs and let the Croats reign." These are samples of the slogans that have won wide popular acceptance in our time. Even a modicum of philosophy would make it impossible to accept such blood-thirsty nonsense. But so long as men are not trained to withhold judgment in the absence of evidence, they will be led astray by cocksure prophets, and it is likely that their leaders will be either ignorant fanatics or dishonest charlatans. To endure uncertainty is difficult, but so are most of the other virtues. For the learning of every virtue there is an appropriate discipline, and for the learning of suspended judgment the best discipline is philosophy.

But if philosophy is to serve a positive purpose, it must not teach mere skepticism, for while the dogmatist is harmful, the skeptic is useless. Dogmatism and skepticism are both, in a sense, absolute philosophies; one is certain of knowing, the other of not knowing. What philosophy should dissipate is *certainty*, whether of knowledge or of ignorance. Knowledge is not so precise a concept as is commonly thought. Instead of saying "I know this," we ought to say, "I more or less know something more or less like this." It is true that this proviso is hardly necessary as regards the multiplication table, but knowledge in practical affairs has not the certainty or the precision of arithmetic. Suppose I say, "Democracy is a good thing." I must admit, first, that I am less sure of this than I am that two and two are four, and secondly, that "democracy" is a somewhat vague term which I cannot define precisely. We ought to say, therefore: "I am fairly certain that it is a good thing if a government has something of the characteristics that are common to the British and American Constitutions," or something of this sort. And one of the aims of education ought to be to make such a statement more effective from a platform than the usual type of political slogan.

For it is not enough to recognize that all our knowledge is, in a greater or less degree, uncertain and vague; it is necessary, at the same time, to learn to act upon the best hypothesis without dogmatically believing it. To revert to the picnic: even though you admit that it may rain, you start out if you think fine weather probable, but you allow for the opposite possibility by taking mackintoshes. If you were a dogmatist you would leave the mackintoshes at home. The same principles apply to more important issues. One may say broadly: all that passes for knowledge can be arranged in a hierarchy of degrees of certainty, with arithmetic and the facts of perception at the top. That two and two are four, and that I am sitting in my room writing, are statements as to which any serious doubt on my part would be pathological. I am nearly as certain that yesterday was a fine day, but not quite, because memory does sometimes play odd tricks. More distant memories are more doubtful, particularly if there is some strong emotional reason for remembering falsely, such, for instance, as made George IV remember being at the battle of Waterloo. Scientific laws may be very nearly certain, or only slightly probable, according to the state of the evidence.

When you act upon a hypothesis which you know to be uncertain, your action should be such as will not have *very* harmful results if your hypothesis is false. In the matter of the picnic, you may risk a wetting if all your party are robust, but not if one of them is so delicate as to run a risk of pneumonia. Or suppose you meet a Muggletonian. You will be justified in arguing with him, because not much harm will have been done if Mr. Muggleton was in fact as great a man as his disciples suppose; but you will not be justified in burning him at the stake, because the evil of being burned alive is more certain than any proposition of theology. Of course if the Muggletonians were so numerous and so fanatical that either you or they must be killed, the question would grow more difficult, but the general principle remains that an uncertain hypothesis cannot justify a certain evil unless an equal evil is equally certain on the opposite hypothesis.

Critical Philosophy
Paves the Way for Science

Moritz Schlick

Moritz Schlick (1882–1936), trained in physics, was Professor of Philosophy in the University of Vienna and led in the founding of the Vienna circle of logical positivist philosophers. His writings are mostly in the theory of knowledge and ethics.

The study of the history of philosophy is perhaps the most fascinating pursuit for anyone who is eager to understand the civilization and culture of the human race, for all of the different elements of human nature that help to build up the culture of a certain epoch or a nation mirror themselves in one way or another in the philosophy of that epoch or of that nation.

The history of philosophy can be studied from two distinct points of view. The first point of view is that of the historian; the second one is that of the philosopher. They will each approach the study of the history of philosophy with different feelings. The historian will be excited to the greatest enthusiasm by the great works of the thinkers of all times, by the spectacle of the immense mental energy and imagination, zeal and unselfishness which they have devoted to their creations, and the historian will derive the highest enjoyment from all of these achievements. The philosopher, of course, when he studies the history of philosophy will also be delighted, and he cannot help being inspired by the wonderful display of genius throughout all the ages. But he will not be able to rejoice at the sight that philosophy presents to him with exactly the same feelings as the historian. He will not be able to enjoy the thoughts of ancient and modern times without being disturbed by feelings of an entirely different nature.

The philosopher cannot be satisfied to ask, as the historian would ask of all the systems of thought—are they beautiful, are they brilliant, are they historically important? and so on. The only question which will interest him is the question, "What truth is there in these systems?" And the moment he asks it he will be discouraged when he looks at the history of philosophy, because, as you all know, there is so much contradiction between the various systems—so much quarreling and strife between the different opinions that have been advanced in different periods by different philosophers belonging to different nations—that it seems at first quite impossible to believe that there is anything like a steady advance in the history of philosophy as there seems to be in other pursuits of the human mind, for example, science or technique.

The question which we are going to ask tonight is "Will this chaos that has existed so far continue to exist in the future?" Will philosophers go on contradicting each other, ridiculing each other's opinions, or will there finally be some kind of universal agreement, a unity of philosophical belief in the world?

All of the great philosophers believed that with their own systems a new epoch of thinking had begun, that they, at last, had discovered the final truth. If they had not believed this they could hardly have accomplished anything. This was true of Descartes, for instance, when he introduced the method which made him "the father of modern philosophy," as he is usually called; of Spinoza when he tried to introduce the mathematical method into philosophy; or even of Kant when he said in the preface to his greatest work that from now on philosophy might begin to work as securely as only science had worked thus far. They all believed that they had been able to bring the chaos to an end and start something entirely new which would at last bring about a rise in the worth of philosophical opinions. But the historian cannot usually share such a belief; it may even seem ridiculous to him.

We want to ask the question, "What will be the future of philosophy?" entirely from the point of view of the philosopher. However, to answer the question we shall have to use the method of the historian, because we shall not be able to say what the future of philosophy will be except insofar as our conclusions are derived from our knowledge of its past and its present.

The first effect of a historical consideration of philosophical opinions is that we feel sure we cannot have any confidence in any one system. If this is so—if we cannot be Cartesians, Spinozists, Kantians, and so forth—it seems that the only alternative is that we become skeptics, and we become inclined to believe that there can be no true system of philosophy, because if there were any such system it seems that at least it must have been suspected and would have shown itself in some way. However, when we examine the history of philosophy honestly, it seems as if there were no traces of any discovery that might lead to unanimous philosophical opinion.

This skeptical inference, in fact, has been drawn by a good many historians, and even some philosophers have come to the conclusion that there is no such thing as philosophical advancement and that philosophy itself is nothing but the history of philosophy. This view was advocated by more than one philosopher in the beginning of the century, and it has been called "historicism." That philosophy consists only of its own history is a strange view to take, but it has been advocated and defended with apparently striking arguments. However, we shall not find ourselves compelled to take such a skeptical view.

We have thus far considered two possible alternatives that one may believe in. First, that the ultimate truth is really presented in some one system of philosophy, and secondly, that there is no philosophy at all, but only a history of thought. I do not . . . propose to choose either of these two alternatives; but I should like to propose a third view which is neither skeptical nor based on the belief that there can be any system of philosophy as a system of ultimate truths. I intend to take an entirely different view of philosophy, and it is, of course, my opinion that this view of philosophy will some time in the future be adopted by everybody. In fact, it would seem strange to me if philosophy, that noblest of intellectual pursuits, the tremendous human achievement that has so often been called the "queen of all sciences," were nothing at all but one great deception. Therefore, it seems likely that a third view can be found by careful analysis, and I believe that the view which I am going to advance here will do full justice to all the skeptical arguments against the possibility of a philosophical system and yet will not deprive philosophy of any of its nobility and grandeur.

Of course, the mere fact that thus far the great systems of philosophy have not been successful and have not been able to gain general acknowledgment is no sufficient reason why there should not be some philosophical system discovered in the future that would universally be regarded as the ultimate solution of the great problems. This might, indeed, be expected to happen if philosophy were a "science." For in science we continually find that unexpected satisfactory solutions for great problems are found, and when it is not possible to see clearly in any particular point on a scientific question, we do not despair. We believe that future scientists will be more fortunate and discover what we have failed to discover. In this respect, however, the great difference between science and philosophy reveals itself. Science shows a gradual development. There is not the slightest doubt that science has advanced and continues to advance, although some people speak skeptically about science. It cannot be seriously doubted for an instant that we know very much more about nature, for example, than people living in former centuries knew. There is unquestionably some kind of advance shown in science, but if we are perfectly honest, a similar kind of advance cannot be discovered in philosophy.

The same great issues are discussed nowadays that were discussed in the time of Plato. When for a time it seemed as though a certain question were definitely settled, soon the same question comes up again and has to be discussed and reconsidered. It was characteristic of the work of the philosopher that he always had to begin at the beginning again. He never takes anything for granted. He feels that every solution to any philosophical problem is not certain or sure enough, and he feels that he must begin all over again in settling the problem. There is, then, this difference between science and philosophy, which makes us very skeptical about any future advance of philosophy. Still we might believe that times may change and that we might possibly find the true philosophical system. But this hope is in vain, for we can find reasons why philosophy has failed, and must fail, to produce lasting scientific results as science has done. If these reasons are good, then we shall be justified in not trusting in any system of philosophy, and in believing that no such system will come forward in the future.

Let me say at once that these reasons do not lie in the difficulty of the problems with which philosophy deals; neither are they to be found in the weakness and incapacity of human understanding. If they lay there, it could easily be conceived that human understanding and reason might develop, that if we are not intelligent enough now our successors might be intelligent enough to develop a system. No, the real reason is to be found in a curious misunderstanding and misinterpretation of the nature of philosophy; it lies in the failure to distinguish between the scientific attitude and the philosophical attitude. It lies in the idea that the nature of philosophy and science are more or less the same, that they both consist of systems of true propositions about the world. In reality, philosophy is never a system of propositions and, therefore, quite different from science. The proper understanding of the relationship between philosophy on one side and of the sciences on the other side is, I think, the best way of gaining insight into the nature of philosophy. We will, therefore, start with an investigation of this relationship and its historical development. This will furnish us the necessary facts in order to predict the future of philosophy. The future, of course, is always a matter of historical conjecture, because it can be calculated only from past and present experiences. So we ask now: what has the nature of philosophy been conceived to be in comparison with that of the sciences? And how has it developed in the course of history?

In its beginnings, as you perhaps know, philosophy was considered to be simply another name for the "search for truth"—it was identical with science. Men who pursued the truth for its own sake were called philosophers, and there was no distinction made between men of science and philosophers.

A little change was brought about in this situation by Socrates. Socrates, one might say, despised science. He did not believe in all the speculations about astronomy and about the structure of the universe in which the early philosophers indulged. He believed one could never gain any certain knowledge about these matters and he restricted his investigations to the nature of human character. He was not a man of science, he had no faith in it, and yet we all acknowledge him to be one of the greatest philosophers who ever lived. It is not Socrates, however, who created the antagonism that we find to exist later on between science and philosophy. In fact, his successor combined very well the study of human nature with the science of the stars and of the universe.

Philosophy remained united with the various sciences until gradually the latter branched off from philosophy. In this way, perhaps, mathematics, astronomy, mechanics, and medicine became independent one after the other and a difference between philosophy and science was created. Nevertheless, some kind of unity or identity of the two persisted, we might say, almost to modern times, i.e., until the nineteenth century. I believe we can say truthfully that there are certain sciences—I am thinking particularly of physics—which were not completely separated from philosophy until the nineteenth century. Even now some university chairs for theoretical physics are officially labeled chairs of "natural philosophy."

It was in the nineteenth century, also, that the real antagonism began, with a certain feeling of unfriendliness developing on the part of the philosopher toward the scientist and the scientist toward the philosopher. This feeling arose when philosophy claimed to possess a nobler and better method of discovering truth than the scientific method of observation and experiment. In Germany, at the beginning of the nineteenth century, Schelling, Fichte, and Hegel believed that there was some kind of royal path leading to truth which was reserved for the philosopher, whereas the scientist walked the pathway of the vulgar and very tedious experimental method, which required so much merely mechanical technique. They thought that they could attain the same truth that the scientist was trying to find out, but could discover it in a much easier way by taking a short cut that was reserved for the very highest minds, only for the philosophical genius. About this, however, I will not speak, because it may be regarded, I think, as having been superseded.

There is another view, however, which tried to distinguish between science and philosophy by saying that philosophy dealt with the most general truths that could be known about the world, and that science dealt with the more particular truths. It is this last view of the nature of philosophy that I must discuss shortly . . . as it will help us to understand what will follow.

This opinion that philosophy is the science that deals with those most general truths which do not belong to the field of any special science is the most common view that you find in nearly all of the textbooks; it has been adopted by the majority of philosophical writers in our present day. It is generally believed that as, for example, chemistry concerns itself with the true propositions about the different chemical compounds and physics with the truth about physical behavior, so philosophy deals with the most general questions concerning the nature of matter. Similarly, as history investigates the various chains of single happenings which determine the fate of the human race, so philosophy (as "philosophy of history") is supposed to discover the general principles which govern all those happenings.

In this way, philosophy, conceived as the science dealing with the most general truths, is believed to give us what might be called a universal picture of the world, a general world view in which all the different truths of the special sciences find their places and are unified into one great picture—a goal which the special sciences themselves are thought incapable of reaching as they are not general enough and are concerned only with particular features and parts of the great whole.

This so-called "synoptic view" of philosophy, holding as it does that philosophy is also a science, only one of a more general character than the special sciences, has, it seems to me, led to terrible confusion. On the one hand it has given to the philosopher the character of the scientist. He sits in his library, he consults innumerable books, he works at his desk and studies various opinions of many philosophers as a historian would compare his different sources, or as a scientist would do while engaged in some particular pursuit in any special domain of knowledge; he has all the bearing of a scientist and really believes that he is using in some way the scientific method, only doing so on a more general scale. He regards philosophy as a more distinguished and much nobler science than the others, but not as essentially different from them.

On the other hand, with this picture of the philosopher in mind, we find a very great contrast when we look at the results that have been really achieved by philosophical work carried on in this manner. There is all the outward appearance of the scientist in the philosopher's mode of work, but there is no similarity of results. Scientific results go on developing, combining themselves with other achievements, and receiving general acknowledgment, but there is no such thing to be discovered in the work of the philosopher.

What are we to think of the situation? It has led to very curious and rather ridiculous results. When we open a textbook on philosophy or when we view one of the large works of a present-day philosopher, we often find an immense amount of energy devoted to the task of finding out what philosophy is. We do not find this in any of the other sciences. Physicists or historians do not have to spend pages to find out what physics or history is. Even those who agree that philosophy in some way is the system of the most general truths explain this generality in rather different ways. I will not go into detail with respect to these varying definitions. Let me just mention that some say that philosophy is the "science of values" because they believe that the most general issues to which all questions finally lead have to do with value in some way or another. Others say that it is epistemology, that is, the theory of knowledge, because the theory of knowledge is supposed to deal with the most general principles on which all particular truths rest. One of the consequences usually drawn by the adherents of the view we are discussing is that philosophy is either partly or entirely metaphysics. And metaphysics is supposed to be some kind of a structure built over and partly resting on the structure of science but towering into lofty heights which are far beyond the reach of all the sciences and of experience.

We see from all this that even those who adopt the definition of philosophy as the most general science cannot agree about its essential nature. This is certainly a little ridiculous, and some future historian a few hundred or a thousand years from now will think it very curious that discussion about the nature of philosophy was taken so seriously in our days. There must be something wrong when a discussion leads to such confusion. There are also very definite positive reasons why "generality" cannot be used as the characteristic that distinguishes philosophy from the "special" sciences, but I will not dwell upon them, but try to reach a positive conclusion in some shorter way.

When I spoke of Socrates a little while ago, I pointed out that his thoughts were, in a certain sense, opposed to the natural sciences; his philosophy, therefore, was certainly not identical with the sciences, and it was not the "most general" one of them. It was rather a sort of Wisdom of Life. But the important feature which we should observe in Socrates, in order to understand his particular attitude as well as the nature of philosophy, is that this wisdom that dealt with human nature and human behavior consists essentially of a special method, different from the method of science and, therefore, not leading to any "scientific" results.

All of you have probably read some of Plato's Dialogues, wherein he pictures Socrates as giving and receiving questions and answers. If you observe what was really done—or what Socrates tried to do—you discover that he did usually not arrive at certain definite truths which would appear at the end of the dialogue, but the whole investigation was carried on for the primary purpose of making clear what was meant when certain questions were asked or when certain words were used. In one of the Platonic Dialogues, for instance, Socrates asks "What is Justice?"; he receives various answers to his question, and in turn he asks what was meant by these answers, why a particular word was used in this way or that way, and it usually turns out that his disciple or opponent is not at all clear about his own opinion. In short, Socrates' philosophy consists of what we may call "The Pursuit of Meaning." He tried to clarify thought by analyzing the meaning of our expressions and the real sense of our propositions.

Here, then, we find a definite contrast between this philosophic method, which has for its object the discovery of meaning, and the method of the sciences, which have for their object the discovery of truth. In fact, before I go any farther, let me state shortly and clearly that I believe Science should be defined as the "pursuit of truth" and Philosophy as the "pursuit of meaning." Socrates has set the example of the true philosophic method for all times. But I shall have to explain this method from the modern point of view.

When we make a statement about anything, we do this by pronouncing a sentence, and the sentence stands for the proposition. This proposition is either true or false, but before we can know or decide whether it is true or false, we must know what this proposition says. We must know the meaning of the proposition first. After we know its sense, we may be able to find out whether it is true or not. These two things, of course, are inseparably connected. I cannot find out the truth without knowing the meaning, and if I know the meaning of the proposition I shall at least know the beginning of some path that will lead to the discovery of the truth or falsity of the proposition, even if I am unable to find it at present. It is my opinion that the future of philosophy hinges on this distinction between the discovery of sense and the discovery of truth.

How do we decide what the sense of a proposition is, or what we mean by a sentence which is spoken, written, or printed? We try to present to ourselves the significance of the different words that we have learned to use, and then endeavor to find sense in the proposition. Sometimes we can do so and sometimes we cannot; the latter case happens, unfortunately, most frequently with propositions which are supposed to be "philosophical." But how can we be quite sure that we really know and understand what we mean when we make an assertion? What is the ultimate criterion of its sense? The answer is this: We know the meaning of a proposition when we are able to indicate exactly the circumstances under which it would be true (or, what amounts to the same, the circumstances which would make it false). The description of these circumstances is absolutely the only way in which the meaning of a sentence can be made clear. After it has been made clear we can proceed to look for the actual circumstances in the world and decide whether they make our proposition true or false. There is no vital difference between the ways we decide about truth and falsity in science and in everyday life. Science develops in the same ways in which does knowledge in daily life. The method of verification is essentially the same; only the facts by which scientific statements are verified are usually more difficult to observe.

It seems evident that a scientist or a philosopher when he propounds a proposition must of necessity know what he is talking about before he proceeds to find out its truth. But it is very remarkable that oftentimes it has happened in the history of human thought that thinkers have tried to find out whether a certain proposition was true or false before being clear about the meaning of it, before really knowing what it was they were desirous of finding out. This has been the case sometimes even in scientific investigations, instances of which I will quote shortly. And it has, I am almost tempted to say, nearly always been the case in traditional philosophy. As I have stated, the scientist has two tasks. He must find out the truth of a proposition and he must also find out the meaning of it, or it must be found out for him, but usually he is able to find it for himself. Insofar as the scientist does find out the hidden meaning of the propositions which he uses in his science, he is a philosopher. All of the great scientists have given wonderful examples of this philosophical method. They have discovered the real significance of words which were used quite commonly in the beginning of science but of which nobody had ever given a perfectly clear and definite account. When Newton discovered the concept of "mass," he was at that time really a philosopher. The greatest example of this type of discovery in modern times is Einstein's analysis of the meaning of the word "simultaneity" as it is used in physics. Continually, something is happening "at the same time" in New York and San Francisco, and although people always thought they knew perfectly well what was meant by such a statement, Einstein was the first one who made it really clear and did away with certain unjustified assumptions concerning time that had been made without anyone being aware of it. This was a real philosophical achievement—the discovery of meaning by a logical clarification of a proposition. I could give more instances, but perhaps these two will be sufficient. We see that meaning and truth are linked together by the process of verification; but the first is found by mere reflection about possible circumstances in the world, while the second is decided by really discovering the existence or nonexistence of those circumstances. The reflection in the first case is the philosophic method of which Socrates' dialectical proceeding has afforded us the simplest example.

From what I have said so far it might seem that philosophy would simply have to be defined as the science of meaning, as, for example, astronomy is the science of the heavenly bodies, or zoology the science of animals, and that philosophy would be a science just as other sciences, only its subject would be different, namely, "Meaning." This is the point of view taken in a very excellent book, *The Practice of Philosophy*, by Susanne K. Langer. The author has seen quite clearly that philosophy has to do with the pursuit of meaning, but she believes the pursuit of meaning can lead to a science, to "a set of true propositions"—for that is the correct interpretation of the term "science." Physics is nothing but a system of truths about physical bodies. Astronomy is a set of true propositions about the heavenly bodies, and so on.

But philosophy is not a science in this sense. There can be no science of meaning, because there cannot be any set of true propositions about meaning. The reason for this is that in order to arrive at the meaning of a sentence or of a proposition we must go beyond propositions. For we cannot hope to explain the meaning of a proposition merely by presenting another proposition. When I ask somebody, "What is the meaning of this or that?" he must answer by a sentence that would try to describe the meaning. But he cannot ultimately succeed in this, for his answering sentence would be but another proposition and I would be perfectly justified in asking, "What do you mean by this?" We would perhaps go on defining what he meant by using different words, and repeat his thought over and over again by using new sentences. I could always go on asking, "But what does this new proposition mean?" You see, there would never be any end to this kind of inquiry; the meaning could never be clarified, if there were no other way of arriving at it than by a series of propositions.

An example will make the above clear, and I believe you will all understand it immediately. Whenever you come across a difficult word for which you desire to find the meaning, you look it up in the *Encyclopaedia Britannica*. The definition of the word is given in various terms. If you don't happen to know them you look up these terms. However, this procedure can't go on indefinitely. Finally, you will arrive at very simple terms for which you will not find any explanation in the encyclopedia. What are these terms? They are the terms which cannot be defined any more. You will admit that there are such terms. If I say, for example, that the lamp shade is yellow, you might ask me to describe what I mean by yellow—and I could not do it. I should have to show you some color and say that this is yellow, but I should be perfectly unable to explain it to you by means of any sentences or words. If you had never seen yellow and I were not in a position to show you any yellow color, it would be absolutely impossible for me to make clear what I meant when I uttered the word. And the blind man, of course, will never be able to understand what the word stands for.

All of our definitions must end by some demonstration, by some activity. There may be certain words at the meaning of which one may arrive by certain mental activities, just as I can arrive at the signification of a word which denotes color by showing the color itself. It is impossible to define a color—it has to be shown. Reflection of some kind is necessary so that we may understand the use of certain words. We have to reflect, perhaps, about the way in which we learn these words, and there are also many ways of reflection which make it clear to us what we mean by various propositions. Think, for example, of the term "simultaneity" of events occurring in different places. To find what is really meant by the term, we have to go into an analysis of the proposition and discover how the simultaneity of events occurring in different places is really determined, as was done by Einstein; we have to point to certain actual experiments and observations. This should lead to the realization that philosophical activities can never be replaced and expressed by a set of propositions. The discovery of the meaning of any proposition must ultimately be achieved by some act, some immediate procedure, for instance, as the showing of yellow; it cannot be given in a proposition. Philosophy, the "pursuit of meaning," therefore, cannot possibly consist of propositions; it cannot be a science. The pursuit of meaning consequently is nothing but a sort of mental activity.

Our conclusion is that philosophy was misunderstood when it was thought that philosophical results could be expressed in propositions, and that there could be a system of philosophy consisting of a system of propositions which would represent the answers to "philosophical" questions. There are no specific "philosophical" truths which would contain the solution of specific "philosophical" problems, but philosophy has the task of finding the meaning of all problems and their solutions. It must be defined as the activity of finding meaning.

Philosophy is an activity, not a science; but this activity, of course, is at work in every single science continually, because before the sciences can discover the truth or falsity of a proposition, they have to get at the meaning first. And sometimes in the course of their work they are surprised to find, by the contradictory results at which they arrive, that they have been using words without a perfectly clear meaning, and then they will have to turn to the philosophical activity of clarification, and they cannot go on with the pursuit of truth before the pursuit of meaning has been successful. In this way philosophy is an extremely important factor within science and it very well deserves to bear the name of "The Queen of Sciences."

The Queen of Sciences is not itself a science. It is an activity which is needed by all scientists and pervades all their other activities. But all real problems are scientific questions; there are no others.

And what was the matter with those great questions that have been looked upon—or rather looked up to—as specific "philosophical problems" for so many centuries? Here we must distinguish two cases. In the first place, there are a great many questions which look like questions because they are formed according to a certain grammatical order, but which, nevertheless, are not real questions, since it can easily be shown that the words, as they are put together, do not make logical sense.

If I should ask, for instance: "Is blue more identical than music?" you would see immediately that there is no meaning in this sentence, although it does not violate the rules of English grammar. The sentence is not a question at all, but just a series of words. Now, a careful analysis shows that this is the case with most so-called philosophical problems. They look like questions and it is very difficult to recognize them as nonsensical, but logical analysis proves them none the less to be merely some kind of confusion of words. After this has been found out, the question itself disappears and we are perfectly peaceful in our philosophical minds; we know that there can be no answers because there were no questions; the problems do not exist any longer.

In the second place, there are some "philosophical" problems which prove to be real questions. But of these it can always be shown by proper analysis that they are capable of being solved by the methods of science, although we may not be able to apply these methods at present for merely technical reasons. We can at least say what would have to be done in order to answer the question even if we cannot actually do it with the means at our disposal. In other words: problems of this kind have no special "philosophical" character, but are simply scientific questions. They are always answerable in principle, if not in practice, and the answer can be given only by scientific investigation.

Thus the fate of all "philosophical problems" is this: Some of them will disappear by being shown to be mistakes and misunderstandings of our language, and the others will be found to be ordinary scientific questions in disguise. These remarks, I think, determine the whole future of philosophy.

Several great philosophers have recognized the essence of philosophical thinking with comparative clarity, although they have given no elaborate expression to it. Kant, for example, used to say in his lectures that philosophy cannot be taught. However, if it were a science such as geology or astronomy, why then should it not be taught? It would then, in fact, be quite possible to teach it. Kant, therefore, had some kind of a suspicion that it was not a science when he stated, "The only thing I can teach is philosophizing." By using the verb and rejecting the noun in this connection, Kant indicated clearly, though almost involuntarily, the peculiar character of philosophy as an activity, thereby to a certain extent contradicting his books, in which he tries to build up philosophy after the manner of a scientific system.

A similar instance of the same insight is afforded by Leibniz. When he founded the Prussian Academy of Science in Berlin and sketched out the plans for its constitution, he assigned a place in it to all the sciences, but Philosophy was not one of them. Leibniz found no place for philosophy in the system of the sciences because he was evidently aware that it is not a pursuit of a particular kind of truth, but an activity that must pervade every search for truth.

The view which I am advocating has at the present time been most clearly expressed by Ludwig Wittgenstein; he states his point in these sentences: "The object of philosophy is the logical clarification of thoughts. Philosophy is not a theory but an activity. The result of philosophy is not a number of 'philosophical propositions,' but to make propositions clear." This is exactly the view which I have been trying to explain here.

We can now understand historically why philosophy could be regarded as a very general science: it was misunderstood in this way because the "meaning" of propositions might seem to be something very "general," since in some way it forms the foundation of all discourse. We can also understand historically why in ancient times philosophy was identical with science: this was because at that time all the concepts which were used in the description of the world were extremely vague. The task of science was determined by the fact that there were no clear concepts. They had to be clarified by slow development; the chief endeavor of scientific investigation had to be directed towards this clarification, that is, it had to be philosophical; no distinction could be made between science and philosophy.

At the present time we also find facts which prove the truth of our statements. In our day certain specific fields of study, such as ethics and esthetics, are called "philosophical" and are supposed to form part of philosophy. However, philosophy, being an activity, is a unit which cannot be divided into parts or independent disciplines. Why, then, are these pursuits called philosophy? Because they are only at the beginnings of the scientific stage; and I think this is true to a certain extent also of psychology. Ethics and esthetics certainly do not yet possess sufficiently clear concepts; most of their work is still devoted to clarifying them, and, therefore, it may justly be called philosophical. But in the future they will, of course, become part of the great system of the sciences.

It is my hope that the philosophers of the future will see that it is impossible for them to adopt, even in outward appearance, the methods of the scientists. Most books on philosophy seem to be, I must confess, ridiculous when judged from the most elevated point of view. They have all the appearance of being extremely scientific books because they seem to use the scientific language. However, the finding of meaning cannot be done in the same way as the finding of truth. This difference will come out much more clearly in the future. There is a good deal of truth in the way in which Schopenhauer (although his own thinking seems to me to be very imperfect indeed) describes the contrast between the real philosopher and the academic scholar who regards philosophy as a subject of scientific pursuit. Schopenhauer had a very clear instinct when he spoke disparagingly of the "professorial philosophy of the professors of philosophy." His opinion was that one should not try to teach philosophy at all but only the history of philosophy and logic; and a good deal may be said in favor of this view.

I hope I have not been misunderstood as though I were advocating an actual separation of scientific and philosophical work. On the contrary, in most cases future philosophers will have to be scientists because it will be necessary for them to have a certain subject matter on which to work—and they will find cases of confused or vague meaning particularly in the foundations of the sciences. But, of course, clarification of meaning will be needed very badly also in a great many questions with which we are concerned in our ordinary human life. Some thinkers, and perhaps some of the strongest minds among them, may be especially gifted in this practical field. In such instances, the philosopher may not have to be a scientist—but in all cases he will have to be a man of deep understanding. In short, he will have to be a wise man.

I am convinced that our view of the nature of philosophy will be generally adopted in the future; and the consequence will be that it will no longer be attempted to teach philosophy as a system. We shall teach the special sciences and their history in the true philosophical spirit of searching for clarity; and by doing this we shall develop the philosophical mind of future generations. This is all we can do, but it will be a great step in the mental progress of our race.

Philosophy As Insight
Into the Games of Life

John Wilson

John Wilson (1928–   ), Director, the Farmington Research Unit, Oxford, is author of several books on many facets of language.

Of course this is an immense subject, and I cannot do it justice; but I hope at least to show that the ordinary person may justifiably be more optimistic about the relevance of philosophy than perhaps some philosophers have led him to expect.

Everything turns on the business of philosophy. One view, perhaps still the most popular, is that philosophy is directly and immediately concerned with a way of life and with the truth about reality. It has to do with what people are, what they do, and what they feel: with their behavior, their emotions, their beliefs and moral judgments. By this account a man's philosophy is a sort of blend between his motives, his behavior, and his values. Thus one may pursue pleasure, think pleasure good, and be labeled a hedonist or a utilitarian; another may listen to the dictates of conscience, act from a sense of duty, and be labeled a Kantian or an intuitionist. These are their philosophies. Philosophy as a whole makes a living, on this theory, by outlining various philosophies and attempting to judge between them. Plato will paint you one kind of life, Aristotle another, Bertrand Russell a third: different philosophers will criticize different ways of life, and the individual reads them and then chooses for himself. This is still perhaps the

Reprinted by permission of Cambridge University Press from *Thinking With Concepts* by John Wilson, 1963, pp. 126–141 (with brief omission at beginning).

most common view of philosophy. Some people declare themselves "on the side of logic," others "on the side of the emotions"; some believe in duty, others in happiness; some in mysticism, others in hard fact.

The objection to this picture is that it makes of the philosopher no more than the manager of an art gallery in which paintings of different ways of life are displayed, held up to the light, criticized, valued, and finally bought. The philosopher exhibits these, explains them, assesses them, and so forth. People buy what suits them. There appears to be no real place for *rational* assessment, no criteria by which one painting may be firmly judged better than another. Various alternative choices are offered: you can buy an Epicurus or one of the Stoic school of painting, a Bentham or a Kant, a D. H. Lawrence or an Archbishop of Canterbury. Debate over which to buy becomes desultory and purposeless. All this may be amusing, and may improve mutual tolerance; but it signally fails to satisfy the intense demand for truth, the need to know as exactly as possible what is so and what is not so, and the desire for some effective tool or method by which to judge, all of which are as common in the twentieth century as they ever were.

The second view, which is still practiced if not preached by the modern linguistic philosophers of Oxbridge, is a sharp and radical reaction from the first. On this view the philosopher has no *direct* connection with ways of life, motives, behavior or values at all. He is an analyst of language, concerned with the verification and meaning of statements and with the logical use of words. The philosopher is not interested in what people think about life (much less how they choose to behave), but only in the words in which they express their thoughts. Do statements about God have meaning? Is the notion of truth applicable to moral judgments? What is meant by saying that a man acts freely? These are linguistic questions, which turn on the use of words like "meaning," "truth," "freely," and so forth.

Plainly such radicalism has a lot to be said for it. For some thousands of years men have been discussing God, right and wrong, truth and falsehood, beauty, intuition, freedom, and so on; and it is both plausible and probably true to say that in an important sense they did not know what they were talking about, in that none of the concepts which they used in their philosophies were ever properly subjected to analytic scrutiny. Plainly there is little point in discussing what is right and wrong unless we know what is meant by the words "right" and "wrong": and so with all questions. Moreover, it is a dangerous illusion to suppose that we do, in all senses, know the meanings of words. We may use them correctly, but we are not fully conscious of how they function logically in language; and to be unconscious of this may lead us into asking mistaken or even meaningless questions.

But as a complete program for philosophy this will not do. It will not do primarily because language is not an abstract activity, but a form of life. It is something used by people; and not only this, but something much more close to people, much more *a part of them*, than most linguistic philosophers suppose. A man's language is *only a symptom* of his conceptual equipment, just as his neurotic behavior-patterns are only symptoms of his inner psychic state. The phrase "conceptual equipment" covers far more ground than "language": though the analysis of language is one way—and a good way—of investigating conceptual equipment. To discover the stance in which a man faces the world, and to make him conscious of it so that he can change it, one good method is to see how he talks and make him conscious of his language.

Yet words represent only one part of the equipment with which people face life. When we say, for instance, "He sees life differently from the way I see it," we do not mean *either* (as the first view claims) that he has a different way of life from me, that his behavior-patterns, motives, and values are different, *or* (according to the second view) just that he makes different sorts of statements from the ones I make, that he uses language differently. Of course both these may be true, and probably will be true; yet this is not what we mean when we say, "He sees life differently." We mean that his conceptual equipment is different. It is as if we said, as we frequently do, "He speaks a different language," using this sentence metaphorically, or "It's no good, we don't speak the same language." Here we are, significantly and interestingly, extending the notion of language to cover far more than the spoken symbols of words: we refer to the whole pattern of thought, the categories, concepts, and modes of thinking, which lie behind both the man's way of life and his actual, spoken words.

Of all the beings we know, man alone is capable of entertaining the notion of meaning. This is to say that man has experiences in a different sense from that in which we might say, if we wished, that animals or inanimate objects have experiences. Dogs are beaten, roses suffer blight, lakes are drained, and mountains leveled; but these occurrences do not *mean* anything to their victims; they simply *happen* to them. The victims act and are acted upon: they "have experiences" in this sense, but in this sense only. With men, however, to have the power of saying, "I had a ghastly experience yesterday" is itself to have the power of conscious experience: of being conscious of what happens to one and what one does, of remembering it, naming and describing it, thinking about it, and interpreting it. Man has the freedom to attach, within limits circumscribed by his own nature, whatever force or weight to his experiences he likes: the freedom to give them meaning.

If we give the concept of meaning or interpretation a wide sense, we see that it enters into all activities or occurrences of which we are at any time conscious. We are most inclined, as philosophers, to lay stress on those cases where we are fully conscious of giving and understanding meaning, as, for instance, in the artificially created symbols of mathematics, or, to a lesser extent, in words. But whether we choose to lie in the sun, to watch a blue and sparkling sea, to make love, to read a novel, to order a particular wine, to buy a particular car, or even to smoke one more cigarette, our choices are very obviously governed by the weight or force which these happenings have for our minds; and this is to say, in a sense, that they are governed by our own interpretation or evaluation of them. The sun, the sea, the lovemaking, and so on, all mean something to us; and conflicts arise, preeminently in personal relationships, because different things mean differently to different people.

Many of our interpretations are, no doubt, in some sense forced upon us. We grow up into a world in which, for the sake of survival, we are forced to attach a certain weight to food, warmth, physical objects, and so on; and thereby we uncritically create and accept a framework of interpretation which, for the most part, stays with us for the rest of our lives. Events happen to us in early childhood which unconsciously exercise power over the conscious activities of our later lives, by forcing upon us certain interpretations and evaluations. Some of these may be acceptable and beneficial, like the desire for food; others may be unacceptable and tiresome, like a fear of cats or running water. Later we acquire, more or less consciously, a framework of attitudes and values towards all the aspects of human life that we meet: to men, women, children, and all the roles that these may play (fathers, sisters, lovers, and so on), to money and possessions, to nature, to our own role in society, to music and literature and the arts, to science, mathematics, philosophy, and all the other disciplines of mankind. This framework is our conceptual equipment.

To describe conceptual equipment, to expand the meaning of the phrase, is not easy. One can use many metaphors, each as good or as bad as any other, to give a general idea of what we are talking about. At any particular period of his life, each man faces himself and the world by adopting a certain posture, a certain stance, towards it. Thus he may cower, stand erect, thrust his chin and his fists forward, wait passively for fate to overtake him, and so on. Or else we shall say that he faces things with a certain set of tools: the incisive, straightforward tool-kit of the physicist, the less informative but deeper probes and sounders of psychoanalysis, and so on. Or else we shall say that he sees through different sets of spectacles: rose-tinted spectacles, or the dark glasses of pessimism, or the tough, protective goggles of the skier or motor racer. Or else we shall say that he speaks certain languages and understands them: the language of strict and authoritarian morality or the kinder but more uncertain language of the liberal, the clear-cut vocabulary of the natural scientist or the emotively charged and symbolic language of the poet or the religious believer. Or else we say, finally, that he has the skill to play a certain number of games in life: the game of working with his colleagues, the game of taking part in dramatic or musical productions, the game of love.

Of these metaphors perhaps the most productive is that of a game. Almost all human behavior, and all behavior which has any claim to be in any sense rational, is artificial. Consciously or unconsciously, people obey or try to obey certain rules. These may be rules of procedure, as in a law-court; rules of convention, as in personal relationships at a casual level; rules of reasoning, as in logic or the study of some specific subject; rules of behavior in their moral lives; rules of language in ordinary communication, and so forth. More subtly, but still within the analogy, they follow certain principles in their deeper personal relationships and their approach to the arts. Learning to get on with people, and (less obviously but still truly) learning to love someone or to be a close friend of someone, is like learning to play a game, just as learning to practice law or to play the piano is like learning to play a game. We can describe, and fruitfully, people who fail in one way or another as failing because of *lack of skill*. People who do not enjoy music (unless they are tone-deaf) fail to enjoy it because they approach it in the wrong way: they have not the skill to listen properly. Juvenile delinquents simply do not know how to play a life-game in which the criminal and civil law of the land forms part of the rules. New nations, trying democracy for the first time, often fail because they lack the feel of democratic procedure: there are certain tacit assumptions which must be observed if parliamentary debates are not to break down, and these are like rules in a game which some players do not understand. A final example from a field which is more obviously connected with our present conception of philosophy: people who reject religion *in toto* often do so because, as it were, they cannot find their way around the conceptual landscape of religion. The concepts and experiences of religion (like those of poetry or music) form a game which it takes skill, practice, and study to play.

To produce a rough approximation; the business of philosophy is to make people conscious of the rules of these games. For unless they are conscious of them, they will be unable to play them better, and also unable to see which new games they want to learn to play, and which old games they want to continue to play or to discard. With certain games, the logic of which is fairly simple, philosophy has already succeeded. The rules or principles by which one does science, or mathematics, or formal logic, are now fairly clearly established: and this is partly why these studies have prospered. Other games present more difficulty. How, for instance, does one decide about moral problems, or problems of personal relationships? How is one to assess works of art? How is one to decide whether to have a religion, and which one to have? In all these cases the philosopher's business is neither (as the first view holds) simply to put forward a moral view, a view about personal relationships, a theory of aesthetics or religion, and compare it with other views, leaving the individual to choose for himself—for on what criteria can he choose?—nor (the second view) simply to analyze the language of morals, aesthetics, and religion, for this alone does not clarify the rules of the games with sufficient depth. His business is, first and foremost, to make clear how the games are in fact played: to clarify *what it is* to settle a moral issue, *what it is* to have a religion, *what it is* to love or be friends with someone, in the same way as we are now clear about what it is to do science or mathematics.

What kind of process is this clarification? To use the example of science: we might feel that the clarification of the science-game was actually very simple. After all, we are all familiar nowadays with the standard technique of observation with our senses, the formulation of hypotheses, making crucial experiments, framing theories and laws, and making predictions from them. But in fact and in history, it took humanity till the Renaissance to gain a clear idea of this game. The change from a view of the world according to which nature was magical and mysterious to a view which regarded nature as essentially explicable and predictable was long and arduous: men gradually grew out of a belief in magic, and came to have the power to see nature as a collection of *things*, depersonalised objects which could be weighed, measured, analyzed, and so forth. This sort of change has various aspects to it. Depth psychologists such as O. Mannoni[1] have given a clear ac-

---

[1] *Prospero and Caliban*, by O. Mannoni (Methuen).

count of its psychological nature (the security required to free oneself from the desire to people nature with little men, magical forces, ghosts, spirits, and so on). But it has also an important *conceptual* aspect; and it is this which is the business of philosophy. It is not just a question of how we feel about the world and ourselves; it is a question of *in what terms we conceive them.* This is something which is amenable to rational discussion, in which we may become more conscious of our own concepts, our own language, our own pictures of the world, and hence learn to change them. All of us are largely unaware of the conceptual principles by which we work: we have, in this century, a reasonably firm grasp of the world of sense-experience, and feel at home with science. But with morals, religion, literature, and the arts, and above all in personal relationships, we feel lost and bewildered (unless we are already so blind that we think there is nothing to see). Neither of the two views I have criticized earlier cater adequately for this blindness or bewilderment. It is inept to say that we must just try harder or behave better or follow more sensible ways of life; and it is inadequate to say that we must scrutinize our language and become more clever about the logic of words. For our difficulties do not arise either because we are not good or virtuous enough, or because we are not clever enough. They arise because we feel *lost,* out of our depth, groping, trying to learn how to play the various games of life. It is the same sort of feeling that one might have when about to step on to the dance floor without knowing how to dance: one doesn't know how to *start.*

Philosophy, then, is clarification of *method,* of the way in which these games are played. Philosophers are already aware of this in the way they handle certain metaphysical problems, questions like "Are any of our actions really free?" or "Can we ever be certain about anything?" We feel about these questions that the most difficult thing is to know how we should *start* setting about giving them an answer. We feel basically puzzled by them: we have no method ready to hand by which we can deal with them. But there are hundreds of questions in life which are in this sense "metaphysical": hundreds of questions, that is, which arise because we are trying to play games without being clear about the rules. The classical metaphysical questions—questions about free will, reality, truth, and so on—have always formed only a small intellectual arena in which academicians fight. Meanwhile in the square outside, in the public streets, in the homes and the dance-halls, ordinary people are puzzled by parts of their lives in precisely the same *kind* of way, a way which necessitates education in self-consciousness, in awareness of how they are in fact facing the world and themselves, in overhauling their conceptual equipment. It is this process which I have described as philosophy.

It would require much more careful consideration to investigate the forms which philosophy, in this sense, will take in the future. But it is certainly true that, even if it splits up into various departments designed to clarify and deal with different games, it will still retain more coherence than, say, the physical sciences. For the links between our depth-psychology, our behaviour, our ways of life, our conceptual equipment, our actual beliefs, and the language in which we express them are very binding; and it is doubtful whether any competent philosopher will be able to afford ignorance in any department. For this reason the training of philosophers as linguistic analysts merely is grotesquely inadequate: and one is not surprised at the appearance of counter-symptoms in the shape of thinkers who care nothing for analysis, but who open the door to experiences and life-games that linguistic philosophers prefer to leave standing in the corridor—as for instance the Existentialist school, or the school of German metaphysical theologians. One should also notice groups which plainly ought to connect with philosophy, but which our appalling communications have virtually servered: the two most obvious examples are, first, the psychoanalysts, and second, the Cambridge literary critics.

For these reasons the philosopher should be familiar with, and sympathetic to, all the major fields which relate directly to human concepts: all the studies and forms of creation which can teach, influence, or otherwise affect our conceptual equipment. Obvious candidates for study are literature (particularly the novel and drama), music, psychology, the social sciences, and history. All these bear directly—and, for most people, much more effectively than philosophy—on our conceptual equipment: on our stance towards life, the spectacles we wear, the game-playing skills we have, the tools we use, the pictures we form. One suspects that academic philosophers have made an obvious error: the error of supposing that only those disciplines which result in true propositions have any bearing upon truth. Thus, it is plain that in the normal sense of "true," music, painting, drama, and even novels do not make "true" statements; but it is wrong to conclude that they have nothing to do with truth. They may indirectly generate factually true statements by a complex process, which no one has properly studied, which consists roughly in giving us certain experiences and affecting our feelings and emotions in a certain way, and hence disturbing and illuminating us, so that we can then change our pictures of the world and our concepts and eventually make or assent to statements which would previously have cut no ice with us at all. Even though the arts do not assert facts, they still teach us—and teach us rationally. It is this kind of rational teaching that philosophy needs to include within its ambience. Insofar as rational discussion takes place in words, the basic and essential parts of the philosopher's tool-kit will, of course, be linguistic. But there will be other tools: instead of merely being able to analyze statements, he will learn to relate them to the general world-pictures and the conceptual equipment as a whole of individuals.

This process of philosophy is, of course, itself a game, and a particularly difficult one to play. It is as if philosophy had to move up to a higher story and watch the people on the ground floor playing their various games with more or less success, and then assess and criticize their rules; or as if one were presented with a compendium of games in a box, like a Christmas present, only the rules had been left out—one has to try and work out what the games are, how they should be played, and whether they are worth playing at all. All this makes the most stringent demands: a demand for logical rigor, so that the game of philosophy should be purposive and not a mere art-gallery comparison of different concepts, and yet also a demand for breadth of understanding, so that we can keep good communications with all the games that actually exist. Yet the importance of philosophy, at any level of life and in any context, is obvious: for without this process of becoming more aware, more conscious of the rules, it is perhaps impossible to assess or make any deliberate rational change in one's life. Certainly we may change, and live, without philosophy, just as we may without common sense, or without some of the five senses. But we cannot do so effectively. We desperately need a technique to handle the problems involved; and it may be possible, without much further research, for the first time to establish such a technique on a firm footing. For at least we recognize the fields of activity involved—literature, the arts, social science, and so forth —and can begin to think about the methods of each, and the way in which they bear upon the problems of life. We may yet live to see the philosopher really earning his keep.

The analysis of concepts, then, emerges as only one tool in the philosopher's equipment, but a very necessary tool, because it is a very good way of generating consciousness. One thing, at least, everyone can always do: he can always say, "What does that mean?" But if he is content with what we may call a purely *logical* analysis, his increase of consciousness, though helpful, will not be as profound as it might be. For meaning goes deeper than usage: it stems from a man's whole conceptual equipment, which itself is rooted in his personality and past experiences. For this reason we have far more than a purely verbal landscape to map: just as, perhaps, someone who really wished to understand the geography of a country would have to go below the surface of its landscape and understand its geology also—the nature of the subsoil, the history of the rock strata, and so forth. Of course geography is a different subject from geology; and of course, for the sake of simplicity at least, we must count philosophy as a different subject from psychology, history, sociology, and so on. But even this is a little misleading. We deceive ourselves if we suppose that these humane studies possess totally separate and discrete subject-matters; it is better to say that there are human problems which can and must be approached both philosophically, psychologically, sociologically, and so forth. We need a harmonious team of experts, who are experts in particular methods of approach: not a number of disjoined specialists working in their own studies and laboratories.

Given an approach of this kind, I believe it would be possible to make the methods of philosophy as real and important to the ordinary person as, say, the methods of elementary mathematics, or of reading and writing. The danger, of course, is that the closer union of these varied disciplines may result in none of them being practiced with a proper rigor and forcefulness: we may get a kind of optimistic, liberal muddle of vaguely cultural subjects that relate in some way—but not very forcefully or directly—to human problems. This is one of the reasons why I think that the analysis of concepts, which if properly practiced is a very exacting discipline, is a good tool to acquire first. But I hope it will also be realized that if we use it in conjunction with other tools, we may achieve results beyond our present expectations.

6

Freedom, Determinism, and Responsibility

The notion that all man's actions, even his thoughts, are governed by immutable laws probably goes back to prehistory. The Greeks had their *moira*, a plot or lot which even the gods must obey, the Romans, Fate, Christians predestination, Moslems *kismet*, Hindus and Buddhists their *karma*. Each of these concepts has peculiarities all its own. It seems almost inevitable that man's insatiable desire to make life intelligible would result in some theory which explains events in terms of an orderly, law-abiding scheme, even though its details might be inscrutable. In some theories life is not presided over by any supreme personal being, and one reaps what one sows. In others an all-knowing, all-powerful being directs events.

Scientific determinism grew out of a concept of law which was parasitic upon the impersonal scheme of justice and the laws decreed by human rulers or handed down from the gods. Baron D'Holbach's materialistic science is used to support "hard determinism" in which the laws of science are very much like the decrees of despots. Whatever anyone did was in obedience to such laws. Moritz Schlick, himself trained in physics, points out how different scientific law is from the law of man, but how easy it is to confuse them in our thoughts and language. He is a "soft determinist" who, like David Hume and John Stuart Mill, believes that scientific laws, as primarily statistical entities, are perfectly compatible with freedom of choice. C. A. Campbell, contemporary British philosopher, gives a very trenchant criticism of soft determinism, arguing that its confusions compromise genuine human freedom too much. R. S. Peters, British philosopher of education, moving in a fairly new realm of inquiry, the relation between the physiological and psychological causes of our behavior and the justifications for our actions, argues that the free-will problem has not kept the genuine differences between these two types of causes clearly in mind.

Free Will Is an Illusion

Paul H. D. Holbach

Paul Henri D. (or T.) Holbach, Baron D'Holbach (1723–1789), a French Encyclopaedist, whose materialist and atheist views often shocked his contemporaries, was nevertheless widely respected for them even during his lifetime.

Motives and the Determination of the Will

In whatever manner man is considered, he is connected to universal nature, and submitted to the necessary and immutable laws that she imposes on all the beings she contains, according to their peculiar essences or to the respective properties with which, without consulting them, she endows each particular species. Man's life is a line that nature commands him to describe upon the surface of the earth, without his ever being able to swerve from it, even for an instant. He is born without his own consent; his organization does in nowise depend upon himself; his ideas come to him involuntarily; his habits are in the power of those who cause him to contract them; he is unceasingly modified by causes, whether visible or concealed, over which he has no control, which necessarily regulate his mode of existence, give the hue to his way

From Paul H. D. Holbach, *The System of Nature,* translated by H. D. Robinson, 1770, Chapters 11 and 12, with omissions.

of thinking, and determine his manner of acting. He is good or bad, happy or miserable, wise or foolish, reasonable or irrational, without his will being for anything in these various states. Nevertheless, in spite of the shackles by which he is bound, it is pretended he is a free agent, or that independent of the causes by which he is moved, he determines his own will, and regulates his own condition.

However slender the foundation of this opinion, of which everything ought to point out to him the error, it is current at this day and passes for an incontestable truth with a great number of people, otherwise extremely enlightened; it is the basis of religion, which, supposing relations between man and the unknown being she has placed above nature, has been incapable of imagining how man could merit reward or deserve punishment from this being, if he was not a free agent. Society has been believed interested in this system because an idea has gone abroad that if all the actions of man were to be contemplated as necessary, the right of punishing those who injure their associates would no longer exist. At length human vanity accommodated itself to a hypothesis which, unquestionably, appears to distinguish man from all other physical beings, by assigning to him the special privilege of a total independence of all other causes, but of which a very little reflection would have shown him the impossibility. . . .

The will, as we have elsewhere said, is a modification of the brain, by which it is disposed to action, or prepared to give play to the organs. This will is necessarily determined by the qualities, good or bad, agreeable or painful, of the object or the motive that acts upon his senses, or of which the idea remains with him, and is resuscitated by his memory. In consequence, he acts necessarily; his action is the result of the impulse he receives either from the motive, from the object, or from the idea which has modified his brain, or disposed his will. When he does not act according to this impulse, it is because there comes some new cause, some new motive, some new idea, which modifies his brain in a different manner, gives him a new impulse, determines his will in another way, by which the action of the former impulse is suspended: thus, the sight of an agreeable object, or its idea, determines his will to set him in action to procure it; but if a new object or a new idea more powerfully attracts him, it gives a new direction to his will, annihilates the effect of the former, and prevents the action by which it was to be procured. This is the mode in which reflection, experience, reason, necessarily arrests or suspends the action of man's will: without this he would of necessity have followed the anterior impulse which carried him towards a then desirable object. In all this he always acts according to necessary laws from which he has no means of emancipating himself.

If when tormented with violent thirst, he figures to himself in idea, or really perceives a fountain, whose limpid streams might cool his feverish want, is he sufficient master of himself to desire or not to desire the object competent to satisfy so lively a want? It will no doubt be conceded, that it is impossible he should not be desirous to satisfy it; but it will be said—if at this moment it is announced to him that the water he so ardently desires is poisoned, he will, notwithstanding his vehement thirst, abstain from drinking it: and it has, therefore, been falsely concluded that he is a free agent. The fact, however, is, that the motive in either case is exactly the same: his own conservation. The same necessity that determined him to drink before he knew the water was deleterious, upon this new discovery equally determined him not to drink; the desire of conserving himself either annihilates or suspends the former impulse; the second motive becomes stronger than the preceding, that is, the fear of death, or the desire of preserving himself, necessarily prevails over the painful sensation caused by his eagerness to drink: but, it will be said, if the thirst is very parching, an inconsiderate man without regarding the danger will risk swallowing the water. Nothing is gained by this remark: in this case, the anterior impulse only regains the ascendency; he is persuaded that life may possibly be longer preserved, or that he shall derive a greater good by drinking the poisoned water than by enduring the torment, which, to his mind, threatens instant dissolution: thus the first becomes the strongest and necessarily urges him on to action. Nevertheless, in either case, whether he partakes of the water, or whether he does not, the two actions will be equally necessary; they will be the effect of that motive which finds itself most puissant, which consequently acts in the most coercive manner upon his will.

This example will serve to explain the whole phenomena of the human will. This will, or rather the brain, finds itself in the same situation as a bowl, which, although it has received an impulse that drives it forward in a straight line, is deranged in its course whenever a force superior to the first obliges it to change its direction. The man who drinks the poisoned water appears a madman; but the actions of fools are as necessary as those of the most prudent individuals. The motives that determine the voluptuary and the debauchee to risk their health, are as powerful, and their actions are as necessary, as those which decide the wise man to manage his. But, it will be insisted, the debauchee may be prevailed on to change his conduct: this does not imply that he is a free agent; but that motives may be found sufficiently powerful to annihilate the effect of those that previously acted upon him; then these new motives determine his will to the new mode of conduct he may adopt as necessarily as the former did to the old mode. . . .

The errors of philosophers on the free agency of man, have arisen from their regarding his will as the *primum mobile*, the original motive of his actions; for want of recurring back, they have not perceived the multiplied, the complicated causes which, independently of him, give motion to the will itself; or which dispose and modify his brain, whilst he himself is purely passive in the motion he receives. Is he the master of desiring or not desiring an object that appears desirable to him? Without doubt it will be answered, no: but he is the master of resisting his desire, if he reflects on the consequences. But, I ask, is he capable of reflecting on these consequences, when his soul is hurried along by a very lively passion, which entirely depends upon his natural organization, and the causes by which he is modified? Is it in his power to add to these consequences all the weight necessary to counterbalance his desire? Is he the master of preventing the qualities which render an object desirable from residing in it? I shall be told: he ought to have learned to resist his passions; to contract a habit of putting a curb on his desires. I agree to it without any difficulty. But in reply, I again ask, is his nature susceptible of this modification? Does his boiling blood, his unruly imagination, the igneous fluid that circulates in his veins, permit him to make, enable him to apply true experience in the moment when it is wanted? And even when his temperament has capacitated him, has his education, the examples set before him, the ideas with which he has been inspired in early life, been suitable to make him contract this habit of repressing his desires? Have not all these things rather contributed to induce him to seek with avidity, to make him actually desire those objects which you say he ought to resist?

The *ambitious man* cries out: you will have me resist my passion; but have they not unceasingly repeated to me that rank, honors, power are the most desirable advantages in life? Have I not seen my fellow citizens envy them, the nobles of my country sacrifice every thing to obtain them? In the society in which I live, am I not obliged to feel, that if I am deprived of these advantages, I must expect to languish in contempt; to cringe under the rod of oppression?

The *miser* says: you forbid me to love money, to seek after the means of acquiring it: alas! does not every thing tell me that, in this world, money is the greatest blessing; that it is amply sufficient to render me happy? In the country I inhabit, do I not see all my fellow citizens covetous of riches? but do I not also witness that they are little scrupulous in the means of obtaining wealth? As soon as they are enriched by the means which you censure, are they not cherished, considered, and respected? By what authority, then, do you defend me from amassing treasure? What right have you to prevent my using means, which, although you call them sordid and criminal, I see approved by the sovereign? Will you have me renounce my happiness?

The *voluptuary* argues: you pretend that I should resist my desires; but was I the maker of my own temperament, which unceasingly invites me to pleasure? You call my pleasures disgraceful; but in the country in which I live, do I not witness the most dissipated men enjoying the most distinguished rank? Do I not behold that no one is ashamed of adultery but the husband it has outraged? Do not I see men making trophies of their debaucheries, boasting of their libertinism, rewarded with applause?

The *choleric man* vociferates: you advise me to put a curb on my passions, and to resist the desire of avenging myself: but can I conquer my nature? Can I alter the received opinions of the world? Shall I not be forever disgraced, infallibly dishonored in society, if I do not wash out in the blood of my fellow creatures the injuries I have received?

The *zealous enthusiast* exclaims: you recommend me mildness; you advise me to be tolerant; to be indulgent to the opinions of my fellow men; but is not my temperament violent? Do I not ardently love my God? Do they not assure me, that zeal is pleasing to him; that sanguinary inhuman persecutors have been his friends? As I wish to render myself acceptable in his sight, I therefore adopt the same means.

In short, the actions of man are never free; they are always the necessary consequence of his temperament, of the received ideas, and of the notions, either true or false, which he has formed to himself of happiness; of his opinions, strengthened by example, by education, and by daily experience. So many crimes are witnessed on the earth only because every thing conspires to render man vicious and criminal; the religion he has adopted, his government, his education, the examples set before him, irresistibly drive him on to evil: under these circumstances, morality preaches virtue to him in vain. In those societies where vice is esteemed, where crime is crowned, where venality is constantly recompensed, where the most deadful disorders are punished only in those who are too weak to enjoy the privilege of committing them with impunity, the practice of virtue is considered nothing more than a painful sacrifice of happiness. Such societies chastise, in the lower orders, those excesses which they respect in the higher ranks; and frequently have the injustice to condemn those in the penalty of death, whom public prejudices, maintained by constant example, have rendered criminal.

Man, then, is not a free agent in any one instant of his life; he is necessarily guided in each step by those advantages, whether real or fictitious, that he attaches to the objects by which his passions are roused: these passions themselves are necessary in a being who unceasingly tends towards his own happiness; their energy is necessary, since that depends on his temperament; his temperament is necessary, because it depends on the physical elements which enter into his composition; the modification of this temperament is necessary, as it is the infallible and inevitable consequence of the impulse he receives from the incessant action of moral and physical beings.

Choice Does Not Prove Freedom

In spite of these proofs of the want of free agency in man, so clear to unprejudiced minds, it will, perhaps, be insisted upon with no small feeling of triumph, that if it be proposed to any one, to move or not to move his hand, an action in the number of those called indifferent, he evidently appears to be the master of choosing; from which it is concluded that evidence has been offered of free agency. The reply is, this example is perfectly simple; man in performing some action which he is resolved on doing, does not by any means prove his free agency: the very desire of displaying this quality, excited by the dispute, becomes a necessary motive, which decides his will either for the one or the other of these actions. What deludes him in this instance, or that which persuades him he is a free agent at this moment, is, that he does not discern the true motive which sets him in action, namely, the desire of convincing his opponent: if in the heat of the dispute he insists and asks, "Am I not the master of throwing myself out of the window?" I shall answer him, no; that whilst he preserves his reason there is no probability that the desire of proving his free agency will become a motive sufficiently powerful to make him sacrifice his life to the attempt: if, notwithstanding this, to prove he is a free agent, he should actually precipitate himself from the window, it would not be a sufficient warranty to conclude he acted freely, but rather that it was the violence of his temperament which spurred him on to this folly. Madness is a state, that depends upon the heat of the blood, not upon the will. A fanatic or a hero, braves death as necessarily as a more phlegmatic man or coward flies from it.

There is, in point of fact, no difference between the man that is cast out of the window by another, and the man who throws himself out of it, except that the impulse in the first instance comes immediately from without whilst that which determines the fall in the second case, springs from within his own peculiar machine, having its more remote cause also exterior. When Mutius Scaevola held his hand in the fire, he was as much acting under the influence of necessity (caused by interior motives) that urged him to this strange action, as if his arm had been held by strong men: pride, despair, the desire of braving his enemy, a wish to astonish him, and anxiety to intimidate him, and so forth, were the invisible chains that held his hand bound to the fire. The love of glory, enthusiasm for their country, in like manner caused Codrus and Decius to devote themselves for their fellow-citizens. The Indian Colanus and the philosopher Peregrinus were equally obliged to burn themselves, by desire of exciting the astonishment of the Grecian assembly.

It is said that free agency is the absence of those obstacles competent to oppose themselves to the actions of man, or to the exercise of his faculties: it is pretended that he is a free agent whenever, making use of these faculties, he produces the effect he has proposed to himself. In reply to this reasoning, it is sufficient to consider that it in nowise depends upon himself to place or remove the obstacles that either determine or resist him; the motive that causes his action is no more in his own power than the obstacle that impedes him, whether this obstacle or motive be within his own machine or exterior of his person: he is not master of the thought presented to his mind, which determines his will; this thought is excited by some cause independent of himself.

To be undeceived on the system of his free agency, man has simply to recur to the motive by which his will is determined; he will always find this motive is out of his own control. It is said: that in consequence of an idea to which the mind gives birth, man acts freely if he encounters no obstacle. But the question is, what gives birth to this idea is his brain? Was he the master either to prevent it from presenting itself, or from renewing itself in his brain? Does not this idea depend either upon objects that strike him exteriorly and in despite of himself, or upon causes, that without his knowledge, act within himself and modify his brain? Can he prevent his eyes, cast without design upon any object whatever, from giving him an idea of this object, and from moving his brain? He is not more master of the obstacles; they are the necessary effects of either interior or exterior causes, which always act according to their given properties. A man insults a coward; this necessarily irritates him against his insulter; but his will cannot vanquish the obstacle that cowardice places to the object of his desire, because his natural conformation, which does not depend upon himself, prevents his having courage. In this case, the coward is insulted in spite of himself; and against his will is obliged patiently to brook the insult he has received.

Absence of Restraint
Is Not Absence of Necessity

The partisans of the system of free agency appear ever to have confounded constraint with necessity. Man believes he acts as a free agent, every time he does not see any thing that places obstacles to his actions; he does not perceive that the motive which causes him to will, is always necessary and independent of himself. A prisoner loaded with chains is compelled to remain in prison; but he is not a free agent in the desire to emancipate himself; his chains prevent him from acting, but they do not prevent him from willing; he would save himself if they would loose his fetters; but he would not save himself as a free agent; fear or the idea of punishment would be sufficient motives for his action.

Man may, therefore, cease to be restrained, without, for that reason, becoming a free agent: in whatever manner he acts, he will act necessarily, according to motives by which he shall be determined. He may be compared to a heavy body that finds itself arrested in its descent by any obstacle whatever: take away this obstacle, it will gravitate or continue to fall; but who shall say this dense body is free to fall or not? Is not its descent the necessary effect of its own specific gravity? The virtuous Socrates submitted to the laws of his country, although they were unjust; and though the doors of his jail were left open to him, he would not save himself; but in this he did not act as a free agent: the invisible chains of opinion, the secret love of decorum, the inward respect for the laws, even when they were iniquitous, the fear of tarnishing his glory, kept him in his prison; they were motives sufficiently powerful with this enthusiast for virtue, to induce him to wait death with tranquility; it was not in his power to save himself, because he could find no potential motive to bring him to depart, even for an instant, from those principles to which his mind was accustomed.

Man, it is said, frequently acts against his inclination, from whence it is falsely concluded he is a free agent; but when he appears to act contrary to his inclination, he is always determined to it by some motive sufficiently efficacious to vanquish this inclination. A sick man, with a view to his cure, arrives at conquering his repugnance to the most disgusting remedies: the fear of pain, or the dread of death, then become necessary motives; consequently this sick man cannot be said to act freely.

When it is said, that man is not a free agent, it is not pretended to compare him to a body moved by a simple impulsive cause: he contains within himself causes inherent to his existence; he is moved by an interior organ, which has its own peculiar laws, and is itself necessarily determined in consequence of ideas formed from perception resulting from sensation which it receives from exterior objects. As the mechanism of these sensations, of these perceptions, and the manner they engrave ideas on the brain of man, are not known to him; because he is unable to unravel all these motions; because he cannot perceive the chain of operations in his soul, or the motive principle that acts within him, he supposes himself a free agent; which literally translated, signifies, that he moves himself by himself; that he determines himself without cause: when he rather ought to say, that he is ignorant how or why he acts in the manner he does. It is true the soul enjoys an activity peculiar to itself: but it is equally certain that this activity would never be displayed, if some motive or some cause did not put it in a condition to exercise itself: at least it will not be pretended that the soul is able either to love or to hate without being moved, without knowing the objects, without having some idea of their qualities. Gunpowder has unquestionably a particular activity, but this activity will never display itself, unless fire be applied to it; this, however, immediately sets it in motion.

The Complexity
of Human Conduct
and the Illusion of Free Agency

It is the great complication of motion in man, it is the variety of his action, it is the multiplicity of causes that move him, whether simultaneously or in continual succession, that persuades him he is a free agent: if all his motions were simple, if the causes that move him did not confound themselves with each other, if they were distinct, if his machine were less complicated, he would perceive that all his actions were necessary, because he would be enabled to recur instantly to the cause that made him act. A man who should be always obliged to go towards the west, would always go on that side; but he would feel that, in so going, he was not a free agent: if he had another sense, as his actions or his motion, augmented by a sixth, would be still more varied and much more complicated, he would believe himself still more a free agent than he does with his five senses.

It is, then, for want of recurring to the causes that move him; for want of being able to analyze, from not being competent to decompose the complicated motion of his machine, that man believes himself a free agent: it is only upon his own ignorance that he founds the profound yet deceitful notion he has of his free agency; that he builds those opinions which he brings forward as a striking proof of his pretended freedom of action. If, for a short time, each man was willing to examine his own peculiar actions, search out their true motives to discover their concatenation, he would remain convinced that the sentiment he has of his natural free agency, is a chimera that must speedily be destroyed by experience.

Nevertheless it must be acknowledged that the multiplicity and diversity of the causes which continually act upon man, frequently without even his knowledge, render it impossible, or at least extremely difficult for him to recur to the true principles of his own peculiar actions, much less the actions of others: they frequently depend upon causes so fugitive, so remote from their effects, and which, superficially examined, appear to have so little analogy, so slender a relation with them, that it requires singular sagacity to bring them into light. This is what renders the study of the moral man a task of such difficulty; this is the reason why his heart is an abyss, of which it is frequently impossible for him to fathom the depth. . . .

If he understood the play of his organs, if he were able to recall to himself all the impulsions they have received, all the modifications they have undergone, all the effects they have produced, he would perceive that all his actions are submitted to that fatality, which regulates his own particular system, as it does the entire system of the universe: no one effect in him, any more than in nature, produces itself by chance; this, as has been before proved, is word void of sense. All that passes in him; all that is done by him; as well as all that happens in nature, or that is attributed to her, is derived from necessary causes, which act according to necessary laws, and which produce necessary effects from whence necessarily flow others.

Fatality, is the eternal, the immutable, the necessary order, established in nature; or the indispensable connection of causes that act, with the effects they operate. Conforming to this order, heavy bodies fall; light bodies rise; that which is analogous in matter reciprocally attracts; that which is heterogeneous mutually repels; man congregates himself in society, modifies each his fellow; becomes either virtuous or wicked; either contributes to his mutual happiness, or reciprocates his misery; either loves his neighbor, or hates his companion necessarily, according to the manner in which the one acts upon the other. From whence it may be seen, that the same necessity which regulates the physical, also regulates the moral world, in which every thing is in consequence submitted to fatality. Man, in running over, frequently without his own knowledge, often in spite of himself, the route which nature has marked out for him, resembles a swimmer who is obliged to follow the current that carries him along: he believes himself a free agent, because he sometimes consents, sometimes does not consent, to glide with the stream, which, notwithstanding, always hurries him forward; he believes himself the master of his condition, because he is obliged to use his arms under the fear of sinking. . . .

Soft Determinism

Moritz Schlick*

The Pseudo-Problem
of Freedom of the Will

With hesitation and reluctance I prepare to add this chapter
to the discussion of ethical problems. For in it I must speak of
a matter which, even at present, is thought to be a fundamental
ethical question, but which got into ethics and has become a much
discussed problem only because of a misunderstanding. This is
the so-called problem of the freedom of the will. Moreover, this
pseudo-problem has long since been settled by the efforts of certain sensible persons; and, above all, the state of affairs just described has been often disclosed—with exceptional clarity by
Hume. Hence it is really one of the greatest scandals of philosophy that again and again so much paper and printer's ink is devoted to this matter, to say nothing of the expenditure of thought,
which could have been applied to more important problems (assuming that it would have sufficed for these). Thus I should
truly be ashamed to write a chapter on "freedom." In the chapter

Reprinted by permission of Dover Publications, Inc., New York, from
The Problems of Ethics by Moritz Schlick, (1939).

* For biographical note, see p. 125.

heading,* the word "responsible" indicates what concerns ethics, and designates the point at which misunderstanding arises. Therefore the concept of responsibility constitutes our theme, and if in the process of its clarification I also must speak of the concept of freedom I shall, of course, say only what others have already said better, consoling myself with the thought that in this way alone can anything be done to put an end at last to that scandal.

The main task of ethics (of which we convinced ourselves in Chapter I) is to explain moral behavior. To explain means to refer back to laws: every science, including psychology, is possible only in so far as there are such laws to which the events can be referred. Since the assumption that *all* events are subject to universal laws is called the principle of causality, one can also say, "Every science presupposes the principle of causality." Therefore every explanation of human behavior must also assume the validity of causal laws, in this case the existence of psychological laws. (If for example our law of motivation of Chapter II were incorrect, then human conduct would be quite unexplained.) All of our experience strengthens us in the belief that this presupposition is realized, at least to the extent required for all purposes of practical life in intercourse with nature and human beings, and also for the most precise demands of technique. Whether, indeed, the principle of causality holds universally, whether, that is, *determinism* is true, we do not know; no one knows. But we do know that it is impossible to settle the dispute between determinism and indeterminism by mere reflection and speculation, by the consideration of so many reasons for and so many reasons against (which collectively and individually are but pseudo-reasons). Such an attempt becomes especially ridiculous when one considers with what enormous expenditure of experimental and logical skill contemporary physics carefully approaches the question of whether causality can be maintained for the most minute intra-atomic events.

But the dispute concerning "freedom of the will" generally proceeds in such fashion that its advocates attempt to refute, and its opponents to prove, the validity of the causal principle, both using hackneyed arguments, and neither in the least abashed by the magnitude of the undertaking. (I can exclude only Bergson from this criticism, with whom, however, this whole question is not an ethical but a metaphysical problem. His ideas, which in my opinion will not stand epistemological analysis, are of no significance for us.) Others distinguish two realms, in one of which

* Original chapter title, "When Is a Man Responsible?" [ed.]

determinism holds, but not in the other. This line of thought (which was unfortunately taken by Kant) is, however, quite the most worthless (though Schopenhauer considered it to be Kant's most profound idea).

Fortunately, it is not necessary to lay claim to a final solution of the causal problem in order to say what is necessary in ethics concerning responsibility; there is required only an analysis of the concept, the careful determination of the meaning which is in fact joined to the words "responsibility" and "freedom" as these are actually used. If men had made clear to themselves the sense of those propositions, which we use in everyday life, that pseudo-argument which lies at the root of the pseudo-problem, and which recurs thousands of times within and outside of philosophical books, would never have arisen.

The argument runs as follows: "If determinism is true, if, that is, all events obey immutable laws, then my will too is always determined, by my innate character and my motives. Hence my decisions are necessary, not free. But if so, then I am not responsible for my acts, for I would be accountable for them only if I could do something about the way my decisions went; but I can do nothing about it, since they proceed with necessity from my character and the motives. And I have made neither, and have no power over them: the motives come from without, and my character is the necessary product of the innate tendencies and the external influences which have been effective during my lifetime. Thus determinism and moral responsibility are incompatible. Moral responsibility presupposes freedom, that is, exemption from causality."

This process of reasoning rests upon a whole series of confusions, just as the links of a chain hang together. We must show these confusions to be such, and thus destroy them.

Two Meanings of the Word "Law"

It all begins with an erroneous interpretation of the meaning of "law." In practice this is understood as a rule by which the state prescribes certain behavior to its citizens. These rules often contradict the natural desires of the citizens (for if they did not do so, there would be no reason for making them), and are in fact not followed by many of them, while others obey, but under *compulsion.* The state does in fact compel its citizens by imposing certain sanctions (punishments) which serve to bring their desires into harmony with the prescribed laws.

In natural science, on the other hand, the word "law" means something quite different. The natural law is not a *prescription* as to how something should behave, but a formula, a *description* of how something does in fact behave. The two forms of "laws" have only this in common: both tend to be expressed in *formulae.* Otherwise they have absolutely nothing to do with one another, and it is very blameworthy that the same word has been used for two such different things, but even more so that philosophers have allowed themselves to be led into serious errors by this usage. Since natural laws are only descriptions of what happens, there can be in regard to them no talk of "compulsion." The laws of celestial mechanics do not prescribe to the planets how they have to move, as though the planets would actually like to move quite otherwise, and are only forced by these burdensome laws of Kepler to move in orderly paths; no, these laws do not in any way "compel" the planets, but express only what in fact planets actually do.

If we apply this to volition, we are enlightened at once, even before the other confusions are discovered. When we say that a man's will "obeys psychological laws," these are not civic laws, which compel him to make certain decisions, or dictate desires to him, which he would in fact prefer not to have. They are laws of nature, merely expressing which desires he *actually has* under given conditions; they describe the nature of the will in the same manner as the astronomical laws describe the nature of planets. "Compulsion" occurs where man is prevented from realizing his natural desires. How could the rule according to which these natural desires arise itself be considered as "compulsion"?

Compulsion and Necessity

But this is the second confusion to which the first leads almost inevitably: after conceiving the laws of nature, anthropomorphically, as order imposed *nolens volens* upon the events, one adds to them the concept of "necessity." This word, derived from "need," also comes to us from practice, and is used there in the sense of inescapable compulsion. To apply the word with this meaning to natural laws is of course senseless, for the presupposition of an opposing desire is lacking; and it is then confused with something altogether different, which is actually an attribute of natural laws. That is, universality. It is of the essence of natural laws to be universally valid, for only when we have found a rule which holds of events without exception do we *call* the rule a law of nature. Thus when we say "a natural law holds necessarily," this has but one legitimate meaning: "It holds in *all* cases where it is applicable." It is again very deplorable that the word "necessary" has been applied to natural laws (or, what amounts to the same thing, with reference to causality), for it is quite superfluous, since the expression "universally valid" is available. Universal validity is something altogether different from "compulsion"; these concepts belong to spheres so remote from each other that once insight into the error has been gained one can no longer conceive the possibility of a confusion.

The confusion of two concepts always carries with it the confusion of their contradictory opposites. The opposite of the universal validity of a formula, of the existence of a law, is the nonexistence of a law, indeterminism, acausality; while the opposite of compulsion is what in practice everyone calls "freedom." Here emerges the nonsense, trailing through centuries, that freedom means "exemption from the causal principle," or "not subject to the laws of nature." Hence it is believed necessary to vindicate indeterminism in order to save human freedom.

Freedom and Indeterminism

This is quite mistaken. Ethics has, so to speak, no moral interest in the purely theoretical question of "determinism or indeterminism?," but only a theoretical interest, namely, insofar as it seeks the laws of conduct, and can find them only to the extent that causality holds. But the question of whether man is morally free (that is, has that freedom which, as we shall show, is the presupposition of moral responsibility) is altogether different from the problem of determinism. Hume was especially clear on this point. He indicated the inadmissible confusion of the concepts of "indeterminism" and "freedom"; but he retained, inappropriately, the word "freedom" for both, calling the one "freedom of the will," the other, genuine kind, "freedom of conduct." He showed that morality is interested only in the latter, and that such freedom, in general, is unquestionably to be attributed to mankind. And this is quite correct. Freedom means the opposite of compulsion; a man is *free* if he does not act under *compulsion*, and he is compelled or unfree when he is hindered from without in the realization of his natural desires. Hence he is unfree when he is locked up, or chained, or when someone forces him at the point of a gun to do what otherwise he would not do. This is quite clear, and everyone will admit that the everyday or legal notion of the lack of freedom is thus correctly interpreted, and that a man will be considered quite free and responsible if no such external compulsion is exerted upon him. There are certain cases which lie between these clearly described ones, as, say, when someone acts under the influence of alcohol or a narcotic. In such cases we consider the man to be more or less unfree, and hold him less accountable, because we rightly view the influence of the drug as "external," even though it is found within the body; it prevents him from making decisions in the manner peculiar to his nature. If he takes the narcotic of his own will, we make him completely responsible for *this* act and transfer a part of the responsibility to the consequences, making, as it were, an average or mean condemnation of the whole. In the case also of a person who is mentally ill we do not consider him free with respect to those acts in which the disease expresses itself, because we view the illness as a disturbing factor which hinders the normal functioning of his natural tendencies. We make not him but his disease responsible.

The Nature of Responsibility

But what does this really signify? What do we mean by this concept of responsibility which goes along with that of "freedom," and which plays such an important role in morality? It is easy to attain complete clarity in this matter; we need only carefully determine the manner in which the concept is used. What is the case in practice when we impute "responsibility" to a person? What is our aim in doing this? The judge has to discover who is responsible for a given act in order that he may *punish* him. We are inclined to be less concerned with the inquiry as to who deserves *reward* for an act, and we have no special officials for this; but of course the principle would be the same. But let us stick to punishment in order to make the idea clear. What is punishment, actually? The view still often expressed, that it is a natural *retaliation* for past wrong, ought no longer to be defended in cultivated society; for the opinion that an increase in sorrow can be "made good again" by further sorrow is altogether barbarous. Certainly the origin of punishment may lie in an impulse of retaliation or vengeance; but what is such an impulse except the instinctive desire to destroy the *cause* of the deed to be avenged, by the destruction of or injury to the malefactor? Punishment is concerned only with the institution of causes, of *motives* of conduct, and this alone is its meaning. Punishment is an educative measure, and as such is a means to the formation of motives, which are in part to prevent the wrongdoer from repeating the act (reformation) and in part to prevent others from committing a similar act (intimidation). Analogously, in the case of reward we are concerned with an incentive.

Hence the question regarding responsibility is the question: Who, in a given case, is to be punished? Who is to be considered the true wrongdoer? This problem is not identical with that regarding the original instigator of the act; for the great-grandparents of the man, from whom he inherited his character, might in the end be the cause, or the statesmen who are responsible for his social milieu, and so forth. But the "doer" is the one *upon whom the motive must have acted* in order, with certainty, to have prevented the act (or called it forth, as the case may be). Consideration of remote causes is of no help here, for in the first place their actual contribution cannot be determined, and in the second place they are generally out of reach. Rather, we must find the person in whom the decisive junction of causes lies. The question of who is responsible is the question concerning the *correct point of application of the motive*. And the important thing is that in this its meaning is completely exhausted; behind it there lurks no mysterious connection between transgression and requital, which is merely *indicated* by the described state of affairs. It is a matter only of knowing who is to be punished or rewarded, in order that punishment and reward function as such—be able to achieve their goal.

Thus, all the facts connected with the concepts of responsibility and imputation are at once made intelligible. We do not charge an insane person with responsibility, for the very reason that he offers no unified point for the application of a motive. It would be pointless to try to affect him by means of promises or threats, when his confused soul fails to respond to such influence because its normal mechanism is out of order. We do not try to give him motives, but try to heal him (metaphorically, we make his sickness responsible, and try to remove its causes). When a man is forced by threats to commit certain acts, we do not blame him, but the one who held the pistol at his breast. The reason is clear: the act would have been prevented had we been able to restrain the person who threatened him; and this person is the one whom we must influence in order to prevent similar acts in the future.

The Consciousness of Responsibility

But much more important than the question of when a man is said to be responsible is that of when he *himself* feels responsible. Our whole treatment would be untenable if it gave no explanation of this. It is, then, a welcome confirmation of the view here developed that the subjective feeling of responsibility coincides with the objective judgment. It is a fact of experience that, in general, the person blamed or condemned is conscious of the fact that he was "rightly" taken to account—of course, under the supposition that no error has been made, that the assumed state of affairs actually occurred. What is this consciousness of having been the true doer of the act, the actual instigator? Evidently not merely that it was he who took the steps required for its performance; but there must be added the awareness that he did it "independently," of his own initiative," or however it be expressed. This feeling is simply the consciousness of *freedom*, which is merely the knowledge of having acted of one's *own* desires. And "one's own desires" are those which have their origin in the regularity of one's character in the given situation, and are not imposed by an external power, as explained above. The absence of the external power expresses itself in the well-known feeling (usually considered characteristic of the consciousness of freedom) *that one could also have acted otherwise.* How this indubitable experience ever came to be an argument in favor of indeterminism is incomprehensible to me. It is of course obvious that I should have acted differently had I *willed* something else;

but the feeling never says that I could also have willed something else, even though this is true, if, that is, other motives had been present. And it says even less that under *exactly the same* inner and outer conditions I could also have willed something else. How could such a feeling inform me of anything regarding the purely theoretical question of whether the principle of causality holds or not? Of course, after what has been said on the subject, I do not undertake to demonstrate the principle, but I do deny that from any such fact of consciousness the least follows regarding the principle's validity. This feeling is not the consciousness of the absence of a cause, but of something altogether different, namely, of *freedom*, which consists in the fact that I can act as I desire.

Thus the feeling of responsibility assumes that I acted freely, that my own desires impelled me; and if because of this feeling I willingly suffer blame for my behavior or reproach myself, and thereby admit that I might have acted otherwise, this means that other behavior was compatible with the laws of volition—of course, granted other motives. And I myself desire the existence of such motives and bear the pain (regret and sorrow) caused me by my behavior so that its repetition will be prevented. To blame oneself means just to apply motives of improvement to oneself, which is usually the task of the educator. But if, for example, one does something under the influence of torture, feelings of guilt and regret are absent, for one knows that according to the laws of volition no other behavior was possible—no matter what ideas, because of their feeling tones, might have functioned as motives. The important thing, always, is that the feeling of responsibility means the realization that one's self, one's own psychic processes, constitute the point at which motives must be applied in order to govern the acts of one's body.

Causality as the Presupposition of Responsibility

We can speak of motives only in a causal context; thus it becomes clear how very much the concept of responsibility rests upon that of causation, that is, upon the regularity of volitional decisions. In fact if we should conceive of a decision as utterly without any cause (this would in all strictness be the indeterministic presupposition) then the act would be entirely a matter of *chance,* for chance is identical with the absence of a cause; there is no other opposite of causality. Could we under such conditions make the agent responsible? Certainly not. Imagine a man, always calm, peaceful, and blameless, who suddenly falls upon and begins to beat a stranger. He is held and questioned regarding the motive of his action, to which he answers, in his opinion truthfully, as we assume: "There was no motive for my behavior. Try as I may I can discover no reason. My volition was without any cause—I desired to do so, and there is simply nothing else to be said about it." We should shake our heads and call him insane, because we have to believe that there was a cause, and lacking any other we must assume some mental disturbance as the only cause remaining; but certainly no one would hold him to be responsible. If decisions were causeless there would be no sense in trying to influence men; and we see at once that this is the reason why we could not bring such a man to account, but would always have only a shrug of the shoulders in answer to his behavior. One can easily determine that in practice we make an agent the more responsible the more motives we can find for his conduct. If a man guilty of an atrocity was an enemy of his victim, if previously he had shown violent tendencies, if some special circumstance angered him, then we impose severe punishment upon him; while the fewer the reasons to be found for an offense the less do we condemn the agent, but make "unlucky chance," a momentary aberration, or something of the sort, responsible. We do not find the causes of misconduct in his character, and therefore we do not try to influence it for the better: this and only this is the significance of the fact that we do not put the responsibility upon him. And he too feels this to be so, and says, "I cannot understand how such a thing could have happened to me."

In general we know very well how to discover the causes of conduct in the characters of our fellow men; and how to use this knowledge in the prediction of their future behavior, often with as much certainty as that with which we know that a lion and a rabbit will behave quite differently in the same situation. From all this it is evident that in practice no one thinks of questioning the principle of causality, that, thus, the attitude of the practical man offers no excuse to the metaphysician for confusing freedom from compulsion with the absence of a cause. If one makes clear to himself that a causeless happening is identical with a chance happening, and that, consequently, an indetermined will would destroy all responsibility, then every desire will cease which might be father to an indeterministic thought. No one can prove determinism, but it is certain that we assume its validity in all of our practical life, and that in particular we can apply the concept of responsibility to human conduct only insofar as the causal principle holds of volitional processes.

For a final clarification I bring together again a list of those concepts which tend, in the traditional treatment of the "problem of freedom," to be confused. In the place of the concepts on the left are put, mistakenly, those of the right, and those in the vertical order form a chain, so that sometimes the previous confusion is the cause of that which follows:

Natural Law	Law of State
Determinism (Causality)	Compulsion
(Universal Validity)	(Necessity)
Indeterminism (Chance)	Freedom
(No Cause)	(No Compulsion)

Errors of Soft Determinism

Charles Arthur Campbell

C. A. Campbell (1897–   ), Professor Emeritus, University of Glasgow, is the most prolific and respected philosophical champion of free will in the English-speaking world since William James.

II

I shall first summarize, as faithfully as I can, what I take to be the distinctive points in Schlick's argument.

The traditional formulation of the problem, Schlick points out, is based on the assumption that to have "free will" entails having a will that is, at least sometimes, exempt from causal law. It is traditionally supposed, quite rightly, that moral responsibility implies freedom in *some* sense: and it is supposed, also quite rightly, that this sense is one which is incompatible with compulsion. But because it is further supposed, quite *wrongly*, that to be subject to causal or natural laws is to be subject to compulsion, the inference is drawn that the free will implied in moral responsibility is incompatible with causal continuity. The ultimate root of the error, Schlick contends, lies in a failure to distinguish between two different kinds of Law, one of which does indeed

Reprinted by permission of the author and the publisher from *Mind*, NS, Vol. LX (1951). Section I is omitted.

"compel," but the other of which does *not*.[1] There are, first, *pre-scriptive* laws, such as the laws imposed by civil authority, which presume contrary desires on the part of those to whom they are applied; and these may fairly be said to exercise "compulsion." And there are, secondly, *descriptive* laws, such as the laws which the sciences seek to formulate; and these merely state what does as a matter of fact always happen. It is perfectly clear that the relation of the latter, the natural, causal laws, to human willing is radically different from the "compulsive" relation of prescriptive laws to human willing, and that it is really an absurdity to talk of a species of natural law like, say, psychological laws, *compelling* us to act in this or that way. The term "compulsion" is totally inept where, as in this case, there are no contrary desires. But the traditional discussions of Free Will, confusing descriptive with prescriptive laws, fallaciously assume "compulsion" to be ingredient in Law as such, and it is contended accordingly that moral freedom, since it certainly implies absence of compulsion, implies also exemption from causal law.

It follows that the problem of Free Will, as traditionally stated, is a mere pseudo-problem. The statement of it in terms of exemption from causal law rests on the assumption that causal law involves "compulsion." And this assumption is demonstrably false. Expose the muddle from which it arises and the so-called "problem" in its traditional form disappears.

But is it quite certain that the freedom which moral responsibility implies is no more than "the absence of compulsion"? This is the premise upon which Schlick's argument proceeds, but Schlick is himself well aware that it stands in need of confirmation from an analysis of the notion of moral responsibility. Otherwise it might be maintained that although "the absence of compulsion" has been shown not to entail a contra-causal type of freedom, there is nevertheless some *other* condition of moral responsibility that *does* entail it. Accordingly Schlick embarks now upon a formal analysis of the nature and conditions of moral responsibility designed to show that the *only* freedom implied by moral responsibility is freedom from compulsion. It was a trifle ambitious, however, even for a master of compression like Professor Schlick, to hope to deal satisfactorily in half a dozen very brief pages with a topic which has been so extensively debated in the literature of moral philosophy: and I cannot pretend that I find what he has to say free from obscurity. But to the best of my belief what follows does reproduce the gist of Schlick's analysis.

[1] *Problems of Ethics*, Ch. VIII, Section 2. (All references are to the English translation by David Rynin, published in New York in 1939.)

What precisely, Schlick asks, does the term "moral responsibility" mean in our ordinary linguistic usage?[2] He begins his answer by insisting upon the close connection for ordinary usage between "moral responsibility" and *punishment* (strictly speaking, punishment and *reward:* but for convenience Schlick virtually confines the discussion to punishment, and we shall do the same). The connection, as Schlick sees it, is this. In ordinary practice our concern with the responsibility for an act (he tells us) is with a view to determining *who is to be punished for it.* Now punishment is (I quote) "an educative measure." It is "a means to the formation of motives, which are in part to prevent the wrongdoer from repeating the act (reformation), and in part to prevent others from committing a similar act (intimidation)."[3] When we ask, then, "Who in a given case is to be punished?"—which is the same as the question "Who is responsible?"—what we are really wanting to discover is some agent in the situation upon whose motives we can bring to bear the appropriate educative influences, so that in similar situations in future his strongest motive will impel him to refrain from, rather than to repeat, the act. "The question of who is responsible," Schlick sums up, "is . . . a matter only of knowing who is to be punished or rewarded, in order that punishment and reward function as such—be able to achieve their goal."[4] It is not a matter, he expressly declares, of trying to ascertain what may be called the "original instigator" of the act. That might be a great-grand-parent, from the consequence of whose behavior vicious tendencies have been inherited by a living person. Such "remote causes" as this are irrelevant to questions of punishment (and so to questions of moral responsibility), "for in the first place their actual contribution cannot be determined, and in the second place they are generally out of reach."[5]

It is a matter for regret that Schlick has not rounded off his discussion, as one had hoped and expected he would, by formulating a precise definition of moral responsibility in terms of what he has been saying. I think, however, that the conclusion to which his argument leads could be not unfairly expressed in some such way as this: "We say that a man is morally responsible for an act if his motives for bringing about the act are such as we can affect favorably in respect of his future behavior by the educative influences of reward and punishment."

[2] *Loc. cit.*, Ch. VII, Section 5.
[3] *Ibid.*, p. 152.
[4] *Ibid.*, p. 153.
[5] *Ibid.*, p. 153.

Given the truth of this analysis of moral responsibility, Schlick's contention follows logically enough that the only freedom that is required for moral responsibility is freedom from compulsion. For what are the cases in which a man's motives are *not* capable of being favorably affected by reward and punishment?—the cases in which, that is, according to Schlick's analysis, we do *not* deem him morally responsible? The only such cases, it would seem, are those in which a man is subjected to some form of external constraint which prevents him from acting according to his "natural desires." For example, if a man is compelled by a pistol at his breast to do a certain act, or induced to do it by an externally administered narcotic, he is not "morally responsible"; or not, at any rate, insofar as punishment would be impotent to affect his motives in respect of his future behavior. External constraint in one form or another seems to be the sole circumstance which absolves a man from moral responsibility. Hence we may say that freedom from external constraint is the only sort of freedom which an agent must possess in order to be morally responsible. The "contra-causal" sort of freedom which so many philosophers and others have supposed to be required is shown by a true analysis of moral responsibility to be irrelevant.

This completes the argument that "Free Will," as traditionally formulated, is a pseudo-problem. The only freedom implied by moral responsibility is freedom from compulsion; and as we have rid ourselves of the myth that subjection to causal law is a form of compulsion, we can see that the only compulsion which absolves from moral responsibility is the external constraint which prevents us from translating our desires into action. The true meaning of the question "Have we free will?" thus becomes simply "Can we translate our desires into action?" And this question does not constitute a "problem" at all, for the answer to it is not in doubt. The obvious answer is "Sometimes we can, sometimes we can't, according to the specific circumstances of the case."

III

Here, then, in substance is Schlick's theory. Let us now examine it.

In the first place, it is surely quite unplausible to suggest that the common assumption that moral freedom postulates some breach of causal continuity arises from a confusion of two different types of law. Schlick's distinction between descriptive and prescriptive law is, of course, sound. It was no doubt worth pointing out, too, that descriptive laws cannot be said to "compel" human behavior in the same way as prescriptive laws do. But it seems to me evident that the usual reason why it is held that moral freedom implies some breach of causal continuity, is not a belief that causal laws "compel" as civil laws "compel," but simply the belief that the admission of unbroken causal continuity entails a *further* admission which is directly incompatible with moral responsibility, namely, the admission that no man could have acted otherwise than he in fact did. Now it may, of course, be an error thus to assume that a man is not morally responsible for an act, a fit subject for moral praise and blame in respect of it, unless he could have acted otherwise than he did. Or, if *this* is not an error, it may still be an error to assume that a man could not have acted otherwise than he did, in the sense of the phrase that is crucial for moral responsibility, without there occurring some breach of causal continuity. Into these matters we shall have to enter very fully at a later stage. But the relevant point at the moment is that these (not *prima facie* absurd) assumptions about the conditions of moral responsibility have very commonly, indeed normally, been made, and that they are entirely adequate to explain why the problem of Free Will finds its usual formulation in terms of partial exemption from causal law. Schlick's distinction between prescriptive and descriptive laws has no bearing at all upon the truth or falsity of these assumptions. Yet if these assumptions are accepted, it is (I suggest) really inevitable that the Free Will problem should be formulated in the way to which Schlick takes exception. Recognition of the distinction upon which Schlick and his followers lay so much stress can make not a jot of difference.

As we have seen, however, Schlick does later proceed to the much more important business of disputing these common assumptions about the conditions of moral responsibility. He offers us an analysis of moral responsibility which flatly contradicts these assumptions; an analysis according to which the only freedom demanded by morality is a freedom which is compatible with Determinism. If this analysis can be sustained, there is certainly no problem of "Free Will" in the traditional sense.

But it seems a simple matter to show that Schlick's analysis is untenable. Let us test it by Schlick's own claim that it gives us what we mean by "moral responsibility" in ordinary linguistic usage.

We do not ordinarily consider the lower animals to be morally responsible. But *ought* we not to do so if Schlick is right about what we mean by moral responsibility? It is quite possible, by punishing the dog who absconds with the succulent chops designed for its master's luncheon, favorably to influence its motives in respect of its future behavior in like circumstances. If moral responsibility is to be linked with punishment as Schlick links it, and punishment conceived as a form of education, we should surely hold the dog morally responsible. The plain fact, of course, is that we don't. We don't, because we suppose that the dog "couldn't help it": that its action (unlike what we usually believe to be true of human beings) was simply a link in a continuous chain of causes and effects. In other words, we do commonly demand the contra-casual sort of freedom as a condition of moral responsibility.

Again, we do ordinarily consider it proper, in certain circumstances, to speak of a person no longer living as morally responsible for some present situation. But *ought* we to do so if we accept Schlick's essentially "forward-looking" interpretation of punishment and responsibility? Clearly we cannot now favorably affect the dead man's motives. No doubt they could *at one time* have been favorably affected. But that cannot be relevant to our judgment of responsibility if, as Schlick insists, the question of who is responsible "is a matter only of knowing who is to be punished or rewarded." Indeed he expressly tells us, as we saw earlier, that in asking this question we are not concerned with a "great-grandparent" who may have been the "original instigator," because, for one reason, this "remote cause" is "out of reach." We cannot bring the appropriate educative influence to bear upon it. But the plain fact, of course, is that we do frequently assign moral responsibility for present situations to persons who have long been inaccessible to any punitive action on our part. And Schlick's position is still more paradoxical in respect of our apportionment of responsibility for occurrences in the distant past. Since in these cases there is no agent whatsoever whom we can favorably influence by punishment, the question of moral responsibility here should have no meaning for us. But of course it has. Historical writings are studded with examples.

Possibly the criticism just made may seem to some to result from taking Schlick's analysis too much *au pied de là lettre*. The absurd consequences deduced, it may be said, would not follow if we interpreted Schlick as meaning that a man is morally responsible where his motive is such as can *in principle* be favorably affected by reward or punishment—whether or not we who pass the judgment are in a position to take such action. But with every desire to be fair to Schlick, I cannot see how he could accept this modification and still retain the essence of his theory. For the essence of his theory seems to be that moral responsibility has its whole meaning and importance for us in relation to our potential control of future conduct in the interests of society. (I agree that it is hard to believe that anybody *really* thinks this. But it is perhaps less hard to believe today than it has ever been before in the history of modern ethics.)

Again, we ordinarily consider that, in certain circumstances, the *degree* of a man's moral responsibility for an act is affected by considerations of his inherited nature, or of his environment, or of both. It is our normal habit to "make allowances" (as we say) when we have reason to believe that a malefactor had a vicious heredity, or was nurtured in his formative years in a harmful environment. We say in such cases, "Poor chap, he is more to be pitied than blamed. We could scarcely expect him to behave like a decent citizen with *his* parentage or upbringing." But this extremely common sort of judgment has no point at all if we mean by moral responsibility what Schlick says that we mean. On *that* meaning the degree of a man's moral responsibility must presumably be dependent upon the degree to which we can favorably affect his future motives, which is quite another matter. Now there is no reason to believe that the motives of a man with a bad heredity or a bad upbringing are either less or more subject to educative influence than those of his more fortunate fellows. Yet it is plain matter of fact that we do commonly consider the degree of a man's moral responsibility to be affected by these two factors.

A final point. The extremity of paradox in Schlick's identification of the question "Who is morally blameworthy?" with the question "Who is to be punished?" is apt to be partially concealed from us just because it is our normal habit to include in the meaning of "punishment" an element of "requital for moral transgression" which Schlick expressly denies to it. On that account we commonly think of "punishment," in its strict sense, as implying moral blameworthiness in the person punished. But if we remember to mean by punishment what Schlick means by it, a purely "educative measure," with no retributive ingredients, his indentification of the two questions loses such plausibility as it might otherwise have. For clearly we often think it proper to "punish" a person, in *Schlick's* sense, where we are not at all prepared to say that the person is morally blameworthy. We may even think him morally commendable. A case in point would be the unmistakably sincere but muddle-headed person who at the cost of great suffering to himself steadfastly pursues as his "duty" a course which, in our judgment, is fraught with danger to the common weal. We should most of us feel entitled, in the public interest, to bring such action to bear upon the man's motives as might induce him to refrain in future from his socially injurious behavior: in other words, to inflict upon him what Schlick would call "punishment." But we should most of us feel perfectly clear that in so "punishing" this misguided citizen we are not proclaiming his moral blameworthiness for moral wickedness.

Adopting Schlick's own criterion, then, looking simply "to the manner in which the concept is used,"[6] we seem bound to admit that constantly people do assign moral responsibility where Schlick's theory says they shouldn't, don't assign moral responsibility where Schlick's theory says they should, and assign degrees of moral responsibility where on Schlick's theory there should be no difference in degree. I think we may reasonably conclude that Schlick's account of what we mean by moral responsibility breaks down.

The rebuttal of Schlick's arguments, however, will not suffice of itself to refute the pseudo-problem theory. The indebtedness to Schlick of most later advocates of the theory may be conceded; but certainly it does not comprehend all of significance that they have to say on the problem. There are recent analyses of the conditions of moral responsibility containing sufficient new matter, or sufficient old matter in a more precise and telling form, to require of us now something of a fresh start. In the section which follows I propose to consider some representative samples of these analyses—all of which, of course, are designed to show that the freedom which moral responsibility implies is not in fact a contra-causal type of freedom.

But before reopening the general question of the nature and conditions of moral responsibility, there is a *caveat* which it seems to me worth while to enter. The difficulties in the way of a clear answer are not slight; but they are apt to seem a good deal more formidable than they really are because of a common tendency to consider in unduly close association two distinct questions: the question "Is a contra-causal type of freedom implied by moral responsibility?" and the question "Does a contra-causal type of freedom anywhere exist?" It seems to me that many philosophers (and I suspect that Moritz Schlick is among them) begin their enquiry with so firm a conviction that the contra-causal sort of free-

---

[6] *Loc. cit.*, Ch. VII, Section 5, p. 151.

dom nowhere exists, that they find it hard to take very seriously the possibility that it is *this* sort of freedom that moral responsibility implies. For they are loth to abandon the commonsense belief that moral responsibility itself is something real. The implicit reasoning I take to be this. Moral responsibility is real. If moral responsibility is real, the freedom implied in it must be a fact. But contra-causal freedom is not a fact. Therefore contra-causal freedom is not the freedom implied in moral responsibility. I think we should be on our guard against allowing this or some similar train of reasoning (whose premises, after all, are far from indubitable) to seduce us into distorting what we actually find when we set about a direct analysis of moral responsibility and its conditions.

IV

The pseudo-problem theorists usually, and naturally, develop their analysis of moral responsibility by way of contrast with a view which, while it has enjoyed a good deal of philosophic support, I can perhaps best describe as the common view. It will be well to remind ourselves, therefore, of the main features of this view.

So far as the *meaning*, as distinct from the *conditions*, of moral responsibility is concerned, the common view is very simple. If we ask ourselves whether a certain person is morally responsible for a given act (or it may be just "in general"), what we are considering, it would be said, is whether or not that person is a fit subject upon whom to pass moral judgment; whether he can fittingly be deemed morally good or bad, morally praiseworthy or blameworthy. This does not take us any great way: but (*pace* Schlick) so far as it goes it does not seem to me seriously disputable. The really interesting and controversial question is about the *conditions* of moral responsibility, and in particular the question whether freedom of a contra-causal kind is among these conditions.

The answer of the common man to the latter question is that it most certainly *is* among the conditions. Why does he feel so sure about this? Not, I argued earlier, because the common man supposes that causal law exercises "compulsion" in the sense that prescriptive laws do, but simply because he does not see how a person can be deemed morally praiseworthy or blameworthy in respect of an act which he could not help performing. From the standpoint of moral praise and blame, he would say—though not necessarily from other standpoints—it is a matter of indifference whether it is by reason of some external constraint or by reason of his own given nature that the man could not help doing what he did. It is quite enough to make moral praise and blame futile that in either case there were no genuine alternatives, no open possibilities, before the man when he acted. He could not have acted otherwise than he did. And the common man might not unreasonably go on to stress the fact that we all, even if we are linguistic philosophers, do in our actual practice of moral judgment appear to accept the common view. He might insist upon the point alluded to earlier in this paper, that we do all, in passing moral censure, "make allowances" for influences in a man's hereditary nature or environmental circumstances which we regard as having made it more than ordinarily difficult for him to act otherwise than he did: the implication being that if we supposed that the man's heredity and environment made it not merely very *difficult* but actually *impossible* for him to act otherwise than he did, we could not properly assign moral blame to him at all.

Let us put the argument implicit in the common view a little more sharply. The moral "ought" implies "can." If we say that A morally ought to have done X, we imply that in our opinion, he could have done X. But we assign moral blame to a man only for failing to do what we think he morally ought to have done. Hence if we morally blame A for not having done X, we imply that he could have done X even though in fact he did not. In other words, we imply that A could have acted otherwise than he did. And that means that we imply, as a necessary condition of a man's being morally blameworthy, that he enjoyed a freedom of a kind not compatible with unbroken causal continuity.

V

Now what is it that is supposed to be wrong with this simple piece of argument?—For, of course, it must be rejected by all these philosophers who tell us that the traditional problem of Free Will is a mere pseudo-problem. The argument looks as though it were doing little more than reading off necessary implications of the fundamental categories of our moral thinking. One's inclination is to ask, "If one is to think morally at all, how else than this *can* we think?"

In point of fact, there is pretty general agreement among the contemporary critics as to what is wrong with the argument. Their answer in general terms is as follows. No doubt *A*'s moral responsibility does imply that he could have acted otherwise. But this expression "could have acted otherwise" stands in dire need of analysis. When we analyze it, we find that it is not, as is so often supposed, simple and unambiguous, and we find that in *some* at least of its possible meanings it implies *no* breach of causal continuity between character and conduct. Having got this clear, we can further discern that only in one of these *latter* meanings is there any compulsion upon our moral thinking to assert that if *A* is morally blameworthy for an act, *A* "could have acted otherwise than he did." It follows that, contrary to common belief, our moral thinking does *not* require us to posit a contra-causal freedom as a condition of moral responsibility.

So much of importance obviously turns upon the validity or otherwise of this line of criticism that we must examine it in some detail and with express regard to the *ipsissima verba* of the critics.

In the course of a recent article in *Mind*[7] entitled "Free Will and Moral Responsibility," Mr. Nowell Smith (having earlier affirmed his belief that "the traditional problem has been solved") explains very concisely the nature of the confusion which, as he thinks, has led to the demand for a contra-causal freedom. He begins by frankly recognising that "It is evident that one of the necessary conditions of moral action is that the agent 'could have acted otherwise,'" and he adds, "it is to this fact that the Libertarian is drawing attention."[8] Then, after showing (unexceptionably, I think) how the relationship of "ought" to "can" warrants the proposition which he has accepted as evident, and how it induces the Libertarian to assert the existence of action that is "uncaused," he proceeds to point out, in a crucial passage, the nature of the Libertarian's error:

> The fallacy in the argument (he contends) lies in supposing that when we say *"A could have acted otherwise"* we mean that *A, being what he was and being placed in the circumstances in which he was placed,* could have done something other than what he did. But in fact we never do mean this.[9]

[7] January, 1948.
[8] *Loc. cit.*, p. 49.
[9] *Loc. cit.*, p. 49.

What then *do* we mean here by "*A* could have acted other-wise"? Mr. Nowell Smith does not tell us in so many words, but the passage I have quoted leaves little doubt how he would an-swer. What we really mean by the expression, he implies, is not a *categorical* but a *hypothetical* proposition. We mean "*A* could have acted otherwise, *if he did not happen to be what he in fact was, or if he were placed in circumstances other than those in which he was in fact placed.*" Now, *these* propositions, it is easy to see, are in no way incompatible with acceptance of the causal principle in its full rigor. Accordingly the claim that our funda-mental moral thinking obliges us to assert a contra-causal freedom as a condition of moral responsibility is disproved.

Such is the "analytical solution" of our problem offered (with obvious confidence) by one able philosopher of today, and entirely representative of the views of many other able philosophers. Yet I make bold to say that its falsity stares one in the face. It seems perfectly plain that the hypothetical propositions which Mr. Nowell Smith proposes to substitute for the categorical proposi-tion cannot express "what we really mean" in this context by "*A* could have acted otherwise," for the simple reason that these hypothetical propositions have no bearing whatsoever upon the question of the moral responsibility of *A*. And it is *A* whose moral responsibility we are talking about—a definite person *A* with a definitive character and in a definitive set of circumstances. What conceivable significance could it have for our attitude to *A*'s re-sponsibility to know that someone with a *different* character (or *A* with a different character, if that collocation of words has any meaning), or *A* in a different set of circumstances from those in which *A* as we are concerned with him was in fact placed, "could have acted otherwise"? No doubt this supposititious being *could* have acted otherwise than the definitive person *A* acted. But the point is that where we are reflecting, as we are supposed in this context to be reflecting, upon the question of *A*'s moral respon-sibility, our interest in this supposititious being is precisely *nil*.

The two hypothetical propositions suggested in Mr. Nowell Smith's account of the matter do not, however, exhaust the specu-lations that have been made along these lines. Another very com-mon suggestion by the analysts is that what we really mean by "*A* could have acted otherwise" is "*A* could have acted otherwise *if he had willed, or chosen, otherwise.*" This was among the suggestions offered by G. E. Moore in the well-known chapter on Free Will in his *Ethics*. It is, I think, the suggestion he most strongly favored; though it is fair to add that neither about this nor about any other of his suggestions is Moore in the least dogmatic. He does claim, for, I think, convincing reasons, that "we *very often* mean by 'could' merely 'would, *if* so-and-so had chosen.' "[10] And he concludes, "I must confess that I cannot feel certain that this may not be all that we usually mean and understand by the assertion that we have Free Will."[11]

This third hypothetical proposition appears to enjoy also the support of Mr. C. L. Stevenson. Mr. Stevenson begins the chapter of *Ethics and Language* entitled "Avoidability-Indeterminism" with the now familiar pronouncement of his School that "controversy about freedom and determinism of the will . . . presents no permanent difficulty to ethics, being largely a product of confusions." A major confusion (if I understand him rightly) he takes to lie in the meaning of the term "avoidable," when we say "*A*'s action was avoidable"—or, I presume, "*A* could have acted otherwise." He himself offers the following definition of "avoidable"— " '*A*'s action was avoidable' has the meaning of 'If *A* had made a certain choice, which in fact he did not make, his action would not have occurred.' "[12] This I think we may regard as in substance identical with the suggestion that what we really mean by "*A* could have acted otherwise" is "*A* could have acted otherwise *if* he had chosen (or willed) otherwise." For clarity's sake we shall here keep to this earlier formulation. In either formulation the special significance of the third hypothetical proposition, as of the two hypothetical propositions already considered, is that it is compatible with strict determinism. If this be indeed all that we mean by the "freedom" that conditions moral responsibility, then those philosophers are certainly wrong who hold that moral freedom is of the contra-causal type.

Now this third hypothetical proposition does at least possess the merit, not shared by its predecessors, of having a real relevance to the question of moral responsibility. If, for example, *A* had promised to meet us at 2 P.M., and he chanced to break his leg at 1 P.M., we should not blame him for his failure to discharge his promise. For we should be satisfied that he *could not* have acted otherwise, even if he had so chosen; or *could not*, at any rate, in a way which would have enabled him to meet us at 2 P.M. The freedom to translate one's choice into action, which we saw earlier is for Schlick the *only* freedom required for moral responsibility, is without doubt *one* of the conditions of moral responsibility.

But it seems easy to show that this third hypothetical proposition does not exhaust what we mean, and *some*times is not even *part* of what we mean, by the expression "could have acted other-

[10] *Ethics*, p. 212.

[11] *Loc. cit.*, p. 217.

[12] *Ethics and Language*, p. 298.

wise" in its moral context. Thus it can hardly be even part of what we mean in the case of that class of wrong actions (and it is a large class) concerning which there is really no question whether the agent could have acted otherwise, *if* he had chosen otherwise. Take lying, for example. Only in some very abnormal situation could it occur to one to doubt whether *A*, whose power of speech was evinced by his telling a lie, was in a position to tell what he took to be the truth *if* he had so chosen. Of *course* he was. Yet it still makes good sense for one's moral thinking to ask whether *A*, when lying, "could have acted otherwise": and we still require an affirmative answer to this question if *A*'s moral blameworthiness is to be established. It seems apparent, therefore, that in this class of cases at any rate one does *not* mean by '*A* could have acted otherwise," "*A* could have acted otherwise *if* he had so chosen."

What then *does* one mean in this class of cases by "*A* could have acted otherwise"? I submit that the expression is taken in its simple, categorical meaning, without any suppressed "if" clause to qualify it. Or perhaps, in order to keep before us the important truth that it is only as expressions of *will* or *choice* that acts are of moral import, it might be better to say that a condition of *A*'s moral responsibility is that he could have *chosen* otherwise. We saw that there is no real question whether A who told a lie could have acted otherwise *if* he had chosen otherwise. But there is a very real question, at least for any person who approaches the question of moral responsibility at a tolerably advanced level of reflection, about whether *A* could have *chosen* otherwise. Such a person will doubtless be acquainted with the claims advanced in some quarters that causal law operates universally: or/and with the theories of some philosophies that the universe is throughout the expression of a single supreme principle; or/and with the doctrines of some theologians that the world is created, sustained, and governed by an Omniscient and Omnipotent Being. Very understandably such world-views awaken in him doubts about the validity of his first, easy, instinctive assumption that there are genuinely open possibilities before a man at the moment of moral choice. It thus becomes for him a real question whether a man could have chosen otherwise than he actually did, and, in consequence, whether man's moral responsibility is really defensible. For how can a man be morally responsible, he asks himself, if his choices, like all other events in the universe, could not have been otherwise than they in fact were? It is precisely against the background of world-views such as these that for reflective people the problem of moral responsibility normally arises.

Furthermore, to the man who has attained this level of reflection, it will in *no* class of cases be a sufficient condition of moral responsibility for an act that one could have acted otherwise *if* one had chosen otherwise—not even in these cases were there *was* some possibility of the operation of "external constraint." In these cases he will, indeed, expressly recognize freedom from external constraint as a *necessary condition*, but not as a *sufficient* condition. For he will be aware that, even granted *this* freedom, it is still conceivable that the agent had no freedom to choose otherwise than he did, and he will therefore require that the latter sort of freedom be added if moral responsibility for the act is to be established.

I have been contending that, for persons at a *tolerably advanced level of reflection*, "A could have acted otherwise," as a condition of *A*'s moral responsibility, means "*A* could have chosen otherwise." The qualification italicized is of some importance. The unreflective or unsophisticated person, the ordinary "man in the street," who does not know or much care what scientists and theologians and philosophers have said about the world, sees well enough that *A* is morally responsibile only if he could have acted otherwise, but in his intellectual innocence he will, very probably, envisage nothing capable of preventing *A* from having acted otherwise except some material impediment—like the broken leg in the example above. Accordingly, for the unreflective person, "*A* could have acted otherwise," as a condition of moral responsibility, *is* apt to mean no more than "*A* could have acted otherwise *if* he had so chosen."

It would appear, then, that the view now favored by many philosophers, that the freedom required for moral responsibility is merely freedom from external constraint, is a view which they share only with the less reflective type of layman. Yet it should be plain that on a matter of this sort the view of the unreflective person is of little value by comparison with the view of the reflective person. There are some contexts, no doubt, in which lack of sophistication is an asset. But this is not one of them. The question at issue here is as to the kind of impediments which might have prevented a man from acting otherwise than he in fact did: and on this question knowledge and reflection are surely prerequisites of any answer that is worth listening to. It is simply on account of the limitations of his mental vision that the unreflective man interprets the expression "could have acted otherwise," in its context as a condition of moral responsibility, solely in terms of external constraint. He has failed (as yet) to reach the intellectual level at which one takes into account the implications for moral choices of the world-views of science, religion, and philosophy. If on a matter of this complexity the philosopher finds that his analysis accords with the utterances of the uneducated, he has, I suggest, better cause for uneasiness than for self-congratulation.

This concludes the main part of what it seems to me necessary to say in answer to the pseudo-problem theorists. My object so far has been to expose the falsity of those innovations (chiefly Positivist) in the way of argument and analysis which are supposed by many to have made it impossible any longer to formulate the problem of Free Will in the traditional manner. My contention is that, at least so far as these innovations are concerned, the simple time-honored argument still holds from the nature of the moral ought to the conclusion that moral responsibility implies a contra-causal type of freedom. The attempts to avoid that conclusion by analyzing the proposition "*A* could have acted otherwise" (acknowledged to be implied in *some* sense in *A*'s moral responsibility) into one or other of certain hypothetical propositions which are compatible with unbroken causal continuity, break down hopelessly when tested against the touchstone of actual moral thinking. It is, I think, not necessary to defend the procedure of testing hypotheses in the ethical field by bringing to bear upon them our actual moral thinking. If there is any other form of test applicable, I should be much interested to learn what it is supposed to be. Certainly "logical analysis" *per se* will not do. That has a function, but a function that can only be ancillary. For what we are seeking to know is the meaning of the expression "could have acted otherwise," not *in the abstract*, but in the context of the question of man's *moral responsibility*. Logical analysis *per se* is impotent to give us this information. It can be of value only insofar as it operates within the orbit of "the moral consciousness." One may admit, with some qualifications, that on a matter of this sort the moral consciousness without logical analysis is blind; but it seems to me to be true without any qualification whatsoever that, on the same problem, logical analysis without the moral consciousness is empty.

VI

There are times when what seems to a critic the very strength of his case breeds mistrust in the critic's own mind. I confess that in making the criticisms that have preceded I have not been altogether free from uncomfortable feelings of this kind. For the arguments I have criticized, and more particularly the analyses of the conditions of moral responsibility, seem to me to be in many cases quite desperately unplausible. Such a state of affairs ought, I think, to give the critic pause. The thought must at least enter his mind (unless he be a total stranger to modesty) that perhaps, despite his best efforts to be fair, he has after all misrepresented what his opponents are saying. No doubt a similar thought will enter, and perhaps find lodgment in, the minds of many readers.

In this situation there is, however, one course by which the critic may reasonably hope to allay these natural suspicions. He should consider whether there may not be certain predisposing influences at work, extrinsic to the specific arguments, which could have the effect of blinding the proponents of these arguments to their intrinsic demerits. If so, he need not be too much disquieted by the seeming weakness of the case against him. For it is a commonplace that, once in the grip of general prepossessions, even very good philosophers sometimes avail themselves of very bad arguments.

Actually, we can, I think, discern at least two such influences operating powerfully in the case before us. One is sympathy with the general tenets of Positivism. The other is the conviction already alluded to, that man does not in fact possess a contra-causal type of freedom; whence follows a strong presumption that no such freedom is necessary to moral responsibility.

About the first of these influences I propose to say very little. I wish merely to indicate how strict adherence to Positivist tenets precludes one in principle from understanding moral responsibility as the ordinary man understands it, and how Positivists are therefore bound, when they attempt to define the conditions of moral responsibility, to say things that seem monstrously unplausible.

That the Positivist—who has certainly not been drawn initially to this way of philosophizing by reflection upon the phenomena of the moral life—should approach the problems of ethical analysis with certain strong prepossessions, is only to be expected. The most crucial of these is that (nontautologous) statements in this field, as in every other field, can have no meaning—or at any rate no cognitive meaning—unless they are, at least in principle, sensibly verifiable. The consequence of that prepossession must be to close the mind in advance, more or less absolutely according to the extent to which the Verifiability principle is maintained as unshakeable dogma, against the common view of the moral ought—

which happens also to be the view in terms of which the problem of moral responsibility historically and habitually arises. For on this view the moral ought as apprehended by the moral consciousness is most certainly an object neither of "outer" nor of "inner" sense. One need not wonder, therefore, that the Positivist should recommend analyses of the conditions of moral responsibility, such as the hypothetical propositions offered as the meaning of the expression "could have acted otherwise," which to anyone who understands the moral ought in the ordinary way seem little short of fantastic. By an *a priori* prejudice he has effectively debarred himself from appreciating what ordinary men mean by moral obligation and moral responsibility. I cannot forbear adding that in view of the doom which has so swiftly attended the very various attempts so far made to define moral obligation in Positivist terms, the case for at least a temporary suspension of belief in Positivist presuppositions in the ethical field would appear to be a strong one.

Of far wider and more permanent interest, in my judgment, is the second of the "predisposing influences"—the conviction that there just *is* no contra-causal freedom such as is commonly alleged to be a condition of moral responsibility. A natural desire to "save" moral responsibility issues, logically enough, in attempts to formulate its conditions in a manner compatible with unbroken causal continuity. The consequent analyses may be, as I have urged, very unsatisfactory. But there is no doubt that the conviction that motivates the analysis is supported by reasons of great weight: well-known arguments that are the property of no particular school and which most of us learned in our philosophical cradles. A very brief summary of what I take to be the most influential of these arguments will suffice for the comments I wish to make upon them.

A contra-causal freedom, it is argued, such as is implied in the "categorical" interpretation of the proposition "*A* could have chosen otherwise than he did," posits a breach of causal continuity between a man's character and his conduct. Now apart from the general presumption in favor of the universality of causal law, there are special reasons for disallowing the breach that is here alleged. It is the common assumption of social intercourse that our acquaintances will act "in character," that their choices will exhibit the "natural" response of their characters to the given situation. And this assumption seems to be amply substantiated, over a wide range of conduct, by the actual success which attends predictions made on this basis. Where there should be, on the contra-causal hypothesis, chaotic variability, there is found in fact a large measure of intelligible continuity. Moreover, what is the alternative to admitting that a person's choices flow from his character? Surely just that the so-called "choice" is not *that person's* choice at all: that, relatively to the person concerned, it is a mere "accident." Now we cannot really believe this. But if it *were* the case, it would certainly not help to establish *moral* freedom, the freedom required for *moral* responsibility. For clearly a man cannot be morally responsible for an act which does not express his own choice but is, on the contrary, attributable simply to chance.

These are clearly considerations worthy of all respect. It is not surprising if they have played a big part in persuading people to respond sympathetically to the view that "Free Will," in its usual contra-causal formulation, is a pseudo-problem. A full answer to them is obviously not practicable in what is little more than an appendix to the body of this paper; but I am hopeful that something can be said, even in a little space, to show that they are very far from being as conclusive against a contra-causal freedom as they are often supposed to be.

To begin with the less troublesome of the two main objections indicated—the objection that the break in causal continuity which free will involves is inconsistent with the predictability of conduct on the basis of the agent's known character. All that is necessary to meet this objection, I suggest, is the frank recognition, which is perfectly open to the Libertarian, that there is a wide area of human conduct, determinable on clear general principles, within which free will does not effectively operate. The most important of these general principles (I have no space to deal here with the others) has often enough been stated by Libertarians. Free will does not operate in these practical situations in which no conflict arises in the agent's mind between what he conceives to be his "duty" and what he feels to be his "strongest desire." It does not operate here because there just is no occasion for it to operate. There is no reason whatever why the agent should here even contemplate choosing any course other than that prescribed by his strongest desire. In all such situations, therefore, he naturally wills in accordance with strongest desire. But his "strongest desire" is simply the specific *ad hoc* expression of that system of conative and emotive dispositions which we call his "character." In all such situations, therefore, whatever may be the case elsewhere, his will is in effect determined by his character as so far formed. Now when we bear in mind that there are an almost immeasurably greater number of situations in a man's life that conform to *this* pattern than there are situations in which an agent is aware of a conflict between strongest desire and duty, it is apparent that a Libertarianism which accepts the limitation of free will to the *latter* type of situation is not open to the stock objection on the score of "predictability." For there still remains a vast area of human behavior in which prediction on the basis of known character may be expected to succeed: an area which will accommodate without difficulty, I think, all these empirical facts about successful prediction which the critic is apt to suppose fatal to Free Will.

So far as I can see, such a delimitation of the field of effective free will denies to the Libertarian absolutely nothing which matters to him. For it is precisely that small sector of the field of choices which our principle of delimitation still leaves open to free will—the sector in which strongest desire clashes with duty—that is crucial for moral responsibility. It is, I believe, with respect to such situations, and in the last resort to such situations alone, that the agent himself recognizes that moral praise and blame are appropriate. They are appropriate, according as he does or does not "rise to duty" in the face of opposing desires, always granted, that is, that he is free to choose between these courses as genuinely open possibilities. If the reality of freedom be conceded *here*, everything is conceded that the Libertarian has any real interest in securing.

But, of course, the most vital question is, can the reality of freedom be conceded even here? In particular, can the standard objection be met which we stated, that if the person's choice does not, in these situations as elsewhere, flow from his *character*, then it is not *that person's* choice at all.

This is, perhaps, of all the objections to a contra-causal freedom, the one which is generally felt to be the most conclusive. For the assumption upon which it is based, namely, that no intelligible meaning can attach to the claim that an act which is not an expression of the self's *character* may nevertheless be the *self's* act, is apt to be regarded as self-evident. The Libertarian is accordingly charged with being in effect an *In*determinist, whose "free will," insofar as it does not flow from the agent's character, can only be a matter of "chance." Has the Libertarian—who invariably repudiates this charge and claims to be a *Self*-determinist—any way of showing that, contrary to the assumption of his critics, we *can* meaningfully talk of an act as the self's act even though, in an important sense, it is not an expression of the self's "character"?

I think that he has. I want to suggest that what prevents the critics from finding a meaning in this way of talking is that they are looking for it in the wrong way, or better, perhaps, with the wrong orientation. They are looking for it from the standpoint of the *external observer:* the standpoint proper to, because alone possible for, apprehension of the physical world. Now from the external standpoint we may observe processes of change. But one thing which, by common consent, *cannot* be observed from without is *creative activity.* Yet—and here lies the crux of the whole matter—it is precisely creative activity which we are trying to understand when we are trying to understand what is traditionally designated by "free will." For if there should be an act which is genuinely the self's act and is nevertheless not an expression of its character, such an act, in which the self "transcends" its character as so far formed, would seem to be essentially of the nature of creative activity. It follows that to look for a meaning in "free will" from the external standpoint is absurd. It is to look for it in a way that ensures that it will not be found. Granted that a creative activity of any kind is at least *possible* (and I know of no ground for its *a priori* rejection), there is one way, and one way only, in which we can hope to apprehend it, and that is from the *inner* standpoint of direct participation.

It seems to me therefore, that if the Libertarian's claim to find a meaning in a "free" will which is genuinely the self's will, though not an expression of the self's character, is to be subjected to any test that is worth applying, that test must be undertaken from the inner standpoint. We ought to place ourselves imaginatively at the standpoint of the agent engaged in the typical moral situation in which free will is claimed, and ask ourselves whether from *this* standpoint the claim in question does or does not have meaning for us. That the appeal must be to introspection is no doubt unfortunate. But he would be a very doctrinaire critic of introspection who declined to make use of it when in the nature of the case no other means of apprehension is available. Everyone must make the introspective experiment for himself; but I may perhaps venture to report, though at this late stage with extreme brevity, what I at least seem to find when I make the experiment myself.

In the situation of moral conflict, then, I (as agent) have before my mind a course of action X, which I believe to be my duty, and also a course of action Y, incompatible with X, which I feel to be that which I most strongly desire. Y is, as it is sometimes expressed, "in the line of least resistance" for me—the course which I am aware I should take if I let my purely desiring nature operate without hindrance. It is the course towards which I am aware that my *character*, as so far formed, naturally inclines me. Now, as actually engaged in this situation, I find that I cannot help believing that I *can* rise to duty and choose X, the "rising to duty" being effected by what is commonly called "effort of will." And I further find, if I ask myself just what it is I am believing when I believe that I "can" rise to duty, that I cannot help believing that it lies with me here and now, quite absolutely, which of two genuinely open possibilities I adopt: whether, that is, I make the effort of will and choose *X*, or, on the other hand, let my desiring nature, my character as so far formed, "have its way," and choose *Y*, the course "in the line of least resistance." These beliefs may, of course, be illusory, but that is not at present in point. For the present argument all that matters is whether beliefs of this sort are in fact discoverable in the moral agent in the situation of "moral temptation." For my own part, I cannot doubt the introspective evidence that they are.

Now here is the vital point. No matter which course, *X* or *Y*, I choose in this situation, I cannot doubt, *qua* practical being engaged in it, that my choice is *not* just the expression of my formed character, and yet *is* a choice made by my *self*. For suppose I make the effort and choose *X* (my "duty"). Since my very purpose in making the "effort" is to enable me to act against the existing "set" of desire, which is the expression of my character as so far formed, I cannot possibly regard the act itself as the expression of my *character*. On the other hand, introspection makes it equally clear that I am certain that it is *I* who choose; that the act is not an "accident," but is genuinely *my* act. Or suppose that I choose *Y* (the end of "strongest desire"). The course chosen here is, it is true, in conformity with my "character." But since I find myself unable to doubt that I *could* have made the effort and chosen *X*, I cannot possibly regard the choice of *Y* as *just* the expression of my character. Yet here again I find that I cannot doubt that the choice is *my* choice, a choice for which *I* am justly to be blamed.

What this amounts to is that I *can* and *do* attach meaning, *qua* moral agent, to an act which is not the self's character and yet is genuinely the self's act. And having no good reason to suppose that other persons have a fundamentally different mental constitution, it seems to me probable that anyone else who undertakes a similar experiment will be obliged to submit a similar report. I conclude, therefore, that the argument against "free will" on the score of its "meaninglessness" must be held to fail. "Free Will" does have meaning; though, because it is of the nature of a creative activity, its meaning is discoverable only in an intuition of the practical consciousness of the participating agent. To the agent making a moral choice in the situation where duty clashes with desire, his "self" is known to him as a creatively active self, a self which declines to be identified with his "character" as so formed. Not, of course, that the self's character—let it be added to obviate misunderstanding—either is, or is supposed by the agent to be, devoid of bearing upon his choices, even in the "sector" in which free will is held to operate. On the contrary, such a bearing is manifest in the empirically verifiable fact that we find it "harder" (as we say) to make the effort of will required to "rise to duty" in proportion to the extent that the "dutiful" course conflicts with the course to which our character as so far formed inclines us. It is only in the polemics of the critics that a "free" will is supposed to be incompatible with recognizing the bearing of "character" upon choice.

"But what" (it may be asked) "of the all-important question of the *value* of this 'subjective certainty'? Even if what you say is sound as 'phenomenology,' is there any reason to suppose that the conviction on which you lay so much stress is in fact *true?*" I agree that the question is important, far more important, indeed, than is always realized, for it is not always realized that the only direct evidence there *could* be for a creative activity like "free will" is an intuition of the practical consciousness. But this question falls outside the purview of the present paper. The aim of the paper has not been to offer a constructive defense of free will. It has been to show that the problem as traditionally posed is a real, and not a pseudo, problem. A serious threat to that thesis, it was acknowledged, arises from the apparent difficulty of attaching meaning to an act which is not the expression of the self's character and yet *is* the self's own act. The object of my brief phenomenological analysis was to provide evidence that such an act *does* have meaning for us in the one context in which there is any sense in *expecting* it to have meaning.

VII

My general conclusion is, I fear, very unexciting. It is merely that it is an error to suppose that the "Free Will" problem, when correctly formulated, turns out not to be a "problem" at all. Laboring to reinstate an old problem is dull work enough. But I am disposed to think that the philosophic situation today calls for a good deal more dull work of a similar sort.

Causes, Reasons, and Human Actions

R. S. Peters

R. S. Peters (1919–   ), Professor of Philosophy in the Research School of Social Sciences, Australian National University, has taught in the School of Education, University of London, and has written on political philosophy and allied subjects.

Introductory

Ever since Hobbes was fired by the imaginative idea that *all* human behavior might be explained in terms of mechanical principles, there have been sporadic attempts to provide over-all theories of human behavior. Such theories have been instigated more by the desire to develop an ambitious theory than by puzzlement about concrete problems of human behavior. This was true of Hobbes who pictured himself doing for psychology what Harvey had done for physiology by extending the new science of motion to the most intimate spheres of human thought and endeavor. It was also true of later theorists who, under the influence of Darwin rather than of Galileo, were excited by the thought that men were animals as well as mere bodies. McDougall, for instance, did not provide any startling answers to concrete questions about human behavior; rather he concocted a sort of dynamic atomism to show that man's social behavior could be explained in terms of biological principles. In fact the inspiration behind theorizing in psychology has been, in the main, the success of other sciences like physiology, chemistry, and mechanics and the idea that there could be an all-inclusive theory of human behavior if psychology were to adopt the postulates and methods of other sciences.

A contributory factor, too, has been the understandable determination of psychologists to make their enquiries "scientific." This has led them to cast their theories in a mold dictated by the current conception of scientific method. For a long time this was thought to be the method of induction; and so systems of psychology like introspectionism and behaviorism developed, which were products of what Popper calls "inductivism"—attempts to build up generalizations on the basis of carefully scrutinized data. The methodologists then proclaimed that scientific method was really deductive. So an enormity like Hull's *Principles of Behavior* emerged, scientifically impeccable because it was a hypothetico-deductive system. Hull boldly proclaimed his program of starting from "colorless movements and mere receptor impulses as such" and eventually explaining everything in terms of such concepts—

> familial behavior, individual adaptive efficiency (intelligence), the formal educative processes, psychogenic disorders, social control and delinquency, character and personality, culture and acculturation, magic and religious practices, custom, law and jurisprudence, politics and government, and many other specialized fields of behavior.

In fact Hull developed some simple postulates which gave dubious answers to limited questions about particular species of rats. He never asked, let alone tried to answer, any concrete questions about human behavior. He was in love with the idea of a science of behavior; he was not acutely worried about concrete questions of explaining *human* behavior.

Freud was perhaps the great exception. For he was genuinely puzzled about concrete phenomena and developed some very fertile assumptions to explain them. Also, in his early work especially, he was very much aware of the limitations of his assumptions and defined carefully the types of phenomena that could be explained by the postulation of unconscious mental processes. In other words he seemed to be aware of the *sort* of questions about human behavior which he was answering. For there are many *different* sorts of questions which can be asked about human behavior and the differences, as I shall hope to show, are such that an all-embracing theory is inappropriate. These different sorts of questions are especially confused in theories of motivation. It is this thesis which I now hope to substantiate.

Types of Questions
About Human Behavior

"His Reason" Explanations

The over-riding aim of a scientist should be explanation. This sounds rather obvious, but it has many important consequences in relation to psychological theorizing. For the general question "Why did Jones do that?" is capable of being asked and answered in a variety of different ways. The particular formula employed in asking the question usually dictates the sort of answer which is expected and which counts as an explanation.[1] The paradigm case of a human action is when something is done in order to bring about an end. So the usual way of explaining an action is to describe it as an action of a certain sort by indicating the end which Jones had in mind. We therefore ask the "why" question in a more specific form. We ask what was his *reason* for doing that or what was the *point* of it, what *end* he had in mind. If we ask why Jones walked across the road, the obvious answer will be something like "To buy tobacco." Instead of saying this we could say "because he wanted some tobacco." This is, logically speaking, another way of giving the same sort of answer; for the answer "to buy some tobacco" is only an explanation because we assume in Jones some sort of directive disposition—a general tendency to obtain and use tobacco.

Even in this very simple sort of explanation in terms of a man's reason for doing something there are, as a matter of fact, concealed assumptions. We assume, for instance, that walking across the street is an efficient way of getting to the tobacconist. This counts as an explanation not simply because Jones envisaged walking across the street as a means to getting the tobacco but because it really is a means to getting it. We assume, too, that a man who has this information will act on it if he wants some

---

[1] I am indebted to J. O. Urmson (1952) for some of these distinctions.

tobacco. We assume that men are rational in that they will take means which lead to ends if they have the information and want the ends. "His reason" is an explanation in terms of what Popper calls "the logic of the situation."

But it is not only norms of efficiency and consistency that are implicit in the concept of "his reason." There are also norms or standards of social appropriateness. After all Jones might have crawled or run across the road. But "to get some tobacco" would be a very odd answer to the question "Why did Jones *run* across the road?" Yet running would be quite an efficient way of getting across the road. It would, however, be socially odd as a way of crossing the road to get some tobacco. *Man is a rule-following animal.* His actions are not simply directed towards ends; they also conform to social standards and conventions, and unlike a calculating machine he acts because of his knowledge of rules and objectives. For instance, we ascribe to people *traits* of character like honesty, punctuality, considerateness, and meanness. Such terms do not, like ambition or hunger or sexual desire, indicate the sorts of goals that a man tends to pursue; rather they indicate the type of regulation that he imposes on his conduct whatever his goals may be. A man who is ruthless, selfish, punctual, considerate, persistent, and honest does not have any particular goals; rather he pursues whatever goals he has in particular sorts of ways.

This simple purposive model of a man taking means to bring about an end is further complicated by the fact that norms enter into and often entirely define the end. Ends like passing an examination, getting married, becoming a professor, and reading a paper explain quite adequately a great deal of the goings on in the precincts of a university; yet they are defined almost entirely by social convention. It is a gross over-simplification to think of ends merely as terminating points of activity. Actually even a rat, after eating or achieving some other end, will continue being active in a variety of ways—sniffing, preening, and so on. If eating can be regarded as an end, this is not because it is a definite terminating point of activity, but because activity *previous* to it varies concomitantly with changes in the conditions necessary to define it as an end. The concept of means is just as necessary to bring out what is meant by an end as the concept of end is to bring out what is meant by a means. Ends are not given as natural terminating points like a chain of oases distributed across a desert. And, to a large extent, what counts as falling within a means-to-end explanatory framework is determined by convention. Even those ends, like eating and sexual intercourse, which are universal and which have an obvious biological basis, can scarcely be specified without recourse to norms. For there are countless ways of performing the acts which can be regarded as ends, and in every culture a few particular ways are stamped with the hallmark of conventionality. Eating is not just getting food into the stomach. Jones' movements across the road are classifiable as means to the end of buying tobacco because of a vast system of norms defining "buying tobacco" as an end as well as a system of norms regulating what is an efficient and socially appropriate way of attaining it.

My reasons for stressing this rule-following purposive pattern into which we fit our common-sense explanations are twofold. In the first place I want to insist that most of our explanations are couched in terms of this model, and our predictions of people's behavior presuppose it. We know what the parson will do when he begins to walk towards the pulpit because we know the conventions regulating church services. And we can make such predictions without knowing anything about the *causes* of people's behavior unless we include under "causes" things like the parson's training and grasp of the rules, which are things of a different order from "causes" in the sense of antecedent movements. Man in society is like a chess-player writ large. Requests for explanation are usually reflections of our ignorance about the particular rule or goal which is relevant to the behavior in question. We usually know the general pattern but are unsure which part of it is relevant. Sometimes, of course, we are in the position of a free-thinker at a Roman Catholic mass. The question "Why did X do that?" is then usually a request for an elucidation of the whole pattern of conventions. In explaining human actions we, like anthropologists, must all, in the first place, be structuralists. Indeed I would go so far as to say that anthropology or sociology must be the basic sciences of human action in that they exhibit the systematic framework of norms and goals which are necessary to classify actions as being of a certain sort. They both—like classical economics— presuppose the purposive, rule-following model; in this respect they are quite unlike sciences which imply a mechanical model of explanation.

In the second place this rule-following purposive pattern of explanation must be sketched in some detail because a proper understanding of what is meant by a human action has very important logical consequences. It shows, for instance . . . that human actions cannot be sufficiently explained in terms of causal concepts like "colorless movements." Indeed to claim that we are confronted with an action is *ipso facto* to rule out such mechanical explanations as being sufficient.

"The Reason" Explanations

But, of course, as psychologists will be the first to point out, people often invent reasons for doing things or delude themselves into thinking that the reasons they offer for their actions are operative reasons. We therefore often say of a man that *his* reason may have been *x* but *the* reason why he acted like that was *y*. For instance we might say that Jones said that he crossed the road in order to buy some tobacco but the reason why he did it was not really his desire for tobacco; it was sex. There was a pretty girl looking in the window of the tobacconist. This explanation may of course be erroneous. For instance a psychologist once told me that I delayed crossing the road to College because of an aversion to getting down to work. I replied, and I think more convincingly, that I stayed on the other side in order to look at the row of glistening cars drawn up opposite. But whether the explanation in question is correct or incorrect does not much matter; the point is that to speak of *the* reason why a person does something is different in that it is a way of calling attention to the law or assumed law that a given case actually falls under. *His* reason may coincide with *the* reason. *The* reason why Jones crossed the road might in fact be his desire for tobacco. He might also be aware that he wanted to inspect the girl at close quarters, but was concealing this by the camouflage of buying tobacco. This would then be his *real* reason. But whereas *his* reason—whether real or not—entails that a man is conscious of his objective, the reason why he did it does not.[2] *The* reason why he did it might well be sex or aversion to work; yet the individual might be quite unaware of pursuing or avoiding the relevant goals. And whereas to say that *he* had a reason for doing something is more or less to rule out a causal explanation, to give *the* reason why he did it is sometimes to subsume it under a law-like proposition of a causal kind. This is not necessarily so. For we can say that sex or aversion to work was *the* reason why he did it and simply be insisting that a different directive disposition is being exercised. But *the* reason why he did

[2] Hamlyn has pointed out to me the use of "the reason for his action" as well as "the reason why he did it." "The reason for" seems to be similar to "his reason" but to imply a coincidence between "his reason" and "the reason why he did it." I am not here concerned with the use of "reason" in the context of *justification* as when we say that *a* reason for giving up smoking is that it causes lung cancer. "His reason" and "the reason for" can be used in contexts both of justification and of explanation. Needless to say, "the reason why he did it" is reserved for contexts of explanation with which I am here concerned.

it might also be that he was pushed or assailed by an attack of giddiness. These would be causal explanations which would rebut the suggestion that he had a reason for crossing the road. Causal explanations, in other words, can count as *the* reason why a person does something; but they are only one type of answer to the question "What was *the* reason why he did it?"

Causal Explanations

There are, however, other questions about particular goings on —I omit to say actions on purpose—to which answers in causal terms are appropriate. Instead of the omnibus question "Why did Jones do that?" we often ask what made, drove, or possessed him to do it. These are usually cases of lapses from action or failure to act—when there is some kind of *deviation* from the purposive rule-following model, when people, as it were, get it wrong. This may be in respect of an efficiency norm—for example, when a person refuses to take the only quick route to his destination by underground train, or when he can't remember a well-known name when he is performing an introduction. Or the behavior may go wrong in respect of a norm governing social appropriateness—as with a business man who runs to work when he is not late or a tutor who crawls round the room sniffing while listening to an undergraduate essay. Or behavior may go wrong by being deflected towards a peculiar goal as with a married man who suddenly makes an advance to a choir boy. In such cases it is as if the man suffers something rather than does something. It is because things seem to be happening to him that it is appropriate to ask what made, drove, or possessed him to do that. The appropriate answer in such cases may be in terms of a causal theory.

These cases of particular goings on which look like breakdowns of action are very similar to a whole class of general activities which seem to have no point or a very odd point—dreams, hallucinations, obsessions, anxieties, and perversions. In such cases the Greeks suggested that the gods intervene and take possession of the individual's mind. Very often recourse is made to crude physiological explanations. It was not till the advent of Freud that any systematic explanation of such goings-on was offered in psychological terms. Indeed Freud claimed in 1913 that the main contribution of psychoanalysis to general psychology was to link together and to give psychological explanations for happenings which had previously been left to physiology or to folklore. Many have claimed that Freud, by reclaiming these phenomena for psychology, was in fact extending the model of purposive rule-following behavior to cover the unconscious. He showed, it is argued, that we have reasons for acts which were previously only explained in terms of causes. I shall argue later that this thesis is mistaken. Freud showed, perhaps, that the concept of "wish" has a wider application than was previously thought. But his account of the working of the primary processes creaks with causality. In maintaining that in the unconscious there is no sense of causal or logical connection, he was *ipso facto* denying that the model of "his reason," implying norms of efficiency and social appropriateness, was relevant. Freud, I shall argue, provides the classic case of giving quasi-causal explanations where causal explanations seem *prima facie* appropriate.

I shall also argue that Freud in fact only intended to explain by reference to unconscious mental processes cases where the purposive rule-following model breaks down or is inappropriate. He did not think—and often explicitly denied—that this sort of explanation can be appropriately given for everything—for cases where a man acts as well as for cases where something happens to a man. In this respect Freud was, from the point of view of my argument, on the side of the angels. For my case is not simply that causal explanations are otiose when we know the point of a person's action in that, life being short and time limited, we no longer feel inclined to ask "why" once we have accommodated a piece of behavior within the rule-following purposive model. It is also that if we are in fact confronted with a case of a genuine action (that is, an act of doing something as opposed to suffering something), then causal explanations are *ipso facto* inappropriate as sufficient explanations. Indeed they may rule out rule-following purposive explanations. To ask what made Jones do something is at least to suggest that he had no good reason for doing it. Similarly to ascribe a point to his action is *ipso facto* to deny that it can be *sufficiently explained* in terms of causes, though, of course, there will be many causes in the sense of *necessary* conditions. A story can always be told about the underlying mechanisms; but this does not add up to a sufficient explanation, if it is an action that has to be explained.

To give a causal *explanation* of an event involves at least showing that, other conditions being presumed unchanged, a change in one variable is a *sufficient* condition for a change in another. In the mechanical conception of "cause" it is also demanded that there should be spatial and temporal contiguity between the movements involved. Now the trouble about giving this sort of explanation of human actions is that we can never specify an action exhaustively in terms of movements of the body or within the body. It is therefore impossible to state sufficient conditions in terms of antecedent movements which may vary concomitantly with subsequent movements. "Signing a contract," for instance, is a typical example of a human action. The movements involved are grouped together because they are seen by the agent to be efficient and appropriate means to an end. But it would be impossible to stipulate exhaustively what the movements *must* be. For if this is a case of a human action the agent must be presumed to be intelligent and he will, accordingly, vary his movements in a great variety of ways. He may hold the pen slightly differently, vary the size of his writing according to the space available, and so on, depending on the sort of ink, paper, and pen available. But provided that he produces a signature which confirms to rough and ready criteria—for example, it must not be typed—more or less *any* movements will do. I suppose he could sign a contract by holding the pen between his toes. A very general range of movements could perhaps be specified, but no specific movements of the muscles, limbs, or nervous system, which *must* occur before it would be conceded that a contract had been signed. This is tantamount to saying that the concept of an action is inseparable from that of intelligence; for part of what we mean by "intelligence" is the ability to vary movements relative to a goal in a way which is appropriate to changes in the situation necessary to define it as a goal and in the conditions relevant to attaining it. So we could never give a sufficient explanation of an action in causal terms because we could never stipulate the movements which would have to count as dependent variables. A precise functional relationship could never be established. Of course, just as we could stipulate a general range of movements necessary to define signing a contract, so also we could lay down certain very general *necessary* conditions. We could, for instance, say that a man could not sign a contract unless he had a brain and nervous system. Such physiological knowledge *might* enable us to predict *bodily movements*. And *if* we had bridging laws to correlate such physiological findings with descriptions of actions, we might *indirectly predict* actions. But we would *first* have to grasp concepts connected with action like "knowing what we are doing" and "grasp of means to an end." As such concepts have no application at the level of mere movement, such predictions would not count as sufficient *explanations* of *actions*.

Furthermore, as I have already argued, general standards or rules are implicit in the concept of an action. We can therefore say that a man is doing something efficiently, correctly, and so on, if he knowingly varies what he does in accordance with changes in the situation conventionally singled out as the goal and the conditions perceived as relevant to attaining it. It only makes sense to talk of actions in this way, not of cases where something happens to a man. A man's action may break down because of a causal condition like a lesion in his brain. But all that can be said of such causal conditions is that they just occur. Movements *qua* movements are neither intelligent, efficient, nor correct. They only become so in the context of an action. There cannot therefore be a sufficient explanation of actions in causal terms because, as Popper has put it, there is a logical gulf between nature and convention. Statements implying norms and standards cannot be deduced from statements about mere movements which have no such normative implications. The contention that man is a rule-following animal must, if taken seriously, entail that the transition from nature to convention occurs whenever we try to give a sufficient explanation of human actions in causal terms. There is, however, no objection to such explanations of what *happens* to a man; for happenings cannot be characterized as intelligent or unintelligent, correct or incorrect, efficient or inefficient. *Prima facie* they are just occurrences. Perhaps Freud showed that some lapses and breakdowns may not be *just* occurrences. But this is another story. The point is that there is a *prima facie* case for treating them as such.

To make explicit the implications of my thesis for psychological theories: If the question is "Why did Jones walk across the road?" a *sufficient* explanation can only be given in terms of the rule-following purposive model—if this is a case of an action rather than of something happening to him. Answers in terms of causal concepts like "receptor impulses" and "colorless movement" are either not explanations because they state not sufficient but only necessary conditions, or they are ways of denying that what has to be explained is a human action. If we ask, "Why did Jones *jump* while he was crossing the road?" it might be appropriate to say, "because of a twinge in his stomach" or "because a car back-fired." The stimulus-response sort of model would perhaps be appropriate and the causal type of explanation in terms of internal or external stimulation might be sufficient because the assumption might be that Jones was suffering something rather than performing an action. This sort of jump would then be quite different from the jump he might perform while competing in an athletic contest.

This is not to deny that causal explanations are *relevant* to human actions. It is only to deny that they are sufficient explanations of them. Causal theories have at least three jobs to do in this context. Firstly they can state *necessary* conditions for human actions to occur. Hebb's physiological speculations, for instance, might well provide a sketch of a typical class of necessary conditions. But this does not mean that such speculations *explain* human actions. Secondly, as a corollary, they could show that some individual differences in performance are dependent on slight differences in such necessary conditions. Hebb's hypothesis of the relationship between the size of the association areas of the brain and the possibility of late learning would be such a hypothesis. Thirdly such theories could be used to give *sufficient* conditions for breakdowns in performance, as in the case of brain lesions, by indicating a necessary condition which was absent. Alternatively lapses and breakdowns could be explained by the postulation of special disrupting conditions—for example, Freud's theory of the unconscious wish.

End-State Explanations

There are, of course, all sorts of higher level questions which can be asked about human actions, most of which are irrelevant to psychology in general and theories of motivation in particular. Questions, for instance, can be raised about the conventions in accordance with which a man acts or which determine his goals. We can ask why Jones is mean or why he eats fish. The way it would be answered would depend on the context. It might be answered in terms of a rule-following type of explanation like "because he is a Scotsman" or "because he is a Roman Catholic." This would assume some *established set of norms* and a system of training for handing them on. It would be radically different from the explanation "because he is an anal character" or "because he is an oral character." For these explanations would presuppose that Jones was in some way a deviant from the norm of the circle in which he had been trained. It would state special conditions in his upbringing which occasioned his deviation. Whether or not such explanations, which presuppose fixation at certain periods of development, are causal or not, will have to be considered later.

Another way of answering the question "Why does Jones eat fish?" would be to state in a tough-minded way, "Because he likes it," or "Because it satisfies him." This could be simply an impatient way of terminating the discussion or it could be an answer to the even more general question "Why does a man eat anything?" At a common-sense level this is a very odd question; for "a man must eat" is regarded as a decisive way of terminating a discussion. If pressed still further, common-sense might reach rock-bottom with the truism that a man would die if he did not eat. The implication is the Hobbesian axiom that every man is afraid of death and that it makes no further sense to ask "why?"

A variant on this type of answer is the assertion that a man needs food, which is very much like saying that a man *must* eat. For, at a common-sense level, the term "need" is mainly normative. It prescribes one of a set of standard goals. It usually functions as a diagnostic term with remedial implications. It implies that something is wrong with a person if certain conditions are absent. We say things like "The trouble with Jones is that he needs a wife" or "Every child needs at least ten hours sleep." The implication is that there is a state of affairs the absence of which is or is likely to be damaging to the individual in question. The individual, like a patient, may well be unaware of what this state of affairs is. Indeed, when we say that a person needs something, we are often indicating a discrepancy between what he actually does and what he ought to be doing. In other words the notion of "need" in ordinary language is seldom *explanatory*. It is used to point out what a person ought to be doing rather than to explain what he is doing. It would only be an observer grossly over-sophisticated by Freudian theory who would say of a man leaping around in a Morris ring that old Jones obviously needs a woman, and who would think that he had *explained* his performance by pointing to the reality beneath the appearances. Reference to needs implies a standard pattern of prescribed goals; but it does not explain actions by reference to them. Whereas causal theories explain deviations from a norm, reference to needs prescribes the norms whose absence is thought to be injurious. It redirects attention to the accepted content of the rule-following purposive model.

Often we hear of "basic needs" and "need-reduction" in the context of explanatory theories in psychology. What has happened here is that conditions whose absence is thought to occasion injury have been interpreted in terms of a biological or physiological model. The answer to questions like "Why does a man eat?" is provided by picturing an organism whose activities are directed towards survival or the preservation of equilibrium or some other such desirable and completely general end-state. This, of course, has to be broken down by giving an account of the particular conditions whose absence is thought to be injurious. Homeostasis, for instance, has to be described in terms of *particular* states like the temperature of the body and the level of blood-sugar. And, no doubt, postulating such conditions restored by various movements of the body in part explains them if the conditions restored are not part of what is meant by the description given to the movements. Sweating, for instance, may be a method of bringing about an optimum level of temperature in the body; but restoration of this level is not part of what is meant when we call certain movements "sweating." So saying that people sweat because it lowers the temperature of the body is explanatory.

But all too often this type of functional or end-state explanation is redescriptive rather than explanatory—especially when it is used for voluntary rather than for involuntary movements. This is when the conditions restored are part of what is meant by the activity to be explained. For instance it might be said that people dominate others because it reduces a need in them to do so. But what is the condition restored apart from that of the presence of others being dominated? What in this type of case is the equivalent of the temperature level which is restored by sweating? The homeostatic model of explanation is retained; but in the absence of specific states required to define what constitutes the equilibrium, it becomes entirely metaphysical. It is true that recourse is made to vague states of quiescence which the activity of dominating or acquiring money is alleged to bring about. But as there are no rules for identifying such states, their explanatory value is nil. Indeed in such cases need-reduction looks like a redescription of goal-seeking in terms which have the normative function of stressing the importance of conventionally prescribed pursuits. It is a justification masquerading as a high-level explanation.

Need-reduction explanations are a particular instance of a very common sort of explanation which will be termed "explanations in terms of end-states." For supervenient states of quiescence and satisfaction abound in psychological theories of motivation. It will probably be found that all such explanations share the logical features revealed in the specific case of need-reduction. These are (*i*) the generalization of a type of explanation that applies properly only to a very limited class of phenomena and (*ii*) the use of a term with highly general normative implications which obscure its emptiness as a highly general *explanation*.

The term "end-state" has been chosen advisedly rather than the term "end." For one of the first things to be pointed out about these highly general sorts of explanation is that the ends postulated are not ends in the sense of "end" or "goal" employed in the purposive rule-following model. They are not—or should not be— postulated as answers to questions like "Why did Jones walk across the road?" but as answers to questions like "Why does a man eat?" or "Why does a man smoke?" They are therefore inappropriate as answers to lower order questions. For a man does not eat *in order to* reduce a need or relieve a tension. By eating, so the theories say, he in fact brings about such an end-state. Such explanations then do not give a man's reason for eating but the reason why he eats. But they differ from other cases of directed behavior where we contrast *his* reason with *the* reason. For in other such cases—for example, explanations in terms of unconscious wishes—we imply a goal *of the same sort* as that implied in *his* reason explanations, but we add the rider that the man does not envisage this goal as a conscious objective. We say, for instance, that *the* reason why he was unintentionally rude to his employer was because of his unconscious desire to injure a man like his father. But end-states are not goals like hurting a man, marrying a girl, or becoming Prime Minister. They are more mysterious states of quiescence, satisfaction, tension-reduction, and so on.

The theoretical interest of these types of explanation is that they are regarded as explaining *all* behavior, whether of the rule-following sort or where there is a breakdown in behavior and a cause is assigned, or when an activity—like dreaming—is of a sort such that it makes no sense to say "What is the point of it?" Freud's pleasure principle is a good example; for he claimed

> In the theory of psychoanalysis we have no hesitation in assuming that the course taken by mental events is automatically regulated by the pleasure principle. We believe, that is to say, that the course of these events is invariably set in motion by an unpleasurable tension, and that it takes a direction such that its final outcome coincides with a lowering of that tension—that is with an avoidance of unpleasure or a production of pleasure.

Some such homeostatic principle is so common in modern psychology that it has reached the standard textbooks. To quote a typical case—Stagner and Karwoski:

> The organism is endowed with an automatic equilibrium-maintaining tendency which helps to preserve existence in the face of many kinds of environmental obstacles and difficulties.

It is assumed that everything we do can somehow be subsumed under this very general principle. This assumption is so widespread and is so important to the claim that an overall theory of motivation can be developed, that much more must be said about its appropriateness.

The assumption, to repeat, is that the reason why men eat, sleep, eliminate, and so on, is that achieving such goals relieves tension, restores equilibrium, produces satisfaction, and other such variations on a theme. This assumption is usually extended to cover all goal-directed behavior—the pursuit of riches and foxes as well as the pursuit of water and women.

I will defer for a moment the problem of whether the postulation of such end-states is *ever* explanatory. For the issue is whether it *always* is. And this seems plainly false. For many goal-directed actions like posting letters, traveling to work, and passing the salt to one's neighbor do not seem invariably to be followed by such end-states. Indeed usually when we *say* that we get satisfaction or pleasure from doing something, we are not referring to some extra subsequent state of mind which we have become aware of by introspection. Rather we are saying two general sorts of things about it. In the first place we are saying that we were not bored, irritated, or distracted while we did it. We put our mind to the job in hand and concentrated on bringing about the required state of affairs. We were absorbed. The reference to satisfaction is not, in this case, an *explanation* of the pursuit of a goal, but a way of emphasizing that it really was a goal in the sense that our movements flowed towards it in an unimpeded and coordinated manner. Secondly the reference to satisfaction can be a way of stressing that the activity in question was done for its own sake and not as a means to something else. If a husband insists doggedly that he does the gardening because of the satisfaction he gets out of it, he may simply be denying that he does it in order to help his wife with the housekeeping. He is not claiming necessarily that he glows and enters into a beatific state when the peas have been staked and the lawn cut. In other words, just as reference to need-reduction is a way of emphasizing the importance of some goals for the avoidance of injury, so reference to satisfaction is often a way of singling out others which are worth pursuing for their own sake. In a context of justification, "Because it satisfies him" is as final as "Because he needs it." What follows the "because" are different facets of the bed-rock of justification. Psychologists have mistaken this bed-rock of justification for the apex of explanation.

Is it to be assumed, then, that reference to such end-states is *never* explanatory? All we have shown is that it is not *always* so. Clearly some such reference is reasonable in answering certain questions about the *body*, as was seen in the case of need-reduction. Cannon, in his *Wisdom of the Body*, was indicating the evidence for bodily mechanisms of regulation and adjustment. The transition to using this type of explanation for voluntary actions rather than for the automatic adjustments of the body, comes about because it is suggested, for example, by Freud—that types of stimulation brought about by departures from these optimum levels or end-states can only be mitigated by contact with the environment. The baby's hunger, for instance, is relieved only by contact with its mother's breast or with some equivalent source of supply. Its movements are at first random; but eventually, through the association of relief of tension with contact with the breast, a directed tendency develops which is activated by the stimulation of hunger. It is therefore concluded, probably erroneously, that whenever we find a case of such directed behavior, it must be sandwiched in between tension and the reduction of tension. Yet even if such tension-reduction were an explanation of *acquiring* such a directed disposition, it would not follow that it also explained its *activation* later on after it had been acquired.

It is, however, significant that the sort of phenomena which have seemed to psychologists to require some sort of an end-state explanation, are those connected with learning and experimental types of situation. Thorndike's Law of Effect, for instance, postulated that successful responses were stamped in because of the satisfaction associated with contact with the correct goal. The pleasure-principle could well be vacuous as an all-embracing postulate, as envisaged by Freud; but it might well be part of the explanation of why certain directed sequences of behavior are *learnt*. And surely it would here coincide with the use of "feeling of satisfaction" in ordinary speech which cannot be analyzed purely in the way described above. For in exploratory and experimental stages of an activity, before a habit has been formed, or when we are confronted with obstacles that impede habitual routines, we do speak of a feeling of satisfaction or a sense of achievement. If we are learning to swim or to play golf or to walk after a long illness, we do get a feeling of satisfaction or sense of achievement on attaining the goal. This is not exactly a supervenient state extra to attaining the goal. The feeling of satisfaction when one hits a good drive is different from that attendant on hitting a good niblick shot; and both are quite different from that attendant on writing a good sentence or doing a good dive. In the same way a hungry man gets satisfaction from eating a beef-steak; but the type of satisfaction is specific to the beef-steak. The end-states are not exactly supervenient; rather they are descriptions of the attainment of certain sorts of goals under certain sorts of conditions. So in some cases which approximate in varying degrees to a learning, experimental, or obstacle type of situation, the postulated sequence of tension, persistent and directed behavior, and relief of tension may well occur. But as most of our days are spent in carrying out habits and routines, they do not occur whenever there is a case of directed behavior. Indeed part of what we want to deny when we call a piece of behavior a habit is that it is a case of the varied, experimental, obstacle-ridden type of behavior.

My point is therefore not that the reduction-of-tension type of explanation is never relevant, but that it explains the directedness of behavior only under certain limited sorts of conditions. My objection to it is that it is so often used as an all-inclusive principle. For most psychological theories seem to accommodate their purposive or causal explanations under some such homeostatic postulate. The quasi-causal concept of drive, for instance, is usually subsumed under the general postulate of homeostasis; so is the purposive concept of the Freudian wish. But the relationship between these types of explanation and a homeostatic postulate is not of this deductive sort. It seems, to say the least of it, misleading to assimilate dreams and playing chess to shivering and sweating by maintaining that they are all particular cases of the maintenance of equilibrium—especially when the theorists, like Stagner and Karwoski, have to go on to distinguish static from dynamic homeostasis to make the suggestion even sound plausible! The quest for an all-inclusive explanation has led repeatedly to the obscuring of important differences by stressing trivial and highly speculative similarities.

7

Causality and the "Problem of Induction"

It is difficult to imagine how seriously philosophers have usually taken Aristotle's dictum that to know anything is to know its causes. Cause and effect has played a major role as the backbone of arguments in metaphysics. Arguments from observed effects to unobserved cause, such as God or substance (mind or matter) have been a staple of speculative philosophy.

But what is a cause, or more properly, what is the cause and effect relationship? Aristotle names four different kinds of causes; for example, he includes among the causes of anything the material of which the thing was made and the plan or form by which it was made. David Hume (d. 1776), Scottish philosopher famed for his skepticism, argues that the notion of cause and effect has no support from observation but is due to a psychological tendency to expect a particular sequence of events because we have seen them following each other time after time. If correct, his arguments would invalidate all arguments to God or substance based on the cause and effect relationship. A. C. Ewing, contemporary British philosopher, challenges Hume's view of causality-as-regular-sequence and gives arguments for an older conception of cause and effect that he calls the entailment conception—rather like the notion of "ground and consequent"—which argues that you cannot really make a distinction between the causes of anything and the reasons for it. His views run contrary to those of R. S. Peters (see Chapter 6) and nearly all analytical philosophers today who argue that logical relations ("reasons") exist only between beliefs, propositions, or statements and that cause and effect relations exist between events.

The "problem of induction" grew out of Hume's doubts that there is a necessary connection between past and future events. Bertrand Russell argues, as does Hume, that predictions, even on the best of evidence, are on shaky ground. Paul Edwards, contemporary American philosopher, accuses Hume and Russell of wanting induction to be like valid deduction, which gives us conclusions that cannot be false.

Cause Is Expected Sequence

David Hume

David Hume (1711–1776) is the most influential of the British empiricists. He set many of the problems in modern philosophy and, many believe, solved or dissolved some of them. The twentieth century has appreciated his ideas more than any previous one.

We have sought in vain for an idea of power or necessary connection in all the sources from which we could suppose it to be derived. It appears that, in single instances of the operation of bodies, we never can, by our utmost scrutiny, discover anything but one event following another, without being able to comprehend any force or power by which the cause operates, or any connection between it and its supposed effect. The same difficulty occurs in contemplating the operations of mind and body—where we observe the motion of the latter to follow upon the volition of the former, but are not able to observe or conceive the tie which binds together the motion and volition, or the energy by which the mind produces this effect. The authority of the will over its own faculties and ideas is not a whit more comprehensible. So that, upon the whole, there appears not, throughout all nature, any one instance of connection which is conceivable by us. All events seem entirely loose and separate. One event follows another; but we can never observe any tie between them. They seem *conjoined*, but never *connected*. And as we can have no idea of anything which never appeared to our outward sense or inward sentiment, the necessary conclusion seems to be that we have no idea of connection or power at all, and that these words are absolutely without any

From *Enquiry Concerning Human Nature,* Section 7, Part ii.

meaning, when employed either in philosophical reasonings or common life.

But there still remains one method of avoiding this conclusion, and one source which we have not yet examined. When any natural object or event is presented, it is impossible for us, by any sagacity or penetration, to discover, or even conjecture, without experience, what event will result from it, or to carry our foresight beyond that object which is immediately present to the memory and senses. Even after one instance or experiment where we have observed a particular event to follow upon another, we are not entitled to form a general rule or foretell what will happen in like cases, it being justly esteemed an unpardonable temerity to judge of the whole course of nature from one single experiment, however accurate or certain. But when one particular species of event has always, in all instances, been conjoined with another, we make no longer any scruple of foretelling one upon the appearance of the other, and of employing that reasoning, which can alone assure us of any matter of fact or existence. We then call the one object, *Cause;* the other, *Effect.* We suppose that there is some connection between them, some power in the one, by which it infallibly produces the other, and operates with the greatest certainty and strongest necessity.

It appears, then, that this idea of a necessary connection among events arises from a number of similar instances which occur of the constant conjunction of these events; nor can that idea ever be suggested by any one of these instances, surveyed in all possible lights and positions. But there is nothing in a number of instances, different from every single instance, which is supposed to be exactly similar; except only, that after a repetition of similar instances, the mind is carried by habit, upon the appearance of one event, to expect its usual attendant, and to believe that it will exist. This connection, therefore, which we *feel* in the mind, this customary transition of the imagination from one object to its usual attendant, is the sentiment or impression from which we form the idea of power or necessary connection. Nothing farther is in the case. Contemplate the subject on all sides; you will never find any other origin of that idea. This is the sole difference between one instance, from which we can never receive the idea of connection, and a number of similar instances, by which it is suggested. The first time a man saw the communication of motion by impulse, as by the shock of two billiard balls, he could not pronounce that the one event was *connected:* but only that it was *conjoined* with the other. After he has observed several instances of this nature, he then pronounces them to be *connected.* What alteration has happened to give rise to this new idea of *connection?* Nothing but that he now *feels* these events to be connected in his imagination, and can readily foretell the existence of the one from the appearance of the other. When we say, therefore, that one object is connected with another, we mean only that they have acquired a connection in our thought, and give rise to this inference, by which they become proofs of each other's existence: a conclusion which is somewhat extraordinary, but which seems founded on sufficient evidence. Nor will its evidence be weakened by any general diffidence of the understanding or skeptical suspicion concerning every conclusion which is new and extraordinary. No conclusions can be made more agreeable to skepticism than such as make discoveries concerning the weakness and narrow limits of human reason and capacity.

And what stronger instance can be produced of the surprising ignorance and weakness of the understanding than the present? For surely, if there be any relation among objects which it imports to us to know perfectly, it is of cause and effect. On this are founded all our reasonings concerning matters of fact and existence. By means of it alone we attain any assurance concerning objects which are removed from the present testimony of our memory and senses. The only immediate utility of all sciences is to teach us how to control and regulate future events by their causes. Our thoughts and enquiries are, therefore, every moment, employed about this relation; yet so imperfect are the ideas which we form concerning it, that it is impossible to give any just definition of cause, except what is drawn from something extraneous and foreign to it. Similar objects are always conjoined with similar. Of this we have experience. Suitably to this experience, therefore, we may define a cause to be *an object, followed by another, and where all the objects similar to the first are followed by objects similar to the second.* Or in other words, *where, if the first object had not been, the second never had existed.* The appearance of a cause always conveys the mind, by a customary transition, to the idea of the effect. Of this also we have experience. We may, therefore, suitably to this experience, form another definition of cause, and call it an object followed by another, and whose appearance always conveys the thought to that other.

Causes Are Reasons

A. C. Ewing

A. C. Ewing (1899–   ) is Reader in Moral Science in Cambridge University. His major books are in ethics, but he has written much in critical evaluation of historical and current trends in philosophy.

Regularity Theory

Let us now consider philosophical theories of what the nature of causation is or, if you prefer to put it that way, what is meant by the term "cause." The philosopher who is inclined to be an empiricist will be likely to adopt a view on this topic which identifies or approximates to identifying causation with regular sequence, since regular sequence is something that can be observed empirically. He will indeed have to assume one principle which he cannot justify empirically, namely, that what has succeeded a certain kind of event regularly in the past is also likely to do so in the future; but the regular sequence or "regularity" view at any rate makes the minimum concessions to the non-empiricist. "*A* causes *B*," if *A* and *B* stand for classes of events, will then mean that *B* usually or always follows *A*. This view is by no means

Reprinted with permission of The Macmillan Company and Routledge & Kegan Paul Ltd from *The Fundamental Questions of Philosophy* by A. C. Ewing, 1951. Printed in Great Britain.

identical with the common-sense view of cause, as is shown by the fact that, if it were true, there would be no more special connection between the striking of a match and the flame which followed it than between the striking of the match and an earthquake which might also occur just afterwards. It would merely be that the striking of a match is usually followed by a flame and not usually followed by earthquakes, and that would be all. We could not then say that the striking *made* the flame follow. All intrinsic necessary connection between cause and effect, all active power on the part of the cause is denied. On this view to give a cause is *toto genere* different from giving a reason; it does not in the least help to explain why the effect happened, it only tells us what preceded the effect. So it is clear that the regularity view stands in very sharp contrast to the common-sense view of causation, though this does not necessarily refute the regularity view. Despite this, the latter theory, or something very like it, is distinctly popular today. It agrees well with the modern empiricist trend, since it makes causation something that can be empirically observed and goes as far as one can towards eliminating the *a priori*. And it is in accord with one fact about causation. Whether causation is merely regular sequence or not, it is clear that at least in the physical world we cannot see any intelligible connection between cause and effect which explains why the latter must occur if the former does so. The chemist may bring propositions such as that wood burns under more general principles about the nature of matter from which they could be deduced, but these more general propositions themselves are not of such a kind that we can see at all why they should be true; we only find that empirically in fact they are true.

But there are other respects in which the theory is less plausible. First, it presents serious difficulties when we start talking about the causation of single events. "I caused the flame by striking the match" might be interpreted as meaning: "Striking a match by me was followed by a flame, and an event of the second class usually does follow an event of the first." But what about events the causation of which is much more complex, such as wars and economic depressions? Nobody has succeeded in discovering a really satisfactory formulation of statements about the causes of these in terms of the regularity view. If we say that Hitler's invasion of Poland caused the second world war to break out when it did we no doubt mean that the war followed it, but the rest of what we mean is not that wars always or usually follow invasions of Poland; it is something much more specific.

Another difficulty about the regularity view is that there are cases of regular sequence which nobody would call cases of causation. For instance, the sounding of a hooter at 8 A.M. in London is regularly followed not only by men going to work at that factory in London but by men going to work at a factory in Manchester which also opens at 8 A.M. Yet everybody would say that, while the arrivals at the factory in London were caused by the hooter in that factory, the arrivals at Manchester were not.

These difficulties might possibly be met by minor amendments of the theory; others are more serious. The theory seems particularly inapplicable in the case of psychology. For instance, when I believe something for a reason, surely my mental state is really determined by the apprehension of the reason and is not merely one of a class of mental states which usually follow the apprehension of similar reasons. If that is all, the belief is not reasonable; for it to be reasonable it must not merely follow on the apprehension of the reason but be determined by the intrinsic character of the reason. Again it is surely incredible that, when I will an action, the action is not determined by my will, or that to say it is "determined" here merely means something like "it is a kind of action which follows most or all states of mind like my own at the time in certain specific respects." Again for memory to be possible one would think that my present state of consciousness must be genuinely determined by, not merely follow on, the past event remembered. There can be no trusting my memory of yesterday's events if it was not really determined by the events said to have been remembered.

Entailment Theory

All this should make one hesitate very much before accepting the regularity theory merely because it is the simplest and keeps closest to what is empirically observed. It seems that besides regularity we must introduce the notion of determination and necessity. There is a sense, it seems, in which the effect not merely does but must follow the cause, and this depends on the specific nature of the cause as such. Can we say anything more to make clearer what it is in which this necessity consists? There is another case of necessity, a clear one, which it is tempting and, I think, reasonable, to take as at least an analogy. That is the necessity underlying valid inference. Where a conclusion follows logically from a premise, this must be because the fact expressed by the premise is so connected with the fact expressed by the conclusion that the former could not possibly occur without the latter occurring. This is logical necessity. The theory according to which the connection between cause and effect is the same as or very like that of logical necessity may be called the rationalist or the entailment theory of causation ("entailment" being the relation between the premises and the conclusion in an argument where the latter follows necessarily from the former or between the objective facts expressed by the premises and by the conclusion).

The entailment theory is a theory of philosophers, but it certainly is more closely akin to the common-sense view than is a purely regularity theory, and though one should not say that causation is just entailment, there is a good case for saying that it involves the entailment relation or else something very similar. It is also true of course that an effect does follow regularly its cause; the regularity theory is not mistaken in what it asserts but only in what it denies. The entailment theory was almost universal among philosophers till the nineteenth century (though they did not use that name). The first leading philosopher to question it was David Hume (1711–76), and at the time his views found little favour, though today the regularity theory is the one most commonly advocated.

However, it seems to me that there are two strong arguments already given against the regularity theory, which did not by themselves suggest another theory to put in its place. The first is that we can after all make legitimate inferences from cause to effect. How could we do this if the case did not in a very important sense entail the effect? The relation need not be exactly the same as the entailment which occurs in formal logical reasoning, but it must at least be analogous to it in the important respect that it justifies the conclusion. It would be a very odd kind of inference in which we were allowed to draw conclusions from premises which in no way entailed their conclusions. This argument gives the main, though usually unexpressed, reason why philosophers have so often believed in the rationalist (or entailment) theory of causation. I do not, of course, in using this argument, mean to imply that a person must consciously assume the entailment theory before he can see that a particular induction is justified, only that the theory is logically presupposed if induction is to be justified. We do not know the ultimate logical presuppositions of our thinking, at any rate till we become philosophers.

The second argument is as follows. The occurrence of regularities is in any case a fact of experience. For instance, whenever solid objects are left unattached in mid-air, they fall to the ground (with certain reservations to cover airplanes, and so forth). Now, if it were not explained in any way, it would be an incredible coincidence that this should happen so constantly. It would be like having all the trumps in one hand at bridge several times running, or more improbable even than this. But what explanation could there be except that the nature of the bodies or the nature of the physical universe as a whole somehow entailed their moving in that way? If causation merely means regular sequence, to say that A causes B gives no explanation of the regular sequence of B on A; it merely affirms that B thus succeeds. Only if the cause is a *reason* for the effect, will it explain why this repeated regularity occurs, and the facts surely cry out for an explanation, since the alternative is to leave it as a mere coincidence which would be incredibly unlikely. But how can the cause be a reason for the effect if its nature does not somehow involve the effect? In that case the latter will logically follow from, that is, be entailed by the former, or at least the relation will be very closely analogous to that of logical entailment.[1]

The following are the main objections brought against the entailment theory.

1. We cannot see any logical connection between cause and effect. This must be admitted as regards the physical world at least. We do not see any ultimate reason why water and not oil should put out a fire or why we should be nourished by bread and not by stones. No doubt a scientist could in a sense give reasons for these laws by explaining, for example, that stones are too hard to digest and that bread contains introgenous matter in an organized form in which it is not present in stones; but the reasons of the scientist only amount either to interpolating intermediate causes so that he explains how A causes B by pointing to an intermediate link C, that is, something which appears between A and B, or to showing that the generalization to be explained is just an instance of wider generalization itself founded on experience, for example, that no animals can extract nutriment direct from inorganic matter. In neither case does he tell us anything which amounts to more than a statement that events of a certain kind

---

[1] Some people prefer not to use the term "entail" of the connection between facts but only of the connection between propositions, but we cannot avoid admitting that, if two true propositions are necessarily connected, the facts for which they stand must also be necessarily connected. Whether we are to call this necessary connection between facts "entailment" or not seems to me only a verbal question.

occur under certain circumstances; he does not explain why they occur. This is made clearer by comparing the conclusions of other sciences with those of mathematics. In the latter alone do we see not merely as an empirical fact that the conclusion is true but why it must be true. No causal law about the physical world even appears to us as logically necessary like the laws of mathematics; we cannot prove any such law *a priori*, but only establish it as an empirical generalization. However, the fact that we cannot see any necessary *a priori* connection behind causal laws is no proof that there is not any. Till comparatively recently most of the logically necessary connections of mathematics had not been discovered by any human being, but they no doubt held all the same in prehistoric days as much as today. We cannot set limits to what is in nature by our ignorance. It would be very different if we were not only unable to see any necessary connection between cause and effect but were able to see positively that there is no such connection. Some philosophers think that they can see this, and if so, they are justified in ruling out the entailment theory; but in the absence of this positive insight the negative argument is only of light weight.

2. The relation between cause and effect is in one respect at least different from that holding in any generally recognized case of necessary connection, that is, cause and effect are not, normally at least, simultaneous, but occur at different times. This of course again does not prove that necessary causal connection cannot occur, but only somewhat lessens the plausibility of the contention that it does. But if there are good positive reasons to suppose it occurs, the fact that it is unlike what happens in other cases is no adequate ground for rejecting the reasons in question.

3. It is objected that in cases of *a priori* reasoning we attain certainty, but in cases of causal reasoning only probability. This may, however, be explained compatibly with the entailment theory. In the first place we never know the whole cause. What common sense calls the cause is only the most striking part of a vast complex of conditions all of which are relevant to the exact manner in which the effect occurs. But, even if the whole cause entails the whole effect, this gives no reason to suppose that a part of it, which is all we know, will do so. The best we can do is to conclude on the ground of previous experience that the factors in the cause of which we are not aware are unlikely to be of such a kind as to counteract the others and prevent the occurrence of something like the expected effect. Secondly, since we cannot see the necessary connection directly even if it is there, we are in any case bound to proceed by employing the recognized methods of induc-

tion, which can logically only yield probability, not certainty. For in the absence of direct insight into it, we can only arrive at conclusions as to when it occurs indirectly by considering what regularities normally occur and inferring from those what are most likely to be the laws underlying them, as on any other view of causation.

The entailment theory is of course incompatible with the view which we earlier rejected that all logically necessary propositions are verbal or analytic in a sense which would make what is entailed part of what entails. Since the effect is a different event from and not part of the cause, the two cannot be necessarily connected unless some propositions not analytic in this sense are *a priori.* Propositions about causation may be analytic in some cases, where something has been defined in terms of its causal properties, but this cannot always be so. If we define a species of thing in terms of one causal property, it will be a synthetic proposition that members of the species have any other causal property they may possess.

So far I have spoken as if it were common ground that we could never have insight into causal entailments, but I should not be ready to admit this. It seems to me true of the physical world, not of the world of psychology. Our insight that the death of a beloved person will tend to cause grief or that insults will tend to cause annoyance does not seem to be based merely on experience. We seem also to see *a priori* that the cause will tend to produce these effects. There is surely something in the thwarting of a desire which entails a tendency to produce pain. Even apart from experience, it would not be as reasonable to expect that the death of a beloved person would cause the lover to jump for joy. We must indeed admit that we can at the best only see a causal *tendency* in these cases. If A loves B now, it is not certain that he will grieve if B dies, for by the time this has happened he may have gone mad or quarreled with B so violently as to rejoice at his death. But we can see, it seems, that the nature of love is such as to tend strongly in the direction mentioned and not in the opposite one. That we can only say what its tendency is and not predict with certainty that this will be fulfilled on a given occasion is presumably because the situation is always very complex and we cannot know that there will not be factors which counteract the tendency in question. It may further be argued that we can easily explain why we should not see entailments in the physical world even if they are really there. For, firstly it is generally held that the internal nature of matter is quite unknown to us, and how can we tell whether what is quite unknown to us does or does not entail something? In psychology alone are we immediately aware of the internal nature of the object with which we are dealing, namely mind, and here we can reasonably claim to see that certain causal entailments hold, as we have just noted. Secondly, we never are in a position to give the whole cause, and it would be the whole cause that entailed the effect, not a part of it. Incidentally it is not necessary to the entailment theory to suppose that there are any causal laws which by themselves would be self-evident even to God. It may be that any causal law depends for its evidence on the whole system to which it belongs, as many have argued to be the case even with the *a priori* propositions of mathematics. It may be that water would not freeze in the way it does in a universe where the chemical constitution of water was the same but the general world system different. The arguments I have used would be compatible even with any law we can discover being only statistical. It has been suggested that the laws of physics do not apply to each single particle but are only statistics about the way in which most particles move, but there still must surely, it seems, be some reason in the nature of things why so many more particles move in one way than in another way.

Whether we are to maintain or reject the entailment theory depends largely on our attitude to the problem of induction. Modern logicians generally have tried to solve the problem of the validity of induction without assuming the entailment theory of causation and generally admit that they have failed. They have not, even according to themselves, shown why we are entitled to make inductive predictions in advance of experience. The main trouble is that there is no reason why we should think that A will be followed by B in the future merely because it has been so in the past. But if we suppose that the repeated experience in the past is an indication of something in the nature of A which entails B, that will be a good reason for expecting B to follow on future occasions also, even if we do not see why the assumed entailment should hold. No detailed theory of induction has been worked out on this basis, but it is significant that modern logicians who will not admit the entailment theory of causation have (usually according to their own admission) failed to produce any rational justification of induction. Nevertheless it has seemed so odd to many philosophers that there should be a relation of logical entailment between different events that they would rather admit all our induction to be irrational than save its rationality in such a fashion. Yet we cannot really suppose it irrational to believe that if we jump from a height we shall fall; and even if we say that all induction is in some sense irrational, it will still be incumbent on us to explain the distinction between scientific inductions and those inductions which would be accepted by no sensible person. What is the difference between the two kinds if they are both irrational?

It has been said that inductive arguments, though not rational in the same way as deductive arguments, are rational in some other way. It is easy enough to say this, but difficult to grasp what this sense of "rational" could be. Inductive arguments are, after all, inferences, and for an inference to be valid the conclusion must follow from the premises. But for this to be so, the premises must entail the conclusion, or at the very least be connected with it by a relation closely analogous to that of logical entailment. It is difficult to escape this argument. Nor have those who try to meet the difficulty by saying that induction is rational but rational in a different sense from deduction succeeded in defining the sense in which induction is rational. They have either left it undefined or defined it in terms of practical utility. In the latter case an inductive inference is rational if it is of a kind which is practically useful. But this seems hardly to solve the problem. It is clear that in order to act in a practically useful way, it is not enough to do what has proved useful in the past unless this is an indication that it is likely to be useful also in the future, and it is just as much an induction to infer that something will have good practical results in the future from the results it has had in the past as it is to infer that something will be true of future events because it has been true of past.

It seems to me, therefore, that there is a strong case for the entailment theory of causation. But I must admit that this is not the opinion of the majority of contemporary philosophers. It is in any case a very important issue metaphysically. One of the most fundamental differences there are in philosophy is between those who think of the world as a rationally connected system and those who regard it as a mere collection of brute facts externally related, and which side we take in this controversy will depend chiefly on whether we, consciously or unconsciously, assume the entailment view of causation or not. One of the chief issues in philosophy through the ages has been that between monism and pluralism, between those who look on the unity of things as more important and those who give a more fundamental position to their plurality; and we shall certainly regard the world as much more of a unity if we adopt the entailment view of causation. If that view is true, everything in the world will be united in a logical system, since everything is causally connected with everything else either directly or indirectly. If that view is true, everything in the world will be a unity in a very important sense, for the very nature of a thing will also involve the other things with which it is causally connected.

The Risks of Induction

Bertrand Russell*

In almost all our previous discussions, we have been concerned in the attempt to get clear as to our data in the way of knowledge of existence. What things are there in the universe whose existence is known to us, owing to our being acquainted with them? So far, our answer has been that we are acquainted with our sense-data, and, probably, with ourselves. These we know to exist. And past sense-data which are remembered are known to have existed in the past. This knowledge supplies our data.

But if we are able to draw inferences from these data—if we are to know of the existence of matter, of other people, of the past before our individual memory begins, or of the future, we must know general principles of some kind by means of which such inferences can be drawn. It must be known to us that the existence of some one sort of thing, A, is a sign of the existence of some other sort of thing, B, either at the same time as A or at some earlier or later time, as, for example, thunder is a sign of the earlier existence of lightning. If this were not known to us, we could never extend our knowledge beyond the sphere of our private experience; and this sphere, as we have seen, is exceedingly limited. The question we have now to consider is whether such an extension is possible, and if so, how it is effected.

Let us take as an illustration a matter about which none of us, in fact, feel the slightest doubt. We are all convinced that the sun will rise tomorrow. Why? Is this belief a mere blind outcome

Reprinted by permission of The Clarendon Press, Oxford, from *The Problems of Philosophy* by Bertrand Russell, 1912.
* For biographical note, see p. 120.

229

of past experience, or can it be justified as a reasonable belief? It is not easy to find a test by which to judge whether a belief of this kind is reasonable or not, but we can at least ascertain what sort of general beliefs would suffice, if true, to justify the judgment that the sun will rise tomorrow, and the many other similar judgments upon which our actions are based.

It is obvious that if we are asked why we believe that the sun will rise tomorrow, we shall naturally answer, "Because it always has risen every day." We have a firm belief that it will rise in the future, because it has risen in the past. If we are challenged as to why we believe that it will continue to rise as heretofore, we may appeal to the laws of motion: the earth, we shall say, is a freely rotating body, and such bodies do not cease to rotate unless something interferes from outside, and there is nothing outside to interfere with the earth between now and tomorrow. Of course it might be doubted whether we are quite certain that there is nothing outside to interfere, but this is not the interesting doubt. The interesting doubt is as to whether the laws of motion will remain in operation until tomorrow. If this doubt is raised, we find ourselves in the same position as when the doubt about the sunrise was first raised.

The *only* reason for believing that the laws of motion will remain in operation is that they have operated hitherto, so far as our knowledge of the past enables us to judge. It is true that we have a greater body of evidence from the past in favor of the laws of motion than we have in favor of the sunrise, because the sunrise is merely a particular case of fulfillment of the laws of motion, and there are countless other particular cases. But the real question is: Do *any* number of cases of a law being fulfilled in the past afford evidence that it will be fulfilled in the future? If not, is becomes plain that we have no ground whatever for expecting the sun to rise tomorrow, or for expecting the bread we shall eat at our next meal not to poison us, or for any of the other scarcely conscious expectations that control our daily lives. It is to be observed that all such expectations are only *probable*; thus we have not to seek for a proof that they *must* be fulfilled, but only for some reason in favor of the view that they are *likely* to be fulfilled.

Now in dealing with this question we must, to begin with, make an important distinction, without which we should soon become involved in hopeless confusions. Experience has shown us that, hitherto, the frequent repetition of some uniform succession or coexistence has been a *cause* of our expecting the same succession or coexistence on the next occasion. Food that has a certain appearance generally has a certain taste, and it is a severe shock to our expectations when the familiar appearance is found to be associated with an unusual taste. Things which we see become associated, by habit, with certain tactile sensations which we expect if we touch them; one of the horrors of a ghost (in many ghost-stories) is that it fails to give us any sensations of touch. Uneducated people who go abroad for the first time are so surprised as to be incredulous when they find their native language not understood.

And this kind of association is not confined to men; in animals also it is very strong. A horse which has been often driven along a certain road resists the attempt to drive him in a different direction. Domestic animals expect food when they see the person who usually feeds them. We know that all these rather crude expectations of uniformity are liable to be misleading. The man who has fed the chicken every day throughout its life at last wrings its neck instead, showing that more refined views as to the uniformity of nature would have been useful to the chicken.

But in spite of the misleadingness of such expectations, they nevertheless exist. The mere fact that something has happened a certain number of times causes animals and men to expect that it will happen again. Thus our instincts certainly cause us to believe that the sun will rise tomorrow, but we may be in no better a position than the chicken which unexpectedly has its neck wrung. We have therefore to distinguish the fact that past uniformities *cause* expectations as to the future, from the question whether there is any reasonable ground for giving weight to such expectations after the question of their validity has been raised.

The problem we have to discuss is whether there is any reason for believing in what is called "the uniformity of nature." The belief in the uniformity of nature is the belief that everything that has happened or will happen is an instance of some general law to which there are *no* exceptions. The crude expectations which we have been considering are all subject to exceptions, and therefore liable to disappoint those who entertain them. But science habitually assumes, at least as a working hypothesis, that general rules which have exceptions can be replaced by general rules which have no exceptions. "Unsupported bodies in air fall" is a general rule to which balloons and airplanes are exceptions. But the laws of motion and the law of gravitation, which account for the fact that most bodies fall, also account for the fact that balloons and airplanes can rise; thus the laws of motion and the law of gravitation are not subject to these exceptions.

The belief that the sun will rise tomorrow might be falsified if the earth came suddenly into contact with a large body which destroyed its rotation; but the laws of motion and the law of gravitation would not be infringed by such an event. The business of science is to find uniformities, such as the laws of motion and the law of gravitation, to which, so far as our experience extends, there are no exceptions. In this search science has been remarkably successful, and it may be conceded that such uniformities have held hitherto. This brings us back to the question: Have we any reason, assuming that they have always held in the past, to suppose that they will hold in the future?

It has been argued that we have reason to know that the future will resemble the past, because what was the future has constantly become the past, and has always been found to resemble the past, so that we really have experience of the future, namely of times which were formerly future, which we may call past futures. But such an argument really begs the very question at issue. We have experience of past futures, but not of future futures, and the question is: Will future futures resemble past futures? This question is not to be answered by an argument which starts from past futures alone. We have therefore still to seek for some principle which shall enable us to know that the future will follow the same laws as the past.

The reference to the future in this question is not essential. The same question arises when we apply the laws that work in our experiences to past things of which we have no experience— as, for example, in geology, or in theories as to the origin of the solar system. The question we really have to ask is: "When two things have been found to be often associated, and no instance is known of the one occurring without the other, does the occurrence of one of the two, in a fresh instance, give any good ground for expecting the other?" On our answer to this question must depend the validity of the whole of our expectations as to the future, the whole of the results obtained by induction, and in fact practically all the beliefs upon which our daily life is based.

It must be conceded, to begin with, that the fact that two things have been found often together and never apart does not, by itself, suffice to *prove* demonstratively that they will be found together in the next case we examine. The most we can hope is that the oftener things are found together, the more probable it becomes that they will be found together another time, and that, if they have been found together often enough, the probability will amount *almost* to certainty. It can never quite reach certainty, because we know that in spite of frequent repetitions there sometimes is a failure at the last, as in the case of the chicken whose neck is wrung. Thus probability is all we ought to seek.

It might be urged, as against the view we are advocating, that we know all natural phenomena to be subject to the reign of law, and that sometimes, on the basis of observation, we can see that only one law can possibly fit the facts of the case. Now to this view there are two answers. The first is that, even if *some* law which has no exceptions applies to our case, we can never, in practice, be sure that we have discovered that law and not one to which there are exceptions. The second is that the reign of law would seem to be itself only probable, and that our belief that it will hold in the future, or in unexamined cases in the past, is itself based upon the very principle we are examining.

The principle we are examining may be called the *principle of induction,* and its two parts may be stated as follows:

(*a*) When a thing of a certain sort A has been found to be associated with a thing of a certain other sort B, and has never been found dissociated from a thing of the sort B, the greater the number of cases in which A and B have been associated, the greater is the probability that they will be associated in a fresh case in which one of them is known to be present;

(*b*) Under the same circumstances, a sufficient number of cases of association will make the probability of a fresh association nearly a certainty, and will make it approach certainty without limit.

As just stated, the principle applies only to the verification of our expectation in a single fresh instance. But we want also to know that there is a probability in favor of the general law that things of the sort A are always associated with things of the sort B, provided a sufficient number of cases of association are known, and no cases of failure of association are known. The probability of the general law is obviously less than the probability of the particular case, since if the general law is true, the particular case must also be true, whereas the particular case may be true without the general law being true. Nevertheless the probability of the general law is increased by repetitions, just as the probability of the particular case is. We may therefore repeat the two parts of our principle as regards the general law, thus:

(*a*) The greater the number of cases in which a thing of the sort A has been found associated with a thing of the sort B, the more probable it is (if no cases of failure of association are known) that A is always associated with B;

(*b*) Under the same circumstances, a sufficient number of cases of the association of A and B will make it nearly certain that A is always associated with B, and will make this general law approach certainty without limit.

It should be noted that probability is always relative to certain data. In our case, the data are merely the known cases of coexistence of *A* and *B*. There may be other data, which *might* be taken into account, which would gravely alter the probability. For example, a man who had seen a great many white swans might argue, by our principle, that on the data it was *probable* that all swans were white, and this might be a perfectly sound argument. The argument is not disproved by the fact that some swans are black, because a thing may very well happen in spite of the fact that some data render it improbable. In the case of the swans, a man might know that color is a very variable characteristic in many species of animals, and that, therefore, an induction as to color is peculiarly liable to error. But this knowledge would be a fresh datum, by no means proving that the probability relatively to our previous data had been wrongly estimated. The fact, therefore, that things often fail to fulfill our expectations is no evidence that our expectations will not *probably* be fulfilled in a given case or a given class of cases. Thus our inductive principle is at any rate not capable of being *disproved* by an appeal to experience.

The inductive principle, however, is equally incapable of being *proved* by an appeal to experience. Experience might conceivably confirm the inductive principle as regards the cases that have been already examined; but as regards unexamined cases, it is the inductive principle alone that can justify any inference from what has been examined to what has not been examined. All arguments which, on the basis of experience, argue as to the future or the unexperienced parts of the past or present, assume the inductive principle; hence we can never use experience to prove the inductive principle without begging the question. Thus we must either accept the inductive principle on the ground of its intrinsic evidence, or forgo all justification of our expectations about the future. If the principle is unsound, we have no reason to expect the sun to rise tomorrow, to expect bread to be more nourishing than a stone, or to expect that if we throw ourselves off the roof we shall fall. When we see what looks like our best friend approaching us, we shall have no reason to suppose that his body is not inhabited by the mind of our worst enemy or of some total stranger. All our conduct is based upon associations which have worked in the past, and which we therefore regard as likely to work in the future; and this likelihood is dependent for its validity upon the inductive principle.

The general principles of science, such as the belief in the reign of law, and the belief that every event must have a cause, are as completely dependent upon the inductive principle as are the beliefs of daily life. All such general principles are believed because mankind has found innumerable instances of their truth and no instances of their falsehood. But this affords no evidence for their truth in the future, unless the inductive principle is assumed.

Thus all knowledge which, on a basis of experience, tells us something about what is not experienced, is based upon a belief which experience can neither confirm nor confute, yet which, at least in its more concrete applications, appears to be as firmly rooted in us as many of the facts of experience. The existence and justification of such beliefs—for the inductive principle, as we shall see, is not the only example—raises some of the most difficult and most debated problems of philosophy. We will, in the next chapter, consider briefly what may be said to account for such knowledge, and what is its scope and its degree of certainty.

Russell's Needless
Doubts About Induction

Paul Edwards

Paul Edwards (1925–   ), Professor of Philosophy in the City College of New York, Brooklyn, is the author of The Logic of Moral Discourse *and editor of the eight-volume* Encyclopaedia of Philosophy.

I

In the celebrated chapter on induction in his *Problems of Philosophy,* Bertrand Russell asks the question: "Have we any reason, assuming that they (laws like the law of gravitation) have always held in the past, to suppose that these laws will hold in the future?"[1] Earlier in the same chapter he raises the more specific question: "Do *any* number of cases of a law being fulfilled in the past afford evidence that it will be fulfilled in the future?"[2] We may reformulate these questions in a way which lends itself more easily to critical discussion as follows:

(1) Assuming that we possess *n* positive instances of a phenomenon, observed in extensively varied circumstances, and that

Reprinted by permission of the author and the publisher from *Mind* (April, 1949), pp. 141–147. The last two sections have been omitted.

[1] p. 100.
[2] p. 96.

we have not observed a single negative instance (where n is a large number), have we any reason to suppose that the $n + 1$st instance will also be positive?

(2) Is there any number n of observed positive instances of a phenomenon which affords evidence that the $n + 1$st instance will also be positive?

It is clear that Russell uses "reason" synonymously with "good reason" and "evidence" with "sufficient evidence." I shall follow the same procedure throughout this article.

Russell asserts that unless we appeal to a non-empirical principle which he calls the "principle of induction," both of his questions must be answered in the negative. "Those who emphasized the scope of induction," he writes, "wished to maintain that all logic is empirical, and therefore could not be expected to realize that induction itself, their own darling, required a logical principle which obviously could not be proved inductively, and must therefore be *a priori* if it could be known at all."[3] "We must either accept the inductive principle on the ground of its intrinsic evidence or forgo all justification of our expectations about the future."[4]

In conjunction with the inductive principle, on the other hand, question (1) at least, he contends, can be answered in the affirmative. "Whether inferences from past to future are valid depends wholly, if our discussion has been sound, upon the inductive principle: if it is true, such inferences are valid."[5] Unfortunately Russell does not make it clear whether in his opinion the same is true about question (2).

As against Russell, I shall try to show in this article that question (1) can be answered in the affirmative without in any way appealing to a non-empirical principle. I shall also attempt to show that, without in any way invoking a non-empirical principle, numbers of observed positive instances do frequently afford us evidence that unobserved instances of the same phenomenon are also positive. At the outset, I shall concentrate on question (1), since this is the more general question. Once we have answered question (1), it will require little further effort to answer question (2).

I want to emphasize here that, to keep this paper within man-

---

[3] *Our Knowledge of the External World* (2nd edition), p. 226.
[4] *Problems of Philosophy*, p. 106; also *Outline of Philosophy*, p. 286.
[5] *External World*, p. 226.

ageable bounds, I shall refrain from discussing, at any rate explicitly, the questions "Are any inductive conclusions probable?" and "Are any inductive conclusions certain?" I hope to fill in this gap on another occasion.

It will be well to conduct our discussion in terms of a concrete example. Supposing a man jumps from a window on the fiftieth floor of the Empire State Building. Is there any reason to suppose that his body will move in the direction of the street rather than say in the direction of the sky or in a flat plane? There can be no doubt that any ordinary person and any philosophically unsophisticated scientist would answer this question in the affirmative without in any way appealing to a non-empirical principle. He would say that there is an excellent reason to suppose that the man's body will move towards the street. This excellent reason, he would say, consists in the fact that whenever in the past a human being jumped out of a window of the Empire State Building, his body moved in a downward direction; that whenever any human being anywhere jumped out of a house, he moved in the direction of the ground; that, more generally, whenever a human body jumped or was thrown off an elevated locality in the neighborhood of the earth, it moved downwards and not either upwards or at an angle of 180°; that the only objects which have been observed to be capable of moving upwards by themselves possess certain special characteristics which human beings lack; and finally in all the other observed confirmations of the theory of gravitation.

The philosophers who reject commonsense answers like the one just described have relied mainly on three arguments. Russell himself explicitly employs two of them and some of his remarks make it clear that he also approves of the third. These three arguments are as follows:

(a) Defenders of commonsense point to the fact that many inferences to unobserved events were subsequently, by means of direct observation, found to have resulted in true conclusions. However, any such appeal to observed results of inductive inferences is irrelevant. For the question at stake is: Have we ever a reason, assuming that all the large number of observed instances of a phenomenon are positive, to suppose that an instance which is still unobserved is also positive? The question is not: Have we ever a reason for supposing that instances which have by now been observed but were at one time unobserved are positive? In Russell's own words: "We have experience of past futures, but not of future futures, and the question is: Will future futures resemble past futures? This question is not to be answered by an argument which starts from past futures alone."[6]

(b) Cases are known where at a certain time a large number of positive instances and not a single negative instance had been observed and where the next instance nevertheless turned out to be negative. "We know that in spite of frequent repetitions there sometimes is a failure at the last."[7] The man, for instance, "who has fed the chicken every day throughout its life at last wrings its neck instead."[8] Even in the case of the human being who is jumping out of the Empire State Building, "we may be in no better position than the chicken which unexpectedly has its neck wrung."[9]

(c) The number of positive and negative necessary conditions for the occurrence of any event is infinite or at any rate too large to be directly observed by a human being or indeed by all human beings put together. None of us, for example, has explored every corner of the universe to make sure that there nowhere exists a malicious but powerful individual who controls the movements of the sun by means of wires which are too fine to be detected by any of our microscopes. None of us can be sure that there is no such Controller who, in order to play a joke with the human race, will prevent the sun from rising tomorrow. Equally, none of us can be sure that there is nowhere a powerful individual who can, if he wishes, regulate the movement of human bodies by means of ropes which are too thin to be detected by any of our present instruments. None of us therefore can be sure that when a man jumps out of the Empire State Building he will not be drawn skyward by the Controller of Motion. Hence we have no reason to suppose that the man's body will move in the direction of the street and not in the direction of the sky.

In connection with the last of these three arguments, attention ought to be drawn to a distinction which Russell makes between what he calls the "interesting" and the "uninteresting" doubt about induction.[10] The uninteresting doubt is doubt about the occurrence of a given event on the ground that not all the conditions which are known to be necessary are in fact known to be present. What Russell calls the interesting doubt is the doubt

[6] *Problems of Philosophy*, p. 100.
[7] *Loc. cit.*, p. 102.
[8] *Loc. cit.*, p. 98.
[9] *Ibid.*
[10] *Loc. cit.*, p. 95.

whether an event will take place although all the conditions known to be necessary are known to obtain. Russell's "interesting doubt," if I am not mistaken, is identical with Donald William's "tragic problem of induction."[11]

II

As I indicated above, it is my object in this article to defend the commonsense answers to both of Russell's questions. I propose to show, in other words, that, without in any way calling upon a non-empirical principle for assistance, we often have a reason for supposing that a generalization will be confirmed in the future as it has been confirmed in the past. I also propose to show that numbers "of cases of a law being fulfilled in the past" do often afford evidence that it will be fulfilled in the future.

However, what I have to say in support of these answers is so exceedingly simple that I am afraid it will not impress the philosophers who are looking for elaborate and complicated theories to answer these questions. But I think I can make my case appear plausible even in the eyes of some of these philosophers if I describe at some length the general method of resolving philosophical puzzles which I shall apply to the problem of induction.

Let us consider a simple statement like "There are several thousand physicians in New York." We may call this a statement of commonsense, meaning thereby no more than that anybody above a certain very moderate level of instruction and intelligence would confidently give his assent to it.

The word "physician," as ordinarily used, is not entirely free from ambiguity. At times it simply means "person who possesses a medical degree from a recognized academic institution." At other times, though less often, it means the same as "person who possesses what is by ordinary standards a considerable skill in curing diseases." On yet other occasions when people say about somebody that he is a physician, they mean both that he has a medical degree and that he possesses a skill in curing diseases which considerably exceeds that of the average layman.

[11] "Induction and the Future," *Mind,* 1948, p. 227.

Let us suppose that in the commonsense statement "There are several thousand physicians in New York" the word "physician" is used exclusively in the last-mentioned sense. This assumption will simplify our discussion, but it is not at all essential to any of the points I am about to make. It is essential, however, to realize that when somebody asserts in ordinary life that there are several thousand physicians in New York, he is using the word "physician" in one or other of the ordinary senses just listed. By "physician" he does not mean, for example, "person who can speedily repair bicycles" or "person who can cure any conceivable illness in less than two minutes."

Now, supposing somebody were to say, "Really, there are no physicians at all in New York," in the belief that he was contradicting and refuting commonsense. Supposing that on investigation it turns out that by "physician" he does not mean "person who has a medical degree and who has considerably more skill in curing disease than the average layman." It turns out that by "physician" he means "person who has a medical degree and who can cure any conceivable illness in less than two minutes."

What would be an adequate reply to such an "enemy of commonsense"? Clearly it would be along the following lines: "What you say is true. There are no physicians in New York—in *your* sense of the word. There are no persons in New York who can cure any conceivable disease in less than two minutes. But this in no way contradicts the commonsense view expressed by 'There are several thousand physicians in New York.' For the latter asserts no more than that there are several thousand people in New York who have a medical degree and who possess a skill in curing disease which considerably exceeds that of the average layman. You are guilty of *ignoratio elenchi*, since the proposition you refute is different from the proposition you set out to refute."

Our discussion from here on will be greatly simplified by introducing a few technical terms. Let us, firstly, call *"ignoratio elenchi* by *redefinition"* any instance of *ignoratio elenchi* in which (i) the same sentence expresses both the proposition which ought to be proved and the proposition which is confused with it and where (ii) in the latter employment of the sentence one or more of its parts are used in a sense which is different from their ordinary sense or senses. Secondly, let us refer to any redefinition of a word which includes all that the ordinary definition of the word includes but which includes something else as well as a *"high* redefinition"; and to the sense which is defined by a high redefinition we shall refer as a high sense of the word. Thus "person who has a medical degree and who is capable of curing any conceivable disease in less than two minutes" is a high redefinition of "physician," and anybody using the word in that fashion is using it in a high sense. Thirdly, we shall refer to a redefinition of a word which includes something but not all of what the ordinary definition includes and which includes nothing else as a *"low* redefinition"; and the sense which is defined by a low redefinition we shall call a low sense of the word. "Person capable of giving first aid" or "person who knows means of alleviating pain" would be low redefinitions of "physician." Finally, it will be convenient to call a statement in which a word is used in a high or in a low sense a *redefinitional statement*. If the word is used in a high sense we shall speak of a highdefinitional statement; if it is used in a low sense we shall speak of a lowdefinitional statement.

A short while ago, I pointed out that the man who says, "There are no physicians in New York," meaning that there are no people in New York who have a medical degree and who can cure any conceivable illness in less than two minutes, is not really contradicting the commonsense view that there are physicians in New York. I pointed out that he would be guilty of what in our technical language is called an *ignoratio elenchi* by redefinition. Now, it seems to me that the relation between the assertion of various philosophers that past experience never constitutes a reason for prediction or generalization except perhaps in conjunction with a non-empirical principle and the commonsense view that past experience does often by itself constitute a reason for inferences to unobserved events has some striking resemblances to the relation between the redefinitional statement about physicians in New York and the commonsense view which this redefinitional statement fails to refute. And more generally, it strongly seems to me that almost all the bizarre pronouncements of philosophers— their "paradoxes," their "silly" theories—are in certain respects strikingly like the statement that there are no physicians in New York, made by one who means to assert that there are no people in New York who have medical degrees and who are capable of curing any conceivable disease in less than two minutes.

In making the last statement I do not mean to deny that there are also important differences between philosophical paradoxes and the highdefinitional statement about physicians. There are three differences in particular which have to be mentioned if my subsequent remarks are not to be seriously misleading. Firstly, many of the philosophical paradoxes are not without some point; they do often draw attention to likenesses and differences which ordinary usage obscures. Secondly, the redefinitions which are implicit in philosophical paradoxes do quite often, though by no means always, receive a certain backing from ordinary usage. Frequently, that is to say, there is a secondary sense or trend in ordinary usage which corresponds to the philosophical redefinition, the "real" sense of the word.[12] Thirdly, philosophical paradoxes are invariably ambiguous in a sense in which the highdefinitional statement about the physicians is not ambiguous.[13]

Now, while fully admitting all these (and other) differences, I wish to insist on the great likenesses between philosophical paradoxes and the redefinitional statement about the physicians. And in this article I am mainly concerned with the likenesses, not with the differences. My main object of course is to point out the likenesses between the highdefinitional statement "There are no physicians in New York" and the statement that past experience never by itself affords a reason for making inferences to unobserved events. However, my points there will be clearer if I first make them in connection with another celebrated paradox.

Following Plato, Berkeley[14] argued in favor of the view that heat and cold are not really "in the object." Ordinary people would unhesitatingly say that water of, for example, 50° Centigrade is hot. Against this, Plato and Berkeley would point out that to a man who a moment before had held his hands in a jug of water with a temperature of 80° C., the water of 50° C. would appear cold. Similarly, to a race of individuals whose body-temperature was say 75° C., water of 50° would regularly appear cold. But the percepts of those to whom the water of 50° appears cold are just as genuine as the percepts of people to whom the water appears hot. Now, since it would be wrong to say that the water of 50° is really cold simply because of these genuine percepts of cold, it cannot any more rationally be said to be hot. The cold has "just as good a right to be considered real" as the hot; and therefore, "to avoid favoritism, we are compelled to deny that in itself"[15] the water is either hot or cold.

It is not difficult to show that this argument is a case of *ignoratio elenchi* by redefinition. When an ordinary person says that water of 50° C. is hot, all he means is that human beings, with

---

[12] Prominent instances of this phenomenon are "real certainty," "real knowledge," "real sameness," "real freedom," and "really contemporaneous events."

[13] The last of these points seems to me to be of enormous importance for understanding the phenomenon of philosophical paradoxes.

[14] *Three Dialogues between Hylas and Philonous*, p. 208 (Everyman edit.).

[15] The phrases are Russell's, used in a very similar context (*Problems*, p. 14).

their body-temperature being what it is, would in *all ordinary circumstances* have sense-impressions of heat on coming into contact with such water. In saying that water of 50° is hot, is *really* hot, an ordinary person in no way denies that under certain *special* conditions a human being would have genuine sense-impressions of cold. He also in no way denies that to a race of individuals whose body-temperature is 75° the water would genuinely appear cold. Pointing to these facts does therefore not refute the ordinary man. Berkeley is clearly guilty of a high redefinition of "hot" or "really hot." To him something is hot only if, in addition to appearing hot to human beings in ordinary circumstances, it also appears hot to them under special circumstances and if it appears hot to beings with a body-temperature which is much greater than the actual body-temperature of human beings.

However, this is not quite accurate since, like most other philosophical paradoxes, the paradox about heat and cold has a double meaning. It would be inaccurate simply to say that Berkeley is guilty of *ignoratio elenchi* by redefinition. On the other hand, without in any way being inaccurate, it can be said that Berkeley and Plato have laid themselves open to the following dilemma: "Either you mean by 'hot' what is ordinarily meant by it—if you do, then what you say is plainly false; or else you are using 'hot' in a high sense—if so, what you say is true, but in that case you are guilty of *ignoratio elenchi* by redefinition. In either event you have failed to refute commonsense." Very similar answers can also be made to Berkeley's and Russell's arguments concerning colors, shapes, and the other qualities which commonsense believes to exist independently of being perceived.

At the same time it must be admitted that Berkeley's arguments have a certain value. In ordinary speech we make a fairly rigid distinction between "real" and "unreal" data. Among the unreal data, we lump together both the percepts which we have under special conditions (and percepts which do and would appear to beings differently constituted from ourselves) and what we experience, for example, in dreams and hallucinations. "Real" we call only those percepts which a normal observer has under certain standard conditions.

A classification of this sort obscures the many likenesses between the "real" percepts and percepts appearing under special conditions, while also hiding the many differences between the latter and data which are experienced in dreams and hallucinations.

The situation becomes quite clear if we divide data into three and not merely into two groups, as follows:

the R-data: percepts appearing to a normal observer under standard conditions,

the A-data: percepts appearing to a normal observer under special conditions or to an abnormal observer in certain normal or special circumstances, and

the D-data: data appearing in dreams, hallucinations, and so forth.

It is unnecessary for our purposes to discuss exactly what are the likenesses between the R-data and the A-data. It is unnecessary, too, to discuss what exactly are the differences between the A-data and the D-data. It is sufficient to point out that while Berkeley is wrong in believing or suggesting that there are no differences between the R-data and the A-data, he is right in insisting that the differences between the R-data and the A-data are not nearly as great as ordinary speech suggests. In the case of colors, Berkeley's argument has the further merit of bringing out the fact that the expression "*X*'s real color" has *two* perfectly proper senses. His argument helps one to realise that "*X*'s real color" may mean "the color which *X* exhibits to a normal observer under certain standard conditions" *as well as* "the color which *X* exhibits to a normal observer under a finer instrument than the human eye, for example, a microscope."

III

Supposing a man, let us call him *M*, said to us, "I have not yet found any physicians in New York." Suppose we take him to Park Avenue and introduce him to Brown, a man who has a medical degree and who has cured many people suffering from diseases of the ear. Brown admits, however, that he has not been able to cure *all* the patients who ever consulted him. He also admits that many of his cures took a long time, some as long as eight years. On hearing this, *M* says, "Brown certainly isn't a physician."

Supposing we next take *M* to meet Black, who has a medical degree and who can prove to *M*'s and to our satisfaction that he has cured every patient who ever consulted him. Moreover, none of Black's cures took more than three years. However, on hearing that some of Black's cures took as long as two years and ten months, *M* says, "Black certainly isn't a physician either."

Finally we introduce *M* to White, who has a medical degree and who has cured every one of his patients in less than six months. When *M* hears that some of White's cures took as long as five and a half months, he is adamant and exclaims, "White— what a ridiculous error to call him a physician!"

At this stage, if not much sooner, all of us would impatiently ask *M:* "What on earth do you mean by 'physician'?" And we would plainly be justified in adding: "Whatever you may mean by 'physician,' in any sense in which we ever use the word, Black and Brown and White are physicians and very excellent ones at that."

Let us return now to Russell's doubt about the sun's rising tomorrow or about what would happen to a man who jumps out of the Empire State Building. Let us consider what Russell would say in reply to the following question: Supposing that the observed confirmatory instances for the theory of gravitation were a million or ten million times as extensive as they now are and that they were drawn from a very much wider field; would we then have a reason to suppose that the man will fall into the street and not move up into the sky? It is obvious that Russell and anybody taking his view would say "No." He would reply that though our *expectation* that the man's body will move in the direction of the street would be even stronger then than it is at present, we would still be without a *reason*.

Next, let us imagine ourselves to be putting the following question to Russell: Supposing the world were such that no accumulation of more than five hundred observed positive instances of a phenomenon has ever been found to be followed by a negative instance; supposing, for instance, that all the chickens who have ever been fed by the same man for 501 days in succession or more are still alive and that all the men, too, are still alive feeding the chickens every day—would the observed confirmations of the law of gravity in that case be a reason to suppose that the man jumping out of the Empire State Building will move in the direction of the street and not in the direction of the sky? I am not quite sure what Russell would say in reply to this question. Let us assume he would once again answer, "No—past experience would not even then ever be a *reason*."

Thirdly, and finally, we have to consider what Russell would say to the following question: Supposing we had explored every corner of the universe with instruments millions of times as fine and accurate as any we now possess and that we had yet failed to discover any Controller of the movements of human bodies— would we then in our predictions about the man jumping out of the Empire State Building be in a better position than the chicken is in predicting its meals? Would our past observations then be a reason for our prediction? Whatever Russell would in fact say to this, it is clear that his remarks concerning the "interesting" doubt about induction require him to answer our question in the negative. He would have to say something like this: "Our *expectation* that the man's body will move in a downward direction will be even stronger than it is now. However, without invoking a non-empirical principle, we shall not *really* be in a better position than the chicken. We should still fail to possess a *reason*."

As in the case of the man who refused to say that Brown, Black, and White were doctors, our natural response to all this will be to turn to Russell and say: "What do you mean by 'being in a better position'? What on earth do you mean by 'a reason'? And, furthermore, why should anybody be interested in a reason in your sense of the word?"

Russell's remarks about the need for a general principle like his principle of induction to serve as major premise in every inductive argument make it clear what he means by a reason: like the Rationalists and Hume (in most places), he means by "reason" a *logically conclusive* reason and by "evidence" *deductively conclusive* evidence. When "reason" is used in this sense, it must be admitted that past observations can never by themselves be a reason for any prediction whatsoever. But "reason" is not used in this sense when, in science or in ordinary life, people claim to have a reason for a prediction.

So far as I can see, there are three different trends in the ordinary usage of "reason for an inductive conclusion," and according to none of them does the word mean "logically conclusive reason." Among the three trends one is much more prominent than the others. It may fitly be called the main sense of the word. According to this main sense, what we mean when we claim that we have a reason for a prediction is that the past observations of this phenomenon or of analogical phenomena are of a certain kind; they are exclusively or predominantly positive, the number of the positive observations is at least fairly large, and they come from extensively varied sets of circumstances. This is of course a very crude formulation. But for the purposes of this article it is, I think, sufficient.[16]

Next, there is a number of trends according to which we mean very much less than this. Occasionally, for instance, we simply mean that it is *reasonable* to infer the inductive conclusion. And

---

[16] I have so far left out one important element in the main sense of "reason for an inductive conclusion." I shall come to that in Section IV. In the meantime this omission will not affect any of my points.

clearly it may be reasonable to infer an inductive conclusion for which we have no reason in the main sense. Thus let us suppose I know that Parker will meet Schroeder in a game in the near future and that it is imperative for me not to suspend my judgment but to come to a conclusion as to who will win. Supposing I know nothing about their present form and nothing also about the type of court on which the match is to be played. All I know is that Parker and Schroeder have in the previous two seasons met six times, Parker scoring four victories to Schroeder's two. In these circumstances it would be reasonable for me to predict that Parker will win and unreasonable to predict that Schroeder will win. Clearly however, in the main sense of the word I have no reason for either prediction.

Again there is a trend according to which any positive instance of a phenomenon is *a* reason for concluding that the next instance of the phenomenon will be positive. Thus in the circumstances described in the preceding paragraph, it would be quite proper to say we have *more reason* for supposing that Parker will win than for predicting Schroeder's victory. It would be quite proper also to say that we have *some reason* for supposing that Schroeder will win. It would be proper to say this even if Schroeder had won only one of the six matches. To all these and similar trends in the ordinary usage of "reason for an inductive conclusion" I shall from now on refer as the second ordinary sense of the word.

There can be no doubt that in both these ordinary senses of the word, we frequently have a reason for an inductive conclusion. In these senses we have an excellent reason for supposing that the man jumping out of the Empire State Building will move in the direction of the street, that the sun will rise tomorrow, and that Stalin will die before the year 2000. The answer to question (1) is therefore a firm and clear "Yes": in many domains we have a multitude of exclusively positive instances coming from extensively different circumstances.

The same is true if "reason" is used in the third ordinary sense. However, I propose to reserve our discussion of that sense for Section V below [not included here]. For the time being it will be convenient and, I think, not at all misleading to speak as if what I have called the main sense is the *only* ordinary sense of "reason for an inductive conclusion."

It should now be clear that, when Russell says that observed instances are never by themselves a reason for an inductive conclusion, he is guilty of an *ignoratio elenchi* by redefinition. His assertion that the premises of an inductive argument never by themselves constitute a *logically conclusive* reason for an inductive conclusion in no way contradicts the commonsense assertion that they frequently constitute a reason *in the ordinary sense of the word*. Russell's definition of "reason" is indeed in one respect not a redefinition, since in certain contexts we do use "reason" to mean "deductively conclusive reason." However, it is a redefinition in that we never in ordinary life use "reason" in Russell's sense when we are talking about inductive arguments.

Moreover, if "reason" means "deductively conclusive reason," Russell's questions are no more genuinely questions than, for example, the sentence "Is a father a female parent?" For, since part of the definition of "inductive inference" is inference from something observed to something unobserved, it is a *contradiction* to say that an inference is both inductive and at the same time in the same respect deductively conclusive. Russell's "interesting" doubt, then, is no more sensible or interesting than the "doubt" whether we shall ever see something invisible or find an object which is a father and also female or an object which is a man but not a human being.

In a similar fashion, Russell's remarks about the future future which we quoted in Section I constitute an *ignoratio elenchi* by redefinition.[17] If the word "future" is used in its ordinary sense in the statement "the future will resemble the past and the present in certain respects," then we have plenty of evidence to support it. For in the ordinary sense of the word, "future" simply means "period which has to the past and the present the relation of happening after it." In its ordinary sense, "future" does *not* mean "period which has to the past and the present the relation of happening after it *and* which can never itself be experienced *as a present*." The period which is referred to by "future" in its ordinary sense may very well one day be experienced as a present.

In the ordinary sense of the word "future," therefore, what Russell calls past futures *are* futures. They are futures in relation to certain other periods which preceded them. Now, the appeal to the fact that past futures resembled past pasts and past presents constitutes excellent inductive evidence for the conclusion that the future will resemble the past and the present. Stated fully, the argument is as follows: a period which has to the past and present the relation of happening after it will resemble the past and the present in certain respects because in the past periods which stood in the same temporal relation to other periods were found to resemble those periods in these respects.

[17] The paragraphs which follow are a summary in my own words of the main point of F. L. Will's delightful article "Will the Future be like the Past?" (*Mind*, 1947).

It should be emphasized that in the conclusion of this argument "future" means "future future," as that phrase would normally be understood. It refers to a period which by the time at which the statement is made has not yet been experienced, that is, has not yet become a present or a past.

The appeal to the resemblance between past futures and past pasts and presents is not to the point only if in the sentence, "The future will resemble the past and the present," the word "future" means "period which has to the present the relation of occurring after it *and* which can never be experienced as a present." In that case, of course past futures are not really futures. For, when they were experienced they were experienced as presents. However, anybody who in ordinary life or in science says or implies that the future will resemble the past and the present does not use "future" in this sense. He means to assert something about a future which may one day be experienced as a present.

If Russell had answered in the affirmative any of the three questions which we imagined ourselves to be addressing to him, his question (1) would be a genuine question in the sense that it could then not be disposed of by an examination of definitions alone. But even then Russell would have been guilty of *ignoratio elenchi* by high redefinition. For in order to have a reason, in the ordinary sense of the word, for inferring that the next instance of a certain phenomenon is positive, it is not necessary to observe all the positive and negative necessary conditions for the occurrence of this instance. Nor is it necessary that the collection of positive observed instances should be larger or taken from more extensively different circumstances than many we actually have. Nor, finally, is it necessary that breakdowns should never have occurred in *any* domain. All that is necessary in this connection is that there should have been no breakdowns in the same domain. Or if any did occur in the same domain, they must have proved capable of correlation with certain special features which are known not to be present in the subject of the prediction.

Anybody who takes the trouble to observe the ordinary usage of the word "reason" in connection with inductive arguments can easily check up on these claims.

It may be interesting to return for a moment to the case of the chicken which finally had its neck wrung. If we had explored every corner of the universe with wonderfully fine instruments and failed to discover a Controller of human movements, then in any ordinary sense of "being in a better position" we should, undoubtedly, be in a better position in the case of the man jumping out of the Empire State Building than the chicken in regard to its meals. If Russell even then denied that we are in a better position, he is surely using the phrase "being in a better position" in a strange sense. Or else he is asserting a very plain falsehood. For to say that possession of one set of observed facts, say P, puts one in a better position with regard to a certain inductive conclusion, say c, than possession of another set of observed facts, say Q, simply means that P is a reason for c while Q is not, or that P is a better reason than Q.

Moreover, even without having explored every corner of the universe, we *are* in a very much better position in the case of predicting the sun's rising or the movement of a man jumping from the Empire State Building than the chicken is regarding its meals. The truth is that Russell's analogy, although it is not wholly pointless, is very weak indeed. Its only merit consists in bringing out the fact that neither we nor the chicken have explored every corner of the universe. On the other hand, there are two important differences which Russell obscures when he says that even in the case of our most trusted scientific theories we may be in no better a position than the chicken. Firstly, the number of observed instances supporting our prediction in a case like the man's jumping from the Empire State Building is obviously much greater than the number of positive instances observed by the chicken. And secondly, although we cannot definitely say that there is nowhere a Controller of human motions, we certainly have no reason whatsoever to suppose that one exists. We have no reason whatsoever to suppose that a living individual, in any ordinary sense of "control," controls the movements of human beings who jump out of a house. The chicken, on the other hand, if it knows anything, knows that it depends for its meals on another living object.

Let us now turn to question (2): Is there any number, n, of observed positive instances of a phenomenon which affords evidence that the $n + 1$st instance will also be positive? I have already mentioned the familiar fact that scientists as well as ordinary people of a certain level of intelligence do not rely for their inductive conclusions on the number of observed positive instances exclusively. However, it will be easier to discuss the question before us if we proceed on the assumption that according to commonsense the strength of the past experience as evidence depends on the number of observed positive instances and on nothing else. All important points can be made more easily if we proceed on this assumption.

Now, in two senses the answer to question (2) must be admitted to be a clear "No." Firstly, even if there were in every domain or in some domains a number of observed positive instances which constitutes the dividing line between evidence and non-evidence or, as it is more commonly expressed, between sufficient and insufficient evidence, there is no reason whatsoever to suppose that the number would be the same for different domains. There is no reason to suppose that in the domain of animal learning, for example, the number is the same as in the domain of the movements of the heavenly bodies. But, secondly, there is no such number in *any* domain. For we are here clearly faced with a case of what is sometimes called "continuous variation." There is no more a number dividing sufficient from insufficient evidence than there is a number dividing bald people from those who are not bald or poor people from people who are not poor.

These facts, however, imply nothing against commonsense. For, from the fact that there is no rigid division between sufficient and insufficient evidence it does not follow that there are no cases of sufficient evidence. From the fact that there is no number which constitutes the borderline between adequate collections of positive instances and those which are not adequate it does not follow that no number of positive instances is adequate. Although we cannot point to a number which divides bald people from people who are not bald, we can without any hesitation say that a man without a single hair on his head is bald while one with a million hairs on his head is not bald.

Furthermore, just as we can say about many people that they are bald and about many others that they are not bald, although we have not counted the number of hairs on their heads, and just as we can say that Rockefeller is rich, although we cannot even approximately say what is the dollar-equivalent of his total possessions, so we can very often say *that* a number of observed instances constitutes sufficient evidence, although we cannot say *what* this number is. The number of instances supporting the theory of gravitation which human beings have observed is, for example, more than sufficient evidence—in any ordinary sense of the word— for supposing that the man jumping out of the Empire State Building will move in a downward direction. But nobody knows what this number is. Human beings simply do not bother to keep records of all instances which confirm the law of gravity.

8

Religious Language
and the Existence of God

The twentieth-century scene in theology and philosophy of religion has been an exciting and rapidly changing one, marked by abrupt changes of styles in doing theology, and far-reaching criticisms in the philosophy of religion. The articles by Paul Tillich, a refugee from Hitler's Germany and late professor of theology at Harvard and the University of Chicago, and by Huston Smith, professor of religion at M.I.T., stress some of the contemporary background and frame of reference in religion. The articles by Antony Flew, British analytical philosopher, and John Hick, British theologian, stress the linguistic frame of reference in which contemporary philosophy of religion is done. Flew's contribution follows up the work of the logical positivists in suggesting that religious discourse is not empirical, in other words, that it is not facts or observations about which theists and atheists disagree, but about the sense or nonsense of words. Hick, on the other hand, argues that the existence of God is indeed an empirical question and that there is a sense in which people who say that God exists do know what would be evidence to verify their belief. If Flew is right, it is in principle impossible to say what would count as evidence for religious beliefs.

The readings on the proofs of the existence of God are a debate between Father F. C. Copleston, one of the most respected Catholic historians of philosophy and commentator on contemporary philosophy, and Bertrand Russell, and a proof by Richard Taylor, contemporary American philosopher.

The Religious Attitude in an Age of Science

Paul Tillich

Paul Tillich (1886–1965), as a Protestant chaplain in the Kaiser's army, was deeply aware of the cultural and religious malaise of the modern world. Successor of Max Scheler at Frankfurt, he was expelled by the Nazis and fled to New York where he was given a teaching post in the Union Theological Seminary. Later he taught at Harvard and the University of Chicago. A theologian who was also a leader in existentialist philosophy, his main work is the three-volume Systematic Theology.

Every observer of our Western civilization is aware of the fact that something has happened to religion. It especially strikes the observer of the American scene. Everywhere he finds symptoms of what one has called religious revival, or more modestly, the revival of interest in religion. He finds them in the churches with their rapidly increasing membership. He finds them in the mushroom-like growth of sects. He finds them on college campuses and in the theological faculties of universities. Most conspicuously, he finds them in the tremendous success of men like Billy Graham and Norman Vincent Peale, who attract masses of people Sunday after Sunday, meeting after meeting. The facts cannot be denied, but how should they be interpreted? It is my intention to show that these facts must be seen as expressions of the predicament of Western man in the second half of the twentieth century. But I would even go a step further. I believe that the predicament of man in our period gives us also an important insight into the

Reprinted by permission of the estate of Paul Tillich from *The Saturday Evening Post*, June 14, 1958, p. 29.

predicament of man generally—at all times and in all parts of the earth.

There are many analyses of man and society in our time. Most of them show important traits in the picture, but few of them succeed in giving a general key to our present situation. Although it is not easy to find such a key, I shall attempt it and, in so doing, will make an assertion which may be somewhat mystifying at first hearing. The decisive element in the predicament of Western man in our period is his loss of the dimension of depth. Of course, "dimension of depth" is a metaphor. It is taken from the spatial realm and applied to man's spiritual life. What does it mean?

It means that man has lost an answer to the question: What is the meaning of life? Where do we come from, where do we go to? What shall we do, what should we become in the short stretch between birth and death? Such questions are not answered or even asked if the "dimension of depth" is lost. And this is precisely what has happened to man in our period of history. He has lost the courage to ask such questions with an infinite seriousness—as former generations did—and he has lost the courage to receive answers to these questions, wherever they may come from.

I suggest that we call the dimension of depth the religious dimension in man's nature. Being religious means asking passionately the question of the meaning of our existence and being willing to receive answers, even if the answers hurt. Such an idea of religion makes religion universally human, but it certainly differs from what is usually called religion. It does not describe religion as the belief in the existence of gods or one God, and as a set of activities and institutions for the sake of relating oneself to these beings in thought, devotion, and obedience. No one can deny that the religions which have appeared in history are religions in this sense. Nevertheless, religion in its innermost nature is more than religion in this narrower sense. It is the state of being concerned about one's own being and being universally.

There are many people who are ultimately concerned in this way who feel far removed, however, from religion in the narrower sense, and therefore from every historical religion. It often happens that such people take the question of the meaning of their life infinitely seriously and reject any historical religion just for this reason. They feel that the concrete religions fail to express their profound concern adequately. They are religious while rejecting the religions. It is this experience which forces us to distinguish the meaning of religion as living in the dimension of depth from particular expressions of one's ultimate concern in the symbols and institutions of a concrete religion. If we now turn to the concrete analysis of the religious situation of our time, it is obvious that our key must be the basic meaning of religion and not any particular religion, not even Christianity. What does this key disclose about the predicament of man in our period?

If we define religion as the state of being grasped by an infinite concern, we must say: Man in our time has lost such infinite concern. And the resurgence of religion is nothing but a desperate and mostly futile attempt to regain what has been lost.

How did the dimension of depth become lost? Like any important event, it has many causes, but certainly not the one which one hears often mentioned from ministers' pulpits and evangelists' platforms, namely, that a widespread impiety of modern man is responsible. Modern man is neither more pious nor more impious than man in any other period. The loss of the dimension of depth is caused by the relation of man to his world and to himself in our period, the period in which nature is being subjected scientifically and technically to the control of man. In this period, life in the dimension of depth is replaced by life in the horizontal dimension. The driving forces of the industrial society of which we are a part go ahead horizontally and not vertically. In popular terms this is expressed in phrases like "better and better," "bigger and bigger," "more and more." One should not disparage the feeling which lies behind such speech. Man is right in feeling that he is able to know and transform the world he encounters without a foreseeable limit. He can go ahead in all directions without a definite boundary.

A most expressive symbol of this attitude of going ahead in the horizontal dimension is the breaking through of the space which is controlled by the gravitational power of the earth into the world-space. It is interesting that one calls this world-space simply "space" and speaks, for instance, of space travel, as if every trip were not travel into space. Perhaps one feels that the true nature of space has been discovered only through our entering into in-definite world-space. In any case, the predominance of the horizontal dimension over the dimension of depth has been immensely increased by the opening up of the space beyond the space of the earth.

If we now ask what does man do and seek if he goes ahead in the horizontal dimension, the answer is difficult. Sometimes one is inclined to say that the mere movement ahead without an end, the intoxication with speeding forward without limits, is what satisfies him. But this answer is by no means sufficient. For on his way into space and time man changes the world he encounters. And the changes made by him change himself. He transforms everything he encounters into a tool; and in doing so, he himself becomes a tool. But if he asks, a tool for what, there is no answer.

One does not need to look far beyond everyone's daily experience in order to find examples to describe this predicament. Indeed our daily life in office and home, in cars and airplanes, at parties and conferences, while reading magazines and watching television, while looking at advertisements and hearing radio, are in themselves continuous examples of a life which has lost the dimension of depth. It runs ahead; every moment is filled with something which must be done or seen or said or planned. But no one can experience depth without stopping and becoming aware of himself. Only if he has moments in which he does not care about what comes next can he experience the meaning of this moment here and now and ask himself about the meaning of his life. As long as the preliminary, transitory concerns are not silenced, no matter how interesting and valuable and important they may be, the voice of the ultimate concern cannot be heard. This is the deepest root of the loss of the dimension of depth in our period—the loss of religion in its basic and universal meaning.

If the dimension of depth is lost, the symbols in which life in this dimension has expressed itself must also disappear. I am speaking of the great symbols of the historical religions in our Western world, of Judaism and Christianity. The reason that the religious symbols become lost is not primarily scientific criticism, but it is a complete misunderstanding of their meaning; and only because of this misunderstanding was scientific critique able, and even justified, in attacking them. The first step toward the nonreligion of the Western world was made by religion itself. When it defended its great symbols, not as symbols, but as literal stories, it had already lost the battle. In doing so, the theologians (and today many religious laymen) helped to transfer the powerful expressions of the dimension of depth into objects or happenings on the horizontal plane. There the symbols lose their power and meaning and become an easy prey to physical, biological, and historical attack.

If the symbol of creation which points to the divine ground of everything is transferred to the horizontal plane, it becomes a story of events in a removed past for which there is no evidence, but which contradicts every piece of scientific evidence. If the symbol of the Fall of Man, which points to the tragic estrangement of man and his world from their true being is transferred to the horizontal plane, it becomes a story of a human couple a few thousand years ago in what is now present-day Iraq. One of the most profound psychological descriptions of the general human predicament becomes an absurdity on the horizontal plane. If the symbols of the Saviour and the salvation through Him which point to the healing power in history and personal life are transferred to the horizontal plane, they become stories of a half-divine being coming from a heavenly place and returning to it. Obviously, in this form, they have no meaning whatsoever for people whose view of the universe is determined by scientific astronomy.

If the idea of God (and the symbols applied to Him) which expresses man's ultimate concern is transferred to the horizontal plane, God becomes a being among others whose existence or non-existence is a matter of inquiry. Nothing, perhaps, is more symptomatic of the loss of the dimension of depth than the permanent discussion about the existence or nonexistence of God—a discussion in which both sides are equally wrong, because the discussion itself is wrong and possible only after the loss of the dimension of depth.

When in this way man has deprived himself of the dimension of depth and the symbols expressing it, he then becomes a part of the horizontal plane. He loses his self and becomes a thing among things. He becomes an element in the process of manipulated production and manipulated consumption. This is now a matter of public knowledge. We have become aware of the degree to which everyone in our social structure is managed, even if one knows it and even if one belongs himself to the managing group. The influence of the gang mentality on adolescents, of the corporation's demands on the executives, of the conditioning of everyone by public communication, by propaganda and advertising under the guidance of motivation research, and so forth, have all been described in many books and articles.

Under these pressures, man can hardly escape the fate of becoming a thing among the things he produces, a bundle of conditioned reflexes without a free, deciding, and responsible self. The immense mechanism, set up by man to produce objects for his use, transforms man himself into an object used by the same mechanism of production and consumption.

But man has not ceased to be man. He resists this fate anxiously, desperately, courageously. He asks the question, for what? And he realizes that there is no answer. He becomes aware of the emptiness which is covered by the continuous movement ahead and the production of means for ends which become means again without an ultimate end. Without knowing what has happened to him, he feels that he has lost the meaning of life, the dimension of depth.

Out of this awareness the religious question arises and religious answers are received or rejected. Therefore, in order to describe the contemporary attitude toward religion, we must first point to the places where the awareness of the predicament of Western man in our period is most sharply expressed. These places are the great art, literature, and, partly at least, the philosophy of our time. It is both the subject matter and the style of these creations which show the passionate and often tragic struggle about the meaning of life in a period in which man has lost the dimension of depth. This art, literature, philosophy is not religious in the narrower sense of the word; but it asks the religious question more radically and more profoundly than most directly religious expressions of our time.

It is the religious question which is asked when the novelist describes a man who tries in vain to reach the only place which could solve the problem of his life, or a man who disintegrates under the memory of a guilt which persecutes him, or a man who never had a real self and is pushed by his fate without resistance to death, or a man who experiences a profound disgust of everything he encounters.

It is the religious question which is asked when the poet opens up the horror and the fascination of the demonic regions of his soul, or if he leads us into the deserts and empty places of our being, or if he shows the physical and moral mud under the surface of life, or if he sings the song of transitoriness, giving words to the ever-present anxiety of our hearts.

It is the religious question which is asked when the playwright shows the illusion of a life in a ridiculous symbol, or if he lets the emptiness of a life's work end in self-destruction, or if he confronts us with the inescapable bondage to mutual hate and guilt, or if he leads us into the dark cellar of lost hopes and slow disintegration.

It is the religious question which is asked when the painter breaks the visible surface into pieces, then reunites them into a great picture which has little similarity with the world at which we normally look, but which expresses our anxiety and our courage to face reality.

It is the religious question which is asked when the architect, in creating office buildings or churches, removes the trimmings taken over from past styles because they cannot be considered an honest expression of our own period. He prefers the seeming poverty of a purpose-determined style to the deceptive richness of imitated styles of the past. He knows that he gives no final answer, but he does give an honest answer.

The philosophy of our time shows the same hiddenly religious traits. It is divided into two main schools of thought, the analytic and the existentialist. The former tries to analyze logical and lin-

guistic forms which are always used and which underlie all scientific research. One may compare them with the painters who
dissolve the natural forms of bodies into cubes, planes, and lines;
or with those architects who want the structural "bones" of their
buildings to be conspicuously visible and not hidden by covering
features. This self-restriction produces the almost monastic poverty and seriousness of this philosophy. It is religious—without
any contact with religion in its method—by exercising the humility
of "learned ignorance."

In contrast to this school, the existentialist philosophers have
much to say about the problems of human existence. They bring
into rational concepts what the writers and poets, the painters and
architects, are expressing in their particular material. What they
express is the human predicament in time and space, in anxiety
and guilt and the feeling of meaninglessness. From Pascal in the
seventeenth century to Heidegger and Sartre in our time, philosophers have emphasized the contrast between human dignity and
human misery. And by doing so, they have raised the religious
question. Some have tried to answer the question they have asked.
But if they did so, they turned back to past traditions and offered
to our time that which does not fit our time. Is it possible for our
time to receive answers which are born out of our time?

Answers given today are in danger of strengthening the present
situation and with it the questions to which they are supposed to
be the answers. This refers to some of the previously mentioned
major representatives of the so-called resurgence of religion, as,
for instance, the evangelist Billy Graham and the counseling and
healing minister, Norman Vincent Peale. Against the validity of
the answers given by the former, one must say that, in spite of his
personal integrity, his propagandistic methods and his primitive
theological fundamentalism fall short of what is needed to give an
answer to the religious question of our period. In spite of all his
seriousness, he does not take the radical questions of our period
seriously.

The effect that Norman Peale has on large groups of people is
rooted in the fact that he confirms the situation which he is supposed to help overcome. He heals people with the purpose of
making them fit again for the demands of the competitive and
conformist society in which we are living. He helps them to become adapted to the situation which is characterized by the loss
of the dimension of depth. Therefore, his advice is valid on this
level; but it is the validity of this level that is the true religious
question of our time. And this question he neither raises nor
answers.

In many cases the increase of church membership and interest in religious activities does not mean much more than the religious consecration of a state of things in which the religious dimension has been lost. It is the desire to participate in activities which are socially strongly approved and give internal and a certain amount of external security. This is not necessarily bad, but it certainly is not an answer to the religious question of our period.

Is there an answer? There is always an answer, but the answer may not be available to us. We may be too deeply steeped in the predicament out of which the question arises to be able to answer it. To acknowledge this is certainly a better way toward a real answer than to bar the way to it by deceptive answers. And it may be that in this attitude the real answer (within available limits) is given. The real answer to the question of how to regain the dimension of depth is not given by increased church membership or church attendance, nor by conversion or healing experiences. But it is given by the awareness that we have lost the decisive dimension of life, the dimension of depth, and that there is no easy way of getting it back. Such awareness is in itself a state of being grasped by that which is symbolized in the term "dimension of depth." He who realizes that he is separated from the ultimate source of meaning shows by this realization that he is not only separated but also reunited. And this is just our situation. What we need above all—and partly have—is the radical realization of our predicament, without trying to cover it up by secular or religious ideologies. The revival of religious interest would be a creative power in our culture if it would develop into a movement of search for the lost dimension of depth.

This does not mean that the traditional religious symbols should be dismissed. They certainly have lost their meaning in the literalistic form into which they have been distorted, thus producing the critical reaction against them. But they have not lost their genuine meaning, namely, of answering the question which is implied in man's very existence in powerful, revealing, and saving symbols. If the resurgence of religion would produce a new understanding of the symbols of the past and their relevance for our situation, instead of premature and deceptive answers, it would become a creative factor in our culture and a saving factor for many who live in estrangement, anxiety, and despair. The religious answer has always the character of "in spite of." In spite of the loss of dimension of depth, its power is present, and most present in those who are aware of the loss and are striving to regain it with ultimate seriousness.

The Religious
Significance of Drugs

Huston Smith

*Huston Smith (1919–   ), Professor of Philosophy, Massachu-
setts Institute of Technology, is best known as a scholar of world
religions and of religious experience.*

Until six months ago, if I picked up my phone in the Cambridge area and dialed KISS-BIG, a voice would answer, "If-if."
These were coincidences: KISS-BIG happened to be the letter
equivalents of an arbitrarily assigned telephone number, and
I.F.I.F. represented the initials of an organization with the improbable name of the International Federation for Internal Freedom. But the coincidences were apposite to the point of being
poetic. "Kiss big" caught the euphoric, manic, life-embracing attitude that characterized this most publicized of the organizations
formed to explore the newly synthesized consciousness-changing
substances; the organization itself was surely one of the "iffy-est"
phenomena to appear on our social and intellectual scene in some
time. It produced the first firings in Harvard's history, an ulti-
matum to get out of Mexico in five days, and "the miracle of Marsh
Chapel," in which, during a two-and-one-half-hour Good Friday
service, ten theological students and professors ingested psilocybin and were visited by what they generally reported to be the
deepest religious experiences of their lives.

Despite the last of these phenomena and its numerous if less

Reprinted by permission of the author and the publisher from the *Journal
of Philosophy*, Vol. LXI, No. 18 (October 1, 1964), pp. 517–530. This is an
emended version of a paper presented to the Woodrow Wilson Society,
Princeton University, on May 16, 1964.

263

dramatic parallels, students of religion appear by and large to be dismissing the psychedelic drugs that have sprung to our attention in the '60s as having little religious relevance. The position taken in one of the most forward-looking volumes of theological essays to have appeared in recent years—*Soundings,* edited by A. R. Vidler[1]—accepts R. C. Zaehner's *Mysticism Sacred and Profane* as having "fully examined and refuted" the religious claims for mescalin which Aldous Huxley sketched in *The Doors of Perception.* The closing of the case strikes me as premature, for it looks as if the drugs have light to throw on the history of religion, the phenomenology of religion, the philosophy of religion, and the practice of the religious life itself.

Drugs and Religion
Viewed Historically

In his trial-and-error life explorations, man almost everywhere has stumbled upon connections between vegetables (eaten or brewed) and actions (yogi breathing exercises, whirling-dervish dances, flagellations) that alter states of consciousness. From the psychopharmacological standpoint we now understand these states to be the products of changes in brain chemistry. From the sociological perspective we see that they tend to be connected in some way with religion. If we discount the wine used in Christian communion services, the instances closest to us in time and space are the peyote of The Native American [Indian] Church and Mexico's 2000-year-old "sacred mushrooms," the latter rendered in Aztec as "God's Flesh"—striking parallel to "the body of our Lord" in the Christian eucharist. Beyond these neighboring instances lie the *soma* of the Hindus, the *haoma* and hemp of the Zoroastrians, the Dionysus of the Greeks who "everywhere . . . taught men the culture of the vine and the mysteries of his worship and everywhere [was] accepted as a god,"[2] the *benzoin* of Southeast Asia, Zen's tea whose fifth cup purifies and whose sixth

[1] *Soundings: Essays concerning Christian Understandings,* A. R. Vidler, ed. (Cambridge: University Press, 1962). The statement cited appears on page 72, in H. A. Williams's essay on "Theology and Self-awareness."

[2] Edith Hamilton, *Mythology* (New York: Mentor, 1953), p. 55.

"calls to the realm of the immortals,"[3] the *pituri* of the Australian aborigines, and probably the mystic *kykeon* that was eaten and drunk at the climactic close of the sixth day of the Eleusinian mysteries.[4] There is no need to extend the list, as a reasonably complete account is available in Philippe de Félice's comprehensive study of the subject, *Poisons sacrés, ivresses divines*.

More interesting than the fact that consciousness-changing devices have been linked with religion is the possibility that they actually initiated many of the religious perspectives which, taking root in history, continued after their psychedelic origins were forgotten. Bergson saw the first movement of Hindus and Greeks toward "dynamic religion" as associated with the "divine rapture" found in intoxicating beverages;[5] more recently Robert Graves, Gordon Wasson, and Alan Watts have suggested that most religions arose from such chemically induced theophanies. Mary Barnard is the most explicit proponent of this thesis. "Which . . . was more likely to happen first," she asks,[6] "the spontaneously generated idea of an afterlife in which the disembodied soul, liberated from the restrictions of time and space, experiences eternal bliss, or the accidental discovery of hallucinogenic plants that give a sense of euphoria, dislocate the center of consciousness, and distort time and space, making them balloon outward in greatly expanded vistas?" Her own answer is that "the [latter] experience might have had . . . an almost explosive effect on the largely dormant minds of men, causing them to think of things they had never thought of before. This, if you like, is direct revelation." Her use of the subjunctive "might" renders this formulation of her answer equivocal, but she concludes her essay on a note that is completely unequivocal: "Looking at the matter coldly, unintoxicated and unentranced, I am willing to prophesy that fifty theobotanists working for fifty years would make the current theories concerning the origins of much mythology and theology as out-of-date as pre-Copernican astronomy."

This is an important hypothesis—one which must surely engage the attention of historians of religion for some time to come. But as I am concerned here only to spot the points at which the

[3] Quoted in Alan Watts, *The Spirit of Zen* (New York: Grove Press, 1958), p. 110.

[4] George Mylonas, *Eleusis and the Eleusinian Mysteries* (Princeton, N.J.: Princeton Univ. Press, 1961), p. 284.

[5] *Two Sources of Morality and Religion* (New York: Holt, 1935), pp. 206–212.

[6] "The God in the Flowerpot," *The American Scholar* 32, 4 (Autumn, 1963): 584, 586.

drugs erupt onto the field of serious religious study, not to ride the geysers to whatever heights, I shall not pursue Miss Barnard's thesis. Having located what appears to be the crux of the historical question, namely the extent to which drugs not merely duplicate or simulate theologically sponsored experiences but generate or shape theologies themselves, I turn to phenomenology.

Drugs and Religion
Viewed Phenomenologically

Phenomenology attempts a careful description of human experience. The question the drugs pose for the phenomenology of religion, therfore, is whether the experiences they induce differ from religious experiences reached naturally, and if so, how.

Even the Bible notes that chemically induced psychic states bear *some* resemblance to religious ones. Peter had to appeal to a circumstantial criterion—the early hour of the day—to defend those who were caught up in the Pentecostal experience against the charge that they were merely drunk: "These men are not drunk, as you suppose, since it is only the third hour of the day" (Acts 2:15); and Paul initiates the comparison when he admonishes the Ephesians not to "get drunk with wine . . . but [to] be filled with the spirit" (Ephesians 5:18). Are such comparisons, paralleled in the accounts of virtually every religion, superficial? How far can they be pushed?

Not all the way, students of religion have thus far insisted. With respect to the new drugs, Prof. R. C. Zaehner has drawn the line emphatically. "The importance of Huxley's *Doors of Perception*," he writes, "is that in it the author clearly makes the claim that what he experienced under the influence of mescalin is closely comparable to a genuine mystical experience. If he is right, . . . the conclusions . . . are alarming."[7] Zaehner thinks that Huxley is not right, but I fear that it is Zaehner who is mistaken.

There are, of course, innumerable drug experiences that have no religious feature; they can be sensual as readily as spiritual, trivial as readily as transforming, capricious as readily as sacramental. If there is one point about which every student of the drugs agrees, it is that there is no such thing as the drug experi-

[7] *Mysticism, Sacred and Profane* (New York: Oxford, 1961), p. 12.

ence *per se*—no experience that the drugs, as it were, merely secrete. Every experience is a mix of three ingredients: drug, set (the psychological make-up of the individual), and setting (the social and physical environment in which it is taken). But given the right set and setting, the drugs can induce religious experiences indistinguishable from experiences that occur spontaneously. Nor need set and setting be exceptional. The way the statistics are currently running, it looks as if from one-fourth to one-third of the general population will have religious experiences if they take the drugs under naturalistic conditions, meaning by this, conditions in which the researcher supports the subject but does not try to influence the direction his experience will take. Among subjects who have strong religious inclinations to begin with, the proportion of those having religious experiences jumps to three-fourths. If they take the drugs in settings that are religious too, the ratio soars to nine in ten.

How do we know that the experiences these people have really are religious? We can begin with the fact that they say they are. The "one-fourth to one-third of the general population" figure is drawn from two sources. Ten months after they had had their experiences, 24 per cent of the 194 subjects in a study by the California psychiatrist Oscar Janiger characterized their experiences as having been religious.[8] Thirty-two per cent of the 74 subjects in Ditman and Hayman's study reported, looking back on their LSD experience, that it looked as if it had been "very much" or "quite a bit" a religious experience; 42 per cent checked as true the statement that they "were left with a greater awareness of God, or a higher power, or ultimate reality."[9] The statement that three-fourths of subjects having religious "sets" will have religious experiences comes from the reports of sixty-nine religious professionals who took the drugs while the Harvard project was in progress.[10]

In the absence of (a) a single definition of religious experience acceptable to psychologists of religion generally and (b) foolproof ways of ascertaining whether actual experiences exemplify any definition, I am not sure there is any better way of telling whether the experiences of the 333 men and women involved in the above studies were religious than by noting whether they

[8] Quoted in William H. McGlothlin, "Long-lasting Effects of LSD on Certain Attitudes in Normals," printed for private distribution by the RAND Corporation, May, 1962, p. 16.

[9] *Ibid.*, pp. 45, 46.

[10] Timothy Leary, "The Religious Experience: Its Production and Interpretation," *The Psychedelic Review*, 1, 3 (1964): 325.

seemed so to them. But if more rigorous methods are preferred, they exist; they have been utilized, and they confirm the conviction of the man in the street that drug experiences can indeed be religious. In his doctoral study at Harvard University, Walter Pahnke worked out a typology of religious experience (in this instance of the mystical variety) based on the classic cases of mystical experiences as summarized in Walter Stace's *Mysticism and Philosophy*. He then administered psilocybin to ten theology students and professors in the setting of a Good Friday service. The drug was given "double-blind," meaning that neither Dr. Pahnke nor his subjects knew which ten were getting psilocybin and which ten placebos to constitute a control group. Subsequently the reports the subjects wrote of their experiences were laid successively before three college-graduate housewives who, without being informed about the nature of the study, were asked to rate each statement as to the degree (strong, moderate, slight, or none) to which it exemplified each of the nine traits of mystical experience enumerated in the typology of mysticism worked out in advance. When the test of significance was applied to their statistics, it showed that "those subjects who received psilocybin experienced phenomena which were indistinguishable from, if not identical with . . . the categories defined by our typology of mysticism."[11]

With the thought that the reader might like to test his own powers of discernment on the question being considered, I insert here a simple test I gave to a group of Princeton students following a recent discussion sponsored by the Woodrow Wilson Society:

> Below are accounts of two religious experiences. One occurred under the influence of drugs, one without their influence. Check the one you think *was* drug-induced.
>
> I
>
> Suddenly I burst into a vast, new, indescribably wonderful universe. Although I am writing this over a year later, the thrill of the surprise and amazement, the awesomeness of the revelation, the engulfment in an overwhelming feeling-wave of gratitude and blessed wonderment, are as fresh, and the memory of the experience is as vivid, as if it had happened five minutes ago. And yet to concoct anything by way of description that would even hint

[11] "Drugs and Mysticism: An Analysis of the Relationship between Psychedelic Drugs and the Mystical Consciousness," a thesis presented to the Committee on Higher Degrees in History and Philosophy of Religion, Harvard University, June 1963.

at the magnitude, the sense of ultimate reality . . . this seems such an impossible task. The knowledge which has infused and affected every aspect of my life came instantaneously and with such complete force of certainty that it was impossible, then or since, to doubt its validity.

II

All at once, without warning of any kind, I found myself wrapped in a flame-colored cloud. For an instant I thought of fire . . . the next, I knew that the fire was within myself. Directly afterward there came upon me a sense of exultation, of immense joyousness accompanied or immediately followed by an intellectual illumination impossible to describe. Among other things, I did not merely come to believe, but I saw that the universe is not composed of dead matter, but is, on the contrary, a living Presence; I became conscious in myself of eternal life. . . . I saw that all men are immortal: that the cosmic order is such that without any peradventure all things work together for the good of each and all; that the foundation principle of the world . . . is what we call love, and that the happiness of each and all is in the long run absolutely certain.

On the occasion referred to, twice as many students (46) answered incorrectly as answered correctly (23). I bury the correct answer in a footnote to preserve the reader's opportunity to test himself.[12]

Why, in the face of this considerable evidence, does Zaehner hold that drug experiences cannot be authentically religious? There appear to be three reasons:

1. His own experience was "utterly trivial." This of course proves that not all drug experiences are religious; it does not prove that no drug experiences are religious.

2. He thinks the experiences of others that appear religious to them are not truly so. Zaehner distinguishes three kinds of mysticism: nature mysticism, in which the soul is united with the natural world; monistic mysticism, in which the soul merges with an impersonal absolute; and theism, in which the soul confronts the living, personal God. He concedes that drugs can induce the first two species of mysticism, but not its supreme instance, the theistic. As proof, he analyzes Huxley's experience as recounted in

[12] The first account is quoted anonymously in "The Issue of the Consciousness-expanding Drugs," *Main Currents in Modern Thought*, 20, 1 (September–October, 1963): 10–11. The second experience was that of Dr. R. M. Bucke, the author of *Cosmic Consciousness*, as quoted in William James, *The Varieties of Religious Experience* (New York: Modern Library, 1902), pp. 390–391. The former experience occurred under the influence of drugs; the latter did not.

The Doors of Perception to show that it produced at best a blend of nature and monistic mysticism. Even if we were to accept Zaehner's evaluation of the three forms of mysticism, Huxley's case, and indeed Zaehner's entire book, would prove only that not every mystical experience induced by the drugs is theistic. Insofar as Zaehner goes beyond this to imply that drugs do not and cannot induce theistic mysticism, he not only goes beyond the evidence but proceeds in the face of it. James Slotkin reports that the peyote Indians "see visions, which may be of Christ Himself. Sometimes they hear the voice of the Great Spirit. Sometimes they become aware of the presence of God and of those personal shortcomings which must be corrected if they are to do His will."[13] And G. M. Carstairs, reporting on the use of psychedelic *bhang* in India, quotes a Brahmin as saying, "It gives good bhakti. . . . You get a very good bhakti with bhang," *bhakti* being precisely Hinduism's theistic variant.[14]

3. There is a third reason why Zaehner might doubt that drugs can induce genuinely mystical experiences. Zaehner is a Roman Catholic, and Roman Catholic doctrine teaches that mystical rapture is a gift of grace and as such can never be reduced to man's control. This may be true; certainly the empirical evidence cited does not preclude the possibility of a genuine ontological or theological difference between natural and drug-induced religious experiences. At this point, however, we are considering phenomenology rather than ontology, description rather than interpretation, and on this level there is no difference. Descriptively, drug experiences cannot be distinguished from their natural religious counterpart. When the current philosophical authority on mysticism, W. T. Stace, was asked whether the drug experience is similar to the mystical experience, he answered, "It's not a matter of its being *similar* to mystical experience; it *is* mystical experience."

What we seem to be witnessing in Zaehner's *Mysticism Sacred and Profane* is a reenactment of the age-old pattern in the conflict between science and religion. Whenever a new controversy arises, religion's first impulse is to deny the disturbing evidence science has produced. Seen in perspective, Zaehner's refusal to admit that drugs can induce experiences descriptively indistinguishable from those which are spontaneously religious is the cur-

---

[13] James S. Slotkin, *Peyote Religion* (New York: Free Press of Glencoe, 1956).

[14] "Daru and Bhang," *Quarterly Journal of the Study of Alcohol*, 15 (1954): 229.

rent counterpart of the seventeenth-century theologians' refusal to look through Galileo's telescope or, when they did, their persistence on dismissing what they saw as machinations of the devil. When the fact that drugs can trigger religious experiences becomes incontrovertible, discussion will move to the more difficult question of how this new fact is to be interpreted. The latter question leads beyond phenomenology into philosophy.

Drugs and Religion
Viewed Philosophically

Why do people reject evidence? Because they find it threatening, we may suppose. Theologians are not the only professionals to utilize this mode of defense. In his *Personal Knowledge*,[15] Michael Polanyi recounts the way the medical profession ignored such palpable facts as the painless amputation of human limbs, performed before their own eyes in hundreds of successive cases, concluding that the subjects were imposters who were either deluding their physicians or colluding with them. One physician, Esdaile, carried out about 300 major operations painlessly under mesmeric trance in India, but neither in India nor in Great Britain could he get medical journals to print accounts of his work. Polanyi attributes this closed-mindedness to "lack of a conceptual framework in which their discoveries could be separated from specious and untenable admixtures."

The "untenable admixture" in the fact that psychotomimetic drugs can induce religious experience is its apparent implicate: that religious disclosures are no more veridical than psychotic ones. For religious skeptics, this conclusion is obviously not untenable at all; it fits in beautifully with their thesis that *all* religion is at heart an escape from reality. Psychotics avoid reality by retiring into dream worlds of make-believe; what better evidence that religious visionaries do the same than the fact that identical changes in brain chemistry produce both states of mind? Had not Marx already warned us that religion is the "opiate" of the people?—apparently he was more literally accurate than he supposed. Freud was likewise too mild. He "never doubted that religious phenomena are to be understood only on the model of

---

[15] Chicago: Univ. of Chicago Press, 1958.

the neurotic symptoms of the individual."[16] He should have said "psychotic symptoms."

So the religious skeptic is likely to reason. What about the religious believer? Convinced that religious experiences are not fundamentally delusory, can he admit that psychotomimetic drugs can occasion them? To do so he needs (to return to Polanyi's words) "a conceptual framework in which [the discoveries can] be separated from specious and untenable admixtures," the "untenable admixture" being in this case the conclusion that religious experiences are in general delusory.

One way to effect the separation would be to argue that, despite phenomenological similarities between natural and drug-induced religious experiences, they are separated by a crucial *ontological* difference. Such an argument would follow the pattern of theologians who argue for the "real presence" of Christ's body and blood in the bread and wine of the Eucharist despite their admission that chemical analysis, confined as it is to the level of "accidents" rather than "essences," would not disclose this presence. But this distinction will not appeal to many today, for it turns on an essence-accident metaphysics which is not widely accepted. Instead of fighting a rear-guard action by insisting that if drug and non-drug religious experiences cannot be distinguished empirically there must be some transempirical factor that distinguishes them and renders the drug experience profane, I wish to explore the possibility of accepting drug-induced experiences as religious without relinquishing confidence in the truth-claims of religious experience generally.

To begin with the weakest of all arguments, the argument from authority: William James did not discount *his* insights that occurred while his brain chemistry was altered. The paragraph in which he retrospectively evaluates his nitrous oxide experiences has become classic, but it is so pertinent to the present discussion that it merits quoting once again.

> One conclusion was forced upon my mind at that time, and my impression of its truth has ever since remained unshaken. It is that our normal waking consciousness, rational consciousness as we call it, is but one special type of consciousness, whilst all about it, parted from it by the filmiest of screens, there lie potential forms of consciousness entirely different. We may go through life without suspecting their existence; but apply the requisite stimulus, and at a touch they are there in all their completeness, definite types of mentality which probably somewhere have their field of application and adaptation. No account of the

[16] *Totem and Taboo* (New York: Modern Library, 1938).

universe in its totality can be final which leaves these other forms of consciousness quite disregarded. How to regard them is the question—for they are so discontinuous with ordinary consciousness. Yet they may determine attitudes though they cannot furnish formulas, and open a region though they fail to give a map. At any rate, they forbid a premature closing of our accounts with reality. Looking back on my own experiences, they all converge toward a kind of insight to which I cannot help ascribing some metaphysical significance (*op. cit.*, 378–379).

To this argument from authority, I add two arguments that try to provide something by way of reasons. Drug experiences that assume a religious cast tend to have fearful and/or beatific features, and each of my hypotheses relates to one of these aspects of the experience.

Beginning with the ominous, "fear of the Lord," awe-ful features, Gordon Wasson, the New York banker-turned-mycologist, describes these as he encountered them in his psilocybin experience as follows: "Ecstasy! In common parlance . . . ecstasy is fun. . . . But ecstasy is not fun. Your very soul is seized and shaken until it tingles. After all, who will choose to feel undiluted awe? . . . The unknowing vulgar abuse the word; we must recapture its full and terrifying sense."[17] Emotionally the drug experience can be like having forty-foot waves crash over you for several hours while you cling desperately to a life-raft which may be swept from under you at any minute. It seems quite possible that such an ordeal, like any experience of a close call, could awaken rather fundamental sentiments respecting life and death and destiny and trigger the "no atheists in foxholes" effect. Similarly, as the subject emerges from the trauma and realizes that he is not going to be insane as he had feared, there may come over him an intensified appreciation like that frequently reported by patients recovering from critical illness. "It happened on the day when my bed was pushed out of doors to the open gallery of the hospital," reads one such report:

> I cannot now recall whether the revelation came suddenly or gradually; I only remember finding myself in the very midst of those wonderful moments, beholding life for the first time in all its young intoxication of loveliness, in its unspeakable joy, beauty, and importance. I cannot say exactly what the mysterious change was. I saw no new thing, but I saw all the usual things in a miraculous new light—in what I believe is their true light. I saw for the first time how wildly beautiful and joyous, beyond any words of mine to describe, is the whole of life. Every

[17] "The Hallucinogenic Fungi of Mexico: An Inquiry into the Origins of the Religious Idea among Primitive Peoples," *Harvard Botanical Museum Leaflets*, 19, 7 (1961).

> human being moving across that porch, every sparrow that flew, every branch tossing in the wind, was caught in and was a part of the whole mad ecstasy of loveliness, of joy, of importance, of intoxication of life.[18]

If we do not discount religious intuitions because they are prompted by battlefields and *physical* crises; if we regard the latter as "calling us to our senses" more often than they seduce us into delusions, need comparable intuitions be discounted simply because the crises that trigger them are of an inner, *psychic* variety?

Turning from the hellish to the heavenly aspects of the drug experience, *some* of the latter may be explainable by the hypothesis just stated; that is, they may be occasioned by the relief that attends the sense of escape from high danger. But this hypothesis cannot possibly account for *all* the beatific episodes, for the simple reason that the positive episodes often come first, or to persons who experience no negative episodes whatever. Dr. Sanford Unger of the National Institute of Mental Health reports that among his subjects "50 to 60% will not manifest any real disturbance worthy of discussion," yet "around 75% will have at least one episode in which exaltation, rapture, and joy are the key descriptions."[19] How are we to account for the drug's capacity to induce peak experiences, such as the following, which are *not* preceded by fear?

> A feeling of great peace and contentment seemed to flow through my entire body. All sound ceased and I seemed to be floating in a great, very very still void or hemisphere. It is impossible to describe the overpowering feeling of peace, contentment, and being a part of goodness itself that I felt. I could feel my body dissolving and actually becoming a part of the goodness and peace that was all around me. Words can't describe this. I feel an awe and wonder that such a feeling could have occurred to me.[20]

Consider the following line of argument. Like every other form of life, man's nature has become distinctive through specialization. Man has specialized in developing a cerebral cortex. The analytic powers of this instrument are a standing wonder, but the instrument seems less able to provide man with the sense that he is meaningfully related to his environment: to life, the world, and history in their wholeness. As Albert Camus describes the situa-

[18] Margaret Prescott Montague, *Twenty Minutes of Reality* (St. Paul, Minn.: Macalester Park, 1947), pp. 15, 17.

[19] "The Current Scientific Status of Psychedelic Drug Research," read at the Conference on Methods in Philosophy and the Sciences, New School for Social Research, May 3, 1964, and scheduled for publication in David Solomon, ed., *The Conscious Expanders* (New York: Putnam, fall of 1964).

[20] Quoted by Dr. Unger in the paper just mentioned.

tion, "If I were . . . a cat among animals, this life would have a meaning, or rather this problem would not arise, for I should belong to this world. I would *be* this world to which I am now opposed by my whole consciousness."[21] Note that it is Camus' consciousness that opposes him to his world. The drugs do not knock this consciousness out, but while they leave it operative they also activate areas of the brain that normally lie below its threshold of awareness. One of the clearest objective signs that the drugs are taking effect is the dilation they produce in the pupils of the eyes, and one of the most predictable subjective signs is the intensification of visual perception. Both of these responses are controlled by portions of the brain that lie deep, further to the rear than the mechanisms that govern consciousness. Meanwhile we know that the human organism is interlaced with its world in innumerable ways it normally cannot sense—through gravitational fields, body respiration, and the like: the list could be multiplied until man's skin began to seem more like a thoroughfare than a boundary. Perhaps the deeper regions of the brain which evolved earlier and are more like those of the lower animals—"If I were . . . a cat . . . I should belong to this world"—can sense this relatedness better than can the cerebral cortex which now dominates our awareness. If so, when the drugs rearrange the neurohumors that chemically transmit impulses across synapses between neurons, man's consciousness and his submerged, intuitive, ecological awareness might for a spell become interlaced. This is, of course, no more than a hypothesis, but how else are we to account for the extraordinary incidence under the drugs of that kind of insight the keynote of which James described as "invariably a reconciliation"? "It is as if the opposites of the world, whose contradictoriness and conflict make all our difficulties and troubles, were melted into one and the same genus, but *one of the species,* the nobler and better one, *is itself the genus, and so soaks up and absorbs its opposites into itself*" (*op. cit.,* 379).

The Drugs and
Religion Viewed "Religiously"

Suppose that drugs can induce experiences indistinguishable from religious experiences and that we can respect their reports.

[21] *The Myth of Sisyphus* (New York: Vintage, 1955), p. 38.

Do they shed any light, not (we now ask) on life, but on the nature of the religious life?

One thing they may do is throw religious experience itself into perspective by clarifying its relation to the religious life as a whole. Drugs appear able to induce religious experiences; it is less evident that they can produce religious lives. It follows that religion is more than religious experiences. This is hardly news, but it may be a useful reminder, especially to those who incline toward "the religion of religious experience"; which is to say toward lives bent on the acquisition of desired states of experience irrespective of their relation to life's other demands and components.

Despite the dangers of faulty psychology, it remains useful to regard man as having a mind, a will, and feelings. One of the lessons of religious history is that, to be adequate, a faith must rouse and involve all three components of man's nature. Religions of reason grow arid; religions of duty, leaden. Religions of experience have their comparable pitfalls, as evidenced by Taoism's struggle (not always successful) to keep from degenerating into quietism, and the vehemence with which Zen Buddhism has insisted that once students have attained *satori*, they must be driven out of it, back into the world. The case of Zen is especially pertinent here, for it pivots on an enlightenment experience—*satori*, or *kensho*—which some (but not all) Zennists say resembles LSD. Alike or different, the point is that Zen recognizes that unless the experience is joined to discipline, it will come to naught:

> Even the Buddha . . . had to sit. . . . Without *joriki*, the particular power developed through *zazen* [seated meditation], the vision of oneness attained in enlightenment . . . in time becomes clouded and eventually fades into a pleasant memory instead of remaining an omnipresent reality shaping our daily life. . . . To be able to live in accordance with what the Mind's eye has revealed through *satori* requires, like the purification of character and the development of personality, a ripening period of *zazen*.[22]

If the religion of religious experience is a snare and a delusion, it follows that no religion that fixes its faith primarily in substances that induce religious experiences can be expected to come to a good end. What promised to be a short cut will prove to be a short circuit; what began as a religion will end as a religion surrogate. Whether chemical substances can be helpful *adjuncts* to

[22] Philip Kapleau, *Zen Practice and Attainment*, a manuscript in process of publication.

faith is another question. The peyote-using Native American Church seems to indicate that they can be; anthropologists give this church a good report, noting among other things that members resist alcohol and alcoholism better than do nonmembers.[23] The conclusion to which evidence currently points would seem to be that chemicals *can* aid the religious life, but only where set within a context of faith (meaning by this the conviction that what they disclose is true) and discipline (meaning diligent exercise of the will in the attempt to work out the implications of the disclosures for the living of life in the everyday, common-sense world).

Nowhere today in Western civilization are these two conditions jointly fulfilled. Churches lack faith in the sense just mentioned; hipsters lack discipline. This might lead us to forget about the drugs, were it not for one fact: the distinctive religious emotion and the emotion that drugs unquestionably can occasion— Otto's *mysterium tremendum, majestas, mysterium fascinans;* in a phrase, the phenomenon of religious awe—seems to be declining sharply. As Paul Tillich said in an address to the Hillel Society at Harvard several years ago:

> The question our century puts before us [is]: Is it possible to regain the lost dimension, the encounter with the Holy, the dimension which cuts through the world of subjectivity and objectivity and goes down to that which is not world but is the mystery of the Ground of Being?

Tillich may be right; this may be the religious question of our century. For if (as we have insisted) religion cannot be equated with religious experiences, neither can it long survive their absence.

[23] Slotkin, *op. cit.*

The Existence
of God—A Debate

F. C. Copleston
and Bertrand Russell

F. C. Copleston, S. J. (1907–   ), Professor in the Gregorian University, Rome, and Heythrop College, Oxford, is the most widely known Roman Catholic historian of philosophy in the English-speaking world and respected critic of antimetaphysical trends in recent philosophy.
For biographical note on Bertrand Russell, see p. 120.

COPLESTON: As we are going to discuss the existence of God, it might perhaps be as well to come to some provisional agreement as to what we understand by the term "God." I presume that we mean a supreme personal being—distinct from the world and creator of the world. Would you agree—provisionally at least—to accept this statement as the meaning of the term "God"?

RUSSELL: Yes, I accept this definition.

COPLESTON: Well, my position is the affirmative position that such a being actually exists, and that His existence can be proved philosophically. Perhaps you would tell me if your position is that of agnosticism or of atheism. I mean, would you say that the non-existence of God can be proved?

RUSSELL: No, I should not say that: my position is agnostic.

COPLESTON: Would you agree with me that the problem of God is a problem of great importance? For example, would you agree that if God does not exist, human beings and human history can

Broadcast in 1948 on the Third Programme of the British Broadcasting Corporation, and published in *Humanitas* (Manchester) and *Why I Am Not a Christian* by Bertrand Russell. Reprinted by permission of Father F. C. Copleston and George Allen & Unwin Ltd.

have no other purpose than the purpose they choose to give themselves, which—in practice—is likely to mean the purpose which those impose who have the power to impose it?

RUSSELL: Roughly speaking, yes, though I should have to place some limitation on your last clause.

COPLESTON: Would you agree that if there is no God—no absolute Being—there can be no absolute values? I mean, would you agree that if there is no absolute good that the relativity of values results?

RUSSELL: No, I think these questions are logically distinct. Take, for instance, G. E. Moore's *Principia Ethica*, where he maintains that there is a distinction of good and evil, that both of these are definite concepts. But he does not bring in the idea of God to support that contention.

COPLESTON: Well, suppose we leave the question of good till later, till we come to the moral argument, and I give first a metaphysical argument. I'd like to put the main weight on the metaphysical argument based on Leibniz's argument from "Contingency" and then later we might discuss the moral argument. Suppose I give a brief statement on the metaphysical argument and that then we go on to discuss it?

RUSSELL: That seems to me to be a very good plan.

The Argument from Contingency

COPLESTON: Well, for clarity's sake, I'll divide the argument into distinct stages. First of all, I should say, we know that there are at least some beings in the world which do not contain in themselves the reason for their existence. For example, I depend on my parents, and now on the air, and on food, and so on. Now, secondly, the world is simply the real or imagined totality or aggregate of individual objects, none of which contain in themselves alone the reason for their existence. There isn't any world distinct from the objects which form it, any more than the human race is something apart from the members. Therefore, I should say, since objects or events exist, and since no object of experience contains within itself the reason of its existence, this reason, the totality of objects, must have a reason external to itself. That reason must be an existent being. Well, this being is either itself the reason for its own existence, or it is not. If it is, well and good. If it is not, then we must proceed farther. But if we proceed to infinity in that sense, then there's no explanation of existence at all. So, I should say, in order to explain existence, we must come to a being which contains within itself the reason for its own existence, that is to say, which cannot not exist.

RUSSELL: This raises a great many points and it is not altogether easy to know where to begin, but I think that, perhaps, in answering your argument, the best point at which to begin is the question of necessary being. The word "necessary," I should maintain, can only be applied significantly to propositions. And, in fact, only to such as are analytic—that is to say—such as it is self-contradictory to deny. I could only admit a necessary being if there were a being whose existence it is self-contradictory to deny. I should like to know whether you would accept Leibniz's division of propositions into truths of reason and truths of fact. The former —the truths of reason—being necessary.

COPLESTON: Well I certainly should not subscribe to what seems to be Leibniz's idea of truths of reason and truths of fact, since it would appear that, for him, there are in the long run only analytic propositions. It would seem that for Leibniz truths of fact are ultimately reducible to truths of reason. That is to say, to analytic propositions, at least for an omniscient mind. Well, I couldn't agree with that. For one thing, it would fail to meet the requirements of the experience of freedom. I don't want to uphold the whole philosophy of Leibniz. I have made use of his argument from contingent to necessary being, basing the argument on the principle of sufficient reason, simply because it seems to me a brief and clear formulation of what is, in my opinion, the fundamental metaphysical argument for God's existence.

RUSSELL: But, to my mind, "a necessary proposition" has got to be analytic. I don't see what else it can mean. And analytic propositions are always complex and logically somewhat late. "Irrational animals are animals" is an analytic proposition; but a proposition such as "This is an animal" can never be analytic. In fact, all the propositions that can be analytic are somewhat late in the build-up of propositions.

COPLESTON: Take the proposition, "If there is a contingent being then there is a necessary being." I consider that that proposition hypothetically expressed is a necessary proposition. If you are going to call every necessary proposition an analytic proposition, then—in order to avoid a dispute in terminology—I would agree to call it analytic, though I don't consider it a tautological proposition. But the proposition is a necessary proposition only on the supposition that there is a contingent being. That there is a contingent being actually existing has to be discovered by experience, and the proposition that there is a contingent being is certainly not an analytic proposition, though once you know, I should maintain, that there is a contingent being, it follows of necessity that there is a necessary being.

RUSSELL: The difficulty of this argument is that I don't admit the idea of a necessary being and I don't admit that there is any particular meaning in calling other beings "contingent." These phrases don't for me have a significance except within a logic that I reject.

COPLESTON: Do you mean that you reject these terms because they won't fit in with what is called "modern logic"?

RUSSELL: Well, I can't find anything that they could mean. The word "necessary," it seems to me, is a useless word, except as applied to analytic propositions, not to things.

COPLESTON: In the first place, what do you mean by "modern logic"? As far as I know, there are somewhat differing systems. In the second place, not all modern logicians surely would admit the meaninglessness of metaphysics. We both know, at any rate, one very eminent modern thinker whose knowledge of modern logic was profound, but who certainly did not think that metaphysics are meaningless or, in particular, that the problem of God is meaningless. Again, even if all modern logicians held that metaphysical terms are meaningless, it would not follow that they were right. The proposition that metaphysical terms are meaningless seems to me to be a proposition based on an assumed philosophy. The dogmatic position behind it seems to be this: What will not go into my machine is non-existent, or it is meaningless; it is the expression of emotion. I am simply trying to point out that anybody who says that a particular system of modern logic is the sole criterion of meaning is saying something that is over-dogmatic; he is dogmatically insisting that a part of philosophy is the whole of philosophy. After all, a "contingent" being is a being which has not in itself the complete reason for its existence; that's what I mean by a contingent being. You know, as well as I do, that the existence of neither of us can be explained without reference to something or somebody outside us, our parents, for example. A "necessary" being, on the other hand, means a being that must and cannot not exist. You may say that there is no such being, but you will find it hard to convince me that you do not understand the terms I am using. If you do not understand them, then how can you be entitled to say that such a being does not exist, if that is what you do say?

RUSSELL: Well, there are points here that I don't propose to go into at length. I don't maintain the meaninglessness of metaphysics in general at all. I maintain the meaninglessness of certain particular terms—not on any general ground, but simply because I've not been able to see an interpretation of those particular terms. It's not a general dogma—it's a particular thing. But those points I will leave out for the moment. And I will say that what you have been saying brings us back, it seems to me, to the ontological argument that there is a being whose essence involves existence, so that his existence is analytic. That seems to me to be impossible, and it raises, of course, the question what one means by existence, and as to this, I think a subject named can never be significantly said to exist but only a subject described. And that existence, in fact, quite definitely is not a predicate.

COPLESTON: Well, you say, I believe, that it is bad grammar, or rather bad syntax to say for example "T. S. Eliot exists"; one ought to say, for example, "He, the author of *Murder in the Cathedral*, exists." Are you going to say that the proposition, "The cause of the world exists," is without meaning? You may say that the world has no cause; but I fail to see how you can say that the proposition that "the cause of the world exists" is meaningless. Put it in the form of a question: "Has the world a cause?" or "Does a cause of the world exist?" Most people surely would understand the question, even if they don't agree about the answer.

RUSSELL: Well, certainly the question "Does the cause of the world exist?" is a question that has meaning. But if you say "Yes, God is the cause of the world," you're using God as a proper name; then "God exists" will not be a statement that has meaning; that is the position that I'm maintaining. Because, therefore, it will follow that it cannot be an analytic proposition ever to say that this or that exists. For example, suppose you take as your subject "the existent round-square," it would look like an analytic proposition that "the existent round-square exists," but it doesn't exist.

COPLESTON: No, it doesn't; then surely you can't say it doesn't exist unless you have a conception of what existence is. As to the phrase "existent round-square," I should say that it has no meaning at all.

RUSSELL: I quite agree. Then I should say the same thing in another context in reference to a "necessary being."

COPLESTON: Well, we seem to have arrived at an impasse. To say that a necessary being is a being that must exist and cannot not exist has for me a definite meaning. For you it has no meaning.

RUSSELL: Well, we can press the point a little, I think. A being that must exist and cannot not exist would surely, according to you, be a being whose essence involves existence.

COPLESTON: Yes, a being the essence of which is to exist. But I should not be willing to argue the existence of God simply from the idea of His essence because I don't think we have any clear intuition of God's essence as yet. I think we have to argue from the world of experience to God.

RUSSELL: Yes, I quite see the distinction. But, at the same time, for a being with sufficient knowledge it would be true to say, "Here is this being whose essence involves existence!"

COPLESTON: Yes, certainly if anybody saw God, he would see that God must exist.

RUSSELL: So that I mean there is a being whose essence involves existence although we don't know that essence. We only know there is such a being.

COPLESTON: Yes, I should add we don't know the essence *a priori*. It is only *a posteriori* through our experience of the world that we come to a knowledge of the existence of that being. And then one argues, the essence and existence must be identical. Because if God's essence and God's existence were not identical, then some sufficient reason for this existence would have to be found beyond God.

RUSSELL: So it all turns on this question of sufficient reason, and I must say you haven't defined "sufficient reason" in a way that I can understand—what do you mean by sufficient reason? You don't mean cause?

COPLESTON: Not necessarily. Cause is a kind of sufficient reason. Only contingent being can have a cause. God is His own sufficient reason; and He is not cause of Himself. By sufficient reason in the full sense I mean an explanation adequate for the existence of some particular being.

RUSSELL: But when is an explanation adequate? Suppose I am about to make a flame with a match. You may say that the adequate explanation of that is that I rub it on the box.

COPLESTON: Well, for practical purposes—but theoretically, that is only a partial explanation. An adequate explanation must ultimately be a total explanation, to which nothing further can be added.

RUSSELL: Then I can only say that you're looking for something which can't be got, and which one ought not to expect to get.

COPLESTON: To say that one has not found it is one thing; to say that one should not look for it seems to me rather dogmatic.

RUSSELL: Well, I don't know. I mean, the explanation of one thing is another thing which makes the other thing dependent on yet another, and you have to grasp this sorry scheme of things entire to do what you want, and that we can't do.

COPLESTON: But are you going to say that we can't, or we shouldn't even raise the question of the existence of the whole of this sorry scheme of things—of the whole universe?

RUSSELL: Yes. I don't think there's any meaning in it at all. I think the word "universe" is a handy word in some connections, but I don't think it stands for anything that has a meaning.

COPLESTON: If the word is meaningless, it can't be so very handy. In any case, I don't say that the universe is something different from the objects which compose it (I indicated that in my brief summary of the proof); what I'm doing is to look for the reason, in this case the cause of the objects—the real or imagined totality of which constitute what we call the universe. You say, I think, that the universe—or my existence if you prefer, or any other existence—is unintelligible?

RUSSELL: First may I take up the point that if a word is meaningless it can't be handy. That sounds well but isn't in fact correct. Take, say, such a word as "the" or "than." You can't point to any object that those words mean, but they are very useful words; I should say the same of "universe." But leaving that point, you ask whether I consider that the universe is unintelligible. I shouldn't say unintelligible—I think it is without explanation. Intelligible, to my mind, is a different thing. Intelligible has to do with the thing itself intrinsically and not with its relations.

COPLESTON: Well, my point is that what we call the world is intrinsically unintelligible, apart from the existence of God. You see, I don't believe that the infinity of the series of events—I mean a horizontal series, so to speak—if such an infinity could be proved, would be in the slightest degree relevant to the situation. If you add up chocolates you get chocolates after and not a sheep. If you add up chocolates to infinity, you presumably get an infinite number of chocolates. So if you add up contingent beings to infinity, you still get contingent beings, not a necessary being. An infinite series of contingent beings will be, to my way of thinking, as unable to cause itself as one contingent being. However, you say, I think, that it is illegitimate to raise the question of what will explain the existence of any particular object?

RUSSELL: It's quite all right if you mean by explaining it, simply finding a cause for it.

COPLESTON: Well, why stop at one particular object? Why shouldn't one raise the question of the cause of the existence of all particular objects?

RUSSELL: Because I see no reason to think there is any. The whole concept of cause is one we derive from our observation of particular things; I see no reason whatsoever to suppose that the total has any cause whatsoever.

COPLESTON: Well, to say that there isn't any cause is not the same thing as saying that we shouldn't look for a cause. The statement that there isn't any cause should come, if it comes at all, at the end of the inquiry, not the beginning. In any case, if the total has no cause, then to my way of thinking it must be its own cause, which seems to me impossible. Moreover, the statement that the world is simply there, if in answer to a question, presupposes that the question has meaning.

RUSSELL: No, it doesn't need to be its own cause; what I'm saying is that the concept of cause is not applicable to the total.

COPLESTON: Then you would agree with Sartre that the universe is what he calls "gratuitous"?

RUSSELL: Well, the word "gratuitous" suggests that it might be something else; I should say that the universe is just there, and that's all.

COPLESTON: Well, I can't see how you can rule out the legitimacy of asking the question how the total, or anything at all, comes to be there. Why something rather than nothing? That is the question. The fact that we gain our knowledge of causality empirically, from particular causes, does not rule out the possibility of asking what the cause of the series is. If the word "cause" were meaningless or if it could be shown that Kant's view of the matter were correct, the question would be illegitimate, I agree; but you don't seem to hold that the word "cause" is meaningless, and I do not suppose you are a Kantian.

RUSSELL: I can illustrate what seems to me your fallacy. Every man who exists has a mother, and it seems to me your argument is that therefore the human race must have a mother, but obviously the human race hasn't a mother—that's a different logical sphere.

COPLESTON: Well I can't really see any parity. If I were saying every object has a phenomenal cause, therefore the whole series has a phenomenal cause, there would be a parity; but I'm not saying that; I'm saying every object has a phenomenal cause if you insist on the infinity of the series—but the series of phenomenal causes is an insufficient explanation of the series. Therefore, the series has not a phenomenal cause but a transcendent cause.

RUSSELL: That's always assuming that not only every particular thing in the world, but the world as a whole must have a cause. For that assumption I see no ground whatever. If you'll give me a ground I'll listen to it.

COPLESTON: Well, the series of events is either caused or it's not caused. If it is caused, there must obviously be a cause outside the series. If it's not caused, then it's sufficient to itself, and if it's sufficient to itself, it is what I call necessary. But it can't be necessary, since each member is contingent, and we've agreed that the total has no reality apart from its members, therefore it can't be necessary. Therefore, it can't be (caused)—uncaused —therefore it must have a cause. And I should like to observe in passing that the statement "The world is simply there and is inexplicable" can't be got out of logical analysis.

RUSSELL: I don't want to seem arrogant, but it does seem to me that I can conceive things that you say the human mind can't conceive. As for things not having a cause, the physicists assure us that individual quantum transitions in atoms have no cause.

COPLESTON: Well, I wonder now whether that isn't simply a temporary inference.

RUSSELL: It may be, but it does show that physicists' minds can conceive it.

COPLESTON: Yes, I agree, some scientists—physicists—are willing to allow for indetermination within a restricted field. But very many scientists are not so willing. I think that Professor Dingle, of London University, maintains that the Heisenberg uncertainty principle tells us something about the success (or the lack of it) of the present atomic theory in correlating observations, but not about nature in itself, and many physicists would accept this view. In any case, I don't see how physicists can fail to accept the theory in practice, even if they don't do so in theory. I cannot see how science could be conducted on any other assumption than that of order and intelligibility in nature. The physicist presupposes, at least tacitly, that there is some sense in investigating nature and looking for the causes of events, just as the detective presupposes that there is some sense in looking for the cause of a murder. The metaphysician assumes that there is sense in looking for the reason or cause of phenomena, and, not being a Kantian, I consider that the metaphysician is as justified in his assumption as the physicist. When Sartre, for example, says that the world is gratuitous, I think that he has not sufficiently considered what is implied by "gratuitous."

RUSSELL: I think—there seems to me a certain unwarrantable extension here; a physicist looks for causes; that does not necessarily imply that there are causes everywhere. A man may look for gold without assuming that there is gold everywhere; if he finds gold, well and good; if he doesn't, he's had bad luck. The same is true when the physicists look for causes. As for Sartre, I don't profess to know what he means, and I shouldn't like to be thought to interpret him, but for my part, I do think the notion of the world having an explanation is a mistake. I don't see why one should expect it to have, and I think what you say about what the scientist assumes is an over-statement.

COPLESTON: Well, it seems to me that the scientist does make some such assumption. When he experiments to find out some particular truth, behind that experiment lies the assumption that the universe is not simply discontinuous. There is the possibility of finding out a truth by experiment. The experiment may be a bad one, it may lead to no result, or not to the result that he wants, but that at any rate there is the possibility, through experiment, of finding out the truth that he assumes. And that seems to me to assume an ordered and intelligible universe.

RUSSELL: I think you're generalizing more than is necessary. Undoubtedly the scientist assumes that this sort of thing is likely to be found and will often be found. He does not assume that it will be found, and that's a very important matter in modern physics.

COPLESTON: Well, I think he does assume or is bound to assume it tacitly in practice. It may be that, to quote Professor Haldane, "when I light the gas under the kettle, some of the water molecules will fly off as vapor, and there is no way of finding out which will do so," but it doesn't follow necessarily that the idea of chance must be introduced except in relation to our knowledge.

RUSSELL: No it doesn't—at least if I may believe what he says. He's finding out quite a lot of things—the scientist is finding out quite a lot of things that are happening in the world, which are, at first, beginnings of causal chains—first causes which haven't in themselves got causes. He does not assume that everything has a cause.

COPLESTON: Surely that's a first cause within a certain selected field. It's a relatively first cause.

RUSSELL: I don't think he'd say so. If there's a world in which most events, but not all, have causes, he will then be able to depict the probabilities and uncertainties by assuming that this particular event you're interested in probably has a cause. And since in any case you won't get more than probability, that's good enough.

COPLESTON: It may be that the scientist doesn't hope to obtain more than probability, but in raising the question, he assumes that the question of explanation has a meaning. But your general point then, Lord Russell, is that it's illegitimate even to ask the question of the cause of the world?

RUSSELL: Yes, that's my position.

COPLESTON: If it's a question that for you has no meaning, it's of course very difficult to discuss it, isn't it?

RUSSELL: Yes, it is very difficult. What do you say—shall we pass on to some other issue?

Religious Experience

COPLESTON: Let's. Well, perhaps I might say a word about religious experience, and then we can go on to moral experience. I don't regard religious experience as a strict proof of the existence of God, so the character of the discussion changes somewhat, but I think it's true to say that the best explanation of it is the existence of God. By religious experience I don't mean simply feeling good. I mean a loving, but unclear, awareness of some object which irresistibly seems to the experiencer as something transcending the self, something transcending all the normal objects of experience, something which cannot be pictured or conceptualized, but of the reality of which doubt is impossible—at least during the experience. I should claim that cannot be explained adequately and without residue, simply subjectively. The actual basic experience at any rate is most easily explained on the hypothesis that there is actually some objective cause of that experience.

RUSSELL: I should reply to that line of argument that the whole argument from our own mental states to something outside us is a very tricky affair. Even where we all admit its validity, we only feel justified in doing so, I think, because of the consensus of mankind. If there's a crowd in a room and there's a clock in a room, they can all see the clock. The fact that they can all see it tends to make them think that it's not an hallucination: whereas these religious experiences do tend to be very private.

COPLESTON: Yes, they do. I'm speaking strictly of mystical experience proper, and I certainly don't include, by the way, what are called visions. I mean simply the experience, and I quite admit it's indefinable, of the transcendent object or of what seems to be a transcendent object. I remember Julian Huxley in some lecture saying that religious experience, or mystical experience, is as much a real experience as falling in love or appreciating poetry and art. Well, I believe that when we appreciate poetry and art we appreciate definite poems or a definite work of art. If we fall in love, well, we fall in love with somebody and not with nobody.

RUSSELL: May I interrupt for a moment here. That is by no means always the case. Japanese novelists never consider that they have achieved a success unless large numbers of real people commit suicide for love of the imaginary heroine.

COPLESTON: Well, I must take your word for these goings on in Japan. I haven't committed suicide, I'm glad to say, but I have been strongly influenced in the taking of two important steps in my life by two biographies. However, I must say I see little resemblance between the real influence of those books on me and the mystic experience proper, so far, that is, as an outsider can obtain an idea of that experience.

RUSSELL: Well, I mean we wouldn't regard God as being on the same level as the characters in a work of fiction. You'll admit there's a distinction here?

COPLESTON: I certainly should. But what I'd say is that the best explanation seems to be the not purely subjectivist explanation. Of course, a subjectivist explanation is possible in the case of certain people in whom there is little relation between the experience and life, in the case of deluded people and hallucinated people, and so on. But when you get what one might call the pure type, say St. Francis of Assisi, when you get an experience that results in an overflow of dynamic and creative love, the best explanation of that, it seems to me, is the actual existence of an objective cause of the experience.

RUSSELL: Well, I'm not contending in a dogmatic way that there is not a God. What I'm contending is that we don't know that there is. I can only take what is recorded as I should take other records, and I do find that a very great many things are reported, and I am sure you would not accept things about demons and devils and what not—and they're reported in exactly the same tone of voice and with exactly the same conviction. And the mystic, if his vision is veridical, may be said to know that there are devils. But I don't know that there are.

COPLESTON: But surely in the case of the devils there have been people speaking mainly of visions, appearances, angels, or demons, and so on. I should rule out the visual appearances, because I think they can be explained apart from the existence of the object which is supposed to be seen.

RUSSELL: But don't you think there are abundant recorded

cases of people who believe that they've heard Satan speaking to them in their hearts, in just the same way as the mystics assert God—and I'm not talking now of an external vision, I'm talking of a purely mental experience. That seems to be an experience of the same sort as mystics' experience of God, and I don't see that from what mystics tell us you can get any argument for God which is not equally an argument for Satan.

COPLESTON: I quite agree, of course, that people have imagined or thought they have heard or seen Satan. And I have no wish in passing to deny the existence of Satan. But I do not think that people have claimed to have experienced Satan in the precise way in which mystics claim to have experienced God. Take the case of a non-Christian, Plotinus. He admits the experience is something inexpressible, the object is an object of love, and therefore, not an object that causes horror and disgust. And the effect of that experience is, I should say, borne out, or I mean the validity of the experience is borne out, in the records of the life of Plotinus. At any rate it is more reasonable to suppose that he had that experience if we're willing to accept Porphyry's account of Plotinus's general kindness and benevolence.

RUSSELL: The fact that a belief has a good moral effect upon a man is no evidence whatsoever in favor of its truth.

COPLESTON: No, but if it could actually be proved that the belief was actually responsible for a good effect on a man's life, I should consider it a presumption in favor of some truth, at any rate of the positive part of the belief if not of its entire validity. But in any case I am using the character of the life as evidence in favor of the mystic's veracity and sanity rather than as a proof of the truth of his beliefs.

RUSSELL: But even that I don't think is any evidence. I've had experiences myself that have altered my character profoundly. And I thought at the time at any rate that it was altered for the good. Those experiences were important, but they did not involve the existence of something outside me, and I don't think that if I'd thought they did, the fact that they had a wholesome effect would have been any evidence that I was right.

COPLESTON: No, but I think that the good effect would attest your veracity in describing your experience. Please remember that I'm not saying that a mystic's mediation or interpretation of his experience should be immune from discussion or criticism.

RUSSELL: Obviously the character of a young man may be— and often is—immensely affected for good by reading about some great men in history, and it may happen that the great man is a myth and doesn't exist, but the boy is just as much affected for good as if he did. There have been such people. Plutarch's *Lives* take Lycurgus as an example, who certainly did not exist, but you might be very much influenced by reading Lycurgus under the impression that he had previously existed. You would then be influenced by an object that you'd loved, but it wouldn't be an existing object.

COPLESTON: I agree with you on that, of course, that a man may be influenced by a character in fiction. Without going into the question of what it is precisely that influences him (I should say a real value) I think that the situation of that man and of the mystic are different. After all, the man who is influenced by Lycurgus hasn't got the irresistible impression that he's experienced in some way the ultimate reality.

RUSSELL: I don't think you've quite got my point about these historical characters—these unhistorical characters in history. I'm not assuming what you call an effect on the reason. I'm assuming that the young man reading about this person and believing him to be real loves him—which is quite easy to happen, and yet he's loving a phantom.

COPLESTON: In one sense he's loving a phantom, that's perfectly true, in the sense, I mean, that he's loving *X* or *Y* who doesn't exist. But at the same time, it is not, I think, the phantom as such that the young man loves; he perceives a real value, an idea which he recognizes as objectively valid, and that's what excites his love.

RUSSELL: Well, in the same sense we had before about the characters in fiction.

COPLESTON: Yes, in one sense the man's loving a phantom—perfectly true. But in another sense he's loving what he perceives to be a value.

The Moral Argument

RUSSELL: But aren't you now saying in effect, "I mean by God whatever is good or the sum total of what is good—the system of what is good, and, therefore, when a young man loves anything that is good, he is loving God." Is that what you're saying, because if so, it wants a bit of arguing.

COPLESTON: I don't say, of course, that God is the sum total or system of what is good in the pantheistic sense; I'm not a pantheist, but I do think that all goodness reflects God in some way and proceeds from Him, so that in a sense the man who loves what is truly good, loves God even if he doesn't advert to God. But still I agree that the validity of such an interpretation of a man's conduct depends on the recognition of God's existence, obviously.

RUSSELL: Yes, but that's a point to be proved.

COPLESTON: Quite so, but I regard the metaphysical argument as probative, but there we differ.

RUSSELL: You see, I feel that some things are good and that other things are bad. I love the things that are good, that I think are good, and I hate the things that I think are bad. I don't say that these things are good because they participate in the Divine goodness.

COPLESTON: Yes, but what's your justification for distinguishing between good and bad or how do you view the distinction between them?

RUSSELL: I don't have any justification any more than I have when I distinguish between blue and yellow. What is my justification for distinguishing between blue and yellow? I can see they are different.

COPLESTON: Well, that is an excellent justification, I agree. You distinguish blue and yellow by seeing them, so you distinguish good and bad by what faculty?

RUSSELL: By my feelings.

COPLESTON: By your feelings. Well, that's what I was asking. You think that good and evil have reference simply to feeling?

RUSSELL: Well, why does one type of object look yellow and another look blue? I can more or less give an answer to that thanks to the physicists, and as to why I think one sort of thing good and another evil, probably there is an answer of the same sort, but it hasn't been gone into in the same way and I couldn't give it you.

COPLESTON: Well, let's take the behavior of the Commandant of Belsen. That appears to you as undesirable and evil and to me too. To Adolf Hilter we suppose it appeared as something good and desirable. I suppose you'd have to admit that for Hilter it was good and for you it is evil.

RUSSELL: No, I shouldn't quite go so far as that. I mean, I think people can make mistakes in that as they can in other things. If you have jaundice you see things yellow that are not yellow. You're making a mistake.

COPLESTON: Yes, one can make mistakes, but can you make a

mistake if it's simply a question of reference to a feeling or emotion? Surely Hitler would be the only possible judge of what appealed to his emotions.

RUSSELL: It would be quite right to say that it appealed to his emotions, but you can say various things about that; among others, that if that sort of thing makes that sort of appeal to Hitler's emotions, then Hitler makes quite a different appeal to my emotions.

COPLESTON: Granted. But there's no objective criterion outside feeling, then, for condemning the conduct of the Commandant of Belsen, in your view?

RUSSELL: No more than there is for the color-blind person who's in exactly the same state. Why do we intellectually condemn the color-blind man? Isn't it because he's in the minority?

COPLESTON: I would say because he is lacking in a thing which normally belongs to human nature.

RUSSELL: Yes, but if he were in the majority, we shouldn't say that.

COPLESTON: Then you'd say that there's no criterion outside feeling that will enable one to distinguish between the behavior of the Commandant of Belsen and the behavior, say, of Sir Stafford Cripps or the Archbishop of Canterbury.

RUSSELL: The feeling is a little too simplified. You've got to take account of the effects of actions and your feelings towards those effects. You see, you can have an argument about it if you say that certain sorts of occurrences are the sort you like and certain others the sort you don't like. Then you have to take account of the effects of actions. You can very well say that the effects of the actions of the Commandant of Belsen were painful and unpleasant.

COPLESTON: They certainly were, I agree, very painful and unpleasant to all the people in the camp.

RUSSELL: Yes, but not only to the people in the camp, but to outsiders contemplating them also.

COPLESTON: Yes, quite true in imagination. But that's my point. I don't approve of them, and I know you don't approve of them, but I don't see what ground you have for not approving of them, because, after all, to the Commandant of Belsen himself, they're pleasant, those actions.

RUSSELL: Yes, but you see I don't need any more ground in that case than I do in the case of color perception. There are some people who think everything is yellow, there are people suffering from jaundice, and I don't agree with these people. I can't prove that the things are not yellow, there isn't any proof, but most people agree with me that they're not yellow, and most people agree with me that the Commandant of Belsen was making mistakes.

COPLESTON: Well, do you accept any moral obligation?

RUSSELL: Well, I should have to answer at considerable length to answer that. Practically speaking—yes. Theoretically speaking I should have to define moral obligation rather carefully.

COPLESTON: Well, do you think that the word "ought" simply has an emotional connotation?

RUSSELL: No, I don't think that, because you see, as I was saying a moment ago, one has to take account of the effects, and I think right conduct is that which would probably produce the greatest possible balance in intrinsic value of all the acts possible in the circumstances, and you've got to take account of the probable effects of your action in considering what is right.

COPLESTON: Well, I brought in moral obligation because I think that one can approach the question of God's existence in that way. The vast majority of the human race will make, and always have made, some distinction between right and wrong. The vast majority I think has some consciousness of an obligation in the moral sphere. It's my opinion that the perception of values and the consciousness of moral law and obligation are best explained through the hypothesis of a transcendent ground of value and of an author of the moral law. I do mean by "author of the moral law" an arbitrary author of the moral law. I think, in fact, that those modern atheists who have argued in the converse way "There is no God; therefore, there are no absolute values and no absolute law," are quite logical.

RUSSELL: I don't like the word "absolute." I don't think there is anything absolute whatever. The moral law, for example, is always changing. At one period in the development of the human race, almost everybody thought cannibalism was a duty.

COPLESTON: Well, I don't see that differences in particular moral judgments are any conclusive argument against the universality of the moral law. Let's assume for the moment that there are absolute moral values, even on that hypothesis it's only to be expected that different individuals and different groups should enjoy varying degrees of insight into those values.

RUSSELL: I'm inclined to think that "ought," the feeling that one has about "ought," is an echo of what has been told one by one's parents or one's nurses.

COPLESTON: Well, I wonder if you can explain away the idea of the "ought" merely in terms of nurses and parents. I really don't see how it can be conveyed to anybody in other terms than itself.

It seems to me that if there is a moral order bearing upon the human conscience, that that moral order is unintelligible apart from the existence of God.

RUSSELL: Then you have to say one or other of two things. Either God only speaks to a very small percentage of mankind—which happens to include yourself—or He deliberately says things that are not true in talking to the consciences of savages.

COPLESTON: Well, you see, I'm not suggesting that God actually dictates moral precepts to the conscience. The human being's idea of the content of the moral law depends certainly to a large extent on education and environment, and a man has to use his reason in assessing the validity of the actual moral ideas of his social group. But the possibility of criticizing the accepted moral code presupposes that there is an objective standard, that there is an ideal moral order, which imposes itself (I mean the obligatory character of which can be recognized). I think that the recognition of this ideal moral order is part of the recognition of contingency. It implies the existence of a real foundation of God.

RUSSELL: But the law-giver has always been, it seems to me, one's parents or someone like. There are plenty of terrestrial law-givers to account for it, and that would explain why people's consciences are so amazingly different in different times and places.

COPLESTON: It helps to explain differences in the perception of particular moral values, which otherwise are inexplicable. It will help to explain changes in the matter of the moral law in the content of the precepts as accepted by this or that nation, or this or that individual. But the form of it, what Kant calls the categorical imperative, the "ought," I really don't see how that can possibly be conveyed to anybody by nurse or parent because there aren't any possible terms, so far as I can see, with which it can be explained. It can't be defined in other terms than itself, because once you've defined it in other terms than itself you've explained it away. It's no longer a moral "ought." It's something else.

RUSSELL: Well, I think the sense of "ought" is the effect of somebody's imagined disapproval, it may be God's imagined disapproval, but it's somebody's imagined disapproval. And I think that is what is meant by "ought."

COPLESTON: It seems to me to be external customs and taboos and things of that sort which can most easily be explained simply through environment and education, but all that seems to me to belong to what I call the matter of the law, the content. The idea of the "ought" as such can never be conveyed to a man by the tribal chief or by anybody else, because there are no other terms in which it could be conveyed. It seems to me entirely——[Russell breaks in].

RUSSELL: But I don't see any reason to say that—I mean we all know about conditioned reflexes. We know that an animal, if punished habitually for a certain sort of act, after a time will refrain. I don't think the animal refrains from arguing within himself, "Master will be angry if I do this." He has a feeling that that's not the thing to do. That's what we can do with ourselves and nothing more.

COPLESTON: I see no reason to suppose that an animal has a consciousness of moral obligation; and we certainly don't regard an animal as morally responsible for his acts of disobedience. But a man has a consciousness of obligation and of moral values. I see no reason to suppose that one could condition all men as one can "condition" an animal, and I don't suppose you'd really want to do so even if one could. If "behaviorism" were true, there would be no objective moral distinction between the emperor Nero and St. Francis of Assisi. I can't help feeling, Lord Russell, you know, that you regard the conduct of the Commandant at Belsen as morally reprehensible, and that you yourself would never under any circumstances act in that way, even if you thought, or had reason to think, that possibly the balance of the happiness of the human race might be increased through some people being treated in that abominable manner.

RUSSELL: No. I wouldn't imitate the conduct of a mad dog. The fact that I wouldn't do it doesn't really bear on this question we're discussing.

COPLESTON: No, but if you were making a utilitarian explanation of right and wrong in terms of consequences, it might be held, and I suppose some of the Nazis of the better type would have held, that although it's lamentable to have to act in this way, yet the balance in the long run leads to greater happiness. I don't think you'd say that, would you? I think you'd say that that sort of action is wrong—and in itself, quite apart from whether the general balance of happiness is increased or not. Then, if you're prepared to say that, then I think you must have some criterion of right and wrong, that is outside the criterion of feeling, at any rate. To me, that admission would ultimately result in the admission of an ultimate ground of value in God.

RUSSELL: I think we are perhaps getting into confusion. It is not direct feeling about the act by which I should judge, but rather a feeling as to the effects. And I can't admit any circumstances in which certain kinds of behavior, such as you have been discussing, would do good. I can't imagine circumstances in which they would have a beneficial effect. I think the persons who think they do are deceiving themselves. But if there were circumstances in which they would have a beneficial effect, then I might be obliged, however reluctantly, to say—"Well, I don't like these things, but I will acquiesce in them," just as I acquiesce in the Criminal Law, although I profoundly dislike punishment.

COPLESTON: Well, perhaps it's time I summed up my position. I've argued two things. First, that the existence of God can be philosophically proved by a metaphysical argument; secondly, that it is only the existence of God that will make sense of man's moral experience and of religious experience. Personally, I think that your way of accounting for man's moral judgments leads inevitably to a contradiction between what your theory demands and your own spontaneous judgments. Moreover, your theory explains moral obligation away, and explaining away is not explanation. As regards the metaphysical argument, we are apparently in agreement that what we call the world consists simply of contingent beings. That is, of beings no one of which can account for its own existence. You say that the series of events needs no explanation; I say that if there were no necessary being, no being which must exist and cannot not exist, nothing would exist. The infinity of the series of contingent beings, even if proved, would be irrelevant. Something does exist; therefore, there must be something which accounts for this fact, a being which is outside the series of contingent beings. If you had admitted this, we could then have discussed whether that being is personal, good, and so on. On the actual point discussed, whether there is or is not a necessary being, I find myself, I think, in agreement with the great majority of classical philosophers.

You maintain, I think, that existing beings are simply there, and that I have no justification for raising the question of the explanation of their existence. But I would like to point out that this position cannot be substantiated by logical analysis; it expresses a philosophy which itself stands in need of proof. I think we have reached an impasse because our ideas of philosophy are radically different; it seems to me that what I call a part of philosophy, that you call the whole, insofar at least as philosophy is rational. It seems to me, if you will pardon my saying so, that besides your own logical system—which you call "modern" in opposition to antiquated logic (a tendentious adjective)—you maintain a philosophy which cannot be substantiated by logical analysis. After all, the problem of God's existence is an existential problem, whereas logical analysis does not deal directly with problems of existence. So it seems to me, to declare that the terms involved in one set of problems are meaningless because they are not required in dealing with another set of problems, is to settle from the beginning the nature and extent of philosophy, and that is itself a philosophical act which stands in need of justification.

RUSSELL: Well, I should like to say just a few words by way of summary on my side. First, as to the metaphysical argument: I don't admit the connotations of such a term as "contingent" or the possibility of explanation in Father Copleston's sense. I think the word "contingent" inevitably suggests the possibility of something that wouldn't have this what you might call accidental character of just being there, and I don't think this is true except in the purely causal sense. You can sometimes give a causal explanation of one thing as being the effect of something else, but that is merely referring one thing to another thing and there's no—to my mind—explanation in Father Copleston's sense of anything at all, nor is there any meaning in calling things "contingent" because there isn't anything else they could be. That's what I should say about that, but I should like to say a few words about Father Copleston's accusation that I regard logic as all philosophy—that is by no means the case. I don't by any means regard logic as all philosophy. I think logic is an essential part of philosophy and logic has to be used in philosophy, and in that I think he and I are at one. When the logic that he uses was new—namely, in the time of Aristotle, there had to be a great deal of fuss made about it; Aristotle made a lot of fuss about that logic. Nowadays it's become old and respectable, and you don't have to make so much fuss about it. The logic that I believe in is comparatively new, and therefore I have to imitate Aristotle in making a fuss about it; but it's not that I think it's all philosophy by any means—I don't think so. I think it's an important part of philosophy, and when I say that I don't find a meaning for this or that word, that is a position of detail based upon what I've found out about that particular word, from thinking about it. It's not a general position that all words that are used in metaphysics are nonsense, or anything like that which I don't really hold.

As regards the moral argument, I do find that when one studies anthropology or history, there are people who think it their duty to perform acts which I think abominable, and I certainly can't, therefore, attribute Divine origin to the matter of moral obligation, which Father Copleston doesn't ask me to; but I think even the form of moral obligation, when it takes the form of enjoining you to eat your father or what not, doesn't seem to me to be such a very beautiful and noble thing; and, therefore, I cannot attribute a Divine origin to this sense of moral obligation, which I think is quite easily accounted for in quite other ways.

God Has Left
Proof of Himself

Richard Taylor

Richard Taylor (1919–   ) is Professor of Philosophy in the University of Rochester.

Chance and Evidence

The idea we want to develop here is not easy to grasp without misunderstanding, so it will be best to approach it stepwise by considering first an example or two that should make it quite obvious.

Suppose, then, that you are riding in a railway coach and glancing from the window at one of the stops; you see numerous white stones scattered about on a small hillside near the train in a pattern resembling these letters: THE BRITISH RAILWAYS WELCOMES YOU TO WALES. Now you could scarcely doubt that these stones do not just accidentally happen to exhibit that pattern. You would, in fact, feel quite certain that they were purposefully *arranged* that way to convey an intelligible message. At the same time, however, you could not prove, just from a consideration of their arrangement alone, that they were arranged by a purposeful being. It is possible—at least logically so—that there was no guiding hand at

Richard Taylor, *Metaphysics*, © 1963. Reprinted by permission of Prentice-Hall, Inc., Englewood Cliffs, New Jersey.

all in back of this pattern, that it is simply the result of the operations of inanimate nature. It is possible that the stones, one by one, rolled down the hill and, over the course of centuries, finally ended up in that interesting arrangement, or that they came in some other accidental way to be so related to each other. For surely the mere fact that something has an interesting or striking shape or pattern, and thus *seems* purposefully arranged, is no proof that it is. There might always be some other explanation. Snowflakes, viewed under magnification, exhibit symmetrical, interesting, and often beautiful shapes, and yet we know that these are not designed but can be explained simply in terms of the physics of crystallization. We find *apparently* purposeful arrangements and contrivances around us all the time, but we cannot always conclude that these are in fact the expressions of any purpose. Our own bodies and their organs seem purposeful not only in their individual structures but in their relationships to each other, and yet there are well known theories, resting on such nonpurposeful concepts as chance variation, natural selection, and so on, which are able, at least in the opinion of many learned men, to explain these structures without introducing any ideas of purpose and design at all.

Here, however, is the important point which it is easy to overlook; namely, that *if*, upon seeing from the train window a group of stones arranged as described, you were to conclude that you were entering Wales, and *if* your sole reason for thinking this, whether it was in fact good evidence or not, was that the stones were so arranged, *then* you could not, consistently with that, suppose that the arrangement of the stones was accidental. You would, in fact, be presupposing that they were arranged that way by an intelligent and purposeful being or beings, for the purpose of conveying a certain message having nothing to do with the stones themselves. Another way of expressing the same point is that it would be *irrational* for you to regard the arrangement of the stones as evidence that you were entering Wales, and at the same time to suppose that they might have come to have that arrangement accidentally, that is, as the result of the ordinary interactions of natural or physical forces. If, for instance, they came to be so arranged over the course of time, simply by rolling down the hill, one by one, and finally just happening to end up that way, or if they were strewn upon the ground that way by the forces of an earthquake or storm or whatnot, then their arrangement would in no sense constitute evidence that you were entering Wales, or for anything whatever unconnected with themselves.

Consider another example. Suppose a stone were dug up and

found to be covered with interesting marks, all more or less the same size and more or less in rows. Now there is nothing very remarkable about that. Glaciers and volcanoes have produced stones no less interesting, in abundance. They may at first sight seem purposefully fabricated, but a geologist who knows how they came to be there can usually explain their interesting shapes and properties. Suppose further, however, that the marks on this stone are found to resemble the characters of an ancient alphabet. This, too, does not prove that they were purposefully inscribed, for natural forces can leave such marks as these on stones, and over the course of millions of years it is entirely possible that this should occasionally happen. There are places where one can, at will, pick up stones that are almost perfect rectangles and look exactly as though they were hewn by stonecutters, though in fact they resulted from glaciation. But now suppose that these marks are recognized by a scholar having a knowledge of that alphabet, and that with considerable uncertainty due to the obscurity of some of the marks and the obliteration of others, he renders a translation of them as follows: HERE KIMON FELL LEADING A BAND OF ATHENIANS AGAINST THE FORCES OF XERXES. Now one can, to be sure, still maintain that the marks are accidental, that they are only scratches left by volcanic activity, and that it is only a singular coincidence that they resemble, more or less, some intelligible message. Nature sometimes produces effects hardly less interesting and arresting than this. The point to make again, however, is this: if anyone having a knowledge of this stone concludes, solely on the basis of it, that there was someone named Kimon who died in battle near where this stone was found, then he cannot, rationally, suppose that the marks on the stone are the result of the chance or purposeless operations of the forces of nature. He must, on the contrary, assume that they were inscribed there by someone whose purpose was to record an historical fact. If the marks had a purposeless origin, as from volcanic activity or whatnot, then they cannot reveal any fact whatever except, perhaps, certain facts about themselves or their origin. It would, accordingly, be irrational for anyone to suppose *both* that what is seemingly expressed by the marks is true, and *also* that they appeared as the result of nonpurposeful forces, provided the marks are his *sole* evidence for believing that what they seem to say is true.

Sensation and Evidence

Our own organs of sense, to say nothing of our brains and nervous systems, are things of the most amazing and bewildering complexity and delicacy. No matter how far and minutely psychologists and physiologists press their studies of these organs, they seem hardly any closer to a real understanding of them and how they enable us to *perceive* the world around us. At best they discover only how they convey stimuli and impress physical changes upon the brain. Theories of perception, drawing upon all the scientific and physiological knowledge accumulated to date, are hardly less crude than the speculations of the Greeks.

Some of these organs, moreover, strikingly resemble things purposefully designed and fabricated by men, though they greatly exceed in their delicacy and versatility anything men have invented. The parts and structure of the eye, for example, closely resemble those of a camera. Yet the comparison of these, however striking, is superficial, for the eye does not take pictures. Unlike a camera, it somehow enables its possessor to perceive and thereby to understand. Things like this can be more or less imitated by men, but they are usually crude and make-shift in comparison. It is sometimes almost irresistible, when considering such a thing as the eye, to suppose that, however it may have originated, it is constructed in that manner *in order* to enable its possessor to see. Many persons quite naturally think in these terms, without at all realizing the implications of such purposeful or teleological conceptions.

It must be noted, however, that just as it is possible for a collection of stones to present a novel and interesting arrangement on the side of a hill, and for marks to appear on a stone in a manner closely resembling some human artifact, and for these things still to be the accidental results of natural, nonpurposeful forces, so also it is possible for such things as our own organs of sense to be the accidental and unintended results, over ages of time, of perfectly impersonal, nonpurposeful forces. In fact, ever so many biologists believe that this is precisely what has happened, that our organs of sense are in no real sense purposeful things, but only appear so because of our failure to consider how they might have arisen through the normal workings of nature. It is supposed, for example, that if we apply the conceptions of chance mutations and variations, natural selection, and so on, then we can see how it is at least possible—perhaps even almost inevitable—that things of this sort should finally emerge, without any purpose behind them at all.

It would be astonishing indeed if a quantity of stones were hurled into the air and fell to earth in a pattern spelling out some intelligible message. Any man would feel, quite irresistibly, that it had been somehow *arranged* that they should fall that way. It would be less astonishing, however, if those stones were thrown a million times, and sooner or later fell to earth in such a pattern. Our astonishment would be still less if we found some perfectly natural, nonpurposeful explanation why they might sooner or later fall in that manner and, having so fallen, be thus preserved. If, for instance, we found that the stones were of slightly different weights, sizes, and shapes, that these influenced how they were thrown and how they rolled upon landing, that these slight differences tended to favor the likelihood that certain ones would come to rest in the striking manner in which they do come to rest, and that certain obstructions on the ground would tend to preserve them in this arrangement, and so on, then we might find it entirely plausible how they might fall as they do without the intervention of any purposeful being at all. If our explanation were of this kind, however, then, as noted before, their arrangement would constitute no evidence whatever for anything not causally connected with themselves.

The mere complexity, refinement, and seemingly purposeful arrangement of our sense organs do not, accordingly, constitute any conclusive reason for supposing that they are the outcome of any purposeful activity. A natural, nonpurposeful explanation of them is possible, and has been attempted—successfully, in the opinion of many.

The important point, however, and one that is rarely considered is that we do not simply *marvel* at these structures, and wonder how they came to be that way. We do not simply view them as amazing and striking things, and speculate upon their origins. We, in fact, whether justifiably or not, *rely* on them for the discovery of things that we suppose to be true and which we suppose to exist quite independently of those organs themselves. We suppose, without even thinking about it, that they reveal to us things that have nothing to do with themselves, their structures, or their origins. Just as we supposed that the stones on the hill told us that we were entering Wales—a fact having nothing to do with the stones themselves—so also we suppose that our senses in some manner "tell us" what is true, at least sometimes. The stones on the hill could, to be sure, have been an accident, in which case we cannot suppose that they really tell us anything at all. So also, our senses and all our faculties could be accidental in their origins, and in that case they do not really tell us anything either. But the fact remains that we do trust them, without the slightest reflection on the matter. Our seeing something is often thought to be, quite by itself, a good reason for believing that the thing exists, and it would be absurd to suggest that we *infer* this from the structure of our eyes or speculations upon their evolutionary origins. And so it is with our other faculties. Our remembering something is often considered to be, quite by itself, a good reason for believing that the thing remembered did happen. Our hearing a sound is often considered, quite by itself, a good reason for believing that a sound exists; and so on.

We are not here suggesting that our senses are infallible, nor even that we ought to rely upon their testimony. The point is that we do rely upon them. We do not believe merely that our senses are remarkably interesting things. We do not believe merely that they produce interesting effects within us, nor merely that they produce beliefs in us. We assume, rightly or wrongly, that they are *trustworthy* guides with respect to what is true and what exists independently of our senses and their origins; and we still assume this, even when they are our only guides.

We saw that it would be irrational for anyone to say *both* that the marks he found on a stone had a natural, nonpurposeful origin and *also* that they reveal some truth with respect to something other than themselves, something that is not merely inferred from them. One cannot rationally believe both of these things. So also, it is now suggested, it would be irrational for one to say *both* that his sensory and cognitive faculties had a natural, nonpurposeful origin and *also* that they reveal some truth with respect to something other than themselves, something that is not merely inferred from them. *If* their origin can be entirely accounted for in terms of chance variations, natural selection, and so on, without supposing that they somehow embody and express the purposes of some creative being, then the most we can say of them is that they exist, that they are complex and wondrous in their construction, and are perhaps in other respects interesting and remarkable. We cannot say that they are, entirely by themselves, reliable guides to any truth whatever, save only what can be inferred from their own structure and arrangement. If, on the other hand, we do assume that they are guides to some truths having nothing to do with themselves, then it is difficult to see how we can, consistently with that supposition, believe them to have arisen by accident, or by the ordinary workings of purposeless forces, even over ages of time.

At this point persons who have a deep suspicion of all such arguments as this, and particularly persons who are hostile to any of the claims of religion, are likely to seize upon numberless objections of a sort that it would hardly occur to anyone to apply to our first two examples, involving the stones. Thus, it is apt to be said that our cognitive faculties are not so reliable as some would suppose, which is irrelevant; or that arguments from analogy prove nothing, which is also irrelevant, since none of the foregoing is an argument from analogy. Or it is claimed that we rely on our cognitive faculties only because we have found them reliable in the past, and thus have a sound inductive basis for our trust, which is absurd, if not question-begging. The reason I believe there is a world around me is, quite simply, that I see it, feel it, hear it, and am in fact perpetually in cognitive contact with it, or at least assume myself to be, without even considering the matter. To suggest that I *infer* its existence from the effects that it has within me, and that I find the inference justified on the ground that such inner effects have, in the past, been accompanied by external causes, is not only a ridiculous caricature, but begs the question of how, without relying upon my faculties, I could ever confirm such an idea in the first place. Again, it is sometimes said that the capacity to grasp truths has a decided value to the survival of an organism, and that our cognitive faculties have evolved, quite naturally, through the operation of this principle. This appears farfetched, however, even if for no other reason than that man's capacity to understand what is true, through reliance upon his senses and cognitive faculties, far exceeds what is needed for survival. One might as well say that the sign on the hill welcoming tourists to Wales originated over the course of ages purely by accident, and has been preserved by the utility it was then found to possess. This is of course possible, but also immensely implausible.

The Significance of These Arguments

It would be extravagant indeed to suppose that these reflections amount to any sort of confirmation of religion, or even that they have much to do with religion. They are purely metaphysical and philosophical considerations having implications of only a purely speculative kind. Even if they are utterly probative, which is of course controversial, it can still be pointed out, correctly, that they are consistent with ever so many views which are radically inconsistent with religion. They imply almost nothing with respect to any divine attributes, such as benevolence, and one could insist with some justification that even the word "God," which is supposed to be the proper name of a personal being and not just a label to be attached to metaphysically inferred things, is out of place in them.

No more is claimed for these arguments, however, than that they are good arguments, and that they seem to yield the conclusions derived from them. If they are defective, the defects are not gross or obvious. The reader may suit himself whether they yield those conclusions, and if so, what their human significance might be.

God's Existence Not an Empirically Meaningful Question

Antony Flew

Antony Flew (1923–   ), Professor of Philosophy in University College of North Staffordshire, is a frequent contributor to, and editor of, the literature of conceptual analysis.

Let us begin with a parable. It is a parable developed from a tale told by John Wisdom in his haunting and revelatory article "Gods."[1] Once upon a time two explorers came upon a clearing in the jungle. In the clearing were growing many flowers and many weeds. One explorer says, "Some gardener must tend this plot." The other disagrees, "There is no gardener." So they pitch their tents and set a watch. No gardener is ever seen. "But perhaps he is an invisible gardener." So they set up a barbed-wire fence. They electrify it. They patrol with bloodhounds. (For they remember how H. G. Wells's "invisible man" could be both smelt and touched though he could not be seen.) But no shrieks ever suggest that some intruder has received a shock. No movements of the wire ever betray an invisible climber. The bloodhounds never give cry. Yet still the Believer is not convinced. "But there is a gardener, invisible, intangible, insensible to electric shocks, a gardener who has no scent and makes no sound, a gardener who comes secretly to look after the garden which he loves." At last the Skeptic despairs, "But what remains of your original assertion? Just how does what you call an invisible, intangible, eter-

Reprinted with permission of The Macmillan Company and SCM Press Ltd from *New Essays in Philosophical Theology* by A. G. N. Flew and Alasdair MacIntyre. First published in 1955.

nally elusive gardener differ from an imaginary gardener or even from no gardener at all?"

In this parable we can see how what starts as an assertion that something exists or that there is some analogy between certain complexes of phenomena may be reduced step by step to an altogether different status, to an expression perhaps of a "picture preference."[2] The Skeptic says there is no gardener. The Believer says there is a gardener (but invisible, and so forth). One man talks about sexual behavior. Another man prefers to talk of Aphrodite (but knows that there is not really a superhuman person additional to, and somehow responsible for, all sexual phenomena).[3] The process of qualification may be checked at any point before the original assertion is completely withdrawn and something of that first assertion will remain (Tautology). Mr. Wells's invisible man could not, admittedly, be seen, but in all other respects he was a man like the rest of us. But though the process of qualification may be, and of course usually is, checked in time, it is not always judiciously so halted. Someone may dissipate his assertion completely without noticing that he has done so. A fine brash hypothesis may thus be killed by inches, the death by a thousand qualifications.

And in this, it seems to me, lies the peculiar danger, the endemic evil, of theological utterance. Take such utterances as "God has a plan," "God created the world," "God loves us as a father loves his children." They look at first sight very much like assertions, vast cosmological assertions. Of course, this is no sure sign that they either are, or are intended to be, assertions. But let us confine ourselves to the cases where those who utter such sentences intend them to express assertions. (Merely remarking parenthetically that those who intend or interpret such utterances as crypto-commands, expressions of wishes, disguised ejaculations, concealed ethics, or as anything else but assertions, are unlikely to succeed in making them either properly orthodox or practically effective.)

Now to assert that such and such is the case is necessarily equivalent to denying that such and such is not the case.[4] Suppose then that we are in doubt as to what someone who gives vent to an utterance is asserting, or suppose that, more radically, we are skeptical as to whether he is really asserting anything at all, one way of trying to understand (or perhaps it will be to expose) his utterance is to attempt to find what he would regard as counting against, or as being incompatible with, its truth. For if the utterance is indeed an assertion, it will necessarily be equivalent to a denial of the negation of that assertion. And anything which would count against the assertion, or which would induce the speaker to withdraw it and to admit that it had been mistaken, must be part of (or the whole of) the meaning of the negation of that assertion. And to know the meaning of the negation of an assertion is, as near as makes no matter, to know the meaning of that assertion.[5] And if there is nothing which a putative assertion denies, then there is nothing which it asserts either: and so it is not really an assertion. When the Skeptic in the parable asked the Believer, "Just how does what you call an invisible, intangible, eternally elusive gardener differ from an imaginary gardener or even from no gardener at all?" he was suggesting that the Believer's earlier statement had been so eroded by qualification that it was no longer an assertion at all.

Now it often seems to people who are not religious as if there was no conceivable event or series of events the occurrence of which would be admitted by sophisticated religious people to be a sufficient reason for conceding "There wasn't a God after all" or "God does not really love us then." Someone tells us that God loves us as a father loves his children. We are reassured. But then we see a child dying of inoperable cancer of the throat. His earthly father is driven frantic in his efforts to help, but his Heavenly Father reveals no obvious sign of concern. Some qualification is made—God's love is "not a merely human love" or it is "an inscrutable love," perhaps—and we realize that such sufferings are quite compatible with the truth of the assertion that "God loves us as a father (but, of course . . .)." We are reassured again. But then perhaps we ask: what is this assurance of God's (appropriately qualified) love worth, what is this apparent guarantee really a guarantee against? Just what would have to happen not merely (morally and wrongly) to tempt but also (logically and rightly) to entitle us to say "God does not love us" or even "God does not exist"? I therefore put to the succeeding symposiasts the simple central questions, "What would have to occur or to have occurred to constitute for you a disproof of the love of, or of the existence of, God?"

Notes

[1] *Proceedings of the Aristotelian Society*, 1944–5, reprinted as Ch. X of *Logic and Language*, Vol I (Blackwell, 1951), and in his *Philosophy and Psycho-Analysis* (Blackwell, 1953).

[2] Cf. J. Wisdom, "Other Minds," *Mind*, 1940; reprinted in his *Other Minds* (Blackwell, 1952).

[3] Cf. Lucretius, *De Rerum Natura*, II, 655–60.

> *Hic siquis mare Neptunum Cereremque vocare*
> *Constituet fruges et Bacchi nomine abuti*
> *Mavolat quam laticis proprium proferre vocamen*
> *Concedamus ut hic terrarum dictitet orbem*
> *Esse deum matrem dum vera re tamen ipse*
> *Religione animum turpi contingere parcat.*

[4] For those who prefer symbolism: $p \equiv {\sim}{\sim}p$.

[5] For by simply negating ${\sim}p$ we get $p: {\sim}{\sim}p \equiv p$.

Talk About God Is Empirically Meaningful

John Hick

John Hick (1922–   ) is H. G. Wood Professor of Theology in the University of Birmingham, England. He has taught in Cambridge, Cornell, and Princeton universities and authored many books and articles on philosophy of religion and theology.

To ask "Is the existence of God verifiable?" is to pose a question which is too imprecise to be capable of being answered. There are many different concepts of God, and it may be that statements employing some of them are open to verification or falsification while statements employing others of them are not. Again, the notion of verifying is itself by no means perfectly clear and fixed; and it may be that on some views of the nature of verification the existence of God is verifiable whereas on other views it is not.

Instead of seeking to compile a list of the various different concepts of God and the various possible senses of "verify," I wish to argue with regard to one particular concept of deity, namely the Christian concept, that divine existence is in principle verifiable; and as the first stage of this argument I must indicate what I mean by "verifiable."

Reprinted by permission of the author and the publisher from *Theology Today*, Vol. XVII (April, 1960), pp. 12–31.

I

The central core of the concept of verification, I suggest, is the removal of ignorance or uncertainty concerning the truth of some proposition. That *p* is verified (whether *p* embodies a theory, hypothesis, prediction, or straightforward assertion) means that something happens which makes it clear that *p* is true. A question is settled so that there is no longer room for rational doubt concerning it. The way in which grounds for rational doubt are excluded varies of course with the subject matter. But the general feature common to all cases of verification is the ascertaining of truth by the removal of grounds for rational doubt. Where such grounds are removed, we rightly speak of verification having taken place.

To characterize verification in this way is to raise the question whether the notion of verification is purely logical or is both logical and psychological. Is the statement that *p* is verified simply the statement that a certain state of affairs exists (or has existed), or is it the statement also that someone is aware that this state of affairs exists (or has existed) and notes that its existence establishes the truth of *p?* A geologist predicts that the earth's surface will be covered with ice in 15 million years time. Suppose that in 15 million years time the earth's surface *is* covered with ice, but that in the meantime the human race has perished, so that no one is left to observe the event or to draw any conclusion concerning the accuracy of the geologist's prediction. Do we now wish to say that his prediction has been verified, or shall we deny that it has been verified on the ground that there is no one left to do the verifying?

The use of "verify" and its cognates is sufficiently various to permit us to speak in either way. But the only sort of verification of theological propositions which is likely to interest us is one in which human beings participate. We may therefore, for our present purpose, treat verification as a logico-psychological rather than as a purely logical concept. I suggest then that "verify" be construed as a verb which has its primary uses in the active voice: I verify, you verify, we verify, they verify or have verified. The impersonal passive, it is verified, now becomes logically secondary. To say that *p* has been verified is to say that (at least) someone has verified it, often with the implication that his or their report to this effect is generally accepted. But it is impossible, on this usage, for p to have been verified without someone having verified it. "Verification" is thus primarily the name for an event which takes place in human consciousness.[1] It refers to an experience, the experience of ascertaining that a given proposition or set of propositions is true. To this extent verification is a psychological notion. But of course it is also a logical notion. For needless to say, not *any* experience is rightly called an experience of verifying p. Both logical and psychological conditions must be fulfilled in order for verification to have taken place. In this respect, "verify" is like "know." Knowing is an experience which someone has or undergoes, or perhaps a dispositional state in which someone is, and it cannot take place without someone having or undergoing it or being in it; but not by any means every experience which people have, or every dispositional state in which they are, is rightly called knowing.

With regard to this logico-psychological concept of verification, such questions as the following arise. When A, but nobody else, has ascertained that p is true, can p be said to have been verified; or is it required that others also have undergone the same ascertainment? How public, in other words, must verification be? Is it necessary that p could in principle be verified by anyone without restriction even though perhaps only A has in fact verified it? If so, what is meant here by "in principle"; does it signify, for example, that p must be verifiable by anyone who performs a certain operation; and does it imply that to do this is within everyone's power?

These questions cannot, I believe, be given any general answer applicable to all instances of the exclusion of rational doubt. The answers must be derived in each case from an investigation of the particular subject matter. It will be the object of subsequent sections of this article to undertake such an investigation in relation to the Christian concept of God.

Verification is often construed as the verification of a prediction. However verification, as the exclusion of grounds for rational doubt, does not necessarily consist in the proving correct of a prediction; a verifying experience does not always need to have been predicted in order to have the effect of excluding rational doubt. But when we are interested in the verifiability of propositions as the criterion for their having factual meaning, the notion of prediction becomes central. If a proposition contains or entails predictions which can be verified or falsified, its character as an assertion (though not of course its character as a true assertion) is thereby guaranteed.

Such predictions may be and often are conditional. For example, statements about the features of the dark side of the moon are rendered meaningful by the conditional predictions which they entail to the effect that if an observer comes to be in such a position in space, he will make such-and-such observations. It would in fact be more accurate to say that the prediction is always conditional, but that sometimes the conditions are so obvious and so likely to be fulfilled in any case that they require no special mention, while sometimes they require for their fulfillment some unusual expedition or operation. A prediction, for example, that the sun will rise within twenty-four hours is intended unconditionally, at least as concerns conditions to be fulfilled by the observer; he is not required by the terms of the prediction to perform any special operation. Even in this case, however, there is an implied negative condition that he shall not put himself in a situation (such as immuring himself in the depths of a coal mine) from which a sunrise would not be perceptible. Other predictions however are explicitly conditional. In these cases it is true for any particular individual that in order to verify the statement in question he must go through some specified course of action. The prediction is to the effect that if you conduct such an experiment, you will obtain such a result: for example, if you go into the next room, you will have such-and-such visual experiences, and if you then touch the table which you see, you will have such-and-such tactual experiences, and so on. The content of the "if" clause is always determined by the particular subject matter. The logic of "table" determines what you must do to verify statements about tables; the logic of "molecule" determines what you must do to verify statements about molecules; and the logic of "God" determines what you must do to verify statements about God.

In those cases in which the individual who is to verify a proposition must himself first perform some operation, it clearly cannot follow the circumstances that the proposition is true that everybody has in fact verified it, or that everybody will at some future time verify it. For whether or not any particular person performs the requisite operation is a contingent matter.

II

What is the relation between verification and falsification? We are all familiar today with the phrase, "theology and falsification."

Antony Flew[2] and others have raised instead of the question, "What possible experiences would verify 'God exists'?" the matching question, "What possible experiences would falsify 'God exists'? What conceivable state of affairs would be incompatible with the existence of God?" In posing the question in this way, it was apparently assumed that verification and falsification are symmetrically related, and that the latter is apt to be the more accessible of the two.

In the most common cases, certainly, verification and falsification are symmetrically related. The logically simplest case of verification is provided by the crucial instance. Here it is integral to a given hypothesis that if, in specified circumstances, A occurs, the hypothesis is thereby shown to be true, whereas if B occurs, the hypothesis is thereby shown to be false. Verification and falsification are also symmetrically related in the testing of such a proposition as "There is a table in the next room." The verifying experiences in this case are experiences of seeing and touching, predictions of which are entailed by the proposition in question, under the proviso that one goes into the next room; and the absence of such experiences in those circumstances serves to falsify the proposition.

But it would be rash to assume, on this basis, that verification and falsification must always be related in this symmetrical fashion. They do not necessarily stand to one another as do the two sides of a coin, so that once the coin is spun it must fall on one side or the other. There are cases in which verification and falsification each correspond to a side on a different coin, so that one can fail to verify without this failure constituting falsification.

Consider, for example, the proposition that "there are three successive sevens in the decimal determination of π." So far as the value of π has been worked out, it does not contain a series of three sevens, but it will always be true that such a series may occur at a point not yet reached in anyone's calculations. Accordingly, the proposition may one day be verified if it is true, but can never be falsified if it is false.

The hypothesis of continued conscious existence after bodily death provides an instance of a different kind of such asymmetry, and one which has a direct bearing upon the theistic problem. This hypothesis has built into it a prediction that one will after the date of one's bodily death have conscious experiences, including the experience of remembering that death. This is a prediction which will be verified in one's own experience if it is true, but which cannot be falsified if it is false. That is to say, it can be false, but *that* it is false can never be a fact which anyone has experientially verified. But this circumstance does not undermine the meaningfulness of the hypothesis, since it is also such that if it be true, it will be known to be true.

It is important to remember that we do not speak of verifying logically necessary truths, but only propositions concerning matters of fact. Accordingly verification is not to be identified with the concept of logical certification or proof. The exclusion of rational doubt concerning some matter of fact is not equivalent to the exclusion of the logical possibility of error or illusion. For truths concerning fact are not logically necessary. Their contrary is never self-contradictory. But at the same time the bare logical possibility of error does not constitute ground for rational doubt as to the veracity of our experience. If it did, no empirical proposition could ever be verified, and indeed the notion of empirical verification would be without use and therefore without sense. What we rightly seek, when we desire the verification of a factual proposition, is not a demonstration of the logical impossibility of the proposition being false (for this would be a self-contradictory demand), but such kind and degree of evidence as suffices, in the type of case in question, to exclude rational doubt.

III

These features of the concept of verification—that verification consists in the exclusion of grounds for rational doubt concerning the truth of some proposition; that this means its exclusion from particular minds; that the nature of the experience which serves to exclude grounds for rational doubt depends upon the particular subject matter; that verification is often related to predictions and that such predictions are often conditional; that verification and falsification may be asymmetrically related; and finally, that the verification of a factual proposition is not equivalent to logical certification—are all relevant to the verification of the central religious claim, "God exists." I wish now to apply these discriminations to the notion of eschatological verification, which has been briefly employed by Ian Crombie in his contribution to *New Essays in Philosophical Theology*,[3] and by myself in *Faith and Knowledge*.[4] This suggestion has on each occasion been greeted with disapproval by both philosophers and theologians. I am, however, still of the opinion that the notion of eschatological verification is sound; and further, that no viable alternative to it has been offered to establish the factual character of theism.

The strength of the notion of eschatological verification is that it is not an *ad hoc* invention but is based upon an actually operative religious concept of God. In the language of Christian faith, the word "God" stands at the center of a system of terms, such as Spirit, grace, Logos, incarnation, Kingdom of God, and many more; and the distinctly Christian conception of God can only be fully grasped in its connection with these related terms.[5] It belongs to a complex of notions which together constitute a picture of the universe in which we live, of man's place therein, of a comprehensive divine purpose interacting with human purposes, and of the general nature of the eventual fulfillment of that divine purpose. This Christian picture of the universe, entailing as it does certain distinctive expectations concerning the future, is a very different picture from any that can be accepted by one who does not believe that the God of the New Testament exists. Further, these differences are such as to show themselves in human experience. The possibility of experiential confirmation is thus built into the Christian concept of God; and the notion of eschatological verification seeks to relate this fact to the problem of theological meaning.

Let me first give a general theological indication of this suggestion, by repeating a parable which I have related elsewhere,[6] and then try to make it more precise and eligible for discussion. Here, first, is the parable.

Two men are traveling together along a road. One of them believes that it leads to a Celestial City, the other that it leads nowhere; but since this is the only road there is, both must travel it. Neither has been this way before, and therefore neither is able to say what they will find around each next corner. During their journey they meet both with moments of refreshment and delight, and with moments of hardship and danger. All the time one of them thinks of his journey as a pilgrimage to the Celestial City and interprets the pleasant parts as encouragements and the obstacles as trials of his purpose and lessons in endurance, prepared by the king of that city and designed to make of him a worthy citizen of the place when at last he arrives there. The other, however, believes none of this and sees their journey as an unavoidable and aimless ramble. Since he has no choice in the matter, he enjoys the good and endures the bad. But for him there is no Celestial City to be reached, no all-encompassing purpose ordaining their journey; only the road itself and the luck of the road in good weather and in bad.

During the course of the journey the issue between them is

not an experimental one. They do not entertain different expectations about the coming details of the road, but only about its ultimate destination. And yet when they do turn the last corner it will be apparent that one of them has been right all the time and the other wrong. Thus although the issue between them has not been experimental, it has nevertheless from the start been a real issue. They have not merely felt differently about the road; for one was feeling appropriately and the other inappropriately in relation to the actual state of affairs. Their opposed interpretations of the road constituted genuinely rival assertions, though assertions whose assertion-status has the peculiar characteristic of being guaranteed retrospectively by a future crux.

This parable has of course (like all parables) strict limitations. It is designed to make only one point: that Christian doctrine postulates an ultimate unambiguous state of existence *in patria* as well as our present ambiguous existence *in via*. There is a state of having arrived as well as a state of journeying, an eternal heavenly life as well as an earthly pilgrimage. The alleged future experience of this state cannot, of course, be appealed to as evidence for theism as a present interpretation of our experience; but it does suffice to render the choice between theism and atheism a real and not a merely empty or verbal choice. And although this does not affect the logic of the situation, it should be added that the alternative interpretations are more than theoretical, for they render different practical plans and policies appropriate now.

The universe as envisaged by the theist, then, differs as a totality from the universe as envisaged by the atheist. This difference does not, however, from our present standpoint within the universe, involve a difference in the objective content of each or even any of its passing moments. The theist and the atheist do not (or need not) expect different events to occur in the successive details of the temporal process. They do not (or need not) entertain divergent expectations of the course of history viewed from within. But the theist does and the atheist does not expect that when history is completed it will be seen to have led to a particular end-state and to have fulfilled a specific purpose, namely that of creating "children of God."

IV

The idea of an eschatological verification of theism can make sense, however, only if the logically prior idea of continued personal existence after death is intelligible. A desultory debate on this topic has been going on for several years in some of the philosophical periodicals. C. I. Lewis has contended that the hypothesis of immortality "is an hypothesis about our own future experience. And our understanding of what would verify it has no lack of clarity."[7] And Morris Schlick agreed, adding, "We must conclude that immortality, in the sense defined [that is, 'survival after death,' rather than 'never-ending life'], should not be regarded as a 'metaphysical problem,' but is an empirical hypothesis, because it possesses logical verifiability. It could be verified by following the prescription: 'Wait until you die!'"[8] However, others have challenged this conclusion, either on the ground that the phrase "surviving death" is self-contradictory in ordinary language or, more substantially, on the ground that the traditional distinction between soul and body cannot be sustained.[9] I should like to address myself to this latter view. The only self of which we know, it is said, is the empirical self, the walking, talking, acting, sleeping individual who lives, it may be, for some sixty to eighty years and then dies. Mental events and mental characteristics are analyzed into the modes of behavior and behavioral dispositions of this empirical self. The human being is described as an organism capable of acting in the "high-level" ways which we characterize as intelligent, thoughtful, humorous, calculating, and the like. The concept of mind or soul is thus not the concept of a "ghost in the machine" (to use Gilbert Ryle's loaded phrase[10]) but of the more flexible and sophisticated ways in which human beings behave and have it in them to behave. On this view there is no room for the notion of soul in distinction from body; and if there is no soul in distinction from body, there can be no question of the soul surviving the death of the body. Against this philosophical background the specifically Christian (and also Jewish) belief in the resurrection of the flesh or body, in contrast to the Hellenic notion of the survival of a disembodied soul, might be expected to have attracted more attention than it has. For it is consonant with the conception of man as an indissoluble psycho-physical unity, and yet it also offers the possibility of an empirical meaning for the idea of "life after death."

Paul is the chief Biblical expositor of the idea of the resurrection of the body.[11] His view, as I understand it, is this. When someone has died, he is, apart from any special divine action, extinct. A human being is by nature mortal and subject to annihilation by death. But in fact, God, by an act of sovereign power, either sometimes or always resurrects or (better) reconstitutes or recreates him—not, however, as the identical physical organism that he was before death, but as a *soma pneumatikon* ("spiritual body") embodying the dispositional characteristics and memory traces of the deceased physical organism, and inhabiting an environment with which the *soma pneumatikon* is continuous as the ante-mortem body was continuous with our present world. In discussing this notion we may well abandon the word "spiritual," as lacking today any precise established usage, and speak of "resurrection bodies" and of "the resurrection world." The principal questions to be asked concern the relation between the physical world and the resurrection world, and the criteria of personal identity which are operating when it is alleged that a certain inhabitant of the resurrection world is the same person as an individual who once inhabited this present world. The first of these questions turns out on investigation to be the more difficult of the two, and I shall take the easier one first.

Let me sketch a very odd possibility (concerning which, however, I wish to emphasize not so much its oddness as its possibility!), and then see how far it can be stretched in the direction of the notion of the resurrection body. In the process of stretching, it will become even more odd than it was before; but my aim will be to show that, however odd, it remains within the bounds of the logically possible. This progression will be presented in three pictures, arranged in a self-explanatory order.

First picture: Suppose that at some learned gathering in this country one of the company were suddenly and inexplicably to disappear, and that at the same moment an exact replica of him were suddenly and inexplicably to appear at some comparable meeting in Australia. The person who appears in Australia is exactly similar, as to both bodily and mental characteristics, with the person who disappears in America. There is continuity of memory, complete similarity of bodily features, including even fingerprints, hair and eye coloration and stomach contents, and also of beliefs, habits, and mental propensities. In fact there is everything that would lead us to identify the one who appeared with the one who disappeared, except continuity of occupancy of space. We may suppose, for example, that a deputation of the colleagues of the man who disappeared fly to Australia to interview the replica of him which is reported there, and find that he is in all respects but one exactly as though he had traveled from, say, Princeton to Melbourne, by conventional means. The only difference is that he describes how, as he was sitting listening to Dr. Z. reading a paper, on blinking his eyes he suddenly found himself sitting in a different room listening to a different paper by an Australian scholar. He asks his colleagues how the meeting had gone after he ceased to be there, and what they had made of his disappearance, and so on. He clearly thinks of himself as the one who was present with them at their meeting in the United States. I suggest that faced with all these circumstances, his colleagues would soon, if not immediately, find themselves thinking of him and treating him as the individual who had so inexplicably disappeared from their midst. We should be extending our normal use of "same person" in a way which the postulated facts would both demand and justify if we said that the one who appears in Australia is the same person as the one who disappears in America. The factors inclining us to identify them would far outweigh the factors disinclining us to do this. We should have no reasonable alternative but to extend our usage of "the same person" to cover the strange new case.

Second picture: Now let us suppose that the event in America is not a sudden and inexplicable disappearance, and indeed not a disappearance at all, but a sudden death. Only, at the moment when the individual dies, a replica of him as he was at the moment before his death, complete with memory up to that instant, appears in Australia. Even with the corpse on our hands, it would still, I suggest, be an extension of "same person" required and warranted by the postulated facts, to say that the same person who died has been miraculously recreated in Australia. The case would be considerably odder than in the previous picture, because of the existence of the corpse in America contemporaneously with the existence of the living person in Australia. But I submit that, although the oddness of this circumstance may be stated as strongly as you please, and can indeed hardly be overstated, yet it does not exceed the bounds of the logically possible. Once again we must imagine some of the deceased's colleagues going to Australia to interview the person who has suddenly appeared there. He would perfectly remember them and their meeting, be interested in what had happened, and be as amazed and dumb-founded about it as anyone else; and he would perhaps be worried about the possible legal complications if he should return to America to claim his property; and so on. Once again, I believe, they would soon find themselves thinking of him and treating him as the same person as the dead Princetonian. Once again the factors inclining us to say that the one who died and the one who appeared are the same person would outweigh the factors inclining us to say that they are different people. Once again we should have to extend our usage of "the same person" to cover this new case.

Third picture: My third supposal is that the replica, complete with memory, etc., appears, not in Australia, but as a resurrection replica in a different world altogether, a resurrection world inhabited by resurrected persons. This world occupies its own space, distinct from the space with which we are now familiar.[12] That is to say, an object in the resurrection world is not situated at any distance or in any direction from an object in our present world, although each object in either world is spatially related to each other object in the same world.

Mr. X., then, dies. A Mr. X. replica, complete with the set of memory traces which Mr. X. had at the last moment before his death, comes into existence. It is composed of other material than physical matter, and is located in a resurrection world which does not stand in any spatial relationship with the physical world. Let us leave out of consideration St. Paul's hint that the resurrection body may be as unlike the physical body as is a full grain of wheat from the wheat seed, and consider the simpler picture in which the resurrection body has the same shape as the physical body.[13]

In these circumstances, how does Mr. X. know that he has been resurrected or recreated? He remembers dying; or rather he remembers being on what he took to be his death-bed, and becoming progressively weaker until, presumably, he lost consciousness. But how does he know that (to put it Irishly) his "dying" proved fatal; and that he did not, after losing consciousness, begin to recover strength, and has now simply waked up?

The picture is readily enough elaborated to answer this question. Mr. X. meets and recognizes a number of relatives and friends and historical personages whom he knows to have died; and from the fact of their presence, and also from their testimony that he has only just now appeared in their world, he is convinced that he has died. Evidences of this kind could mount up to the point at which they are quite as strong as the evidence which, in pictures one and two, convince the individual in question that he has been miraculously translated to Australia. Resurrected persons would be individually no more in doubt about their own identity than we are now, and would be able to identify one another in the same kinds of ways, and with a like degree of assurance, as we do now.

If it be granted that resurrected persons might be able to arrive at a rationally founded conviction that their existence is *postmortem*, how could they know that the world in which they find themselves is in a different space from that in which their physical bodies were? How could such a one know that he is not in a like situation with the person in picture number two, who dies in America and appears as a full-blooded replica in Australia, leaving his corpse in the U.S.A.—except that now the replica is situated, not in Australia, but on a planet of some other star?

It is of course conceivable that the space of the resurrection world should have properties which are manifestly incompatible with its being a region of physical space. But on the other hand, it is not of the essence of the notion of a resurrection world that its space should have properties different from those of physical space. And supposing it not to have different properties, it is not evident that a resurrected individual could learn from any direct observations that he was not on a planet of some sun which is at so great a distance from our own sun that the stellar scenery visible from it is quite unlike that which we can now see. The grounds that a resurrected person would have for believing that he is in a different space from physical space (supposing there to be no discernible difference in spatial properties) would be the same as the grounds that any of us may have now for believing this concerning resurrected individuals. These grounds are indirect and consist in all those considerations (for example, Luke 16:26) which lead most of those who consider the question to reject as absurd the possibility of, for example, radio communication or rocket travel between earth and heaven.

V

In the present context my only concern is to claim that this doctrine of the divine creation of bodies composed of a material other than that of physical matter, which bodies are endowed with sufficient correspondence of characteristics with our present bodies, and sufficient continuity of memory with our present consciousness, for us to speak of the same person being raised up again to life in a new environment, is not self-contradictory. If, then, it cannot be ruled out *ab initio* as meaningless, we may go on to consider whether and how it is related to the possible verification of Christian theism.

So far I have argued that a survival prediction such as is contained in the *corpus* of Christian belief is in principle subject to future verification. But this does not take the argument by any means as far as it must go if it is to succeed. For survival, simply as such, would not serve to verify theism. It would not necessarily be a state of affairs which is manifestly incompatible with the non-existence of God. It might be taken just as a surprising natural fact. The atheist, in his resurrection body, and able to remember his life on earth, might say that the universe has turned out to be more complex, and perhaps more to be approved of, than he had realized. But the mere fact of survival, with a new body in a new environment, would not demonstrate to him that there is a God. It is fully compatible with the notion of survival that the life to come be, so far as the theistic problem is concerned, essentially a continuation of the present life, and religiously no less ambiguous. And in this event, survival after bodily death would not in the least constitute a final verification of theistic faith.

I shall not spend time in trying to draw a picture of a resurrection existence which would merely prolong the religious ambiguity of our present life. The important question, for our purpose, is not whether one can conceive of after-life experiences which would *not* verify theism (and in point of fact, one can fairly easily conceive them), but whether one can conceive of after-life experiences which *would* serve to verify theism.

I think that we can. In trying to do so I shall not appeal to the traditional doctrine, which figures especially in Catholic and mystical theology, of the Beatific Vision of God. The difficulty presented by this doctrine is not so much that of deciding whether there are grounds for believing it, as of deciding what it means. I shall not, however, elaborate this difficulty, but pass directly to the investigation of a different and, as it seems to me, more intelligible possibility. That is the possibility not of a direct vision of God, whatever that might mean, but of a *situation* which points unambiguously to the existence of a loving God. This would be a situation which, so far as its religious significance is concerned, contrasts in a certain important respect with our present situation. Our present situation is one which in some ways seems to confirm and in other ways to contradict the truth of theism. Some events around us suggest the presence of an unseen benevolent intelligence and others suggest that no such intelligence is at work. Our situation is religiously ambiguous. But in order for us to be aware of this fact, we must already have some idea, however vague, of what it would be for our situation to be not ambiguous, but on the contrary wholly evidential of God. I therefore want to try to make clearer this presupposed concept of a religiously unambiguous situation.

There are, I suggest, two possible developments of our experience such that, if they occurred in conjunction with one another (whether in this life or in another life to come), they would assure us beyond rational doubt of the reality of God, as conceived in the Christian faith. These are, *first*, an experience of the fulfillment of God's purpose for ourselves, as this has been disclosed in the Christian revelation; in conjunction, *second*, with an experience of communion with God as he has revealed himself in the person of Christ.

The divine purpose for human life, as this is depicted in the New Testament documents, is the bringing of the human person, in society with his fellows, to enjoy a certain valuable quality of personal life, the content of which is given in the character of Christ—which quality of life (that is, life in relationship with God, described in the Fourth Gospel as eternal life) is said to be the proper destiny of human nature and the source of man's final self-fulfillment and happiness. The verification situation with regard to such a fulfillment is asymmetrical. On the one hand, so long as the divine purpose remains unfulfilled, we cannot know that it never will be fulfilled in the future; hence no final falsification is possible of the claim that this fulfillment will occur— unless, of course, the prediction contains a specific time clause which, in Christian teaching, it does not. But on the other hand, if and when the divine purpose *is* fulfilled in our own experience, we must be able to recognize and rejoice in that fulfillment. For the fulfillment would not be for us the promised fulfillment without our own conscious participation in it.

It is important to note that one can say this much without being cognizant in advance of the concrete form which such fulfillment will take. The before-and-after situation is analogous to that of a small child looking forward to adult life and then, having grown to adulthood, looking back upon childhood. The child possesses and can use correctly in various contexts the concept of "being grown-up," although he does not know, concretely, what it is like to be grown-up. But when he reaches adulthood he is nevertheless able to know that he has reached it; he is able to recognize the experience of living a grown-up life even though he did not know in advance just what to expect. For his understanding of adult maturity grows as he himself matures. Something similar may be supposed to happen in the case of the fulfillment of the divine purpose for human life. That fulfillment may be as far removed from our present condition as is mature adulthood from the mind of a little child; nevertheless, we possess already a comparatively vague notion of this final fulfillment, and as we move towards it, our concept will itself become more adequate; and if and when we finally reach that fulfillment, the problem of recognizing it will have disappeared in the process.

The other feature that must, I suggest, be present in a state of affairs that would verify theism, is that the fulfillment of God's purpose be apprehended *as* the fulfillment of God's purpose and not simply as a natural state of affairs. To this end it must be accompanied by an experience of communion with God as he has made himself known to men in Christ.

The specifically Christian clause, "as he has made himself known to men in Christ," is essential, for it provides a solution to the problem of recognition in the awareness of God. Several writers have pointed out the logical difficulty involved in any claim to have encountered God.[14] How could one know that it was *God* whom one had encountered? God is described in Christian theology in terms of various absolute qualities, such as omnipotence, omnipresence, perfect goodness, infinite love, and so forth, which cannot as such be observed by us, as can their finite analogues, limited power, local presence, finite goodness, and human love. One can recognize that a being whom one "encounters" has a given finite degree of power, but how does one recognize that he has *un*limited power? How does one observe that an encountered being is *omni*present? How does one perceive that his goodness and love, which one can perhaps see to exceed any human goodness and love, are actually infinite? Such qualities cannot be given in human experience. One might claim, then, to have encountered a Being whom one presumes, or trusts, or hopes to be God; but one cannot claim to have encountered a Being whom one recognized to be the infinite, almighty, eternal Creator.

This difficulty is met in Christianity by the doctrine of the Incarnation—although this was not among the considerations which led to the formulation of that doctrine. The idea of incarnation provides answers to the two related questions: "How do we know that God has certain absolute qualities which, by their very nature, transcend human experience?" and "How can there be an eschatological verification of theism which is based upon a recognition of the presence of God in his Kingdom?"

In Christianity God is known as "the God and Father of our Lord Jesus Christ."[15] God is the Being about whom Jesus taught; the Being in relation to whom Jesus lived, and into a relationship with whom he brought his disciples; the Being whose *agape* to-

ward men was seen on earth in the life of Jesus. In short, God is
the transcendent Creator who has revealed himself in Christ. Now
Jesus' teaching about the Father is a part of that self-disclosure,
and it is from this teaching (together with that of the prophets
who preceded him) that the Christian knowledge of God's transcendent being is derived. Only God himself knows his own infinite nature; and our human belief about that nature is based
upon his self-revelation to men in Christ. As Karl Barth expresses
it, "Jesus Christ is the knowability of God."[16] Our beliefs about
God's infinite being are not capable of observational verification,
being beyond the scope of human experience, but they are susceptible of indirect verification by the removal of rational doubt concerning the authority of Christ. An experience of the reign of the
Son in the Kingdom of the Father would confirm that authority,
and therewith, indirectly, the validity of Jesus' teaching concerning the character of God in his infinite transcendent nature.

The further question as to how an eschatological experience
of the Kingdom of God could be known to be such has already
been answered by implication. It is God's union with man in
Christ that makes possible man's recognition of the fulfillment
of God's purpose for man as being indeed the fulfillment of *God's*
purpose for him. The presence of Christ in his Kingdom marks
this as being beyond doubt the Kingdom of the God and Father
of the Lord Jesus Christ.

It is true that even the experience of the realization of the
promised Kingdom of God, with Christ reigning as Lord of the
New Aeon, would not constitute a logical certification of his claims
nor, accordingly, of the reality of God. But this will not seem remarkable to any philosopher in the empiricist tradition, who
knows that it is only a confusion to demand that a factual proposition be an analytic truth. A set of expectations based upon faith
in the historic Jesus as the incarnation of God, and in his teaching as being divinely authoritative, could be so fully confirmed in
post-mortem experience as to leave no grounds for rational doubt
as to the validity of that faith.

VI

There remains of course the problem (which falls to the New
Testament scholar rather than to the philosopher) whether Chris-

tian tradition, and in particular the New Testament, provides a sufficiently authentic "picture" of the mind and character of Christ to make such recognition possible. I cannot here attempt to enter into the vast field of Biblical criticism, and shall confine myself to the logical point, which only emphasizes the importance of the historical question, that a verification of theism made possible by the Incarnation is dependent upon the Christian's having a genuine contact with the person of Christ, even though this is mediated through the life and tradition of the Church.

One further point remains to be considered. When we ask the question, *"To whom* is theism verified?" one is initially inclined to assume that the answer must be, "To everyone." We are inclined to assume that, as in my parable of the journey, the believer must be confirmed in his belief, and the unbeliever converted from his unbelief. But this assumption is neither demanded by the nature of verification nor by any means unequivocally supported by our Christian sources.

We have already noted that a verifiable prediction may be conditional. "There is a table in the next room" entails conditional predictions of the form: if someone goes into the next room he will see, and so on. But no one is compelled to go into the next room. Now it may be that the predictions concerning human experience which are entailed by the proposition that God exists are conditional predictions and that no one is compelled to fulfill those conditions. Indeed we stress in much of our theology that the manner of the divine self-disclosure to men is such that our human status as free and responsible beings is respected, and an awareness of God is never forced upon us. It may then be a condition of *post-mortem* verification that we be already in some degree conscious of God by an uncompelled response to his modes of revelation in this world. It may be that such a voluntary consciousness of God is an essential element in the fulfillment of the divine purpose for human nature, so that the verification of theism which consists in an experience of the final fulfillment of that purpose can only be experienced by those who have already entered upon an awareness of God by the religious mode of apperception which we call faith.

If this be so, it has the consequence that only the theistic believer can find the vindication of his belief. This circumstance would not of course set any restriction upon who can become a believer, but it would involve that while theistic faith can be verified—found by one who holds it to be beyond rational doubt —yet it cannot be proved to the nonbeliever. Such an asymmetry would connect with that strand of New Testament teaching which speaks of a division of mankind even in the world to come.

Having noted this possibility, I will only express my personal opinion that the logic of the New Testament as a whole, though admittedly not always its explicit content, leads to a belief in ultimate universal salvation. However, my concern here is not to seek to establish the religious facts, but rather to establish that there are such things as religious facts, and in particular that the existence or nonexistence of the God of the New Testament is a matter of fact, and claims as such eventual experiential verification.

Notes

[1] This suggestion is closely related to Carnap's insistence that, in contrast to "true," "confirmed" is time-dependent. To say that a statement is confirmed, or verified, is to say that it has been confirmed at a particular time—and, I would add, by a particular person. *See* Rudolf Carnap, "Truth and Confirmation," Feigl and Sellars, *Readings in Philosophical Analysis*, 1949, pp. 119f.

[2] Antony Flew, "Theology and Falsification," [reprinted above, pp. 307f]. On the philosophical antecedents of this change from the notion of verification to that of falsification, *see* Karl R. Popper, *The Logic of Scientific Discovery* (1934; E.T., 1959).

[3] *Op. cit.*, p. 126.

[4] Ithaca: Cornell University Press and London: Oxford University Press, 1957, pp. 150–62.

[5] Its clear recognition of this fact, with regard not only to Christianity but to any religion, is one of the valuable features of Ninian Smart's *Reasons and Faiths* (1958). He remarks, for example, that "the claim that God exists can only be understood by reference to many, if not all, other propositions in the doctrinal scheme from which it is extrapolated" (p. 12).

[6] *Faith and Knowledge*, pp. 150f.

[7] "Experience and Meaning," *Philosophical Review*, 1934, reprinted in Feigl and Sellars, *Readings in Philosophical Analysis*, 1949, p. 142.

[8] "Meaning and Verification," *Philosophical Review*, 1936, reprinted in Feigl and Sellars, *op. cit.*, p. 160.

[9] *See* e.g., A. G. N. Flew, "Death," *New Essays in Philosophi-*

cal Theology; "Can a Man Witness his own Funeral?" *Hibbert Journal,* 1956.

[10] *The Concept of Mind,* 1949, which contains an important exposition of the interpretation of "mental" qualities as characteristics of behavior.

[11] I Cor. 15.

[12] On this possibility, *see* Anthony Quinton "Spaces and Times," *Philosophy,* XXXVII, No. 140 (April, 1962).

[13] As would seem to be assumed, for example, by Irenaeus (*Adversus Haereses,* Bk. II, Ch. 34, Sec. 1).

[14] For example, H. W. Hepburn, *Christianity and Paradox,* 1958, pp. 56f.

[15] II Cor. 11:31.

[16] *Church Dogmatics,* Vol. II, Pt. I, p. 150.

9

The Nature of Ethical
Judgments and Concepts

Ethics concerns the rightness or wrongness of human actions. But it is one thing to make judgments praising or blaming acts, and quite another to justify these judgments. The latter problem is the sphere of metaethics: what standards shall we use to judge ethical standards as higher or lower, better or worse? What do we mean by the terms we use in making judgments, such as "ought," "duty," and "right?"

Most people hold that an action is right if it produces, or at least aims at, a good result. If this is the case, what *is* a good result? The history of ethical theory in the English-speaking world for almost the entire first half of the twentieth century is a chronicle of preoccupation with "the meaning of 'good'." No word more clearly illustrates the errors of linguistic assumptions than this one. G. E. Moore early saw that there is nothing which all good things have in common that we can observe with our senses. But he assumes that all good things must have something in common, since they are all called good—something perhaps detectable only by some special moral sense. C. L. Stevenson, following the suggestions of A. J. Ayer and, earlier of Bertrand Russell, Edward

Westermarck, and others, argues that what good things have in common is simply that people like them. When people disagree about good, he says, it is not about the qualities of things but about their likes and dislikes. Hence no "scientific" solution to the problem of ethical standards was possible, for there were no observable properties of good things to agree on. W. T. Stace, late professor of philosophy at Princeton, examines cultural relativism and argues for a sane relativism in ethics. R. M. Hare states that although it is true there is nothing all good things have in common except that they are commended, everyone in a given group at a given time knows perfectly well what is meant by, for example, a "good car," or a "good cricket bat."

Many people have agreed, openly or tacitly, that good things are at least things that people want, and maybe they are nothing more. Egoism is a theory arguing that all actions are based on self-interest, and that self-interest cannot often take into consideration the interests of others, except when expedient. Glaucon, speaking in Plato's dialogue, the *Republic*, tells the story of a promising shepherd boy who shows man's true nature when he is given the cloak of invisibility. Lucius Garvin, contemporary American philosopher, analyzes the theory of ethical egoism and shows why most philosophers cannot accept it.

The Acid Test of Morality

Plato

Plato (427–347 B.C.), a young aristocrat, took up Socrates's cause after the latter was put to death for impiety and corrupting the youth of Athens. This cause was to make the Athenian citizen look beyond the surface relativism and subjectivism of Athenian life towards something more objective, stable, and beautiful. Plato's distrust of democracy, reflected in his many dialogues, mellowed slightly in later years. With his pupil, Aristotle, he dominates philosophical tradition in the West.

[Glaucon speaking to Socrates.] I . . . shall begin by speaking . . . of the nature and origin of justice.

They say that to do injustice is, by nature, good; to suffer injustice, evil; but that the evil is greater than the good. And so when men have both done and suffered injustice and have had experience of both, not being able to avoid the one and obtain the other, they think that they had better agree among themselves to have neither; hence there arise laws and mutual covenants; and that which is ordained by law is termed by them lawful and just. This they affirm to be the origin and nature of justice;—it is a mean or compromise, between the best of all, which is to do injustice and not be punished, and the worst of all, which is to suffer injustice without the power of retaliation; and justice, being at a middle point between the two, is tolerated not as a good, but as the lesser evil, and honored by reason of the inability of men to do injustice. For no man who is worthy to be called a man would ever submit to such an agreement if he were able to resist;

From Plato's *Republic,* Book II, Jowett translation.

he would be mad if he did. Such is the received account, Socrates, of the nature and origin of justice.

Now that those who practice justice do so involuntarily and because they have not the power to be unjust will best appear if we imagine something of this kind: having given both to the just and the unjust power to do what they will, let us watch and see whither desire will lead them; then we shall discover in the very act the just and unjust man to be proceeding along the same road, following their interest, which all natures deem to be their good, and are only diverted into the path of justice by the force of law. The liberty which we are supposing may be most completely given to them in the form of such a power as is said to have been possessed by Gyges, the ancestor of Croesus the Lydian. According to the tradition, Gyges was a shepherd in the service of the king of Lydia; there was a great storm, and an earthquake made an opening in the earth at the place where he was feeding his flock. Amazed at the sight, he descended into the opening, where, among other marvels, he beheld a hollow brazen horse, having doors, at which he stooping and looking in saw a dead body of stature, as appeared to him, more than human, and having nothing on but a gold ring; this he took from the finger of the dead and reascended. Now the shepherds met together, according to custom, that they might send their monthly report about the flocks to the king; into their assembly he came having the ring on his finger, and as he was sitting among them he chanced to turn the collet of the ring inside his hand, when instantly he became invisible to the rest of the company and they began to speak of him as if he were no longer present. He was astonished at this, and again touching the ring he turned the collet outwards and reappeared; he made several trials of the ring, and always with the same result—when he turned the collet inwards he became invisible, when outwards he reappeared. Whereupon he contrived to be chosen one of the messengers who were sent to the court; where as soon as he arrived he seduced the queen, and with her help conspired against the king and slew him, and took the kingdom. Suppose now that there were two such magic rings, and the just put on one of them and the unjust the other; no man can be imagined to be of such an iron nature that he would stand fast in justice. No man would keep his hands off what was not his own when he could safely take what he liked out of the market, or go into houses and lie with any one at his pleasure, or kill or release from prison whom he would, and in all respects be like a God among men. Then the actions of the just would be as the actions of the unjust; they would both come at last to the same point. And this we may truly affirm to be a great proof that a man is just, not willingly or because he thinks that justice is any good to him individually, but of necessity, for wherever any one thinks that he can safely be unjust, there he is unjust. For all men believe in their hearts that injustice is far more profitable to the individual than justice, and he who argues as I have been supposing, will say that they are right. If you could imagine any one obtaining this power of becoming invisible, and never doing any wrong or touching what was another's, he would be thought by the lookers-on to be a most wretched idiot, although they would praise him to one another's faces, and keep up appearances with one another from a fear that they too might suffer injustice.

Why Egoism Is
an Untenable Theory

Lucius Garvin

Lucius Garvin (1908–   ), Provost, Macalester College, taught philosophy in the University of Maryland.

Do We Ever Do
What We Don't Want To Do?

Psychological egoism may be described as the view whose essence consists in replying "No" to the above question. Actually the question is phrased very roughly, and those who maintain psychological egoism would certainly wish to explain their stand in much more precise terms. In particular they would want it understood that the question to which they give a negative answer is whether we ever *voluntarily* do what we don't want to do. For it is obvious that the lot of most mortals is not exactly what they would have it be, if it were entirely under their control. The world does not contain—at least not as standard equipment—any Aladdin's lamps by which they may summon kindly genii to do their bidding.

Reprinted by permission of the author and Houghton Mifflin Company, from *A Modern Introduction to Ethics* by Lucius Garvin, pp. 34–52. Copyright 1953.

What the psychological egoist asserts is that men do not, of their own preference and choice, act otherwise than in terms of what they consider their own best interests. It is natural and inevitable, they declare, that men should seek their own well-being; that their ultimate motives should be selfish. Unselfish, disinterested actions simply do not exist.

The view is called "psychological egoism" rather than just plain "egoism" in order to distinguish it from another egoistic doctrine. The other egoism, sometimes referred to as "ethical egoism," asserts that the individual *ought* to act with reference to his own interests. The type of egoism we are considering in this chapter is purely descriptive. It does not say that men *should* consider themselves first, but that men *do* consider themselves first. It offers no evaluation of conduct, only a psychological analysis of conduct.

Yet its implication for ethics is obvious—and apparently quite devastating. For if it should be true that no person ever acts except in a single way—namely, in terms of what he thinks will promote his own good—then genuine moral choice is impossible. For a real choice presupposes alternatives. And there are no real alternatives for individuals who are bound to act in a line of least resistance determined by allegedly selfish forces within their own natures. If it is impossible for me to select any but the largest slice of cake, table morals would seem to be ruled out.

Psychological egoism, then, serves as a natural springboard for moral skepticism. In effect the egoist says, "How can you speak of morality when morality requires unselfishness? For there is no unselfishness. How can you speak of duty or of the beauty of sacrifice when a sacrificial act is a pure illusion? How can you raise questions about various bases of human choice when there is in fact only one basis on which choices are ever made?"

Such is the issue which appears forced on us. A careful scrutiny of this view which would thus rule morality out of the picture is accordingly indicated.

The doctrine of universal selfishness has boasted a distinguished set of supporters. So obviously sound did it seem to Macaulay that when he was asked, "What proposition is there respecting human nature which is absolutely and universally true?" he replied, "We know of only one . . . that men always act from self-interest." And Thomas Hobbes with equal assurance asserted that "No man giveth but with intention of good to himself; because gift is voluntary; and of all voluntary acts the object to every man is his own pleasure."

As far back as the time of Socrates there were numerous spokesmen for the view that men never really have an unselfish thought in their heads. Most notably, Callicles, Glaucon, Thrasymachus, and the other moral dissenters in Plato's dialogues announced their opinion that what passes for justice and morality is no more than a set of conventions adopted by men to serve what they suppose to be their own special interests. If individuals were able to do what they liked and to have what they pleased in defiance of moral codes, they would not feel impelled to pay attention to those codes. Men have set up and respected certain conventions solely out of fear of what would happen to the individual if mankind tried to live in a state of anarchical self-sufficiency. With their mouths they sing the virtues of generosity, sacrifice, and mutuality, since they dare not do otherwise. But deep down in their hearts they envy the tyrant who can ruthlessly work his will without fear of reprisal. Self-interest, then, is the driving force, whether it be that of the strong man who works his will by virtue of his superior power and cleverness, or that of the average man who, by the sheer weight of his number, forces the powerful few into conformity with his democratically designed code of conduct. Social morality and altruism are the products of fear. Group solidarity is as much born of the hostility and selfishness of individuals as is group antagonism. Might is right, since it is only some form of might or force that can rouse sufficiently those fears that make men moral. Civilization in its entirety is conducted on the

> Good old way, the ancient plan
> That he shall take who has the power
> And he shall keep who can.

The Case for Universal Selfishness

From the time of the ancient Greeks to the present, it has always been comparatively easy to convince anyone who has not thought a great deal about the matter that he and everyone else in the world are fundamentally selfish. All that is ordinarily required to establish this thesis is to point out that when men seem to act selflessly and sacrificially to promote the well-being of others, they are really acting in this fashion only because they are pleased to do so, because they gain the recognition, or the satisfaction, or the serenity of mind which these actions produce.

Once the conviction that selfishness is universal finds root in a person's mind, it is very likely to burgeon out in a thousand corroborating generalizations. It will be discovered that a friendly smile is really only an attempt to win an approving nod from a more or less gullible recording angel; that a charitable deed is, for its performer, only an opportunity to congratulate himself on the good fortune or the cleverness that enables him to be charitable; that a public benefaction is just plain good business advertising. It will emerge that gods are worshiped only because they indulge men's selfish fears, or tastes, or hopes; that the "golden rule" is no more than an eminently sound success formula; that social and political codes are created and subscribed to only because they serve to restrain other men's egoism as much as one's own, morality being only a special sort of "racket" or intrigue using weapons of persuasion in place of bombs and machine guns. Under this interpretation of human nature, the categories of commercialism replace those of disinterested service and the spirit of the horse trader broods over the face of the earth.

Interestingly, people seem to be as readily convinced of the basic selfishness of their own motives as of other people's motives —a fact which might in itself suggest the falsity of egotism, if not of egoism. The writer recalls particularly a college student who had come "under conviction" of the truth of psychological egoism as a result of some reading he had done for a course in psychology. Persuaded that nature has provided, through a long process of biological evolution, that human beings should respond solely in terms of pleasure and pain stimuli, this student on one occasion performed a detailed analysis of his activities from morning to night of a particular day. Every single act from brushing his teeth to attending a college pep rally was sedulously and triumphantly construed as an act of unmixed pleasure seeking. Even that act which his friends insisted contained some element of generosity and altruism—the saving of one of his breakfast doughnuts for the dog who, counting on some tidbit, daily awaited his departure from the dining hall—he discounted as really selfish. "For," he said, "I have come to like the dog so well that I should be most miserable if I should disappoint him. My happiness depends upon watching the dog's pleasure when I feed him. So there is nothing in the least generous about what I have done."

A Difficulty
with the Egoistic View

Despite the superficial plausibility of this thesis as just formulated, most present-day critics are of the opinion that the doctrine of universal egoism, far from being true, is merely a complicated kind of intellectual seduction resting upon an argument that is a logical nightmare. This is not to say that there is not a great deal of selfishness in the world. Nor is it to deny that many people are far more selfish than they would be prepared to admit. But a little reflection will suggest that it is a mistake to conclude from the foregoing considerations that unselfish acts are impossible.

In the first place, the argument for egoism, based on the fact that whoever performs a voluntary act is acting in accord with his own wishes, begs the whole question. Since "voluntary" means nothing more than "proceeding from one's own wishes," it represents at best a hollow linguistic victory to show that whenever one's acts proceed from one's own wishes they do, in fact, proceed from one's own wishes.

The error lies in defining selfishness in terms of doing what one wants to do. This is the way to define *voluntary* acts, not *selfish* acts; though it is clear that no act would be called either selfish or unselfish unless it were also voluntary. The spontaneous blinking of one's eye when an object passes close to it is a "self-protective" reflex, but it is not selfish.

An egoistic or selfish act may be defined as one which the agent performs with a view to benefiting himself. An altruistic or unselfish act is one which the agent performs with a view to conferring some benefit on others than himself. To define acts as selfish because they are voluntary is to rule unselfishness out of the picture from the start. Or rather it is not to rule it out, because the opposite of voluntary action is not unselfish action. A person is not unselfish when he does something he does not wish to do. Unselfishness implies willingness to act on the part of the actor quite as much as does selfishness. There is no law against an altruist's enjoying his altruism. Indeed, the high-water mark of the unselfish spirit is the joy with which it moves into action. A person who makes his gifts with a leaden heart can make no honest claim to magnanimity.

In other words, the fallacy in the egoist's argument lies in the supposition that the apparently unselfish desire to benefit others is transformed into a selfish one by the fact that we derive pleasure from carrying it out. But to say that an act proceeds from our own pleasure or desire is only to say that the act is our own. To demand that we should act on motives that are not our own is to ask us to make ourselves living contradictions in terms.

Selfishness, then, is not to be distinguished from unselfishness by the fact that it takes pleasure in what it does, but rather by what sort of thing it takes pleasure in doing. Not where an action comes from, but what it aims at, determines its classification in this regard. Thus the fact that the student referred to above took pleasure and fulfilled his own wishes in feeding the dog did not really make this act a selfish one. For the purpose of his action was to do the dog a favor by seeing to it that he did not share the fate of Mother Hubbard's less fortunate animal.

The student might reply, of course, that even though his aim was to benefit the dog, his desire to do so existed only because of the satisfaction he found in carrying it out. If he did not *enjoy* seeing the dog wag his tail, then he would have no *desire* to have him wag it. The desire, that is to say, is itself selfish, since the whole point in having it is that it may be fulfilled.

This answer, however, is plainly untrue to the facts and only reveals its maker's confusion. We cannot create a desire simply by thinking how much fun it would be to fulfill it if we had it. The student's affection for the dog, his desire to see it fed, must have existed before any satisfaction could be obtained from providing the food. An altruistic desire, since it is by definition— at least by the definition we have just proposed—one which is directed at another's good, remains altruistic no matter how it is used. Even when it is overcome by an egoistic desire, it none the less remains undeniably and disturbingly real—as in the case of the person who liked to monopolize the family newspaper, but who always retired to his room when he did so because it bothered him to see the longing expressions of those whose use of the paper he was preventing.

One is reminded, in this connection, of one of George Bernard Shaw's more cynical remarks, to the effect that the only thing good about self-sacrifice is that it enables us to sacrifice other people without blushing. But the very capacity to blush suggests that there is in us a latent set of scruples that needs artificially to be choked off.

In any case, referring once more to the student skeptic, it is quite unlikely that he ever consciously said to himself, "How unhappy I should be if I failed this dog. I simply must save him one of my doughnuts or else the sight of his disappointment will leave me utterly miserable." While people who have embarked on a professional career in egoism may indulge in reflections of this sort, most people, including probably our donor of doughnuts, would not ordinarily admit to such elaborate calculations except perhaps as they reconstructed their own motives in retrospect. At least a good portion of generous acts are spontaneous and quite free from guile or duplicity. Possibly it is because most people represent admixtures, in varying proportions, of selfish and unselfish tendencies that the presence of a clean-cut case of altruism is so difficult to detect.

Selfishness and Unselfishness As Intentions

It is also true that no one can ever be really certain to what extent an act is selfish or unselfish except the person who performs it. For he alone can know the motive that lies behind it. Consequently it is difficult to refute egoism merely by conjuring up instances in the actions of others where altruism seems most plainly to be present. Take such examples as that of the woman under torture who, according to the classical account, rather than inform on her friends, bites off her own tongue and spits it in the face of her torturer; or that of the young man who gives his life for his country; or that of the old man who makes a secret will providing benefactions for others whose gratitude he does not expect to enjoy. Since one cannot be certain of inner motivations, each instance is capable of being interpreted as a case of egoism. The woman might be held to have acted as she did because the thought of what might happen to her friends brought her more pain than her own act of self-violence—or perhaps because she enjoyed the glory of figuring in a heroic role more than she regretted the womanly discomfiture of being unable to talk about it afterwards. Similarly, soldiers might be held to risk their lives for the sake of social approval, or because they selfishly prefer to die than to relinquish the privileges and ideals represented in the cause for which they fight (thus producing what Dickinson refers to as the "charming paradox" of "individuals sacrificing in defense of the community those very lives which they originally entered the community to protect"). As for the gentleman whose posthumous reputation for generosity was supposed to do him no good, it might be argued that, while he may not have believed in a post-existence during which he could bask in the afterglow of a splendid liberality, nevertheless he might have counted on living out his declining years in contented anticipation of the joys of those on whom his benefactions would fall.

If some of these explanations seem weird and exaggerated in the extreme, they suggest, in any case, the difficulties which face those who would try to demonstrate the presence of disinterestedness *in others*. On the other hand, because it is possible in any given instance to find a selfish construction for acts of apparent generosity, it does not follow that a considerable bulk of such acts are not exactly what they appear to be. From the fact that some men at some times have taken credit for a good will they have not felt, it is not to be concluded that honest good will never enters into the composition of men's natures.

It may be objected, at this point, that to define egoism and altruism in terms of the agent's intention leaves us without an objective test of their presence. One can only guess what another person means to be doing. Why not, therefore, define these qualities in terms, not of intention, but of accomplishment: a selfish act as one that benefits or tends to benefit the self, an unselfish act one that benefits or tends to benefit others?

The difficulty with this suggestion is that it does not seem to give us what we mean when we use the terms. Loving another may confer benefits on the lover, but we should say, ordinarily, that a person who loves for the sake of derived benefits is no true lover at all. "Disinterested" desires by their very nature are defined in terms of intentions. Likewise, selfish desires. If a person attempting a robbery accidentally saves his victims from a fire which would have destroyed them had they not been awakened by the sounds made by the burglar, the latter confers a benefit on those rescued. But his enterprise is hardly to be termed unselfish. (It must, of course, be admitted that from the standpoint of moral education we are interested in the agent's intentions primarily for the results they produce. And for practical purposes we may have to judge intentions by results. The law sometimes has to do this. It may be added that so far as society is concerned, a person who always bungled his selfishness would—assuming selfishness socially undesirable—perhaps be preferable to one who always bungled his unselfishness. But for the most part we assume that people's acts afford some evidence of their intentions.)

Freud, Darwin, and Egoism

But the objector may still be dissatisfied with our definition and turn his attack in another direction. In so doing, another argument for egoism presents itself.

The trouble with the definition in terms of intentions, it may be said, is that no one can really be trusted to interpret his own intentions. All he can know are his conscious motives and these are more than likely to be specious and superficial, mere rationalizations of underlying motives which are subconscious. These subconscious motives or drives are the effective and significant factors in the determination of human behavior and are better understood by the scientific analyst than by their own possessors. Appeal is made to the psychoanalysts, following Freud, and to the evolutionists, following Darwin, to show that the main forces which dominate human conduct must be egocentric. Both psychologically and biologically we are conditioned to selfishness, which may now be construed in terms of tendencies to self-assertion and self-satisfaction.

Psychologically, it is held, our behavior is explainable in terms of such primary instincts as sex, hunger, and self-preservation. These instincts, operating in the experience of the developing organism, produce a store of effects which, though not recognized, are not inactive. These constitute what Freud called the unconscious. Here in the unconscious will be found man's deepest wishes, his strongest instinctive desires, especially powerful when they are repressed, but determinative, in any case, of his behavior. To these basically selfish drives, and not to any consciously held motives, we must look for the real source of our actions.

Biologically, we are end products of an evolutionary development in which survival has been possible only for those species who proved themselves superior in a dog-eat-dog process of natural selection. Such a process, it is insisted, could scarcely throw up a race of human beings fit for anything but rugged individualism. Appeal is made to the fact that the lower invertebrates show not the slightest indication of unselfish behavior. This being the case, the appearance of true altruism higher in the scale would, so it is argued, be sheer magic, incompatible with the whole mechanism of evolution. Hence what appears as altruism must be a disguised form of self-seeking.

It will not be possible to make here a detailed analysis of these arguments from psychology and biology. However, a few comments may serve to indicate that they are far from conclusive.

In the first place, it is arguable whether motivations that are entirely unconscious should be attributed to the self in a sense that implies its responsibility for them. What is not under the self's deliberate control may be said to be nothing on which a judgment of selfishness or unselfishness should be made. It would be like calling a person selfish because he had naturally wavy hair—or like calling a bird selfish because it flew to a warm climate in the fall. On the other hand, there are many motives, often referred to as subconscious, which are not subconscious at all. We may, it is true, ignore them or refuse to acknowledge them; but they are not so deeply buried or so subtly disguised that a little conscientious probing will not bring them to light. And often they will be properly designated as selfish in comparison with our rationalizations of them: as when we discover that our anxiety to attend Aunt Bertha's funeral is due in considerable degree to the pleasant prospect of a day away from the office, or that our conviction as to the superiority of pinochle over contract bridge is not unrelated to the fact that we have spent the greater part of our life in acquiring a practically unbeatable prowess in the former game. Indeed, if anybody is looking for one more trait to add to those which have traditionally been cited as distinguishing man from the other animals, no better candidate is available than the ability to rationalize any and every unlovely human tendency, from pride to prejudice.

But even if it be granted that there are subconscious determining tendencies within us, either deep down or near the surface, it does not follow that they always determine us to egoistic behavior. Gregariousness, for example, has frequently been listed among the basic instincts, animal and human, and might be expected to lead to unselfish behavior. Moreover, the fact that many animals— such as the honey bees, the beavers, and the ants—form mutual benefit societies suggests that cooperative action has a natural precedent rather well back in the animal kingdom. Such mutuality of behavior may have been quite as valuable a variation for certain species in the struggle for existence as pugnacity or self-assertiveness. Some experts in comparative psychology have found in the reproductive instinct and parental care the earliest forms of altruistic behavior. In some cases reproduction and its accompanying activities—nest-building, incubation, feeding—involve considerable burden and danger. There are even cases where reproduction always means the death of the mother, as with the female thread worm whose young, hatched within her body, eat their way out after devouring her internal organs.

As with the animals, so also with primitive (and modern) men. Whereas they may quarrel and fight both as individuals and as groups, yet they also band together in tribes or clans or nations, and in so doing display intrasocietal loyalties as strong as their intersocietal and interindividual animosities. Reinhold Neibuhr, in his *Moral Man and Immoral Society*, has made a great deal of the fact that men have been able to utilize their positions as members of societies to satisfy at one stroke both their pugnacious and their gregarious urges. Patriotism, for example, can be in time of war a stone that kills two birds, that of loyal devotion (to one's country) and that of pitiless animosity (against the enemy).

We may conclude, then, that the theory of basic instincts or inherited drives in animal organisms does not necessarily exclude the possibility of altruistic behavior at the human level.

Selfishness Not Necessarily Evil

We must now consider one final objection which is almost sure to be raised against our definitions of selfishness and unselfishness.

Selfishness, it will be said, is something more than just the desire to benefit one's self. It is the desire to benefit one's self at the expense of others. A person is not selfish because he keeps himself warm, or because he nourishes himself with good food, or because he decides to educate himself. These acts become selfish only when the supply of blankets, or food, or colleges, or of what it takes to acquire them, is in a particular case so limited that the use of them deprives others of their fair share.

What is really meant by selfishness, then, on this view, is what William James called "hoggishness"—the tendency to reserve for ourselves more than our share of goods of limited availability.

While it must probably be agreed that something of this sort is what many people have in mind when they use the word "selfishness," it is nevertheless a question whether this meaning should be preferred to our more general definition. Certainly adopting it would not help the argument for universal egoism. For whereas before it was necessary to show that people always acted to benefit themselves, it would with this definition become necessary to show not only that they sought to benefit themselves but that they hurt others in the process.

There is the additional disadvantage that the new definition appears to include a moral notion, that of "fair sharing," which is left out of the earlier one. While it is true that a great number of people think of the term "selfishness" as carrying ethical overtones—if not, indeed, as equivalent to "wrong"—there is something to be said for using the term in a morally neutral sense. Considerable confusion has resulted because people have thought of selfishness as being always bad and unselfishness as being always good.

Actually, if by selfishness we mean concern for one's own good, such concern has its place. This is true even when our main desire is to be of use to others. A physician, when his community is in the grip of an epidemic, cannot afford to neglect his own need for sleep, food, and the taking of various personal precautions. To spend himself in unremitting service to his patients so completely as to destroy his own capacity to serve, we should recognize as more foolish than noble. Sometimes the most merciful missions require the most merciless use of common sense.

So it frequently occurs that what appears to be a meritorious altruism is a case of well-intentioned blindness; and that what may appear as selfishness is a case of needed self-education or self-reconstruction. No one is required to make of himself any less of a self in order to meet the demands of social morality. To abandon self-development, and even self-assertion, is to leave oneself with no real self to assert, with nothing of strength, or discipline, or skill to offer the society one wishes to serve. I am no good to my football team if I refuse to exercise my body; no good to my debating team if I refuse to exercise my wits.

A distinction frequently made is that between naïve and enlightened egoism and naïve and enlightened altruism. The naïve egoist acts upon every impulse to further his own good, without examining the long-run consequences of his acts. The naïve altruist unreflectively suppresses every such impulse. The former would find himself, typically, a social outcast, living a life of narrowly restricted interests and learning too late that we cannot live happily with ourselves until we have entered sympathetically into the lives of others. The latter would normally betray the very interests he sought to serve by such self-sacrifice as would leave him a giver with no gifts to give. As someone has sagely remarked, it is impossible, really, to remain a completely naïve altruist for very long, since such a person, if he would free himself from all suspicion of selfishness, would have to give up breathing.

Enlightened egoism and altruism are characterized by the fact that they each recognize deficiencies of the naïve forms. The enlightened egoist emphasizes the social nature of the self. Appealing to psychology, he points out that we are essentially social products. As babies, we had no real selfhood, no personality, but were just centers of a "buzzing, blooming confusion." We grew into selves or persons by imitation and suggestion and by projecting ourselves into others. And in general, so long as we remain in isolation, in solitude, we are literally and figuratively next to nothing; our personalities shrink and become sick and deformed. The naïve egoist would, in effect, cut off his nose to spite his face. He has not perceived that, just as it takes two to quarrel, it takes two to make love. To resist the pressure of our social nature is spiritual death. Thus, it is the custom today to rehabilitate men psychiatrically in a social environment, rather than in solitude.

The enlightened altruist, correspondingly, condemns the naïve altruist for his shortsightedness. If one is to treat other people decently, he must have taken time to educate himself to be a decent person. A person who has starved himself does not make a pleasant companion. To tend to one's own requirements is perfectly consistent with altruism. And the fact that most people do not have to be urged or cajoled into doing this is not wholly to be deplored. For the most part, and allowing for obvious exceptions, no one can take better care of a person than the person himself can. For no one else is so closely and constantly associated with him or has such ready access to what is taking place in his mind.

It is no paradox that the enlightened altruist would be the first to admit that we are often not selfish enough—intelligently so, that is. Most of us have not learned at all well the art of living happily with ourselves. We don't even begin to go "all out" for selfishness. The most consummate egoist, boasting of his self-devotion, is often a scoundrel unto himself, failing miserably to achieve such results as would reflect credit on his capacities for self-fulfillment. Laziness, inertia, neglect of the most elementary principles underlying the achievement of health of body and richness of experience, get in our way. We could all, if we would, live more zestfully, feel more keenly, enjoy a more vivid store of memories and anticipations, stock our imaginations with more colorful and variegated contents, undertake more challenging and exciting pursuits.

It is further noted by the enlightened altruist that persistent, unremitting, and indiscriminate benevolence can be disastrous in its results. We may again cite George Bernard Shaw—this time his remark to the effect that if everyone tried to do a good turn daily, it would make for an intolerable situation. It would be as though the members of a basketball team were each so anxious to yield the glory of point-making to the others that they simply passed the ball back and forth without ever taking a shot at the basket. The great difficulty with altruism is that it is so often misdirected and clumsy. Benevolence, as has frequently been noted, can kill the initiative of its recipient. And because people tend to restrict their altruism to certain favorite groups, their giving may take the form of a narrowly conceived fanaticism, a form of devotion to others which comes nearer to being large-scale egoism than genuine altruism.

To be sure, it would not occur to most people to regard an overdose of unselfishness as a cause for moral anxiety. Yet the likelihood is that the chief reason for the high esteem commonly attached to unselfishness is the same as that which explains the general respect for a million dollar fortune—namely, that it is so hard to produce. Were it not for the fact that people are usually more ready to feel concern for themselves than for others, especially when those others are not closely associated with them, it would be much easier to see that both egoism and altruism have their merits and defects.

The Opposition
of the Individual and Society

We may conclude, then, that an enlightened practice of egoism involves a large use of altruism and that an intelligent altruism recognizes the indispensability of egoism. Indeed, the view has frequently been taken that if we compare the enlightened egoist's emphasis on benevolence and the enlightened altruist's emphasis an self-development, we will find positions that actually coincide. Thus, on any particular problem the judgment of altruist and egoist would be identical, so long as you concede to each of them a maximum of "enlightenment." For the intelligent individual would see that his own good was tied in with that of society in such a way that service to either would mean service to the other, and injury to either would mean injury to the other. Self-sacrifice would be impossible, since society's good could never require the individual's hurt.

If such a harmony of goods really were the case, then, for all practical purposes, the contrast between egoism and altruism would break down and there would be no problem about the former's giving rise to moral skepticism. The problem would resolve itself into determining what were the best interests of self or of society. (It wouldn't matter which of these we concentrated on, since, on this view, if we secured either one we would necessarily also have secured the other.) This problem might be a difficult one, but it would, at any rate, be a real problem requiring—and permitting—a real choice. For even if everyone *were* selfishly interested in his own good, he would still face the problem of how most rationally to secure it.

It is by no means clear, however, that individual and general interests are identical. We shall return to this question later, but some brief observations concerning it may not be inappropriate at this place. Is it true that the smart egoist would never need to exploit others unjustly in order to secure his own good? And would the intelligent altruist really never need to sacrifice his own desires for the sake of the general welfare?

As we have seen, the principle usually appealed to by those who deny any opposition between self and society is that of the social nature of the self. If the self is really tied up with society, it is maintained, then it is not a thing which can be opposed to society without causing trouble for itself. We are, after all, whatever we identify ourselves with, whatever we call our own. We speak of our bodies, our clothes, our books, our religion, our friends, our ideas—even of our world. And to the extent that we mean this and act on this, these things may be regarded as a part of us. Injury to them means injury to us; their good is automatically our good. Challenge our ideas and you challenge us. Insult our friends and we are insulted. Ridicule our religious faith and we are made ridiculous. Let those about us be unhappy and we are unhappy. And this, it is held, occurs spontaneously and naturally so long as our selves really embrace these objects, so long as our sympathies are sufficiently encompassing. It does not occur merely as the result of cold egoistic calculations. The blackmailer who rescues his intended victim has not identified himself with that victim, since he proposes to harm him in short order. Even the banker who, interested in sound investments, is anxious for the health and success of those to whom he had made loans, and the salesman who, with an eye to future sales, refuses to show his customers shoddy goods, may be said to have fallen somewhat

short of that complete identification which would mark fully enlightened egoism. Where we have failed to make the good of
others wholly our own good, we have failed to make our natures
completely social. We have been living under wraps, so to speak,
as spiritual hermits, capable, to be sure, of opposing our "good"
to society's, but wholly unaware of the paltriness of the good we
cherished. We have been, in some degree, naïve egoists, cheating
ourselves of potential riches which could be ours if we would but
expand our concerns.

There is so much of truth and wisdom in this view that one
hesitates to suggest that it may not be completely true. Even those
who would not accept the view without qualification would be
likely to agree that if they could be shown a way of educating the
people of the world to actions based on an enlightened egoism,
they would, in the present state of things, be more than happy to
settle for that.

The difficulty is, however, that until we have considered more
fully what is good, for the individual and for society, it is not quite
obvious that we shall invariably be serving ourselves best when we
"identify" ourselves with others. I may call my appendix *my* appendix, thus identifying myself with it, in terms of the above
view. But let it behave in the unfriendly way appendixes have of
behaving, and I shall want to disown it, feeling that I am better
off without it.

Of course my appendix is not really a friend. But not infre-
quently even the taking on of new human associates brings added
sorrows and difficulties. For the most part we are willing to take
the risk—or we would never marry, have children, or invite new
responsibilities of any kind—but we do recognize that it is a risk.
Thus, although our social nature may dictate that we shall not be
happy unless we see others happy, it also dictates that the unhap-
piness of others will distress us. And while this may impel us to
work the harder for their happiness, it is not always clear that
social responsibilities of this kind can be successfully undertaken
without greater sacrifice on our part than would be consistent
with the truth of the theory we are examining.

There is the additional difficulty that it is somewhat hard to
see what the identification of self and society would mean. "Society" itself is too complicated, too much broken up into diverse,
antagonistic elements, for one to be sure quite how to swing into
tune with it. To identify one's self with some part or movement or
idea is inevitably to bring one's self into violent opposition with
other parts, movements, or ideas. That these various vortices
within society, with their several interests and claims, are not as

utterly opposed in the last analysis as they think they are, we may readily accept. But that none of them can be even slightly better off by the sacrifice or hardship of some others is not *prima facie* apparent. In any case, the question must be left undecided until we have considered more fully what "better-offness" may be.

Having said this, however, we should perhaps not close without reiterating that no more important practical moral problem exists than that of convincing people that their interests really are far more nearly identical with the good of society than they suppose them to be; and that they do not serve themselves best by opposing themselves to others. To make this more convincing it is desirable so to mold human institutions and train human beings as to provide a basis in truth for the encouragement thus given. If society is so arranged as to afford people no chance to expand themselves and their tastes and sympathies in such a way as to find useful and satisfying places for themselves, the most impassioned plea for harmonizing one's interests with society's will be bound to ring hollow.

Cultural Relativism: Pros and Cons

W. T. Stace

W. T. Stace (1886–1967), during twenty-two years in the British Civil Service in Ceylon, wrote books on history of philosophy and aesthetics. Later, as Professor of Philosophy in Princeton, he wrote on most of the other major fields of philosophy.

Any ethical position which denies that there is a single moral standard which is equally applicable to all men at all times may fairly be called a species of ethical relativity. There is not, the relativist asserts, merely one moral law, one code, one standard. There are many moral laws, codes, standards. What morality ordains in one place or age may be quite different from what morality ordains in another place or age. The moral code of Chinamen is quite different from that of Europeans, that of African savages quite different from both. Any morality, therefore, is relative to the age, the place, and the circumstances in which it is found. It is in no sense absolute.

This does not mean merely—as one might at first sight be inclined to suppose—that the very same kind of action which is *thought* right in one country and period may be *thought* wrong in another. This would be a mere platitude, the truth of which everyone would have to admit. Even the absolutist would admit this—would even wish to emphasize it—since he is well aware that different peoples have different sets of moral ideas, and his whole point is that some of these sets of ideas are false. What the relativist means to assert is, not this platitude, but that the very same kind of action which *is* right in one country and period may *be* wrong in another. And this, far from being a platitude, is a very startling assertion.

It is very important to grasp thoroughly the difference between the two ideas. For there is reason to think that many minds tend to find ethical relativity attractive because they fail to keep them clearly apart. It is so very obvious that moral ideas differ from country to country and from age to age. And it is so very easy, if you are mentally lazy, to suppose that to say this means the same as to say that no universal moral standard exists—or in other words that it implies ethical relativity. We fail to see that the word "standard" is used in two different senses. It is perfectly true that, in one sense, there are many variable moral standards. We speak of judging a man by the standard of his time. And this implies that different times have different standards. And this, of course, is quite true. But when the word "standard" is used in this sense, it means simply the set of moral ideas current during the period in question. It means what people *think* right, whether as a matter of fact it *is* right or not. On the other hand, when the absolutist asserts that there exists a single universal moral "standard," he is not using the word in this sense at all. He means by "standard" what *is* right as distinct from what people merely think right. His point is that although what people think right varies in different countries and periods, yet what actually is right is everywhere and always the same. And it follows that when the ethical relativist disputes the position of the absolutist and denies that any universal moral standard exists, he too means by "standard" what actually is right. But it is exceedingly easy, if we are not careful, to slip loosely from using the word in the first sense to using it in the second sense; and to suppose that the variability of moral beliefs is the same thing as the variability of what really is moral. And unless we keep the two senses of the word "standard" distinct, we are likely to think the creed of ethical relativity much more plausible than it actually is.

The genuine relativist, then, does not merely mean that Chinamen may think right what Frenchmen think wrong. He means that what *is* wrong for the Frenchman may *be* right for the Chinaman. And if one enquires how, in those circumstances, one is to know what actually is right in China or in France, the answer comes quite glibly. What is right in China is the same as what people think right in China; and what is right in France is the same as what people think right in France. So that, if you want to know what is moral in any particular country or age, all you have to do is to ascertain what are the moral ideas current in that age or country. Those ideas are, *for that age or country,* right. Thus what is morally right is identified with what is thought to be morally right, and the distinction which we made above between these two is simply denied. To put the same thing in another way, it is denied that there can be or ought to be any distinction between the two senses of the word "standard." There is only one kind of standard of right and wrong, namely, the moral ideas current in any particular age or country.

Moral right *means* what people think morally right. It has no other meaning. What Frenchmen think right is, therefore, right *for Frenchmen.* And evidently one must conclude—though I am not aware that relativists are anxious to draw one's attention to such unsavoury but yet absolutely necessary conclusions from their creed—that cannibalism is right for people who believe in it, that human sacrifice is right for those races which practice it, and that burning widows alive was right for Hindus until the British stepped in and compelled the Hindus to behave immorally by allowing their widows to remain alive.

When it is said that, according to the ethical relativist, what is thought right in any social group is right for that group, one must be careful not to misinterpret this. The relativist does not, of course, mean that there actually is an objective moral standard in France and a different objective standard in England, and that French and British opinions respectively give us correct information about these different standards. His point is rather that there are no objectively true moral standards at all. There is no single universal objective standard. Nor are there a variety of local objective standards. All standards are subjective. People's subjective feelings about morality are the only standards which exist.

To sum up. The ethical relativist consistently denies, it would seem, whatever the ethical absolutist asserts. For the absolutist there is a single universal moral standard. For the relativist there is no such standard. There are only local, ephemeral, and variable standards. For the absolutist there are two senses of the word "standard." Standards in the sense of sets of current moral ideas are relative and changeable. But the standard in the sense of what is actually morally right is absolute and unchanging. For the relativist no such distinction can be made. There is only one meaning of the word "standard," namely, that which refers to local and variable sets of moral ideas. Or if it is insisted that the word must be allowed two meanings, then the relativist will say that there is at any rate no actual example of a standard in the absolute sense, and that the word as thus used is an empty name to which nothing in reality corresponds; so that the distinction between the two meanings becomes empty and useless. Finally—though this is merely saying the same thing in another way—the absolutist makes a distinction between what actually is right and what is thought right. The relativist rejects this distinction and identifies what is moral with what is thought moral by certain human beings or groups of human beings.

· · ·

It was easy enough to believe in a single absolute morality in older times when there was no anthropology, when all humanity was divided clearly into two groups, Christian peoples and the "heathen." Christian peoples knew and possessed the one true morality. The rest were savages whose moral ideas could be ignored. But all this is changed. Greater knowledge has brought greater tolerance. We can no longer exalt our own morality as alone true, while dismissing all other moralities as false or inferior. The investigations of anthropologists have shown that there exist side by side in the world a bewildering variety of moral codes. On this topic endless volumes have been written, masses of evidence piled up. Anthropologists have ransacked the Melanesian Islands, the jungles of New Guinea, the steppes of Siberia, the deserts of Australia, the forests of central Africa, and have brought back with them countless examples of weird, extravagant, and fantastic "moral" customs with which to confound us. We learn that all kinds of horrible practices are, in this, that, or the other place, regarded as essential to virtue. We find that there is nothing, or next to nothing, which has always and everywhere been regarded as morally good by all men. Where then is our universal morality? Can we, in face of all this evidence, deny that it is nothing but an empty dream?

This argument, taken by itself, is a very weak one. It relies upon a single set of facts—the variable moral customs of the world. But this variability of moral ideas is admitted by both parties to the dispute, and is capable of ready explanation upon the hypothesis of either party. The relativist says that the facts are to be explained by the non-existence of any absolute moral standard. The absolutist says that they are to be explained by human ignorance of what the absolute moral standard is. And he can truly point out that men have differed widely in their opinions about all manner of topics including the subject matters of the physical sciences—just as much as they differ about morals. And if the various different opinions which men have held about the shape of the earth do not prove that it has no one real shape, neither do the various opinions which they have held about morality prove that there is no one true morality.

Thus the facts can be explained equally plausibly on either hypothesis. There is nothing in the facts themselves which compels us to prefer the relativistic hypothesis to that of the absolutist. And therefore the argument fails to prove the relativist conclusion. If that conclusion is to be established, it must be by means of other considerations.

This is the essential point. But I will add some supplementary remarks. The work of the anthropologists, upon which ethical relativists seem to rely so heavily, has as a matter of fact added absolutely nothing *in principle* to what has always been known about the variability of moral ideas. Educated people have known all along that the Greeks tolerated sodomy, which in modern times has been regarded in some countries as an abominable crime; that the Hindus thought it a sacred duty to burn their widows; that trickery, now thought despicable, was once believed to be a virtue; that terrible torture was thought by our own ancestors only a few centuries ago to be a justifiable weapon of justice; that it was only yesterday that western peoples came to believe that slavery is immoral. Even the ancients knew very well that moral customs and ideas vary—witness the writings of Herodotus. Thus the principle of the variability of moral ideas was well understood long before modern anthropology was ever heard of. Anthropology has added nothing to the knowledge of this principle except a mass of new and extreme examples of it drawn from very remote sources. But to multiply examples of a principle already well known and universally admitted adds nothing to the argument which is built upon that principle. The discoveries of the anthropologists have no doubt been of the highest importance in their own sphere. But in my considered opinion they have thrown no new light upon the special problems of the moral philosopher.

Although the multiplication of examples has no logical bearing on the argument, it does have an immense *psychological* effect upon people's minds. These masses of anthropological learning are impressive. They are propounded in the sacred name of "science." If they are quoted in support of ethical relativity—as they often are—people *think* that they must prove something important. They bewilder and over-awe the simple-minded, batter down their resistance, make them ready to receive humbly the doctrine of ethical relativity from those who have acquired a reputation by their immense learning and their claims to be "scientific." Perhaps this is why so much ado is made by ethical relativists regarding the anthropological evidence. But we must refuse to be impressed.

We must discount all this mass of evidence about the extraordinary moral customs of remote peoples. Once we have admitted—as everyone who is instructed must have admitted these last two thousand years without any anthropology at all—the principle that moral ideas vary, all this new evidence adds nothing to the argument. And the argument itself proves nothing for the reasons already given.

. . .

It is time that we turned our attention from the case in favor of ethical relativity to the case against it. Now the case against it consists, to a very large extent, in urging that, if taken seriously and pressed to its logical conclusion, ethical relativity can only end in destroying the conception of morality altogether, in undermining its practical efficacy, in rendering meaningless many almost universally accepted truths about human affairs, in robbing human beings of any incentive to strive for a better world, in taking the life-blood out of every ideal and every aspiration which has ever ennobled the life of man. In short, the charge against it is that it revolts and outrages man's moral *feelings*.

To all such arguments it is always possible to reply that they are merely pragmatic, mere appeals to feeling which have no logical cogency and no scientific value. I will not for the moment argue the question whether feelings have any value at all in the search for truth, or whether they ought to be utterly disregarded. That matter may be left for a later page. For the moment let us rather see what these arguments of the anti-relativist are. We will frankly recognize from the outset their quasi-emotional character. If we do this, we shall perhaps be saved from disappointment and misunderstanding. The reader should not be either disappointed or surprised if in what follows I seem to him to be merely appealing to feelings and not to facts or logic. This in fact is what I shall be doing. And I shall be doing it because it is the only way in which the case of the anti-relativist can be communicated to the reader. We can judge of all this afterwards. Perhaps we shall find that the purely logical and scientific procedure, which would rule out all feeling as irrelevant, is not wholly applicable to the subject matter of morals; that it rests upon a too rigorous dichotomy between feeling and cognition. But however that may be, let us hear what the anti-relativist has to say. It cannot be wrong, it cannot be irrelevant for us, and for the relativist himself, to see what his doctrine actually implies in the way of practical consequences; to see how it tallies with the demands of the "moral consciousness." Other arguments, of a more definitely empirical and scientific character, can be left for discussion in later chapters.

First of all, then, ethical relativity, in asserting that the moral standards of particular social groups are the only standards which exist, renders meaningless all propositions which attempt to compare these standards with one another in respect of their moral worth. And this is a very serious matter indeed. We are accustomed to think that the moral ideas of one nation or social group may be "higher" or "lower" than those of another. We believe, for example, that Christian ethical ideals are nobler than those of the savage races of central Africa. Probably most of us would think that the Chinese moral standards are higher than those of the inhabitants of New Guinea. In short we habitually compare one civilization with another and judge the sets of ethical ideas to be found in them to be some better, some worse. The fact that such judgments are very difficult to make with any justice, and that they are frequently made on very superficial and prejudiced grounds, has no bearing on the question now at issue. The question is whether such judgments have any *meaning*. We habitually assume that they have.

But on the basis of ethical relativity they can have none whatever. For the relativist must hold that there is no *common* standard which can be applied to the various civilizations judged. Any such comparison of moral standards implies the existence of some superior standard which is applicable to both. And the existence of any such standard is precisely what the relativist denies. According to him the Christian standard is applicable only to Christians, the Chinese standard only to Chinese, the New Guinea standard only to the inhabitants of New Guinea.

What is true of comparisons between the moral standards of different races will also be true of comparisons between those of different ages. It is not unusual to ask such questions as whether the standard of our own day is superior to that which existed among our ancestors five hundred years ago. And when we remember that our ancestors employed slaves, practiced barbaric physical tortures, and burnt people alive, we may be inclined to think that it is. At any rate we assume that the question is one which has meaning and is capable of rational discussion. But if the ethical relativist is right, whatever we assert on this subject must be totally meaningless. For here again there is no common standard which could form the basis of any such judgments.

This in its turn implies that the whole notion of moral *progress* is a sheer delusion. Progress means an advance from lower to higher, from worse to better. But on the basis of ethical relativity it has no meaning to say that the standards of this age are better (or worse) than those of a previous age. For there is no common standard by which both can be measured. Thus it is nonsense to say that the morality of the New Testament is higher than that of the Old. And Jesus Christ, if he imagined that he was introducing into the world a higher ethical standard than existed before his time, was merely deluded.

There is indeed one way in which the ethical relativist can give some sort of meaning to judgments of higher or lower as applied to the moral ideas of different races or ages. What he will have to say is that we assume *our* standards to be the best simply because they are ours. And we judge other standards by our own. If we say that Chinese moral codes are better than those of African cannibals, what we *mean* by this is that they are better *according to our standards*. We mean, that is to say, that Chinese standards are *more like our own* than African standards are. "Better" accordingly *means* "more like us." "Worse" means "less like us." It thus becomes clear that judgments of better and worse in such cases do not express anything that is really true at all. They merely give expression to our perfectly groundless satisfaction with our own ideas. In short, they give expression to nothing but our egotism and self-conceit. Our moral ideals are not really better than those of the savage. We are simply deluded by our egotism into thinking they are. The African savage has just as good a right to think his morality the best as we have to think ours the best. His opinion is just as well grounded as ours, or rather both opinions are equally groundless. And on this view Jesus Christ can only have been led to the quite absurd belief that his ethical precepts were better than those of Moses by his personal vanity. If only he had read Westermarck and Dewey he would have understood that, so long as people continued to believe in the doctrine of an eye for an eye and a tooth for a tooth, that doctrine was morally *right;* and that there could not be any point whatever in trying to make them believe in his new-fangled theory of loving one's enemies. True, the new morality would *become* right as soon as people came to believe in it, for it would then be the accepted standard. And what people think right is right. But then, if only Jesus Christ and persons with similar ideas had kept these ideas to themselves, people might have gone on believing that the old morality was right. And in that case it would have *been* right, and would have remained so till this day. And that would have saved a lot of useless trouble. For the change which Jesus Christ actually brought about was merely a change from one set of moral ideas to another. And as the new set of ideas was in no way better than the set it displaced—to say that it was better would be meaningless for the reasons already given—the change was really a sheer waste of time. And of course it likewise follows that anyone who in the future tries to improve the moral ideas of humanity will also be wasting his time.

Thus the ethical relativist must treat all judgments comparing different moralities as either entirely meaningless; or, if this course appears too drastic, he has the alternative of declaring that they have for their meaning-content nothing except the vanity and egotism of those who pass them. We are asked to believe that the highest moral ideas of humanity are not really any better than those of an Australian bushman. But if this is so, why strive for higher ideals? Thus the heart is taken out of all effort, and the meaning out of all human ideals and aspirations.

The ethical relativist may perhaps say that he is being misjudged. It is not true that, on the basis of his doctrine, all effort for moral improvement is vain. For if we take such a civilization as our own, and if we assume that the standard of morals theoretically accepted by it is that of Christian ethics, then there is surely plenty of room for improvement and "progress" in the way of making our practice accord with our theory. Effort may legitimately be directed towards getting people to live up to whatever standards they profess to honor. Such effort will be, on the relativistic basis, perfectly meaningful; for it does not imply a comparison of standards by reference to a common standard, but only a comparison of actual achievements with an admitted and accepted standard within a social group.

Now I do not believe that even this plea can be accepted. For as soon as it comes to be effectively realized that our moral standard is no better than that of barbarians, why should anyone trouble to live up to it? It would be much easier to adopt some lower standard, to preach it assiduously until everyone believes it, when it would automatically become right. But even if we waive this point, and admit that the exhortation to practice what we preach may be meaningful, this does not touch the issue which was raised above. It will still be true that efforts to improve moral *beliefs*, as distinguished from moral *practice*, will be futile. It will still be true that Jesus Christ would have done better had he tried only to persuade humanity to live up to the old barbaric standards than he did in trying to propagate among them a new and more enlightened moral code. It will still be true that any reformer in the future who attempts to make men see even more noble ideals than those which we have inherited from the reformers of the past will be wasting his time.

I come now to a second point. Up to the present I have

allowed it to be taken tacitly for granted that, though judgments comparing different races and ages in respect of the worth of their moral codes are impossible for the ethical relativist, yet judgments of comparison between individuals living within the same social group would be quite possible. For individuals living within the same social group would presumably be subject to the same moral code, that of their group, and this would therefore constitute, as between these individuals, a common standard by which they could both be measured. We have not here, as we had in the other case, the difficulty of the absence of any common standard of comparison. It should therefore be possible for the ethical relativist to say quite meaningfully that President Lincoln was a better man than some criminal or moral imbecile of his own time and country, or that Jesus was a better man than Judas Iscariot.

But is even this minimum of moral judgment really possible on relativist grounds? It seems to me that it is not. For when once the whole of humanity is abandoned as the area covered by a single moral standard, what smaller areas are to be adopted as the *loci* of different standards? Where are we to draw the lines of demarcation? We can split up humanity, perhaps,—though the procedure will be very arbitrary—into races, races into nations, nations into tribes, tribes into families, families into individuals. Where are we going to draw the *moral* boundaries? Does the *locus* of a particular moral standard reside in a race, a nation, a tribe, a family, or an individual? Perhaps the blessed phrase "social group" will be dragged in to save the situation. Each such group, we shall be told, has its own moral code which is, for it, right. But what *is* a "group"? Can anyone define it or give its boundaries? This is the seat of that ambiguity in the theory of ethical relativity to which reference was made on an earlier page.[1]

The difficulty is not, as might be thought, merely an academic difficulty of logical definition. If that were all, I should not press the point. But the ambiguity has practical consequences which are disastrous for morality. No one is likely to say that moral codes are confined within the arbitrary limits of the geographical divisions of countries. Nor are the notions of race, nation, or political state likely to help us. To bring out the essentially practical character of the difficulty let us put it in the form of concrete questions. Does the American nation constitute a "group" having a single moral standard? Or does the standard of what I ought to do change continuously as I cross the continent in a railway train? Do different States of the Union have different moral codes? Per-

[1] Page 12. [Not reprinted here.]

haps every town and village has its own peculiar standard. This may at first sight seem reasonable enough. "In Rome do as Rome does" may seem as good a rule in morals as it is in etiquette. But can we stop there? Within the village are numerous cliques, each having its own set of ideas. Why should not each of these claim to be bound only by its own special and peculiar moral standards? And if it comes to that, why should not the gangsters of Chicago claim to constitute a group having its own morality, so that its murders and debaucheries must be viewed as "right" by the only standard which can legitimately be applied to it? And if it be answered that the nation will not tolerate this, that may be so. But this is to put the foundation of right simply in the superior force of the majority. In that case whoever is stronger will be right, however monstrous his ideas and actions. And if we cannot deny to any set of people the right to have its own morality, is it not clear that, in the end, we cannot even deny this right to the individual? Every individual man and woman can put up, on this view, an irrefutable claim to be judged by no standard except his or her own.

If these arguments are valid, the ethical relativist cannot really maintain that there is anywhere to be found a moral standard binding upon anybody against his will. And he cannot maintain that, even within the social group, there is a common standard as between individuals. And if that is so, then even judgments to the effect that one man is morally better than another become meaningless. All moral valuation thus vanishes. There is nothing to prevent each man from being a rule unto himself. The result will be moral chaos and the collapse of all effective standards.

. . .

A further difficulty presents itself. Suppose that we have now definitely decided what are the exact boundaries of the social group within which a moral standard is to be operative. And we will assume—as is invariably done by relativists themselves—that this group is to be some actually existing social community such as a tribe or nation. How are we to know, even then, what actually *is* the moral standard within that group? How is anyone to know? How is even a member of the group to know? For there are certain to be within the group—at least this will be true among advanced peoples—wide differences of opinion as to what is right, what wrong. Whose opinion, then, is to be taken as representing *the* moral standard of the group? Either we must take the opinion of the majority within the group, or the opinion of some minority. If we rely upon the ideas of the majority, the results will be disastrous. Wherever there is found among a people a small band of select spirits, or perhaps one man, working for the establishment of higher and nobler ideals than those commonly accepted by the group, we shall be compelled to hold that, for that people at that time, the majority are right, and that the reformers are wrong and are preaching what is immoral. We shall have to maintain, for example, that Jesus was preaching immoral doctrines to the Jews. Moral goodness will have to be equated always with the mediocre and sometimes with the definitely base and ignoble. If, on the other hand, we say that the moral standard of the group is to be identified with the moral opinions of some minority, then what minority is this to be? We cannot answer that it is to be the minority composed of the best and most enlightened individuals of the group. This would involve us in a palpably vicious circle. For by what standard are these individuals to be judged the best and the most enlightened? There is no principle by which we could select the right minority. And therefore we should have to consider every minority as good as every other. And this means that we should have no logical right whatever to resist the claim of the gangsters of Chicago—if such a claim were made—that their practices represent the highest standards of American morality. It means in the end that every individual is to be bound by no standard save his own.

The ethical relativists are great empiricists. *What* is the actual moral standard of any group can only be discovered, they tell us, by an examination on the ground of the moral opinions and customs of that group. But will they tell us how they propose to decide, when they get to the ground, which of the many moral opinions they are sure to find there is *the* right one in that group? To some extent they will be able to do this for the Melanesian Islanders—from whom apparently all lessons in the nature of morality are in future to be taken. But it is certain that they cannot do it for advanced peoples whose members have learnt to think for themselves and to entertain among themselves a wide variety of opinions. They cannot do it unless they accept the calamitous view that the ethical opinion of the majority is always right. We are left therefore once more with the conclusion that, even within a particular social group, anybody's moral opinion is as good as anybody else's, and that every man is entitled to be judged by his own standards.

Finally, not only is ethical relativity disastrous in its consequences for moral theory. It cannot be doubted that it must tend to be equally disastrous in its impact upon practical conduct. If men come really to believe that one moral standard is as good as another, they will conclude that their own moral standard has nothing special to recommend it. They might as well then slip down to some lower and easier standard. It is true that, for a time, it may be possible to hold one view in theory and to act practically upon another. But ideas, even philosophical ideas, are not so ineffectual that they can remain forever idle in the upper chambers of the intellect. In the end they seep down to the level of practice. They get themselves acted on.

Speaking of the supposedly dangerous character of ethical relativity, Westermarck says, "Ethical subjectivism instead of being a danger is more likely to be an advantage to morality. Could it be brought home to people that there is no absolute standard in morality, they would perhaps be on the one hand more tolerant, and on the other hand more critical in their judgment."[2] Certainly, if we believe that any one moral standard is as good as any other, we *are* likely to be more tolerant. We shall tolerate widow-burning, human sacrifice, cannibalism, slavery, the infliction of physical torture, or any other of the thousand and one abominations which are, or have been, from time to time approved by one moral code or another. But this is not the kind of toleration that we want, and I do not think its cultivation will prove "an advantage to morality."

These, then, are the main arguments which the anti-relativist will urge against ethical relativity. And perhaps finally he will attempt a diagnosis of the social, intellectual, and psychological conditions of our time to which the emergence of ethical relativism is to be attributed. His diagnosis will be somewhat as follows.

We have abandoned, perhaps with good reason, the oracles of the past. Every age, of course, does this. But in our case it seems that none of us knows any more whither to turn. We do not know what to put in the place of that which has gone. What ought we, supposedly civilized peoples, to aim at? What are to be our ideals? What is right? What is wrong? What is beautiful? What is ugly? No man knows. We drift helplessly in this direction and that. We know not where we stand nor whither we are going.

There are, of course, thousands of voices frantically shouting directions. But they shout one another down, they contradict one another, and the upshot is mere uproar. And because of this confusion there creeps upon us an insidious skepticism and despair. Since no one knows what the truth is, we will deny that there is any truth. Since no one knows what right is, we will deny that there is any right. Since no one knows what the beautiful is, we

---

[2] *Ethical Relativity,* page 59.

will deny that there is any beauty. Or at least we will say—what comes to the same thing—that what people (the people of any particular age, region, society)—think to be true is true *for them;* that what people think morally right is morally right *for them;* that what people think beautiful is beautiful *for them.* There is no common and objective standard in any of these matters. Since all the voices contradict one another, they must be all equally right (or equally wrong, for it makes no difference which we say). It is from the practical confusion of our time that these doctrines issue. When all the despair and defeatism of our distracted age are expressed in abstract concepts, are erected into a philosophy, it is then called relativism—ethical relativism, esthetic relativism, relativity of truth. Ethical relativity is simply defeatism in morals.

And the diagnosis will proceed. Perhaps, it will say, the current pessimism as to our future is unjustified. But there is undoubtedly a wide spread feeling that our civilization is rushing downwards to the abyss. If this should be true, and if nothing should check the headlong descent, then perhaps some historian of the future will seek to disentangle the causes. The causes will, of course, be found to be multitudinous and enormously complicated. And one must not exaggerate the relative importance of any of them. But it can hardly be doubted that our future historian will include somewhere in his list the failure of the men of our generation to hold steadfastly before themselves the notion of an (even comparatively) unchanging moral idea. He will cite that feebleness of intellectual and moral grasp which has led them weakly to harbor the belief that no one moral aim is really any better than any other, that each is good and true for those who entertain it. This meant, he will surely say, that men had given up in despair the struggle to attain moral truth. Civilization lives in and through its upward struggle. Whoever despairs and gives up the struggle, whether it be an individual or a whole civilization, is already inwardly dead.

And the philosophers of our age, where have they stood? They too, as is notorious, speak with many voices. But those who preach the various relativisms have taken upon themselves a heavy load of responsibility. By formulating abstractly the defeatism of the age, they have made themselves the aiders and abettors of death. They are injecting poison into the veins of civilization. Their influence upon practical affairs may indeed be small. But it counts for something. And they cannot avoid their share of the general responsibility. They have failed to do what little they could to stem the tide. They have failed to do what Plato did for the men of his own age—find a way out of at least the intellectual confusions of the time.

"Good" Indefinable but Meaningful

G. E. Moore

G. E. Moore (1873–1958), a pioneer in twentieth-century analysis and revival of realism, argues that philosophers often try to answer questions they have not made sense of and sin needlessly against common sense. He taught in Cambridge University and edited the prestigious journal, Mind.

This question,.how "good" is to be defined, is the most fundamental question in all Ethics. That which is meant by "good" is, in fact, except its converse, "bad," the *only* simple object of thought which is peculiar to Ethics. Its definition is, therefore, the most essential point in the definition of Ethics; and moreover, a mistake with regard to it entails a far larger number of erroneous ethical judgments than any other. Unless this first question be fully understood, and its true answer clearly recognized, the rest of Ethics is as good as useless from the point of view of systematic knowledge. True ethical judgments, of the two kinds last dealt with [not included here], may indeed be made by those who do not know the answer to this question as well as by those who do; and it goes without saying that the two classes of people may lead equally good lives. But it is extremely unlikely that the *most general* ethical judgments will be equally valid, in the absence of a true answer to this question. I shall presently try to show that the gravest errors have been largely due to beliefs in a false answer. And, in any case, it is impossible that, till the answer to this question be known, anyone should know *what is the evidence* for any

Reprinted by permission of Cambridge University Press from *Principia Ethica* by G. E. Moore, pp. 5–17.

ethical judgment whatsoever. But the main object of Ethics, as a systematic science, is to give correct *reasons* for thinking that this or that is good; and, unless this question be answered, such reasons cannot be given. Even, therefore, apart from the fact that a false answer leads to false conclusions, the present enquiry is a most necessary and important part of the science of Ethics.

What, then, is good? How is good to be defined? Now, it may be thought that this is a verbal question. A definition does indeed often mean the expressing of one word's meaning in other words. But this is not the sort of definition I am asking for. Such a definition can never be of ultimate importance in any study except lexicography. If I wanted that kind of definition, I should have to consider in the first place how people generally used the word "good"; but my business is not with its proper usage, as established by custom. I should, indeed, be foolish, if I tried to use it for something which it did not usually denote: if, for instance, I were to announce that, whenever I used the word "good," I must be understood to be thinking of that object which is usually denoted by the word "table." I shall, therefore, use the word in the sense in which I think it is ordinarily used; but at the same time I am not anxious to discuss whether I am right in thinking that it is so used. My business is solely with that object or idea, which I hold, rightly or wrongly, that the word is generally used to stand for. What I want to discover is the nature of that object or idea, and about this I am extremely anxious to arrive at an agreement.

But if we understand the question in this sense, my answer to it may seem a very disappointing one. If I am asked, "What is good?" my answer is that good is good, and that is the end of the matter. Or if I am asked, "How is good to be defined?" my answer is that it cannot be defined, and that is all I have to say about it. But disappointing as these answers may appear, they are of the very last importance. To readers who are familiar with philosophic terminology, I can express their importance by saying that they amount to this: that propositions about the good are all of them synthetic and never analytic; and that is plainly no trivial matter. And the same thing may be expressed more popularly, by saying that if I am right, then nobody can foist upon us such an axiom as that "Pleasure is the only good" or that "The good is the desired" on the pretence that this is "the very meaning of the word."

Let us, then, consider this position. My point is that "good" is a simple notion, just as "yellow" is a simple notion; that, just as you cannot, by any manner of means, explain to anyone who does not already know it, what yellow is, so you cannot explain what good is. Definitions of the kind that I was asking for, definitions which describe the real nature of the object or notion denoted by a word, and which do not merely tell us what the word is used to mean, are only possible when the object or notion in question is something complex. You can give a definition of a horse, because a horse has many different properties and qualities, all of which you can enumerate. But when you have enumerated them all, when you have reduced a horse to his simplest terms, then you can no longer define those terms. They are simply something which you think of or perceive, and to anyone who cannot think of or perceive them, you can never, by any definition, make their nature known. It may perhaps be objected to this that we are able to describe to others, objects which they have never seen or thought of. We can, for instance, make a man understand what a chimaera is, although he has never heard of one or seen one. You can tell him that it is an animal with a lioness's head and body, with a goat's head growing from the middle of its back, and with a snake in place of a tail. But here the object which you are describing is a complex object; it is entirely composed of parts with which we are all perfectly familiar—a snake, a goat, a lioness; and we know, too, the manner in which those parts are to be put together, because we know what is meant by the middle of a lioness's back, and where her tail is wont to grow. And so it is with all objects, not previously known, which we are able to define: they are all complex; all composed of parts, which may themselves, in the first instance, be capable of similar definition, but which must in the end be reducible to simplest parts, which can no longer be defined. But "yellow" and "good," we say, are not complex: they are notions of that simple kind, out of which definitions are composed and with which the power of further defining ceases.

When we say, as Webster says, "The definition of horse is 'A hoofed quadruped of the genus Equus,'" we may, in fact, mean three different things. (1) We may mean merely: "When I say 'horse,' you are to understand that I am talking about a hoofed quadruped of the genus Equus." This might be called the arbitrary verbal definition: and I do not mean that "good" is indefinable in that sense. (2) We may mean, as Webster ought to mean: "When most English people say 'horse,' they mean a hoofed quadruped of the genus Equus." This may be called the verbal definition proper, and I do not say that "good" is indefinable in this sense either; for it is certainly possible to discover how people use a word: otherwise, we could never have known that "good" may be translated by "gut" in German and by "bon" in French. But (3) we may, when we define "horse," mean something much more important. We may mean that a certain object, which we all of us know, is composed in a certain manner: that it has four legs, a head, a heart, a liver, and so forth, and so on, all of them arranged in definite relations to one another. It is in this sense that I deny "good" to be definable. I say that it is not composed of any parts, which we can substitute for it in our minds when we are thinking of it. We might think just as clearly and correctly about a horse, if we thought of all its parts and their arrangement instead of thinking of the whole: we could, I say, think how a horse differed from a donkey just as well, just as truly, in this way, as now we do, only not so easily; but there is nothing whatsoever which we could so substitute for "good"; and that is what I mean when I say that "good" is indefinable.

But I am afraid I have still not removed the chief difficulty which may prevent acceptance of the proposition that "good" is indefinable. I do not mean to say that "*the* good, that which is good," is thus indefinable; if I did think so, I should not be writing on Ethics, for my main object is to help towards discovering that definition. It is just because I think there will be less risk of error in our search for a definition of "the good" that I am now insisting that "*good*" is indefinable. I must try to explain the difference between these two. I suppose it may be granted that "good" is an adjective. Well "the good, that which is good," must therefore be the substantive to which the adjective "good" will apply: it must be the whole of that to which the adjective will apply, and the adjective must *always* truly apply to it. But if it is that to which the adjective will apply, it must be something different from that adjective itself; and the whole of that something different, whatever it is, will be our definition of *the* good. Now it may be that this something will have other adjectives, beside "good," that will apply to it. It may be full of pleasure, for example; it may be intelligent: and if these two adjectives are really part of its definition, then it will certainly be true that pleasure and intelligence are good. And many people appear to think that if we say, "Pleasure and intelligence are good," or if we say, "Only pleasure and intelligence are good," we are defining "good." Well, I cannot deny that propositions of this nature may sometimes be called definitions; I do not know well enough how the word is generally used to decide upon this point. I only wish it to be understood that that is not what I mean when I say there is no possible definition of good, and that I shall not mean this if I use the word again. I do most fully believe that some true proposition of the form "Intelligence is good and intelligence alone is good" can be found; if none could be found, our definition of *the* good would be impossible. As it is,

I believe *the* good to be definable; and yet I still say that good it-self is indefinable.

"Good," then, if we mean by it that quality which we assert to belong to a thing when we say that the thing is good, is incapable of any definition, in the most important sense of that word. The most important sense of "definition" is that in which a definition states what are the parts which invariably compose a certain whole; and in this sense "good" has no definition because it is simple and has no parts. It is one of those innumerable objects of thought which are themselves incapable of definition, because they are the ultimate terms by reference to which whatever *is* capable of definition must be defined. That there must be an indefinite number of such terms is obvious, on reflection; since we cannot define anything except by an analysis, which, when carried as far as it will go, refers us to something, which is simply different from anything else, and which by that ultimate difference explains the peculiarity of the whole which we are defining: for every whole contains some parts which are common to other wholes also. There is, therefore, no intrinsic difficulty in the contention that "good" denotes a simple and indefinable quality. There are many other instances of such qualities.

Consider "yellow," for example. We may try to define it by describing its physical equivalent; we may state what kind of light-vibrations must stimulate the normal eye in order that we may perceive it. But a moment's reflection is sufficient to show that those light-vibrations are not themselves what we mean by yellow. *They* are not what we perceive. Indeed we should never have been able to discover their existence, unless we had first been struck by the patent difference of quality between the different colors. The most we can be entitled to say of those vibrations is that they are what corresponds in space to the yellow which we actually perceive.

Yet a mistake of this simple kind has commonly been made about "good." It may be true that all things which are good are *also* something else, just as it is true that all things which are yellow produce a certain kind of vibration in the light. And it is a fact that Ethics aims at discovering what are those other proper-ties belonging to all things which are good. But far too many philosophers have thought that when they named those other properties they were actually defining good; that these properties, in fact, were simply not "other," but absolutely and entirely the same with goodness. This view I propose to call the "naturalistic fallacy" and of it I shall now endeavor to dispose.

Let us consider what it is such philosophers say. And first it is to be noticed that they do not agree among themselves. They not only say that they are right as to what good is, but they endeavor to prove that other people who say that it is something else, are wrong. One, for instance, will affirm that good is pleasure, another, perhaps, that good is that which is desired; and each of these will argue eagerly to prove that the other is wrong. But how is that possible? One of them says that good is nothing but the object of desire, and at the same time tries to prove that it is not pleasure. But from his first assertion, that good just means the object of desire, one of two things must follow as regards his proof:

1. He may be trying to prove that the object of desire is not pleasure. But, if this be all, where is his Ethics? The position he is maintaining is merely a psychological one. Desire is something which occurs in our minds, and pleasure is something else which so occurs; and our would-be ethical philosopher is merely holding that the latter is not the object of the former. But what has that to do with the question in dispute? His opponent held the ethical proposition that pleasure was the good, and although he should prove a million times over the psychological proposition that pleasure is not the object of desire, he is no nearer proving his opponent to be wrong. The position is like this. One man says a triangle is a circle: another replies, "A triangle is a straight line, and I will prove to you that I am right: *for*" (this is the only argument) "a straight line is not a circle." "That is quite true," the other may reply; "but nevertheless a triangle is a circle, and you have said nothing whatever to prove the contrary. What is proved is that one of us is wrong, for we agree that a triangle cannot be both a straight line and a circle: but which is wrong, there can be no earthly means of proving, since you define triangle as straight line and I define it as circle."—Well, that is one alternative which any naturalistic Ethics has to face; if good is *defined* as something else, it is then impossible either to prove that any other definition is wrong or even to deny such definition.

2. The other alternative will scarcely be more welcome. It is that the discussion is after all a verbal one. When *A* says, "Good means pleasant" and *B* says, "Good means desired," they may merely wish to assert that most people have used the word for what is pleasant and for what is desired respectively. And this is quite an interesting subject for discussion: only it is not a whit more an ethical discussion than the last was. Nor do I think that any exponent of naturalistic Ethics would be willing to allow that this was all he meant. They are all so anxious to persuade us that what they call "the good" is what we really ought to do. "Do, pray,

act so, because the word 'good' is generally used to denote actions of this nature": such, on this view, would be the substance of their teaching. And insofar as they tell us how we ought to act, their teaching is truly ethical, as they mean it to be. But how perfectly absurd is the reason they would give for it! "You are to do this, because most people use a certain word to denote conduct such as this." "You are to say the thing which is not, because most people call it lying." That is an argument just as good!—My dear sirs, what we want to know from you as ethical teachers is not how people use a word; it is not even what kind of actions they approve, which the use of this word "good" may certainly imply: what we want to know is simply what *is* good. We may indeed agree that what most people do think good is actually so; we shall at all events be glad to know their opinions: but when we say their opinions about what *is* good, we do mean what we say; we do not care whether they call that thing which they mean "horse" or "table" or "chair," "gut" or "bon" or "ἀγαθός"; we want to know what it is that they so call. When they say, "Pleasure is good," we cannot believe that they merely mean "Pleasure is pleasure" and nothing more than that.

Suppose a man says, "I am pleased"; and suppose that is not a lie or a mistake but the truth. Well, if it is true, what does that mean? It means that his mind, a certain definite mind, distinguished by certain definite marks from all others, has at this moment a certain definite feeling called pleasure. "Pleased" *means* nothing but having pleasure, and though we may be more pleased or less pleased, and even, we may admit for the present, have one or another kind of pleasure; yet in so far as it is pleasure we have, whether there be more or less of it, and whether it be of one kind or another, what we have is one definite thing, absolutely indefinable, some one thing that is the same in all the various degrees and in all the various kinds of it that there may be. We may be able to say how it is related to other things: that, for example, it is in the mind, that it causes desire, that we are conscious of it, and so on. We can, I say, describe its relations to other things, but define it we can *not*. And if anybody tried to define "pleasure" for us as being any other natural object; if anybody were to say, for instance, that "pleasure" *means* the sensation of red, and were to proceed to deduce from that that pleasure is a color, we should be entitled to laugh at him and to distrust his future statements about pleasure. Well, that would be the same fallacy which I have called the naturalistic fallacy. That "pleased" does not mean "having the sensation of red," or anything else whatever, does not prevent us from understanding what it does mean. It is enough for us to know that "pleased" does mean "having the sensation of pleasure," and though "pleasure" is absolutely indefinable, though pleasure is pleasure and nothing else whatever, yet we feel no difficulty in saying that we are pleased. The reason is, of course, that when I say, "I am pleased," I do *not* mean that "I" am the same thing as "having pleasure." And similarly no difficulty need be found in my saying that "pleasure is good" and yet not meaning that "pleasure" is the same thing as "good," that "pleasure" *means* "good," and that "good" *means* "pleasure." If I were to imagine that when I said, "I am pleased," I meant that I was exactly the same thing as "pleased," I should not indeed call that a naturalistic fallacy, although it would be the same fallacy as I have called naturalistic with reference to Ethics. The reason of this is obvious enough. When a man confuses two natural objects with one another, defining the one by the other, if for instance, he confuses himself, who is one natural object, with "pleased" or with "pleasure," which are others, then there is no reason to call the fallacy naturalistic. But if he confuses "good," which is not in the same sense a natural object, with any natural object whatever, then there is a reason for calling that a naturalistic fallacy; its being made with regard to "good" marks it as something quite specific, and this specific mistake deserves a name because it is so common. As for the reasons why good is not to be considered a natural object, they may be reserved for discussion in another place. But, for the present, it is sufficient to notice this: Even if it were a natural object, that would not alter the nature of the fallacy nor diminish its importance one whit. All that I have said about it would remain quite equally true: only the name which I have called it would not be so appropriate as I think it is. And I do not care about the name: what I do care about is the fallacy. It does not matter what we call it, provided we recognize it when we meet with it. It is to be met with in almost every book on Ethics; and yet it is not recognized: and that is why it is necessary to multiply illustrations of it, and convenient to give it a name. It is a very simply fallacy indeed. When we say that an orange is yellow, we do not think our statement binds us to hold that "orange" means nothing else than "yellow," or that nothing can be yellow but an orange. Supposing the orange is also sweet! Does that bind us to say that "sweet" is exactly the same thing as "yellow," that "sweet" must be defined as "yellow"? And supposing it be recognized that "yellow" just means "yellow" and nothing else whatever; does that make it any more difficult to hold that oranges are yellow? Most certainly it does not: on the contrary, it would be absolutely meaningless to say that oranges were yellow, unless "yellow" did in the end mean just "yellow" and nothing else whatever—unless it was absolutely indefinable. We should not get any very clear notion about things which are yellow—we should not get very far with our science—if we were bound to hold that everything which was yellow *meant* exactly the same thing as "yellow." We should find we had to hold that an orange was exactly the same thing as a stool, a piece of paper, a lemon, anything you like. We could prove any number of absurdities; but should we be the nearer to the truth? Why, then, should it be different with "good"? Why, if good is good and indefinable, should I be held to deny that pleasure is good? Is there any difficulty in holding both to be true at once? On the contrary, there is no meaning in saying that pleasure is good, unless good is something different from pleasure. It is absolutely useless, so far as Ethics is concerned, to prove, as Mr Spencer tries to do, that increase of pleasure coincides with increase of life, unless "good" *means* something different from either life or pleasure. He might just as well try to prove that an orange is yellow by showing that it always is wrapped up in paper.

In fact, if it is not the case that "good" denotes something simple and indefinable, only two alternatives are possible: either it is a complex, a given whole, about the correct analysis of which there may be disagreement; or else it means nothing at all, and there is no such subject as Ethics. In general, however, ethical philosophers have attempted to define good, without recognizing what such an attempt must mean. They actually use arguments which involve one or both of the absurdities considered [above]. We are, therefore, justified in concluding that the attempt to define good is chiefly due to want of clearness as to the possible nature of definition. There are, in fact, only two serious alternatives to be considered, in order to establish the conclusion that "good" does denote a simple and indefinable notion. It might possibly denote a complex, as "horse" does; or it might have no meaning at all. Neither of these possibilities has, however, been clearly conceived and seriously maintained, as such, by those who presume to define "good"; and both may be dismissed by a simple appeal to facts.

1. The hypothesis that disagreement about the meaning of "good" is disagreement with regard to the correct analysis of a given whole, may be most plainly seen to be incorrect by consideration of the fact that, whatever definition be offered, it may be always asked, with significance, of the complex so defined, whether it is itself good. To take, for instance, one of the more plausible, because one of the more complicated, of such proposed definitions, it may easily be thought, at first sight, that to be good may mean

to be that which we desire to desire. Thus if we apply this definition to a particular instance and say, "When we think that *A* is
good, we are thinking that *A* is one of the things which we desire
to desire," our proposition may seem quite plausible. But, if we
carry the investigation further, and ask ourselves, "Is it good to
desire *A*?" it is apparent, on a little reflection, that this question
is itself as intelligible as the original question "Is *A* good?"—that
we are in fact now asking for exactly the same information about
the desire to desire *A* for which we formerly asked with regard to
A itself. But it is also apparent that the meaning of this second
question cannot be correctly analyzed into, "Is the desire to desire
A one of the things which we desire to desire?": we have not before our minds anything so complicated as the question, "Do we
desire to desire to desire to desire *A*?" Moreover, anyone can easily
convince himself by inspection that the predicate of this proposition—"good"—is positively different from the notion of "desiring
to desire" which enters into its subject: "That we should desire
to desire *A* is good" is *not* merely equivalent to "That *A* should be
good is good." It may indeed be true that what we desire to desire
is always also good; perhaps, even the converse may be true: but
it is very doubtful whether this is the case, and the mere fact that
we understand very well what is meant by doubting it, shows
clearly that we have two different notions before our minds.

2. And the same consideration is sufficient to dismiss the hypothesis that "good" has no meaning whatsoever. It is very natural to make the mistake of supposing that what is universally
true is of such a nature that its negation would be self-contradictory: the importance which has been assigned to analytic propositions in the history of philosophy shows how easy such a mistake is. And thus it is very easy to conclude that what seems to be
a universal ethical principle is in fact an identical proposition;
that, if, for example, whatever is called "good" seems to be pleasant, the proposition "Pleasure is the good" does not assert a connection between two different notions, but involves only one, that
of pleasure, which is easily recognized as a distinct entity. But
whoever will attentively consider with himself what is actually
before his mind when he asks the question "Is pleasure (or whatever it may be), after all, good?" can easily satisfy himself that he
is not merely wondering whether pleasure is pleasant. And if he
will try this experiment with each suggested definition in succession, he may become expert enough to recognize that in every case
he has before his mind a unique object, with regard to the connection of which with any other object, a distinct question may be
asked. Everyone does in fact understand the question "Is this

good?" When he thinks of it, his state of mind is different from what it would be were he asked, "Is this pleasant, or desired, or approved?" It has a distinct meaning for him, even though he may not recognize in what respect it is distinct. Whenever he thinks of "intrinsic value," or "intrinsic worth," or says that a thing "ought to exist," he has before his mind the unique object— the unique property of things—which I mean by "good." Everybody is constantly aware of this notion, although he may never become aware at all that it is different from other notions of which he is also aware. But, for correct ethical reasoning, it is extremely important that he should become aware of this fact; and, as soon as the nature of the problem is clearly understood, there should be little difficulty in advancing so far in analysis.

"Good," then, is indefinable.

Ethical Disagreements
Concern Attitudes More Than Facts

Charles L. Stevenson

C. L. Stevenson (1908–   ) is Professor of Philosophy in the University of Michigan. His articles and his book Ethics and Language *have established him as the foremost American advocate of the emotive theory of ethics. Lately, he has written in aesthetics.*

When people disagree about the value of something—one saying that it is good or right, and another that it is bad or wrong—by what methods of argument or inquiry can their disagreement be resolved? Can it be resolved by the methods of science, or does it require methods of some other kind, or is it open to no rational solution at all?

The question must be clarified before it can be answered. And the word that is particularly in need of clarification, as we shall see, is the word "disagreement."

Let us begin by noting that "disagreement" has two broad senses: In the first sense it refers to what I shall call "disagreement in belief." This occurs when Mr. A believes *p*, when Mr. B believes *not-p*, or something incompatible with *p*, and when neither is content to let the belief of the other remain unchallenged. Thus doctors may disagree in belief about the causes of an illness; and friends may disagree in belief about the exact date on which they last met.

In the second sense, the word refers to what I shall call "disagreement in attitude." This occurs when Mr. A has a favorable attitude to something, when Mr. B has an unfavorable or less

Reprinted by permission of the author from *Sigma*, Vols. I–II, Nos. 8–9, 1947–48.

favorable attitude to it, and when neither is content to let the other's attitude remain unchanged. The term "attitude" is here used in much the same sense that R. B. Perry uses "interest"; it designates any psychological disposition of being *for* or *against* something. Hence love and hate are relatively specific kinds of attitudes, as are approval and disapproval, and so on.

This second sense can be illustrated in this way: Two men are planning to have dinner together. One is particularly anxious to eat at a certain restaurant, but the other doesn't like it. Temporarily, then, the men cannot "agree" on where to dine. Their argument may be trivial, and perhaps only half serious; but in any case it represents a disagreement *in attitude*. The men have divergent preferences, and each is trying to redirect the preference of the other.

Further examples are readily found. Mrs. Smith wishes to cultivate only the four hundred; Mr. Smith is loyal to his old poker-playing friends. They accordingly disagree, in attitude, about whom to invite to their party. The progressive mayor wants modern school-buildings and large parks; the older citizens are against these "new-fangled" ways; so they disagree on civic policy. These cases differ from the one about the restaurant only in that the clash of attitudes is more serious, and may lead to more vigorous argument.

The difference between the two senses of "disagreement" is essentially this: the first involves an opposition of beliefs, both of which cannot be true, and the second involves an opposition of attitudes, both of which cannot be satisfied.

Let us apply this distinction to a case that will sharpen it. Mr. A believes that most voters will favor a proposed tax, and Mr. B disagrees with him. The disagreement concerns attitudes—those of the voters—but not that A and B are *not* disagreeing in attitude. Their disagreement is *in belief about* attitudes. It is simply a special kind of disagreement in belief, differing from disagreement in belief about head colds only with regard to subject matter. It implies not an opposition of the actual attitudes of the speakers, but only of their beliefs about certain attitudes. Disagreement *in* attitude, on the other hand, implies that the very attitudes of the speakers are opposed. A and B may have opposed beliefs about attitudes without having opposed attitudes, just as they may have opposed beliefs about head colds without having opposed head colds. Hence we must not, from the fact that an argument is concerned with attitudes, infer that it necessarily involves disagreement *in* attitude.

We may now turn more directly to disagreement about values,

with particular reference to normative ethics. When people argue about what is good, do they disagree in belief, or do they disagree in attitude? A long tradition of ethical theorists strongly suggests, whether they always intend to or not, that the disagreement is one *in belief*. Naturalistic theorists, for instance, identify an ethical judgment with some sort of scientific statement, and so make normative ethics a branch of science. Now a scientific argument typically exemplifies disagreement in belief, and if an ethical argument is simply a scientific one, then it too exemplifies disagreement in belief. The usual naturalistic theories of ethics that stress attitudes—such as those of Hume, Westermarck, Perry, Richards, and so many others—stress disagreement in belief no less than the rest. They imply, of course, that disagreement about what is good is disagreement *in belief* about attitudes; but we have seen that that is simply one sort of disagreement in belief, and by no means the same as disagreement *in* attitude. Analyses that stress disagreement *in* attitude are extremely rare.

If ethical arguments, as we encounter them in everyday life, involved disagreement in belief exclusively—whether the beliefs were about attitudes or about something else—then I should have no quarrel with the ordinary sort of naturalistic analysis. Normative judgments could be taken as scientific proof. But a moment's attention will readily show the disagreement in belief has not the exclusive role that theory has so repeatedly ascribed to it. It must be readily granted that ethical arguments usually involve disagreement in belief; but they *also* involve disagreement in attitude. And the conspicuous role of disagreement in attitude is what we usually take, whether we realize it or not, as the distinguishing feature of ethical arguments. For example: suppose that the representative of a union urges that the wage level in a given company ought to be higher—that it is only right that the workers receive more pay. The company representative urges in reply that the workers ought to receive no more than they get. Such an argument clearly represents a disagreement in attitude. The union is *for* higher wages; the company is *against* them, and neither is content to let the other's attitude remain unchanged. *In addition* to this disagreement in attitude, of course, the argument may represent no little disagreement in belief. Perhaps the parties disagree about how much the cost of living has risen, and how much the workers are suffering under the present wage scale. Or perhaps they disagree about the company's earnings, and the extent to which the company could raise wages and still operate at a profit. Like any typical ethical argument, then, this argument involves both disagreement in attitude and disagreement in belief.

It is easy to see, however, that the disagreement in attitude plays a unifying and predominating role in the argument. This is so in two ways:

In the first place, disagreement in attitude determines what beliefs are *relevant* to the argument. Suppose that the company affirms that the wage scale of fifty years ago was far lower than it is now. The union will immediately urge that this contention, even though true, is irrelevant. And it is irrelevant simply because information about the wage level of fifty years ago, maintained under totally different circumstances, is not likely to affect the present attitudes of either party. To be relevant, any belief that is introduced into the argument must be one that is likely to lead one side or the other to have a different attitude, and so reconcile disagreement in attitude. Attitudes are often functions of beliefs. We often change our attitudes to something when we change our beliefs about it; just as a child ceases to *want* to touch a live coal when he comes to *believe* that it will burn him. Thus in the present argument, any beliefs that are at all likely to alter attitudes, such as those about the increasing cost of living or the financial state of the company, will be considered by both sides to be relevant to the argument. Agreement in belief on these matters may lead to agreement in attitude toward the wage scale. But beliefs that are likely to alter the attitudes of neither side will be declared irrelevant. They will have no bearing on the disagreement in attitude, with which both parties are primarily concerned.

In the second place, ethical argument usually terminates when disagreement in attitude terminates, even though a certain amount of disagreement in belief remains. Suppose, for instance, that the company and the union continue to disagree in belief about the increasing cost of living, but that the company, even so, ends by favoring the higher wage scale. The union will then be content to end the argument, and will cease to press its point about living costs. It may bring up that point again, in some future argument of the same sort, or in urging the righteousness of its victory to the newspaper columnists; but for the moment the fact that the company has agreed in attitude is sufficient to terminate the argument. On the other hand: suppose that both parties agreed on all beliefs that were introduced into the argument, but even so continued to disagree in attitude. In that case neither party would feel that their dispute had been successfully terminated. They might look for other beliefs that could be introduced into the argument. They might use words to play on each other's emotions. They might agree (in attitude) to submit the case to arbitration, both feeling that a decision, even if strongly adverse to one party or the other, would be preferable to a continued impasse. Or, perhaps, they might abandon hope of settling their dispute by any peaceable means.

In many other cases, of course, men discuss ethical topics without having the strong, uncompromising attitudes that the present example has illustrated. They are often as much concerned with redirecting their own attitudes, in the light of greater knowledge, as with redirecting the attitudes of others. And the attitudes involved are often altruistic, rather than selfish. Yet the above example will serve, so long as that is understood, to suggest the nature of ethical disagreement. Both disagreement in attitude and disagreement in belief are involved, but the former predominates in that (1) it determines what sort of disagreement in belief is relevantly disputed in a given ethical argument, and (2) it determines, by its continued presence or its resolution, whether or not the argument has been settled. We may see further how intimately the two sorts of disagreement are related; since attitudes are often functions of beliefs, an agreement in belief may lead people, as a matter of psychological fact, to agree in attitude.

Having discussed disagreement, we may turn to the broad question that was first mentioned, namely: By what methods or argument or inquiry may disagreement about matters of value be resolved?

It will be obvious that to whatever extent an argument involves disagreement in belief, it is open to the usual methods of the sciences. If these methods are the *only* rational methods for supporting beliefs—as I believe to be so, but cannot now take time to discuss—then scientific methods are the only rational methods for resolving the disagreement in *belief* that arguments about values may include.

But if science is granted an undisputed sway in reconciling beliefs, it does not thereby acquire, without qualification, an undisputed sway in reconciling attitudes. We have seen that arguments about values include disagreement in attitude, no less than disagreement in belief, and that in certain ways the disagreement in attitude predominates. By what methods shall the latter sort of disagreement be resolved?

The methods of science are still available for that purpose, but only in an indirect way. Initially, these methods have only to do with establishing agreement in belief. If they serve further to establish agreement in attitude, that will be due simply to the psychological fact that altered beliefs may cause altered attitudes. Hence scientific methods are conclusive in ending arguments about values only to the extent that their success in obtaining agreement in belief will in turn lead to agreement in attitude.

In other words: the extent to which scientific methods can bring about agreement on values depends on the extent to which a commonly accepted body of scientific beliefs would cause us to have a commonly accepted set of attitudes.

How much is the development of science likely to achieve, then, with regard to values? To what extent *would* common beliefs lead to common attitudes? It is, perhaps, a pardonable enthusiasm to *hope* that science will do everything—to hope that in some rosy future, when all men know the consequences of their acts, they will all have common aspirations, and live peaceably in complete moral accord. But if we speak not from our enthusiastic hopes, but from our present knowledge, the answer must be far less exciting. We usually *do not know*, at the beginning of any argument about values, whether an agreement in belief, scientifically established, will lead to an agreement in attitude or not. It is logically possible, at least, that two men should continue to disagree in attitude even though they had all their beliefs in common, and even though neither had made any logical or inductive error, or omitted any relevant evidence. Differences in temperament, or in early training, or in social status, might make the men retain different attitudes even though both were possessed of the complete scientific truth. Whether this logical possibility is an empirical likelihood I shall not presume to say; but it is unquestionably a possibility that must not be left out of account.

To say that science can always settle arguments about value, we have seen, is to make this assumption: Agreement in attitude will always be consequent upon complete agreement in belief, and science can always bring about the latter. Taken as purely heuristic, this assumption has its usefulness. It leads people to discover the discrepancies in their beliefs, and to prolong enlightening argument that *may* lead, as a matter of fact, from commonly accepted beliefs to commonly accepted attitudes. It leads people to reconcile their attitudes in a rational, permanent way, rather than by rhapsody or exhortation. But the assumption is *nothing more*, for present knowledge, than a heuristic maxim. It is wholly without any proper foundation of probability. I conclude, therefore, that scientific methods cannot be guaranteed the definite role in the so-called "normative sciences" that they may have in the natural sciences. Apart from a heuristic assumption to the contrary, it is possible that the growth of scientific knowledge may leave many disputes about values permanently unsolved. Should these disputes persist, there are non-rational methods for dealing with them, of course, such as impassioned, moving oratory. But the purely intellectual methods of science, and, indeed, *all* methods of reasoning, may be insufficient to settle disputes about values, even though they may greatly help to do so.

For the same reasons, I conclude that normative ethics is not a branch of any science. It deliberately deals with a type of disagreement that science deliberately avoids. Ethics is not psychology, for instance; for although psychologists may, of course, agree or disagree in belief about attitudes, they need not, as psychologists, be concerned with whether they agree or disagree with one another *in* attitude. Insofar as normative ethics draws from the sciences, in order to change attitudes *via* changing people's beliefs, it *draws* from *all* the sciences; but a moralist's peculiar aim—that of *redirecting* attitudes—is a type of activity, rather than knowledge, and falls within no science. Science may study that activity, and may help indirectly to forward it; but it is not *identical* with that activity.

I have only a moment to explain why the ethical terms, such as "good," "wrong," "ought," and so on, are so habitually used to deal with disagreement in attitude. On account of their repeated occurrence in emotional situations, they have acquired a strong emotive meaning. This emotive meaning makes them serviceable in initiating changes in a hearer's attitudes. Sheer emotive impact is not likely, under many circumstances, to change attitudes in any permanent way; but it *begins* a process that can then be supported by other means.

There is no occasion for saying that the meaning of ethical terms is *purely* emotive, like that of "alas" or "hurrah." We have seen that ethical *arguments* include many expressions of *belief;* and the rough rules of ordinary language permit us to say that some of these beliefs are expressed by an ethical judgment itself. But the beliefs so expressed are by no means always the same. Ethical terms are notable for their ambiguity, and opponents in an argument may use them in different senses. Sometimes this leads to artificial issues; but it usually does not. So long as one person says "This is good" with emotive praise, and another says "No, it is bad," with emotive condemnation, a disagreement in attitude is manifest. Whether or not the beliefs that these statements express are logically incompatible may not be discovered until later in the argument; but even if they are actually compatible, disagreement in attitude will be preserved by emotive meaning; and this disagreement, so central to ethics, may lead to an argument that is certainly not artificial in its issues, so long as it is taken for what it is.

The many theorists who have refused to identify ethical statements with scientific ones have much to be said in their favor. They have seen that ethical judgments mold or alter attitudes, rather than describe them, and they have seen that ethical judgments can be guaranteed no definitive scientific support. But one need not, on that account, provide ethics with any extramundane, sui generis *subject matter*. The distinguishing features of an ethical judgment can be preserved by a recognition of emotive meaning and disagreement in attitude, rather than by some non-natural quality—and with far greater intelligibility. If an unique subject matter is *postulated*, as it usually is, to preserve the important distinction between normative ethics and science, it serves no purpose that is not served by the very simple analysis I have here suggested. Unless non-natural qualities can be defended by positive arguments, rather than as an "only resort" from the acknowledged weakness of ordinary forms of naturalism, they would seem nothing more than the invisible shadows cast by emotive meaning.

"Good" Commends and Informs

Richard M. Hare

Richard M. Hare (1919–   ) is Fellow in Balliol College, Oxford. In addition to the book from which this reading is taken, he has written Freedom and Reason.

"Naturalism"

Let me illustrate one of the most characteristic features of value-words in terms of a particular example. It is a feature sometimes described by saying that "good" and other such words are the names of "supervenient" or "consequential" properties. Suppose that a picture is hanging upon the wall and we are discussing whether it is a good picture; that is to say, we are debating whether to assent to, or dissent from, the judgment "*P* is a good picture." It must be understood that the context makes it clear that we mean by "good picture" not "good likeness" but "good work of art"—though both these uses would be value-expressions.

First let us notice a very important peculiarity of the word "good" as used in this sentence. Suppose that there is another picture next to *P* in the gallery (I will call it *Q*). Suppose that

Reprinted by permission of the author and The Clarendon Press, Oxford, from *The Language of Morals* by R. M. Hare, pp. 80–134, with many omissions. Copyright 1952.

either *P* is a replica of *Q* or *Q* of *P*, and we do not know which, but do know that both were painted by the same artist at about the same time. Now there is one thing that we cannot say; we cannot say "*P* is exactly like *Q* in all respects save this one, that *P* is a good picture and *Q* not." If we were to say this, we should invite the comment, "But how can one be good and the other not, if they are exactly alike? There must be some *further* difference between them to make one good and the other not." Unless we at least admit the relevance of the question "What makes one good and the other not?" we are bound to puzzle our hearers; they will think that something has gone wrong with our use of the word "good." Sometimes we cannot specify just what it is that makes one good and the other not; but there always must be something. Suppose that in the attempt to explain our meaning we said: "I didn't say that there *was* any other difference between them; there is just this one difference, that one is good and the other not. Surely you would understand me if I said that one was *signed* and the other not, but that there was otherwise no difference? So why shouldn't I say that one was *good* and the other not, but that there was otherwise no difference?" The answer to this protest is that the word "good" is not like the word "signed"; there is a difference in their logic.

The following reason might be suggested for this logical peculiarity: there is some one characteristic or group of characteristics of the two pictures on which the characteristic "good" is logically dependent, so that, of course, one cannot be good and the other not, unless these characteristics vary too. To quote a parallel case, one picture could not be *rectangular* and the other not, unless certain other characteristics also varied, for example the size of at least one of the angles. And so a natural response to the discovery that "good" behaves as it does, is to suspect that there is a set of characteristics which together *entail* a thing being good, and to set out to discover what these characteristics are. This is the genesis of that group of ethical theories which Professor Moore called "naturalist"—an unfortunate term, for as Moore says himself, substantially the same fallacy may be committed by choosing metaphysical or suprasensible characteristics for this purpose.[1] Talking about the supernatural is no prophylactic against "naturalism." The term has, unfortunately, since Moore's introduction of it, been used very loosely. It is best to confine it to those theories against which Moore's refutation (or a recognizable version of it) is valid. In this sense most "emotive" theo-

[1] *Principia Ethica*, p. 39.

ries are not naturalist, though they are often called so. Their error is a quite different one. I shall argue below . . . that what is wrong with naturalist theories is that they leave out the prescriptive or commendatory element in value-judgments, by seeking to make them derivable from statements of fact. If I am right in this opinion, my own theory, which preserves this element, is not naturalist.

. . .

Let us then ask whether "good" behaves in the way that we have noticed for the same reason that "rectangular" does; in other words, whether there are certain characteristics of pictures which are defining characteristics of a good picture, in the same way as "having all its angles 90 degrees and being a rectilinear plane figure" are defining characteristics of a rectangle. Moore thought that he could prove that there were no such defining characteristics for the word "good" as used in morals. His argument has been assailed since he propounded it; and it is certainly true that the formulation of it was at fault. But it seems to me that Moore's argument was not merely plausible; it rests, albeit insecurely, upon a secure foundation; there is indeed something about the way in which, and the purposes for which, we use the word "good" which makes it impossible to hold the sort of position which Moore was attacking, although Moore did not see clearly what this something was. Let us, therefore, try to restate Moore's argument in a way which makes it clear why "naturalism" is untenable, not only for the moral use of "good" as he thought, but also for many other uses.

Let us suppose for the sake of argument that there are some "defining characteristics" of a good picture. It does not matter of what sort they are; they can be a single characteristic, or a conjunction of characteristics, or a disjunction of alternative characteristics. Let us call the group of these characteristics C. "P is a good picture" will then mean the same as "P is a picture and P is C." For example, let C mean "having a tendency to arouse in people who are at that time members of the Royal Academy (or any other definitely specified group of people) a definitely recognizable feeling called 'admiration.'" The words "definitely specified" and "definitely recognizable" have to be inserted, for otherwise we might find that words in the *definiens* were being used evaluatively, and this would make the definition no longer "naturalistic." Now suppose that we wish to say that the members of the Royal Academy have good taste in pictures. To have good taste in pictures means to have this definitely recognizable feeling of admiration for those pictures, and only those pictures, which are good pictures. If, therefore, we wish to say that the members of the Royal Academy have good taste in pictures, we have, according to the definition, to say something which means the same as saying that they have this feeling of admiration for pictures which have a tendency to arouse in them this feeling.

Now this is not what we wanted to say. We wanted to say that they admired good pictures; we have succeeded only in saying that they admired pictures which they admired. Thus if we accept the definition, we debar ourselves from saying something that we do sometimes want to say. What this something is will become apparent later; for the moment let us say that what we wanted to do was to *commend* the pictures which the members of the Royal Academy admired. Something about our definition prevented our doing this. We could no longer commend the pictures which they admired; we could only say that they admired those pictures which they admired. Thus our definition has prevented us, in one crucial case, from commending something which we want to commend. That is what is wrong with it.

Let us generalize. If "*P* is a good picture" is held to mean the same as "*P* is a picture and *P* is *C*," then it will become impossible to commend pictures for being *C*; it will be possible only to say that they are *C*. It is important to realize that this difficulty has nothing to do with the particular example that I have chosen. It is not because we have chosen the wrong defining characteristics; it is because, whatever defining characteristics we choose, this objection arises, that we can no longer commend an object for possessing those characteristics.

Let us illustrate this by another example. I am deliberately excluding for the moment moral examples because I want it to be clear that the logical difficulties which we are encountering have nothing to do with morals in particular, but are due to the general characteristics of value-words. Let us consider the sentence "*S* is a good strawberry." We might naturally suppose that this means nothing more than "*S* is a strawberry and *S* is sweet, juicy, firm, red, and large." But it then becomes impossible for us to say certain things which in our ordinary talk we do say. We sometimes want to say that a strawberry is a good strawberry because it is sweet, and so on. This—as we can at once see if we think of ourselves saying it—does not mean the same as saying that a strawberry is a sweet, and so on, strawberry because it is sweet, and so on. But according to the proposed definition, this is what it would mean. Thus here again the proposed definition would prevent our saying something that we do succeed in saying meaningfully in our ordinary talk.

. . .

Meaning and Criteria

It is characteristic of the word "red" that we can explain its meaning in a certain way. The suggestion that the logical character of words can be investigated by asking how we would explain their meaning comes from Wittgenstein. The point of the method is that it brings out the ways in which the learner could get the meaning *wrong*, and so helps to show what is required in order to get it right. Let us suppose that we are trying to teach English to a foreign philosopher who either deliberately or inadvertently makes all the mistakes that he *logically* can (for what mistakes anyone *actually* makes or avoids is irrelevant.) We must assume that, when we start, he knows no English, and we know nothing of his language. At a certain stage, we shall get to the simple property-words. If we had to explain the meaning of the word "red" to such a person, we might proceed as follows: we might take him to see pillar-boxes, tomatoes, underground trains, and so on, and say, as we showed him each object, "That is red." And then we might take him to see some pairs of things that were like each other in most respects, but unlike in colour (for example pillar-boxes in England and Ireland, ripe and unripe tomatoes, London Transport trains and main line electric trains), and on each occasion say, "This is red; that is not red but green." In this way he would learn the use of the word "red"; he would become conversant with its meaning.

It is tempting to assume that the meaning of all words that are applied in any sense to things could be conveyed (directly or indirectly) in the same way; but this is not so, as is well known. The word "this" could not be treated in this fashion, nor, perhaps, could the word "Quaxo"—if we can call the name of a cat a word at all. It is instructive to ask whether the meaning of "good" could be explained like this, and if not, why not.

It is a characteristic of "good" that it can be applied to any number of different classes of objects. We have good cricket-bats, good chronometers, good fire extinguishers, good pictures, good sunsets, good men. The same is true of the word "red"; all the objects I have just listed might be red. We have to ask first, whether, in explaining the meaning of the word "good," it would be possible to explain its meaning in all of these expressions at once, or whether it would be necessary to explain "good cricket-bat" first, and then go on to explain "good chronometer" in the second lesson, "good fire extinguisher" in the third, and so on; and if the latter, whether in each lesson we should be teaching something entirely new—like teaching the meaning of "fast dye" after we had in a previous lesson taught the meaning of "fast motorcar"—or whether it would be just the same lesson over again, with a different example—like teaching "red dye" after we had taught "red motorcar." Or there might be some third possibility.

The view that "good chronometer" would be a completely new lesson, even though the day before we had taught "good cricket-bat," runs at once into difficulties. For it would mean that at any one time our learner could only use the word "good" in speaking of classes of objects which he had learnt so far. He would never be able to go straight up to a new class of objects and use the word "good" of one of them. When he had learnt "good cricket-bat" and "good chronometer," he would not be able to manage "good fire extinguisher"; and when he had learnt the latter, he would still be unable to manage "good motorcar." But in fact one of the most noticeable things about the way we use "good" is that we are able to use it for entirely new classes of objects that we have never called "good" before. Suppose that someone starts collecting cacti for the first time and puts one on his mantelpiece— the only cactus in the country. Suppose then that a friend sees it, and says, "I must have one of those"; so he sends for one from wherever they grow, and puts it on his mantelpiece, and when his friend comes in, he says, "I've got a better cactus than yours." But how does he know how to apply the word in this way? He has never learnt to apply "good" to cacti; he does not even know any *criteria* for telling a good cactus from a bad one (for as yet there are none); but he has learnt to use the word "good," and having learnt that, he can apply it to any class of objects that he requires to place in order of merit. He and his friend may dispute about the criteria of good cacti; they may attempt to set up rival criteria; but they could not even do this unless they were from that start under no difficulty in using the word "good" for a new class of objects without further instruction. Learning the use of the word for one class of objects cannot be a different lesson from learning it for another class of objects—though learning the criteria of goodness in a new class of objects may be a new lesson each time.

. . .

Description and Evaluation

Of all the problems raised by the preceding argument, the key problem is as follows: there are two sorts of things that we can say, for example, about strawberries; the first sort is usually called *descriptive*, the second sort *evaluative*. Examples of the first sort of remark are, "This strawberry is sweet" and "This strawberry is large, red, and juicy." Examples of the second sort of remark are, "This is a good strawberry" and "This strawberry is just as strawberries ought to be." The first sort of remark is often given as a reason for making the second sort of remark; but the first sort does not by itself entail the second sort, nor vice versa. Yet there seems to be some close logical connection between them. Our problem is: "What is this connection?"; for no light is shed by saying that there is a connection, unless we can say what it is.

The problem may also be put in this way: if we knew all the descriptive properties which a particular strawberry had (knew, of every descriptive sentence relating to the strawberry, whether it was true or false), and if we knew also the meaning of the word "good," then what else should we require to know, in order to be able to tell whether a strawberry was a good one? Once the question is put in this way, the answer should be apparent. We should require to know, what are the criteria in virtue of which a strawberry is to be called a good one, or what are the characteristics that make a strawberry a good one, or what is the standard of goodness in strawberries. We should require to be given the major premise. We have already seen that we can know the meaning of "good strawberry" without knowing any of these latter things—though there is also a sense of the sentence "What does it mean to call a strawberry a good one?" in which we should not know the answer to it, unless we also knew the answer to these other questions. It is now time to elucidate and distinguish these two ways in which we can be said to know what it means to call an object a good member of its class. This will help us to see more clearly both the differences and the similarities between "good" and words like "red" and "sweet."

Since we have been dwelling for some time on the differences, it will do no harm now to mention some of the similarities. For this purpose, let us consider the two sentences "*M* is a red motorcar" and "*M* is a good motorcar." It will be noticed that "motorcar," unlike "strawberry," is a functional word, as defined in the preceding chapter. Reference to the *Shorter Oxford English Dictionary* shows that a motorcar is a carriage, and a carriage a means of conveyance. Thus, if a motorcar will not convey anything, we know from the definition of motorcar that it is not a good one. But when we know this, we know so little, compared with what is required in order to know the full criteria of a good motorcar, that I propose in what follows to ignore, for the sake of simplicity, this complicating factor. I shall treat "motorcar" as if it did not have to be defined functionally: that is to say, I shall assume that we could learn the meaning of "motorcar" (as in a sense we can) simply by being shown examples of motorcars. It is, of course, not always easy to say whether or not a word is a functional word; it depends, like all questions of meaning, on how the word is taken by a particular speaker.

The first similarity between "*M* is a red motorcar" and "*M* is a good motorcar" is that both can be, and often are, used for conveying information of a purely factual or descriptive character. If I say to someone, "*M* is a good motorcar," and he himself has not seen, and knows nothing of *M*, but does on the other hand know what sorts of motorcar we are accustomed to call "good" (knows what is the accepted standard of goodness in motorcars), he undoubtedly receives information from my remark about what sort of motorcar it is. He will complain that I have misled him, if he subsequently discovers that *M* will not go over 30 m.p.h., or uses as much oil as petrol, or is covered with rust, or has large holes in the roof. His reason for complaining will be the same as it would have been if I had said that the car was red and he subsequently discovered that it was black. I should have led him to expect the motorcar to be of a certain description when in fact it was of a quite different description.

The second similarity between the two sentences is this. Sometimes we use them, not for actually conveying information, but for putting our hearer into a position subsequently to use the word "good" or "red" for giving or getting information. Suppose, for example, that he is utterly unfamiliar with motorcars in the same sort of way as most of us are unfamiliar with horses nowadays, and knows no more about motorcars than is necessary in order to distinguish a motorcar from a hansom cab. In that case, my saying to him, "*M* is a good motorcar" will not give him any information about *M*, beyond the information that it is a motorcar. But if he is able then or subsequently to examine *M*, he will have learnt something. He will have learnt that some of the characteristics which *M* has are characteristics which make people—or at any rate me—call it a good motorcar. This may not be to learn very much. But suppose that I make judgments of this sort about a great many motorcars, calling some good and some not good, and he is able to examine all or most of the motorcars about which I am speaking; he will in the end learn quite a lot, always presuming that I observe a consistent standard in calling them good or not good. He will eventually, if he pays careful attention, get into the position in which he knows, after I have said that a motorcar is a good one, what sort of a motorcar he may expect it to be—for example fast, stable on the road, and so on.

Now if we were dealing not with "good," but with "red," we should call this process "explaining the meaning of the word"—and we might indeed, in a sense, say that what I have been doing is explaining what one means by "a good motorcar." This is a sense of "mean" about which, as we have seen, we must be on our guard. The processes, however, are very similar. I might explain the meaning of "red" by continually saying of various motorcars, "*M* is a red motorcar," "*N* is not a red motorcar," and so on. If he were attentive enough, he would soon get into a position in which he was able to use the word "red" for giving or getting information, at any rate about motorcars. And so, both with "good" and with "red," there is this process, which in the case of "red" we may call "explaining the meaning," but in the case of "good" may only call it so loosely and in a secondary sense; to be clear we must call it something like "explaining or conveying or setting forth the standard of goodness in motorcars."

The standard of goodness, like the meaning of "red," is normally something which is public and commonly accepted. When I explain to someone the meaning of "red motorcar," he expects, unless I am known to be very eccentric, that he will find other people using it in the same way. And similarly, at any rate with objects like motorcars where there is a commonly accepted standard, he will expect, having learnt from me what is the standard of goodness in motorcars, to be able, by using the expression "good motorcar," to give information to other people, and get it from them, without confusion.

A third respect in which "good motorcar" resembles "red

motorcar" is the following: both "good" and "red" can vary as regards the exactitude or vagueness of the information which they do or can convey. We normally use the expression "red motorcar" very loosely. Any motorcar that lies somewhere between the unmistakably purple and the unmistakably orange could without abuse of language be called a red motorcar. And similarly, the standard for calling motorcars good is commonly very loose. There are certain characteristics, such as inability to exceed 30 m.p.h., which to anyone but an eccentric would be sufficient conditions for refusing to call it a good motorcar; but there is no precise set of accepted criteria such that we can say, "If a motorcar satisfies these conditions, it is a good one; if not, not." And in both cases we could be precise if we wanted to. We could, for certain purposes, agree not to say that a motorcar was "really red" unless the redness of its paint reached a certain measurable degree of purity and saturation; and similarly, we might adopt a very exact standard of goodness in motorcars. We might refuse the name "good motorcar" to any car that would not go round a certain race-track without mishap in a certain limited time, that did not conform to certain other rigid specifications as regards accommodation, and so on. This sort of thing has not been done for the expression "good motorcar"; but, as Mr. Urmson has pointed out, it has been done by the Ministry of Agriculture for the expression "super apple."[2]

It is important to notice that the exactness or looseness of their criteria does absolutely nothing to distinguish words like "good" from words like "red." Words in both classes may be descriptively loose or exact, according to how rigidly the criteria have been laid down by custom or convention. It certainly is not true that value-words are distinguished from descriptive words in that the former are looser, descriptively, than the latter. There are loose and rigid examples of both sorts of word. Words like "red" can be extremely loose, without becoming to the least degree evaluative; and expressions like "good sewage effluent" can be the subject of very rigid criteria, without in the least ceasing to be evaluative.

It is important to notice also how easy it is, in view of these resemblances between "good" and "red," to think that there are no differences—to think that to set forth the standard of goodness in motorcars is to set forth the meaning, in all senses that there are of that word, of the expression "good motorcar"; to think that *"M* is a good motorcar" means neither more nor less than *"M* has certain characteristics of which good is the name."

---

[2] *Mind,* lix (1950), 152 (also in *Logic and Language,* ii, ed. Flew, 166).

It is worth noticing here that the functions of the word "good" which are concerned with information could be performed equally well if "good" had no commendatory function at all. This can be made clear by substituting another word, made up for the purpose, which is to be supposed to lack the commendatory force of "good." Let us use "doog" as this new word. "Doog," like "good," can be used for conveying information only if the criteria for its application are known; but this makes it, unlike "good," altogether meaningless until these criteria are made known. I make the criteria known by pointing out various motorcars, and saying, "M is a doog motorcar," "N is not a doog motorcar," and so on. We must imagine that, although "doog" has no commendatory force, the criteria for doogness in motorcars which I am employing are the same as those which, in the previous example, I employed for goodness in motorcars. And so, as in the previous example, the learner, if he is sufficiently attentive, becomes able to use the word "doog" for giving or getting information; when I say to him, "Z is a doog motorcar," he knows what characteristics to expect it to have; and if he wants to convey to someone else that a motorcar Y has those same characteristics, he can do so by saying, "Y is a doog motorcar."

Thus the word "doog" does (though only in connection with motor-cars) half the jobs that the word "good" does—namely, all those jobs that are concerned with the giving, or learning to give or get, information. It does not do those jobs which are concerned with commendation. Thus we might say that "doog" functions just like a descriptive word. First my learner learns to use it by my giving him examples of its application, and then he uses it by applying it to fresh examples. It would be quite natural to say that what I was doing was teaching my learner the *meaning* of "doog"; and this shows us again how natural it is to say that, when we are learning a similar lesson for the expression "good motorcar" (that is, learning the criteria of its application), we are learning its meaning. But with the word "good" it is misleading to say this; for the meaning of "good motorcar" (in another sense of "meaning") is something that might be known by someone who did not know the criteria of its application; he would know, if someone said that a motorcar was a good one, that he was commending it; and to know that would be to know the meaning of the expression. Further, as we saw earlier (6. 4) [not included here], someone might know about "good" all the things which my learner learnt about the word "doog" (namely, how to apply the word to the right objects, and use it for giving and getting information) and yet be said not to know its meaning; for he might not know that to call a motorcar good was to commend it.

It may be objected by some readers that to call the descriptive or informative job of "good" its *meaning* in any sense is illegitimate. Such objectors might hold that the meaning of "good" is adequately characterized by saying that it is used for commending, and that any information we get from its use is not a question of meaning at all. When I say, "*M* is a good motorcar," my meaning, on this view, is to commend *M;* if a hearer gets from my remark, together with his knowledge of the standard habitually used by me in assessing the merits of motorcars, information about what description of motorcar it is, this is not part of my meaning; all my hearer has done is to make an inductive inference from "Hare has usually in the past commended motorcars of a certain description" and "Hare has commended *M*" to "*M* is of the same description." I suspect that this objection is largely a verbal one, and I have no wish to take sides against it. On the one hand, we must insist that to know the criteria for applying the word "good" to motorcars is not to know—at any rate in the full or primary sense —the meaning of the expression "good motorcar"; to this extent the objection must be agreed with. On the other hand, the relation of the expression "good motorcar" to the criteria for its application is very like the relation of a descriptive expression to its defining characteristics, and this likeness finds an echo in our language when we ask "What do you mean, good?" and get the answer "I mean it'll do 80 and never break down." In view of this undoubted fact of usage, I deem it best to adopt the term "descriptive meaning." Moreover, it is natural to say that a sentence has descriptive meaning if the speaker intends it primarily to convey information; and when a newspaper says that *X* opened the batting on a good wicket, its intention is not primarily to commend the wicket, but to inform its readers what description of wicket it was.

It is time now to justify my calling the descriptive meaning of "good" secondary to the evaluative meaning. My reasons for doing so are two. First, the evaluative meaning is constant for every class of object for which the word is used. When we call a motorcar or a chronometer or a cricket-bat or a picture good, we are commending all of them. But because we are commending all of them for different reasons, the descriptive meaning is different in all cases. We have knowledge of the evaluative meaning of "good" from our earliest years; but we are constantly learning to use it in new descriptive meanings, as the classes of objects whose virtues we learn to distinguish grow more numerous. Sometimes we learn to use "good" in a new descriptive meaning through being taught it by an expert in a particular field—for example, a horseman might teach me how to recognize a good hunter. Sometimes, on the other hand, we make up a new descriptive meaning for ourselves. This happens when we start having a standard for a class of objects, certain members of which we have started needing to place in order of merit, but for which there has hitherto been no standard, as in the "cactus" example. I shall in the next chapter discuss why we commend things.

The second reason for calling the evaluative meaning primary is that we can use the evaluative force of the word in order to *change* the descriptive meaning for any class of objects. This is what the moral reformer often does in morals; but the same process occurs outside morals. It may happen that motor-cars will in the near future change considerably in design (for example, by our seeking economy at the expense of size). It may be that then we shall cease giving the name "a good motorcar" to a car that now would rightly and with the concurrence of all be allowed that name. How, linguistically speaking, would this have happened? At present, we are roughly agreed (though only roughly) on the necessary and sufficient criteria for calling a motorcar a good one. If what I have described takes place, we may begin to say, "No cars of the nineteen-fifties were really good; there weren't any good ones till 1960." Now here we cannot be using "good" with the same descriptive meaning as it is now generally used with; for some of the cars of 1950 do indubitably have those characteristics which entitle them to the name "good motorcar" in the 1950 descriptive sense of that word. What is happening is that the evaluative meaning of the word is being used in order to shift the descriptive meaning; we are doing what would be called, if "good" were a purely descriptive word, redefining it. But we cannot call it that, for the evaluative meaning remains constant; we are rather altering the standard. This is similar to the process called by Professor Stevenson "persuasive definition"; the process is not necessarily, however, highly colored with emotion.

.   .   .

Commending and Choosing

It is now time to inquire into the reasons for the logical features of "good" that we have been describing, and to ask why it is that it has this peculiar combination of evaluative and descriptive meaning. The reason will be found in the purposes for which it, like other value-words, is used in our discourse. The examination of these purposes will reveal the relevance of the matters discussed in the first part of this book to the study of evaluative language.

I have said that the primary function of the word "good" is to commend. We have, therefore, to inquire what commending is. When we commend or condemn anything, it is always in order, at least indirectly, to guide choices, our own or other people's, now or in the future. Suppose that I say, "The South Bank Exhibition is very good." In what context should I appropriately say this, and what would be my purpose in so doing? It would be natural for me to say it to someone who was wondering whether to go to London to see the Exhibition, or, if he was in London, whether to pay it a visit. It would, however, be too much to say that the reference to choices is always as direct as this. An American returning from London to New York, and speaking to some people who had no intention of going to London in the near future, might still make the same remark. In order, therefore, to show that critical value-judgments are all ultimately related to choices, and would not be made if they were not so related, we require to ask for what purpose we have standards.

It has been pointed out by Mr. Urmson that we do not speak generally of "good" wireworms. This is because we never have any occasion for choosing between wireworms, and therefore require no guidance in so doing. We therefore need to have no standards for wireworms. But it is easy to imagine circumstances in which this situation might alter. Suppose that wireworms came into use as a special kind of bait for fishermen. Then we might speak of having dug up a very good wireworm (one, for example, that was exceptionally fat and attractive to fish), just as now, no doubt, sea-fishermen might talk of having dug up a very good lug-worm. We only have standards for a class of objects, we only talk of the virtues of one specimen as against another, we only use value-words about them, when occasions are known to exist, or are conceivable, in which we, or someone else, would have to choose between specimens. We should not call pictures good or bad if no one ever had the choice of seeing them or not seeing them (or of studying them or not studying them in the way that art students study pictures, or of buying them or not buying them). Lest, by the way, I should seem to have introduced a certain vagueness by specifying so many alternative kinds of choices, it must be pointed out that the matter can, if desired, be made as precise as we require; for we can specify, when we have called a picture a good one, within what class we have called it good; for example, we can say, "I meant a good picture to study, but not to buy."

Some further examples may be given. We should not speak of good sunsets unless sometimes the decision had to be made whether to go to the window to look at the sunset; we should not speak of good billiard-cues unless sometimes we had to choose one billiard-cue in preference to another; we should not speak of good men unless we had the choice what sort of men to try to become. Leibniz, when he spoke of "the best of all possible worlds," had in mind a creator choosing between the possibilities. The choice that is envisaged need not ever occur, nor even be expected ever to occur; it is enough for it to be envisaged as occurring, in order that we should be able to make a value-judgment with reference to it. It must be admitted, however, that the most useful value-judgments are those which have reference to choices that we might very likely have to make.

It should be pointed out that even judgments about past choices do not refer merely to the past. As we shall see, all value-judgments are covertly universal in character, which is the same as to say that they refer to, and express acceptance of, a standard which has an application to other similar instances. If I censure someone for having done something, I envisage the possibility of him, or someone else, or myself, having to make a similar choice again; otherwise there would be no point in censuring him. Thus, if I say to a man whom I am teaching to drive, "You did that maneuvre badly," this is a very typical piece of driving-instruction; and driving-instruction consists in teaching a man to drive not in the past but in the future; to this end we censure or commend past pieces of driving, in order to impart to him the standard which is to guide him in his subsequent conduct.

When we commend an object, our judgment is not solely about that particular object, but is inescapably about objects like it. Thus, if I say that a certain motorcar is a good one, I am not merely saying something about that particular motorcar. To say something about that particular car, merely, would not be to commend. To commend, as we have seen, is to guide choices. Now for guiding a particular choice, we have a linguistic instrument which is not that of commendation, namely, the singular imperative. If I wish merely to tell someone to choose a particular car, with no thought of the kind of car to which it belongs, I can say, "Take that one." If instead of this I say, "That is a good one," I am saying something more. I am implying that if any motorcar were just like that one, it would be a good one too; whereas by saying, "Take that one," I do not imply that, if my hearer sees another car just like that one, he is to take it too. But further, the implication of the judgment "That is a good motorcar" does not extend merely to motorcars *exactly* like that one. If this were so, the implication would be for practical purposes useless; for nothing is exactly like anything else. It extends to every motorcar that is like that one in the *relevant* particulars; and the relevant particulars are its virtues—those of its characteristics for which I was commending it, or which I was calling good about it. Whenever we commend, we have in mind something about the object commended which is the reason for our commendation. It therefore always makes sense, after someone has said, "That is a good motorcar," to ask, "What is good about it?" or "Why do you call it good?" or "What features of it are you commending?" It may not always be easy to answer this question precisely, but it is always a legitimate question. If we did not understand why it was always a legitimate question, we should not understand the way in which the word "good" functions.

We may illustrate this point by comparing two dialogues:
1. *X*. Jones' motorcar is a good one.
   Y. What makes you call it good?
   X. Oh, just that it's good.
   Y. But there must be some *reason* for your calling it good, I mean some property that it has in virtue of which you call it good.
   X. No; the property in virtue of which I call it good is just its goodness and nothing else.
   Y. But do you mean that its shape, speed, weight, maneuverability, and so on, are irrelevant to whether you call it good or not?
   X. Yes, quite irrelevant; the only relevant property is that of goodness, just as, if I called it yellow, the only relevant property would be that of yellowness.
2. The same dialogue, only with "yellow" substituted for "good" and "yellowness" for "goodness" throughout, and the last clause ("just as . . . yellowness") omitted.

The reason why *X*'s position in the first dialogue is eccentric is that since, as we have already remarked, "good" is a "supervenient" or "consequential" epithet, one may always legitimately be asked when one has called something a good something, "What is good about it?" Now to answer this question is to give the properties in virtue of which we call it good. Thus, if I have said, "That is a good motorcar" and someone asks, "Why? What is good about it?" and I reply, "Its high speed combined with its stability on the road," I indicate that I call it good in virtue of its having these properties or virtues. Now to do this is *eo ipso* to say something about other motorcars which have these properties. If any motorcar whatever had these properties, I should have, if I were not to be inconsistent, to agree that it was, *pro tanto*, a good motorcar, though of course it might, although it had these properties in its favor, have other countervailing disadvantages, and so be, taken all in all, not a good motorcar.

This last difficulty can always be got over by specifying in detail why I called the first motorcar a good one. Suppose that a second motorcar were like the first one in speed and stability, but gave its passengers no protection from the rain, and proved difficult to get into and out of. I should not then call it a good motorcar, although it had those characteristics which led me to call the first one good. This shows that I should not have called the first one good either, if it too had had the bad characteristics of the second one; and so in specifying what was good about the first one, I ought to have added, ". . . and the protection it gives to the passengers and the ease with which one can get into and out of it." This process could be repeated indefinitely until I had given a complete list of the characteristics of the first motorcar which were required to make me allow it to be a good one. This, in itself, would not be saying all that there was to be said about my standards for judging motorcars—for there might be other motorcars which, although falling short to a certain extent in these characteristics, had other countervailing good characteristics, for example, soft upholstery, large accommodation, or small consumption of petrol. But it would be at any rate some help to my hearer in building up an idea of my standards in motorcars; and in this lies the importance of such questions and answers, and the importance of recognizing their relevance, whenever a value-judgment has been made. For one of the purposes of making such judgments is to make known the standard.

When I commend a motorcar, I am guiding the choices of my hearer not merely in relation to that particular motorcar but in relation to motorcars in general. What I have said to him will be of assistance to him whenever in the future he has to choose a motorcar or advise anyone else on the choice of a motorcar or even design a motorcar (choose what sort of motorcar to have made) or write a general treatise on the design of motorcars (which involves choosing what sort of motorcars to advise other people to have made). The method whereby I give him this assistance is by making known to him a standard for judging motorcars.

This process has, as we have noticed, certain features in common with the process of defining (making known the meaning or application of) a descriptive word, though there are important differences. We have now to notice a further resemblance between showing the usage of a word and showing how to choose between motorcars. In neither case can the instruction be done successfully unless the instructor is consistent in his teaching. If I use "red" for objects of a wide variety of colors, my hearer will never learn from me a consistent usage of the word. Similarly, if I commend motorcars with widely different or even contrary characteristics, what I say to him will not be of assistance to him in choosing motorcars subsequently, because I am not teaching him any consistent standard—or any standard at all, for a standard is by definition consistent. He will say, "I don't see by what standards you are judging these motorcars; please explain to me why you call them all good, although they are so different." Of course, I might be able to give a satisfactory explanation. I might say, "There are different sorts of motorcars, each good in its way; there are sports cars, whose prime requisites are speed and maneuverability; and family cars, which ought rather to be capacious and economical; and taxis, and so on. So when I say a car is good which is fast and maneuverable, although it is neither capacious nor economical, you must understand that I am commending it as a sports car, not as a family car." But suppose that I did not recognize the relevance of his question; suppose that I was just doling out the predicate "good" entirely haphazard, as the whim took me. It is clear that in this case I should teach him no standard at all.

We thus have to distinguish two questions that can always be asked in elucidation of a judgment containing the word "good." Suppose that someone says, "That is a good one." We can then always ask (1) "Good what—sports car or family car or taxi or example to quote in a logic book?" Or we can ask (2) "What makes you call it good?" To ask the first question is to ask for the class within which evaluative comparisons are being made. Let us call it the class of comparison. To ask the second question is to ask for the virtues or "good-making characteristics." These two questions are, however, not independent; for what distinguishes the class of comparison "sports car" from the class "family car" is the set of virtues which are to be looked for in the respective classes. This is so in all cases where the class of comparison is defined by means of a functional word—for obviously "sports car," "family car," and "taxi" are functional to a very much higher degree than plain "motorcar." Sometimes, however, a class of comparison may be further specified without making it more functional; for example, in explaining the phrase "good wine," we might say, "I mean good wine for this district, not good wine compared with all the wines that there are."

Now since it is the purpose of the word "good" and other value-words to be used for teaching standards, their logic is in accord with this purpose. We are therefore in a position at last to explain the feature of the word "good" which I pointed out at the beginning of this investigation. The reason why I cannot apply the word "good" to one picture, if I refuse to apply it to another picture which I agree to be in all other respects exactly similar, is that by doing this I should be defeating the purpose for which the word is designed. I should be commending one object, and so purporting to teach my hearers one standard, while in the same breath refusing to commend a similar object, and so undoing the lesson just imparted. By seeking to impart two inconsistent standards, I should be imparting no standard at all. The effect of such an utterance is similar to that of a contradiction; for in a contradiction, I say two inconsistent things, and so the effect is that the hearer does not know what I am trying to say.

What I have said so far may also be put into another terminology, that of principles, which we were using in Part I [not included here]. To teach a person—or to decide on for oneself—a standard for judging the merits of objects of a certain class is to teach or decide on principles for choosing between objects of that class. To know the principles for choosing motorcars is to be able to judge between motorcars or to tell a good one from a bad one. If I say, "That isn't a good motorcar," and am asked what virtue it is, the lack of which makes me say this, and reply, "It isn't stable on the road," then I am appealing to a principle.

10

Political Philosophy

Some of the problems of ethics lead to questions about political philosophy. Let us suppose for the sake of argument that so far as possible everyone ought to be allowed to do exactly as he pleases. But what is "so far as possible?" The main objection is mutual frustration: doing the thing that I please deprives you of the opportunity of doing the thing you please, and vice versa. But anarchists have claimed that this problem can be worked out without the institutionalized use of force to restrain one or both of us. Classical communist doctrine aims at anarchy as an eventual goal of socialism, in "the withering away of the state." Virtually all other political persuasions say that some sort of central regulative body is necessary to keep people from coming together in conflict, some institution which will look out for the interests of all. How are those interests determined? How much shall it look out for those interests, and in what ways? Such governments, from family or tribe to the modern superstate, have existed for thousands of years, but big government is modern. The Greek city-state was one city, with its surrounding agricultural land used for economic support and as a buffer against invasion. Many of its inhabitants were not citizens, thus did not have a voice in government. The idea that "the pursuit of happiness" is a *right of all* is modern, and it compounds the problems of an exploding population in a complex, delicately-balanced economy and a society with huge destructive capabilities furnished by weapons technology.

The notion that governments derive their powers from the spoken or silent consent of the governed is a tautology in that no government can have any power if enough people are sufficiently opposed to it. There is bound to be something wrong in any nation which has more than a tiny fraction of its population unable to consent to its laws or their administration.

Do I consent when I am sent to war or put in prison for any cause? This is surely a question which goes to the root of the nature of government and society. With recent political movements stemming from the tactics of Gandhi and the theories of Thoreau, Sidney Hook, a contemporary American philosopher who has pilgrimaged from radicalism to conservatism, explores civil disobedience and protest. But the theoretical questions go back further: What is the justification for the use of the enormous power that is at the disposal of the state? Thomas Hobbes paradoxically finds it in the universal desire of every man for survival and ego aggrandizement. John Locke conceives of man as basically moral and cooperative, a social animal, but both thinkers recognize, willingly or grudgingly, the necessity for "the consent of the governed."

Hobbes and Locke were looking at the logical bases and to some extent the historical origins of government and political and social institutions. Friedrich Engels, the wealthy patron and alter ego of Karl Marx, and B. F. Skinner, the Harvard behaviorist psychologist, look not only at the bases and origins of twentieth-century life but at some more ideal kind of life. Communists have always been leary of "Utopia" but Skinner does not shrink from it. Indeed, he thinks it a necessary human step.

Civil Society Based on Self-Interest

Thomas Hobbes

Thomas Hobbes (1588–1679) was an English materialist philosopher and political theorist whose writings provoked a wave of protest in religious and philosophical circles.

Of the Natural Condition of Mankind

Nature hath made men so equal, in the faculties of the body and the mind, that though there be found one man sometimes manifestly stronger in body, or of quicker mind than another; yet when all is reckoned together, the difference between man, and man, is not so considerable, as that one man can thereupon claim to himself any benefit, to which another may not pretend, as well as he. For as to the strength of body, the weakest has strength enough to kill the strongest, either by secret machination, or by confederacy with others, that are in the same danger with himself.

And as to the faculties of the mind, setting aside the arts grounded upon words, and especially that skill of proceeding upon general, and infallible rules, called science; which very few have, and but in few things; as being not a native faculty, born with us; nor attained, as prudence, while we look after somewhat else, I find yet a greater equality amongst men, than that of strength.

From Thomas Hobbes, *Leviathan*, Chapters 13–15, 17–18.

For prudence, is but experience; which equal time, equally bestows on all men, in those things they equally apply themselves unto. That which may perhaps make such equality incredible, is but a vain conceit of one's wisdom, which almost all men think they have in a greater degree, than the vulgar; that is, than all men but themselves, and a few others, whom by fame, or for concurring with themselves, they approve. For such is the nature of man, that howsoever they may acknowledge many others to be more witty, or more eloquent, or more learned, yet they will hardly believe there be many so wise as themselves; for they see their own wit at hand, and other men's at a distance. But this proveth rather that men are in that point equal, than unequal. For there is not ordinarily a greater sign of the equal distribution of any thing, than that every man is contented with his share.

From this equality of ability, ariseth equality of hope in the attaining of our ends. And therefore if any two men desire the same thing, which nevertheless they cannot both enjoy, they become enemies; and in the way to their end, which is principally their own conservation, and sometimes their delectation only, endeavor to destroy, or subdue one another. And from hence it comes to pass, that where an invader hath no more to fear, than another man's single power; if one plant, sow, build, or possess a convenient seat, others may probably be expected to come prepared with forces united, to dispossess, and deprive him, not only of the fruit of his labor, but also of his life, or liberty. And the invader again is in the like danger of another.

And from this diffidence of one another, there is no way for any man to secure himself, so reasonable, as anticipation; that is, by force, or wiles, to master the persons of all men he can, so long, till he see no other power great enough to endanger him: and this is no more than his own conservation requireth, and is generally allowed. Also because there be some, that taking pleasure in contemplating their own power in the acts of conquest, which they pursue farther than their security requires; if others, that otherwise would be glad to be at ease within modest bounds, should not by invasion increase their power, they would not be able, long time, by standing only on their defence, to subsist. And by consequence, such augmentation of dominion over men being necessary to a man's conservation, it ought to be allowed him.

Again, men have no pleasure, but on the contrary a great deal of grief, in keeping company, where there is no power able to over-awe them all. For every man looketh that his companion should value him, at the same rate he sets upon himself: and upon all signs of contempt, or undervaluing, naturally endeavors, as far as he dares (which amongst them that have no common power to keep them in quiet, is far enough to make them destroy each other), to extort a greater value from his contemners, by damage; and from others, by the example.

So that in the nature of man, we find three principal causes of quarrel. First, competition; secondly, diffidence; thirdly, glory.

The first maketh men invade for gain; the second, for safety; and the third, for reputation. The first use violence, to make themselves masters of other men's persons, wives, children, and cattle; the second, to defend them; the third, for trifles, as a word, a smile, a different opinion, and any other sign of undervalue, either direct in their persons, or by reflection in their kindred, their friends, their nation, their profession, or their name.

Hereby it is manifest, that during the time men live without a common power to keep them all in awe, they are in that condition which is called war; and such a war, as is of every man, against every man. For WAR, consisteth not in battle only, or the act of fighting; but in a tract of time, wherein the will to contend by battle is sufficiently known: and therefore the notion of *Time*, is to be considered in the nature of war; as it is in the nature of weather. For as the nature of foul weather, lieth not in a shower or two of rain, but in an inclination thereto of many days together: so that nature of war, consisteth not in actual fighting, but in the known disposition thereto, during all the time, there is no assurance to the contrary. All other time is PEACE.

Whatsoever therefore is consequent to a time of war, where every man is enemy to every man; the same is consequent to the time, wherein men live without other security, than what their own strength, and their own invention shall furnish them withal. In such condition, there is no place for industry; because the fruit thereof is uncertain: and consequently no culture of the earth; no navigation, nor use of the commodities that may be imported by sea; no commodious building; no instruments of moving, and removing, such things as require much force; no knowledge of the face of the earth; no account of time; no arts; no letters; no society; and which is worst of all, continual fear, and danger of violent death; and the life of man, solitary, poor, nasty, brutish, and short.

It may seem strange to some man, that has not well weighed these things, that nature should thus dissociate, and render men apt to invade, and destroy one another: and he may therefore, not trusting to this inference, made from the passions, desire perhaps to have the same confirmed by experience. Let him therefore consider with himself, when taking a journey, he arms himself, and seeks to go well accompanied; when going to sleep, he locks his doors; when even in his house he locks his chests; and this when he knows there be laws, and public officers, armed, to revenge all injuries shall be done him; what opinion he has of his fellow-subjects, when he rides armed; of his fellow-citizens, when he locks his doors; and of his children, and servants, when he locks his chests. Does he not there as much accuse mankind by his actions, as I do by my words? But neither of us accuse man's nature in it. The desires, and other passions of man, are in themselves no sin. No more are the actions, that proceed from those passions, till they know a law that forbids them: which till laws be made they cannot know: nor can any law be made, till they have agreed upon the person that shall make it.

It may peradventure be thought, there was never such a time, nor condition of war as this: and I believe it was never generally so, over all the world: but there are many places where they live so now. For the savage people in many places of America, except the government of small families, the concord whereof dependeth on natural lust, have no government at all; and live at this day in that brutish manner, as I have said before. Howsoever, it may be perceived what manner of life there would be, where there were no common power to fear, by the manner of life, which men that have formerly lived under a peaceful government, use to degenerate into, in a civil war.

But though there had never been any time, wherein particular men were in a condition of war one against another; yet in all times, kings, and persons of sovereign authority, because of their independency, are in continual jealousies, and in the state and posture of gladiators; having their weapons pointing, and their eyes fixed on one another; that is, their forts, garrisons, and guns upon the frontiers of their kingdoms; and continual spies upon their neighbors; which is a posture of war. But because they uphold thereby, the industry of their subjects; there does not follow from it, that misery, which accompanies the liberty of particular men.

To this war of every man, against every man, this also is consequent; that nothing can be unjust. The notions of right and wrong, justice and injustice have there no place. Where there is no common power, there is no law: where no law, no injustice. Force and fraud are in war the two cardinal virtues. Justice and injustice are none of the faculties neither of the body, nor of the mind. If they were, they might be in a man that were alone in the world, as well as his senses, and passions. They are qualities, that relate to men in society, not in solitude. It is consequent also to the same condition, that there be no propriety, no dominion, no *mine* and *thine* distinct; but only that to be every man's, that he can get; and for so long, as he can keep it. And thus much for the ill condition which man by mere nature is actually placed in; though with a possibility to come out of it, consisting partly in the passions, partly in his reason.

The passions that incline men to peace, are fear of death; desire of such things as are necessary to commodious living; and a hope by their industry to obtain them. And reason suggesteth convenient articles of peace, upon which men may be drawn to agreement. These articles, are they, which otherwise are called the Laws of Nature: whereof I shall speak more particularly in the two following chapters.

Of the First and Second
Natural Laws, and of Contracts

The RIGHT OF NATURE, which writers commonly call *jus naturale*, is the liberty each man hath, to use his own power, as he will himself, for the preservation of his own nature; that is to say, of his own life; and consequently, of doing any thing, which in his own judgment, and reason, he shall conceive to be the aptest means thereunto.

By LIBERTY, is understood, according to the proper signification of the word, the absence of external impediments: which impediments, may oft take away part of a man's power to do what he would; but cannot hinder him from using the power left him, according as his judgment, and reason shall dictate to him.

A LAW OF NATURE, *lex naturalis*, is a precept or general rule, found out by reason, by which a man is forbidden to do that, which is destructive of his life, or taketh away the means of preserving the same; and to omit that, by which he thinketh it may be best preserved. For though they that speak of this subject, use to confound *jus* and *lex*, *right* and *law*: yet they ought to be distinguished; because RIGHT, consisteth in liberty to do, or to forbear; whereas LAW, determineth, and bindeth to one of them: so that law, and right, differ as much, as obligation, and liberty; which in one and the same matter are inconsistent.

And because the conditions of man, as hath been declared in the precedent chapter, is a condition of war of everyone against every one: in which case every one is governed by his own reason;

and there is nothing he can make use of, that may not be a help unto him, in preserving his life against his enemies: it followeth, that in such a condition, every man has a right to every thing; even to one another's body. And therefore, as long as this natural right of every man to every thing endureth, there can be no security to any man, how strong or wise soever he be, of living out the time, which nature ordinarily alloweth men to live. And consequently it is a precept, or general rule of reason, *that every man, ought to endeavor peace, as far as he has hope of obtaining it; and when he cannot obtain it, that he may seek, and use, all helps, and advantages of war.* The first branch of which rule, containeth the first and fundamental law of nature; which is, *to seek peace and follow it.* The second, the sum of the right of nature; which is, *by all means we can, to defend ourselves.*

From this fundamental law of nature, by which men are commanded to endeavor peace, is derived this second law; *that a man be willing, when others are so too, as far-forth, as for peace, and defence of himself he shall think it necessary, to lay down this right to all things; and be contented with so much liberty against other men, as he would allow other men against himself.* For as long as every man holdeth this right of doing any thing he liketh, so long are all men in the condition of war. But if other men will not lay down their right, as well as he, then there is no reason for any one, to divest himself of his: for that were to expose himself to prey, which no man is bound to, rather than to dispose himself to peace. This is that law of the Gospel; *whatsoever you require that others should do to you, that do ye to them. . . .*

To *lay down* a man's *right* to any thing, is to *divest* himself of the *liberty,* of hindering another of the benefit of his own right to the same. For he that renounceth, or passeth away his right, giveth not to any other man a right which he had not before; because there is nothing to which every man had not right by nature: but only standeth out of his way, that he may enjoy his own original right, without hindrance from him; not without hindrance from another. So that the effect which redoundeth to one man, by another man's defect of right, is but so much diminution of impediments to the use of his own right original.

Right is laid aside, either by simply renouncing it; or by transferring it to another. By *simply* RENOUNCING; when he cares not to whom the benefit thereof redoundeth. By TRANSFERRING; when he intendeth the benefit thereof to some certain person, or persons. And when a man hath in either manner abandoned, or granted away his right, then is he said to be OBLIGED, or BOUND, not to hinder those, to whom such right is granted, or abandoned, from the benefit of it: and that he *ought*, and it is his DUTY, not to make void that voluntary act of his own: and that such hindrance is INJUSTICE, and INJURY, as being *sine jure;* the right being before renounced, or transferred. So that *injury,* or *injustice,* in the controversies of the world, is somewhat like to that, which in the disputations of scholars is called *absurdity.* For as it is there called an absurdity, to contradict what one maintained in the beginning: so in the world, it is called injustice, and injury, voluntarily to undo that, which from the beginning he had voluntarily done. The way by which a man either simply renounceth, or transferreth his right, is a declaration, or signification, by some voluntary and sufficient sign, or signs, that he doth so renounce, or transfer; or hath so renounced, or transferred the same, to him that accepteth it. And these signs are either words only, or actions only; or, as it happeneth most often both words, and actions. And the same are the BONDS, by which men are bound, and obliged: bonds, that have their strength, not from their own nature, for nothing is more easily broken than a man's word, but from fear of some evil consequence upon the rupture.

Whensoever a man transferreth his right, or renounceth it; it is either in consideration of some right reciprocally transferred to himself; or for some other good he hopeth for thereby. For it is a voluntary act: and of the voluntary acts of every man, the object is some *good to himself.* And therefore there be some rights, which no man can be understood by any words, or other signs, to have abandoned, or transferred. As first a man cannot lay down the right of resisting them, that assault him by force, to take away his life; because he cannot be understood to aim thereby, at any good to himself. The same may be said of wounds, and chains, and imprisonment; both because there is no benefit consequent to such patience; as there is to the patience of suffering another to be wounded, or imprisoned: as also because a man cannot tell, when he seeth men proceed against him by violence, whether they intend his death or not. And lastly the motive, and end for which this renouncing, and transferring of right is introduced, is nothing else but the security of a man's person, in his life, and in the means of so preserving life, as not to be weary of it. And therefore if a man by words, or other signs, seems to despoil himself of the end, for which those signs were intended, he is not to be understood as if he meant it, or that it was his will; but that he was ignorant of how such words and actions were to be interpreted.

The mutual transferring of right, is that which men call CONTRACT. . . .

Again, one of the contractors, may deliver the thing contracted for on his part, and leave the other to perform his part at some determinate time after, and in the mean time be trusted; and then the contract on his part, is called PACT, or COVENANT: or both parts may contract now, to perform hereafter: in which cases, he that is to perform in time to come, being trusted, his performance is called *keeping of promise,* or faith; and the failing of performance, if it be voluntary, *violation of faith.*

When the transferring of right, is not mutual; but one of the parties transferreth, in hope to gain thereby friendship, or service from another, or from his friends; or in hope to gain the reputation of charity, or magnanimity; or to deliver his mind from the pain of compassion; or in hope of reward in heaven; this is not contract, but GIFT, FREE GIFT, GRACE: which words signify one and the same thing. . . .

If a covenant be made, wherein neither of the parties perform presently, but trust one another; in the condition of mere nature, which is a condition of war of every man against every man, upon any reasonable suspicion, it is void: but if there be a common power set over them both, with right and force sufficient to compel performance, it is not void. For he that performeth first, has no assurance the other will perform after; because the bonds of words are too weak to bridle men's ambition, avarice, anger, and other passions without the fear of some coercive power; which in the condition of mere nature where all men are equal, and judges of the justness of their own fears, cannot possibly be supposed. And therefore he which performeth first, does but betray himself to his enemy; contrary to the right, he can never abandon, of defending his life, and means of living.

But in a civil estate, where there is a power set up to constrain those that would otewise violate their faith, that fear is no more reasonable; and for that cause, he which by the covenant is to perform first, is obliged so to do. . . .

Of Other Laws of Nature

From that law of nature by which we are obliged to transfer to another such rights, as being retained, hinder the peace of mankind, there followeth a third, which is this, *that men perform their covenants made:* without which, covenants are in vain, and but empty words; and the right of all men to all things remaining, we are still in the condition of war.

And in this law of nature consisteth the fountain and original of JUSTICE. For where no covenant hath proceded, there hath no right been transferred, and every man has right to every thing; and consequently, no action can be unjust. But when a covenant is made, then to break it is *unjust:* and the definition of INJUSTICE is no other than the *not performance of covenant.* And whatsoever is not unjust is *just.*

But because covenants of mutual trust, where there is a fear of not performance on either part, as hath been said in the former chapter [in this text, pp. 413–414], are invalid; though the original of justice be the making of covenants; yet injustice actually there can be none, till the cause of such fear be taken away; which, while men are in the natural condition of war, cannot be done. Therefore before the names of just and unjust can have place, there must be some coercive power, to compel men equally to the performance of their covenants, by the terror of some punishment greater than the benefit they expect by the breach of their covenant; and to make good that propriety, which by mutual contract men acquire, in recompense of the universal right they abandon: and such power there is none before the erection of a commonwealth. And this is also to be gathered out of the ordinary definition of justice in the Schools: for they say, that *justice is the constant will of giving to every man his own.* And therefore where there is no *own,* that is, no propriety, there is no injustice; and where there is no coercive power erected, that is, where there is no commonwealth, there is no propriety; all men having right to all things: therefore where there is no commonwealth, there nothing is unjust. So that the nature of justice consisteth in keeping of valid covenants: but the validity of covenants begins not but with the constitution of a civil power, sufficient to compel men to keep them: and then it is also that propriety begins. . . .

Of the Causes, Generation, and Definition of a Commonwealth

The final cause, end, or design of men, who naturally love liberty, and dominion over others, in the introduction of that restraint upon themselves, in which we see them live in commonwealths, is the foresight of their own preservation, and of a more contented life thereby; that is to say, of getting themselves out from that miserable condition of war, which is necessarily consequent, as hath been shown previously, to the natural passions of men, when there is no visible power to keep them in awe, and tie them by fear of punishment to the performance of their covenants, and observation of those laws of nature set down in the fourteenth and fifteenth chapter [pp. 411–415 in this text].

For the laws of nature, as *justice, equity, modesty, mercy* and, in sum, *doing to others, as we would be done to,* of themselves, without the terror of some power, to cause them to be observed, are contrary to our natural passions, that carry us to partiality, pride, revenge, and the like. And covenants, without the sword, are but words, and of no strength to secure a man at all. Therefore notwithstanding the laws of nature, which every man hath then kept, when he has the will to keep them, when he can do it safely, if there be no power erected, or not great enough for our security; every man will, and may lawfully rely on his own strength and art, for caution against all other men. And in all places, where men have lived by small families, to rob and spoil one another, has been a trade, and so far from being reputed against the law of nature, that the greater spoils they gained, the greater was their honor; and men observed no other laws therein, but the laws of honor; that is, to abstain from cruelty, leaving to men their lives, and instruments of husbandry. And as small families did then; so now do cities and kingdoms, which are but greater families, for their own security, enlarge their dominions, upon all pretences of danger, and fear of invasion, or assistance that may be given to invaders, and endeavor as much as they can, to subdue or weaken their neighbors, by open force, and secret arts, for want of other caution, justly; and are remembered for it in after ages with honor.

Nor is it the joining together of a small number of men, that gives them this security; because in small numbers, small additions on the one side or the other, make the advantage of strength so great, as is sufficient to carry the victory; and therefore gives encouragement to an invasion. The multitude sufficient to confide in for our security, is not determined by any certain number, but by comparison with the enemy we fear; and is then sufficient, when the odds of the enemy is not of so visible and conspicuous moment, to determine the event of war, as to move him to attempt.

And be there never so great a multitude; yet if their actions be directed according to their particular judgments, and particular appetites, they can expect thereby no defence, nor protection, neither against a common enemy, nor against the injuries of one another. For being distracted in opinions concerning the best use and application of their strength, they do not help but hinder one another; and reduce their strength by mutual opposition to nothing: whereby they are easily, not only subdued by a very few that agree together; but also when there is no common enemy, they make war upon each other, for their particular interests. For if we could suppose a great multitude of men to consent in the observation of justice, and other laws of nature, without a common power to keep them all in awe; we might as well suppose all mankind to do the same; and then there neither would be, nor need to be any civil government, or commonwealth at all; because there would be peace without subjection.

Nor is it enough for the security which men desire should last all the time of their life, that they be governed, and directed by one judgment, for a limited time; as in one battle, or one war. For though they obtain a victory by their unanimous endeavor against a foreign enemy; yet afterwards, when either they have no common enemy, or he that by one part is held for an enemy, is by another part held for a friend, they must needs by the difference of their interests dissolve, and fall again into a war amongst themselves.

It is true, that certain living creatures, as bees, and ants, live socially one with another, which are therefore by Aristotle numbered amongst political creatures; and yet have no other direction, than their particular judgments and appetites; nor speech, whereby one of them can signify to another, what he thinks expedient for the common benefit: and therefore some man may perhaps desire to know, why mankind cannot do the same. To which I answer,

First, that men are continually in competition for honor and dignity, which these creatures are not; and consequently amongst men there ariseth on that ground envy and hatred, and finally war; but amongst these not so.

Secondly, that amongst these creatures, the common good differeth not from the private; and being by nature inclined to their private, they procure thereby the common benefit. But man, whose joy consisteth in comparing himself with other men, can relish nothing but what is eminent.

Thirdly, that these creatures, having not, as man, the use of reason, do not see, nor think they see any fault in the administration of their common business; whereas amongst men, there are very many, that think themselves wiser, and abler to govern the public, better than the rest; and these strive to reform and innovate, one this way, another that way; and thereby bring it into distraction and civil war.

Fourthly, that these creatures, though they have some use of voice, in making known to one another their desires, and other affections; yet they want that art of words, by which some men can represent to others, that which is good, in the likeness of evil; and evil, in the likeness of good; and augment, or diminish the apparent greatness of good and evil; discontenting men, and troubling their peace at their pleasure.

Fifthly, irrational creatures cannot distinguish between *injury* and *damage;* and therefore as long as they be at ease, they are not offended with their fellows: whereas man is then most troublesome, when he is most at ease: for then it is that he loves to show his wisdom, and control the actions of them that govern the commonwealth.

Lastly, the agreement of these creatures is natural; that of men, is by covenant only, which is artificial: and therefore it is no wonder if there be somewhat else required, besides covenant, to make their agreement constant and lasting; which is a common power, to keep them in awe, and to direct their actions to the common benefit.

The only way to erect such a common power, as may be able to defend them from the invasion of foreigners, and the injuries of one another, and thereby to secure them in such sort, as that by their own industry, and by the fruits of the earth, they may nourish themselves and live contentedly; is, to confer all their power and strength upon one man, or upon one assembly of men, that may reduce all their wills, by plurality of voices, unto one will: which is as much as to say, to appoint one man, or assembly of men, to bear their person; and every one to own, and acknowledge himself to be author of whatsoever he that so beareth their person, shall act, or cause to be acted, in those things which concern the common peace and safety; and therein to submit their wills, every one to his will, and their judgments, to his judgment. This is more than consent, or concord; it is a real unity of them all, in one and the same person, made by covenant of every man with every man, in such manner, as if every man should say to every man, *I authorize and give up my right of governing myself, to this man, or to this assembly of men, on this condition, that thou give up thy right to him, and authorize all his actions in like manner.* This done, the multitude so united in one person is called a COMMONWEALTH, in Latin *civitas.* This is the generation of that great LEVIATHAN, or rather, to speak more reverently, of that *mortal god,* to which we owe under the *immortal God,* our peace and defence.

For by this authority, given him by every particular man in the commonwealth, he hath the use of so much power and strength conferred on him, that by terror thereof, he is enabled to perform the wills of them all, to peace at home, and mutual aid against their enemies abroad. And in him consisteth the essence of the commonwealth; which, to define it, is *one person, of whose acts a great multitude, by mutual covenants one with another, have made themselves every one the author, to the end he may use the strength and means of them all, as he shall think expedient, for their peace and common defence.*

And he that carrieth this person, is called SOVEREIGN, and said to have *sovereign power;* and everyone besides, his SUBJECT.

The attaining to this sovereign power, is by two ways. One, by natural force; as when a man maketh his children, to submit themselves, and their children to his government, as being able to destroy them if they refuse; or by war subdueth his enemies to his will, giving them their lives on that condition. The other, is when men agree amongst themselves, to submit to some man, or assembly of men, voluntarily, on confidence to be protected by him against all others. This latter, may be called a political commonwealth, or commonwealth by *institution;* and the former, a commonwealth by *acquisition.* And first, I shall speak of a commonwealth by institution.

Of the Rights
of Sovereigns by Institution

A *commonwealth* is said to be *instituted,* when a *multitude* of men do agree, and *covenant, every one, with every one,* that to whatsoever *man,* or *assembly of men,* shall be given by the major part, the *right* to *present* the person of them all, that is to say, to be their representative; every one, as well he that *voted* for it, as he that *voted against it,* shall *authorize* all the actions and judgments, of that man, or assembly of men, in the same manner, as if they were his own, to the end, to live peaceably amongst themselves, and be protected against other men.

From this institution of a commonweath are derived all the *rights,* and *faculties* of him, or them, on whom sovereign power is conferred by the consent of the people assembled.

First, because they covenant, it is to be understood, they are not obliged by former covenant to anything repugnant hereunto. And consequently they that have already instituted a commonwealth, being thereby bound by covenant, to own the actions, and judgments of one, cannot lawfully make a new covenant, amongst themselves, to be obedient to any other, in any thing whatsoever, without his permission. And therefore, they that are subject to a monarch, cannot without his leave cast off monarchy, and return to the confusion of a disunited multitude; nor transfer their person from him that beareth it to another man, or other assembly of men: for they are bound, every man to every man, to own, and be reputed author of all, that he that already is their sovereign, shall do, and judge fit to be done: so that any one man dissenting, all the rest should break their covenant made to that man, which is injustice: and they have also every man given the sovereignty to him that beareth their person; and therefore if they depose him, they take from him that which is his own, and so again it is injustice. Besides, if he that attempteth to depose his sovereign, be killed, or punished by him for such attempt, he is author of his own punishment, as being by the institution, author of all his sovereign shall do: and because it is injustice for a man to do anything, for which he may be punished by his own authority, he is also upon that title, unjust. And whereas some men have pretended for their disobedience to their sovereign, a new covenant, made, not with men, but with God; this also is unjust: for there is no covenant with God, but by mediation of somebody that representeth God's person; which none doth but God's lieutenant, who hath the sovereignty under God. But this pretence of covenant with God, is so evident a lie, even in the pretenders' own consciences, that it is not only an act of an unjust, but also of a vile, and unmanly disposition.

Secondly, because the right of bearing the person of them all, is given to him they make sovereign, by covenant only of one to another, and not of him to any of them; there can happen no breach of covenant on the part of the sovereign; and consequently none of his subjects, by any pretence of forfeiture, can be freed from his subjection. That he which is made sovereign maketh no covenant with his subjects beforehand, is manifest; because either he must make it with the whole multitude, as one party to the covenant; or he must make a several covenant with every man. With the whole, as one party, it is impossible; because as yet they are not one person: and if he make so many several covenants as there be men, those covenants after he hath the sovereignty are void; because what act soever can be pretended by any one of them for breach thereof, is the act both of himself, and of all the rest, because done in the person, and by the right of every one of them in particular. Besides, if any one, or more of them, pretend a breach of the covenant made by the sovereign at his institution; and others, or one other of his subjects, or himself alone, pretend there was no such breach, there is in this case, no judge to decide the controversy; it returns therefore to the sword again; and every man recovereth the right of protecting himself by his own strength, contrary to the design they had in the institution. It is therefore in vain to grant sovereignty by way of proceeding covenant. The opinion that any monarch receiveth his power by covenant, that is to say, on condition, proceedeth from want of understanding this easy truth, that covenants being but words and breath, have no force to oblige, contain, constrain, or protect any man, what it has from the public sword; that is, from the united hands of that man, or assembly of men that hath the sovereignty, and whose actions are avouched by them all, and performed by the strength of them all, in him united. But when an assembly of men is made sovereign; then no man imagineth any such covenant to have passed in the institution; for no man is so dull as to say, for example, the people of Rome made a covenant with the Romans, to hold the sovereignty on such and such conditions; which not performed, the Romans might lawfully depose the Roman people. That men see not the reason to be alike in a monarchy, and in a popular government, proceedeth from the ambition of some, that are kinder to the government of an assembly, whereof they may hope to participate, than of monarchy, which they despair to enjoy.

Thirdly, because the major part hath by consenting voices declared a sovereign; he that dissented must now consent with the rest; that is, be contented to avow all the actions he shall do, or else justly be destroyed by the rest. For if he voluntarily entered into the congregation of them that were assembled, he sufficiently declared thereby his will, and therefore tacitly convenanted, to stand to what the major part should ordain: and therefore if he refuse to stand thereto, or make protestation against any of their decrees, he does contrary to his covenant, and therefore unjustly. And whether he be of the congregation or not; and whether his consent be asked, or not, he must either submit to their decrees, or be left in the condition of war he was in before; wherein he might without injustice be destroyed by any man whatsoever. . . . .

Property and Government

John Locke

John Locke (1632–1706), first of the British empiricists, is best known for his associationist psychology, his attack on the theory of innate ideas, and for his political philosophy.

Of the State of Nature

To understand political power right, and derive it from its original, we must consider what state all men are naturally in, and that is a state of perfect freedom to order their actions and dispose of their possessions and persons as they think fit, within the bounds of the law of nature, without asking leave or depending upon the will of any other man.

A state also of equality, wherein all the power and jurisdiction is reciprocal, no one having more than another; there being nothing more evident than that creatures of the same species and rank, promiscuously born to all the same advantages of nature and the use of the same faculties, should also be equal one amongst another without subordination or subjection; unless the lord and master of them all should, by any manifest declaration of his will,

From John Locke, *Second Treatise of Civil Government*, Chapters 2, 3, 5, 8, 19.

set one above another, and confer on him by an evident and clear appointment an undoubted right to dominion and sovereignty. . . .

But though this be a state of liberty, yet it is not a state of license; though man in that state have an uncontrollable liberty to dispose of his persons or possessions, yet he has not liberty to destroy himself, or so much as any creature in his possession, but where some nobler use than its bare preservation calls for it. The state of nature has a law of nature to govern it which obliges every one; and reason, which is that law, teaches all mankind who will but consult it that, being all equal and independent, no one ought to harm another in his life, health, liberty, or possessions; for men being all the workmanship of one omnipotent and infinitely wise Maker—all the servants of one sovereign master, sent into the world by his order, and about his business—they are his property whose workmanship they are, made to last during his, not one another's pleasure; and being furnished with like faculties, sharing all in one community of nature, there cannot be supposed any such subordination among us that may authorize us to destroy one another, as if we were made for one another's uses as the inferior ranks of creatures are for ours. Every one as he is bound to preserve himself and not to quit his station willfully, so by the like reason, when his own preservation comes not in competition, ought he, as much as he can, to preserve the rest of mankind, and may not, unless it be to do justice to an offender, take away or impair the life, or what tends to the preservation of life: the liberty, health, limb, or goods of another.

And that all men may be restrained from invading others' rights and from doing hurt to one another, and the law of nature be observed which willeth the peace and preservation of all mankind, the execution of the law of nature is, in that state, put into every man's hands, whereby everyone has a right to punish the transgressors of that law to such a degree as may hinder its violation; for the law of nature would, as all other laws that concern men in this world, be in vain, if there were nobody that in the state of nature had a power to execute that law and thereby preserve the innocent and restrain offenders. And if any one in the state of nature may punish another for any evil he has done, every one may do so; for in that state of perfect equality where naturally there is no superiority or jurisdiction of one over another, what any may do in prosecution of that law, everyone must needs have a right to do. . . .

And here we have the plain difference between the state of nature and the state of war which, however, some men have confounded, are as far distant as a state of peace, good-will, mutual assistance, and preservation, and a state of enmity, malice, violence, and mutual destruction are one from another. Men living together and according to reason, without a common superior on earth with authority to judge between them, is properly the state of nature. But force, or a declared design of force, upon the person of another, where there is no common superior on earth to appeal to for relief, is the state of war; and it is the want of such an appeal gives a man the right of war even against an aggressor, though he be in society and a fellow subject. Thus a thief, whom I cannot harm but by an appeal to the law for having stolen all that I am worth, I may kill when he sets on me to rob me but of my horse or coat; because the law, which was made for my preservation, where it cannot interpose to secure my life from present force, which, if lost, is capable of no reparation, permits me my own defence and the right of war, a liberty to kill the aggressor, because the aggressor allows not time to appeal to our common judge, nor the decision of the law, for remedy in a case where the mischief may be irreparable. Want of a common judge with authority puts all men in a state of nature; force without right upon a man's person makes a state of war both where there is, and is not, a common judge. . . .

To avoid this state of war—wherein there is no appeal but to heaven, and wherein even the least difference is apt to end in war, where there is no authority to decide between the contenders—is one great reason of men's putting themselves into society and quitting the state of nature; for where there is an authority, a power on earth from which relief can be had by appeal, there the continuance of the state of war is excluded, and the controversy is decided by that power. . . .

Of Property

God, who hath given the world to men in common, hath also given them reason to make use of it to the best advantage of life and convenience. The earth and all that is therein is given to men for the support and comfort of their being. And though all the fruits it naturally produces and beasts it feeds belong to mankind in common, as they are produced by the spontaneous hand of nature; and nobody has originally a private dominion exclusive of the rest of mankind in any of them, as they are thus in their natural state; yet, being given for the use of men, there must of necessity be a means to appropriate them some way or other before they can be of any use or at all beneficial to any particular man. The fruit or venison which nourishes the wild Indian, must be his, and so his, that is, a part of him, that another can no longer have any right to it before it can do him any good for the support of his life.

Though the earth and all inferior creatures be common to all men, yet every man has a property in his own person; this nobody has any right to but himself. The labor of his body and the work of his hands, we may say, are properly his. Whatsoever then he removes out of the state that nature hath provided and left it in, he hath mixed his labor with, and joined to it something that is his own, and thereby makes it his property. It being by him removed from the common state nature hath placed it in, it hath by this labor something annexed to it that excludes the common right of other men. For this labor being the unquestionable property of the laborer, no man but he can have a right to what that is once joined to, at least where there is enough and as good left in common for others.

He that is nourished by the acorns he picked up under an oak, or the apples he gathered from the trees in the wood, has certainly appropriated them to himself. Nobody can deny but the nourishment is his. I ask, then, when did they begin to be his? When he digested? or when he ate? or when he boiled? or when he brought them home? or when he picked them up? And it is plain, if the first gathering made them not his, nothing else could. That labor put a distinction between them and common; that added something to them more than nature, the common mother of all, had done; and so they became his private right. . . .

It will perhaps be objected to this that "if gathering the acorns, or other fruits of the earth, and so on, makes a right to them, then any one may engross as much as he will." To which I answer: not so. The same law of nature that does by this means give us property does also bound that property too. "God has given us all things richly" (1 Tim. vi. 17), is the voice of reason confirmed by inspiration. But how far has he given it to us? To enjoy. As much as any one can make use of to any advantage of life before it spoils, so much he may by his labor fix a property in; whatever is beyond this is more than his share, and belongs to others. Nothing was made by God for man to spoil or destroy. And thus, considering the plenty of natural provisions there was a long time in the world, and the few spenders, and to how small a part of that provision the industry of one man could extend itself and engross it to the prejudice of others, especially keeping within the bounds set by reason of what might serve for his use, there could be then little room for quarrels or contentions about property so established. . . .

God gave the world to men in common; but since he gave it them for their benefit and the greatest conveniences of life they were capable to draw from it, it cannot be supposed he meant it should always remain common and uncultivated. He gave it to the use of the industrious and rational—and labor was to be his title to it—not to the fancy or covetousness of the quarrelsome and contentious. He that had as good left for his improvement as was already taken up needed not complain, ought not to meddle with what was already improved by another's labor; if he did, it is plain he desired the benefit of another's pains which he had no right to, and not the ground which God had given him in common with others to labor on, and whereof there was as good left as that already possessed, and more than he knew what to do with, or his industry could reach to.

Of the Beginning
of Political Societies

Men being, as has been said, by nature all free, equal and independent, no one can be put out of this estate and subjected to the political power of another without his own consent. The only way whereby any one divests himself of his natural liberty, and puts on the bonds of civil society, is by agreeing with other men to join and unite into a community for their comfortable, safe, and peaceable living one amongst another, in a secure enjoyment of their properties and a greater security against any that are not of it. This any number of men may do, because it injures not the freedom of the rest; they are left as they were in the liberty of the state of nature. When any number of men have so consented to make one community or government, they are thereby presently incorporated and make one body politic wherein the majority have a right to act and conclude the rest.

For when any number of men have, by the consent of every

individual, made a community, they have thereby made that community one body, with a power to act as one body, which is only by the will and determination of the majority; for that which acts any community, being only the consent of the individuals of it, and it being necessary to that which is one body to move one way, it is necessary the body should move that way whither the greater force carries it, which is the consent of the majority; or else it is impossible it should act or continue one body, one community, which the consent of every individual that united into it agreed that it should; and so every one is bound by that consent to be concluded by the majority. And therefore we see that in assemblies impowered to act by positive laws, where no number is set by that positive law which impowers them, the act of the majority passes for the act of the whole, and, of course, determines, as having by the law of nature and reason the power of the whole.

And thus every man by consenting with others to make one body politic under one government, puts himself under an obligation to every one of that society to submit to the determination of the majority, and to be concluded by it; or else this original compact, whereby he with others incorporates into one society, would signify nothing, and be no compact, if he be left free and under no other ties than he was in before in the state of nature. For what appearance would there be of any compact? What new engagement if he were no farther tied by any decrees of the society than he himself thought fit and did actually consent to? This would be still as great a liberty as he himself had before his compact, or any one else in the state of nature hath who may submit himself and consent to any acts of it if he thinks fit.

For if the consent of the majority shall not in reason be received as the act of the whole and concluded every individual, nothing but the consent of every individual can make anything to be the act of the whole; but such a consent is next to impossible ever to be had if we consider the infirmities of health and avocations of business which in a number though much less than that of a commonwealth, will necessarily keep many away from the public assembly. To which, if we add the variety of opinions and contrariety of interests which unavoidably happen in all collections of men, the coming into society upon such terms would be only like Cato's coming into the theatre only to go out again. Such a constitution as this would make the mighty leviathan of a shorter duration than the feeblest creatures, and not let it outlast the day it was born in; which cannot be supposed till we can think that rational creatures should desire and constitute societies only to be dissolved; for where the majority cannot conclude the rest, there they cannot act as one body, and consequently will be immediately dissolved again.

Whosoever, therefore, out of a state of nature unite into a community must be understood to give up all the power necessary to the ends for which they unite into society to the majority of the community, unless they expressly agreed in any number greater than the majority. And this is done by barely agreeing to unite into one political society, which is all the compact that is, or needs be, between the individuals that enter into or make up a commonwealth. And thus that which begins and actually constitutes any political society is nothing but the consent of any number of freemen capable of a majority to unite and incorporate into such a society. And this is that, and that only, which did or could give beginning to any lawful government in the world.

Of the Ends of Political Society and Government

If man in the state of nature be so free, as has been said, if he be absolute lord of his own person and possessions, equal to the greatest, and subject to nobody, why will he part with his freedom, why will he give up his empire and subject himself to the dominion and control of any other power? To which it is obvious to answer that though in the state of nature he hath such a right, yet the enjoyment of it is very uncertain and constantly exposed to the invasion of others; for all being kings as much as he, every man his equal, and the greater part no strict observers of equity and justice, the enjoyment of the property he has in this state is very unsafe, very insecure. This makes him willing to quit a condition which, however free, is full of fears and continual dangers; and it is not without reason that he seeks out and is willing to join in society with others who are already united, or have a mind to unite, for the mutual preservation of their liberties, lives, and estates, which I call by the general name "property."

The great and chief end, therefore, of men's uniting into commonwealths and putting themselves under government is the preservation of their property. To which in the state of nature there are many things wanting:

First, There wants an established, settled, known law, received and allowed by common consent to be the standard of right and wrong and the common measure to decide all controversies between them; for though the law of nature be plain and intelligible to all rational creatures, yet men, being biased by their interest as well as ignorant for want of studying it, are not apt to allow of it as a law binding to them in the application of it to their particular cases.

Secondly, In the state of nature there wants a known and indifferent judge with authority to determine all differences according to the established law; for everyone in that state being both judge and executioner of the law of nature, men being partial to themselves, passion and revenge is very apt to carry them too far and with too much heat in their own cases, as well as negligence and unconcernedness to make them too remiss in other men's.

Thirdly, In the state of nature, there often wants power to back and support the sentence when right, and to give it due execution. They who by any injustice offend will seldom fail, where they are able, by force, to make good their injustice; such resistance many times makes the punishment dangerous and frequently destructive to those who attempt it.

Thus mankind, notwithstanding all the privileges of the state of nature, being but in an ill condition while they remain in it, are quickly driven into society. Hence it comes to pass that we seldom find any number of men live any time together in this state. The inconveniences that they are therein exposed to by the irregular and uncertain exercise of the power every man has of punishing the transgressions of others make them take sanctuary under the established laws of government and therein seek the preservation of their property. It is this makes them so willingly give up every one his single power of punishing, to be exercised by such alone as shall be appointed to it amongst them; and by such rules as the community, or those authorized by them to that purpose, shall agree on. And in this we have the original right of both the legislative and executive power, as well as of the governments and societies themselves.

For in the state of nature, to omit the liberty he has of innocent delights, a man has two powers:

The first is to do whatsoever he thinks fit for the preservation of himself and others within the permission of the law of nature, by which law, common to them all, he and all the rest of mankind are one community, make up one society, distinct from all other creatures. And, were it not for the corruption and viciousness of degenerate men, there would be no need of any other, no necessity that men should separate from this great and natural community and by positive agreements combine into smaller and divided associations.

The other power a man has in the state of nature is the power to punish the crimes committed against that law. Both these he gives up when he joins in a private, if I may so call it, or particular political society and incorporates into any commonwealth separate from the rest of mankind.

The *first* power, namely, of doing whatsoever he thought fit for the preservation of himself and the rest of mankind, he gives up to be regulated by laws made by the society, so far forth as the preservation of himself and the rest of that society shall require; which laws of the society in many things confine the liberty he had by the law of nature.

Secondly, The power of punishing he wholly gives up, and engages his natural force—which he might before employ in the execution of the law of nature by his own single authority, as he thought fit—to assist the executive power of the society, as the law thereof shall require; for being now in a new state, wherein he is to enjoy many conveniences from the labor, assistance, and society of others in the same community as well as protection from its whole strength, he is to part also with as much of his natural liberty, in providing for himself, as the good, prosperity, and safety of the society shall require, which is not only necessary, but just, since the other members of the society do the like.

But though men when they enter into society give up the equality, liberty, and executive power they had in the state of nature into the hands of the society, to be so far disposed of by the legislative as the good of the society shall require, yet it being only with an intention in every one the better to preserve himself, his liberty and property—for no rational creature can be supposed to change his condition with an intention to be worse—the power of the society, or legislative constituted by them, can never be supposed to extend farther than the common good, but is obliged to secure every one's property by providing against those three defects above-mentioned that made the state of nature so unsafe and uneasy. And so whoever has the legislative or supreme power of any commonwealth is bound to govern by established standing laws, promulgated and known to the people, and not by extemporary decrees; by indifferent and upright judges who are to decide controversies by those laws; and to employ the force of the community at home only in the execution of such laws, or abroad to prevent or redress foreign injuries, and secure the community from inroads and invasion. And all this to be directed to no other end but the safety, peace, and public good of the people.

Of the Dissolution of Government

The reason why men enter into society is the preservation of their property; and the end why they choose and authorize a legislative is that there may be laws made and rules set as guards and fences to the properties of all the members of the society, to limit the power and moderate the dominion of every part and member of the society; for since it can never be supposed to be the will of the society that the legislative should have a power to destroy that which every one designs to secure by entering into society, and for which the people submitted themselves to legislators of their own making. Whenever the legislators endeavor to take away and destroy the property of the people, or to reduce them to slavery under arbitrary power, they put themselves into a state of war with the people who are thereupon absolved from any further obedience, and are left to the common refuge which God hath provided for all men against force and violence. Whensoever, therefore, the legislative shall transgress this fundamental rule of society, and either by ambition, fear, folly, or corruption, endeavor to grasp themselves, or put into the hands of any other, an absolute power over the lives, liberties, and estates of the people, by this breach of trust they forfeit the power the people had put into their hands for quite contrary ends, and it devolves to the people who have a right to resume their original liberty, and by the establishment of a new legislative, such as they shall think fit, provide for their own safety and security, which is the end for which they are in society. What I have said here concerning the legislative in general holds true also concerning the supreme executor, who having a double trust put in him—both to have a part in the legislative and the supreme execution of the law—acts against both when he goes about to set up his own arbitrary will as the law of the society. . . .

Here, it is likely, the common question will be made: "Who shall be judge whether the prince or legislative act contrary to their trust?" This, perhaps, ill-affected and factious men may spread amongst the people, when the prince only makes use of his due prerogative. To this I reply: The people shall be judge; for who shall be judge whether his trustee or deputy acts well and according to the trust reposed in him but he who deputes him and must, by having deputed him, have still a power to discard him when he fails in his trust? If this be reasonable in particular cases of private men, why should it be otherwise in that of the greatest moment where the welfare of millions is concerned, and also where the evil, if not prevented, is greater and the redress very difficult, dear, and dangerous?

But further, this question, "Who shall be judge?" cannot mean that there is no judge at all; for where there is no judicature on earth to decide controversies amongst men, God in heaven is Judge. He alone, it is true, is Judge of the right. But every man is judge for himself, as in all other cases, so in this, whether another hath put himself into a state of war with him, and whether he should appeal to the Supreme Judge . . .

If a controversy arise betwixt a prince and some of the people in a matter where the law is silent or doubtful, and the thing be of great consequence, I should think the proper umpire in such a case should be the body of the people; for in cases where the prince hath a trust reposed in him and is dispensed from the common ordinary rules of the law, there, if any men find themselves aggrieved and think the prince acts contrary to or beyond that trust, who so proper to judge as the body of the people—who, at first, lodged that trust in him—how far they meant it should extend? But if the prince, or whoever they be in the administration, decline that way of determination, the appeal then lies nowhere but to heaven; force between either persons who have no known superior on earth, or which permits no appeal to a judge on earth, being properly a state of war wherein the appeal lies only to heaven; and in that state the injured party must judge for himself when he will think fit to make use of that appeal and put himself upon it.

To conclude, the power that every individual gave the society when he entered into it can never revert to the individuals again as long as the society lasts, but will always remain in the community, because without this there can be no community, no commonwealth, which is contrary to the original agreement; so also when the society hath placed the legislative in any assembly of men, to continue in them and their successors with direction and authority for providing such successors, the legislative can never revert to the people whilst that government lasts, because having provided a legislative with power to continue for ever, they have given up their political power to the legislative and cannot resume it.

But if they have set limits to the duration of their legislative and made this supreme power in any person or assembly only temporary, or else when by the miscarriages of those in authority it is forfeited, upon the forfeiture, or at the determination of the time set, it reverts to the society, and the people have a right to act as supreme and continue the legislative in themselves, or erect a new form, or under the old form place it in new hands, as they think good.

Theory of Socialism

Friedrich Engels

*Friedrich Engels (1820–1895), German-born, was first an em-
ployee and later partner in his family's cotton-spinning factory in
Manchester, England. He wrote much on socialist causes and
theory, co-authored with Marx the Communist* Manifesto, *and
from Marx's notes completed the last two volumes of* Capital
after Marx's death.

The materialist conception of history starts from the proposition that the production of the means to support human life and,
next to production, the exchange of things produced, is the basis
of all social structure; that in every society that has appeared in
history, the manner in which wealth is distributed and society
divided into classes or orders is dependent upon what is produced,
how it is produced, and how the products are exchanged. From
this point of view the final causes of all social changes and political revolutions are to be sought, not in men's brains, not in man's
better insight into eternal truth and justice, but in changes in the
modes of production and exchange. They are to be sought, not in
the *philosophy*, but in the *economics* of each particular epoch. The
growing perception that existing social institutions are unreasonable and unjust, that reason has become unreason, and right
wrong, is only proof that in the modes of production and exchange
changes have silently taken place, with which the social order,
adapted to earlier economic conditions, is no longer in keeping.
From this it also follows that the means of getting rid of the incon-
gruities that have been brought to light must also be present, in a

From Friedrich Engels: *Anti-Dühring*, Part 3, Chapter 2.

more or less developed condition, within the changed modes of production themselves. These means are not to be invented by deduction from fundamental principles, but are to be discovered in the stubborn facts of the existing system of production.

What is, then, the position of modern socialism in this connection?

The present structure of society—this is now pretty generally conceded—is the creation of the ruling class of today, of the bourgeoisie. The mode of production peculiar to the bourgeoisie, known, since Marx, as the capitalist mode of production, was incompatible with the feudal system, with the privileges it conferred upon individuals, entire social ranks and local corporations, as well as with the hereditary ties of subordination which constituted the framework of its social organization. The bourgeoisie broke up the feudal system and built upon its ruins the capitalist order of society, the kingdom of free competition, of personal liberty, of equality before the law of all commodity owners, and of all the rest of the capitalist blessings. Thenceforward the capitalist mode of production could develop in freedom. Since steam, machinery and the making of machines by machinery transformed the older manufacture into modern industry, the productive forces evolved under the guidance of the bourgeoisie developed with a rapidity and in a degree unheard of before. But just as the older manufacture, in its time, and handicraft, becoming more developed under its influence, had come into collision with the feudal trammels of the guilds, so now modern industry, in its more complete development, comes into collision with the bounds within which the capitalistic mode of production holds it confined. The new productive forces have already outgrown the capitalistic mode of using them. And this conflict between productive forces and modes of production is not a conflict engendered in the mind of man, like that between original sin and divine justice. It exists, in fact, objectively, outside us, independently of the will and actions even of the men that have brought it on. Modern socialism is nothing but the reflex, in thought, of this conflict in fact; its ideal reflection in the minds, first, of the class directly suffering under it, the working class.

Now, in what does this conflict consist?

Before capitalistic production, that is, in the Middle Ages, the system of petty industry obtained generally, based upon the private property of the laborers in their means of production; in the country, the agriculture of the small peasant, freeman or serf; in the towns, the handicrafts organized in guilds. The instruments of labor—land, agricultural implements, the workshop, the tool—

were the instruments of labor of single individuals, adapted for the use of one worker, and, therefore, of necessity, small, dwarfish, circumscribed. But for this very reason they belonged, as a rule, to the producer himself. To concentrate these scattered, limited means of production, to enlarge them, to turn them into the powerful levers of production of the present day—this was precisely the historic rôle of capitalist production and of its upholder, the bourgeoisie. In Part IV of *Capital* Marx has explained in detail, how since the fifteenth century this has been historically worked out through the three phases of simple co-operation, manufacture and modern industry. But the bourgeoisie, as is also shown there, could not transform these puny means of production into mighty productive forces, without transforming them, at the same time, from means of production of the individual into *social* means of production only workable by a collectivity of men. The spinning-wheel, the hand-loom, the blacksmith's hammer were replaced by the spinning machine, the power-loom, the steam-hammer; the individual workshop, by the factory, implying the co-operation of hundreds and thousands of workmen. In like manner, production itself changed from a series of individual into a series of social acts, and the products from individual to social products. The yarn, the cloth, the metal articles that now came out of the factory were the joint product of many workers, through whose hands they had successively to pass before they were ready. No one person could say of them: "I made that; this is *my* product."

But where, in a given society, the fundamental form of production is that spontaneous division of labor which creeps in gradually and not upon any preconceived plan, there the products take on the form of *commodities*, whose mutual exchange, buying and selling, enable the individual producers to satisfy their manifold wants. And this was the case in the Middle Ages. The peasant, for example, sold to the artisan agricultural products and bought from him the products of handicraft. Into this society of individual producers, of commodity producers, the new mode of production thrust itself. In the midst of the old division of labor, grown up spontaneously and upon *no definite plan*, which had governed the whole of society, now arose division of labor upon a *definite plan*, as organized in the factory; side by side with *individual* production appeared *social* production. The products of both were sold in the same market, and, therefore, at prices at least approximately equal. But organization upon a definite plan was stronger than spontaneous division of labor. The factories working with the combined social forces of a collectivity of individuals produced their commodities far more cheaply than the individual small producers. Individual production succumbed in one department after another. Socialized production revolutionized all the old methods of production. But its revolutionary character was, at the same time, so little recognized, that it was, on the contrary, introduced as a means of increasing and developing the production of commodities. When it arose, it found ready-made, and made liberal use of, certain machinery for the production and exchange of commodities: merchants' capital, handicraft, wage labor. Socialized production thus introducing itself as a new form of the production of commodities, it was a matter of course that under it the old forms of appropriation remained in full swing, and were applied to its products as well.

In the medieval stage of evolution of the production of commodities, the question as to the owner of the product of labor could not arise. The individual producer, as a rule, had from raw material belonging to himself, and generally his own handiwork, produced it with his own tools, by the labor of his own hands or of his family. There was no need for him to appropriate the new product. It belonged wholly to him, as a matter of course. His property in the product was, therefore, based *upon his own labor*. Even where external help was used, this was, as a rule, of little importance, and very generally was compensated by something other than wages. The apprentices and journeymen of the guilds worked less for board and wages than for education, in order that they might become master craftsmen themselves.

Then came the concentration of the means of production and of the producers in large workshops and manufactories, their transformation into actual socialized means of production and socialized producers. But the socialized producers and means of production and their products were still treated, after this change, just as they had been before, i.e., as the means of production and the products of individuals. Hitherto, the owner of the instruments of labor had himself appropriated the product, because as a rule it was his own product and the assistance of others was the exception. Now the owner of the instruments of labor always appropriated to himself the product, although it was no longer *his* product but exclusively the product of the *labor of others*. Thus, the products now produced socially were not appropriated by those who had actually set in motion the means of production and actually produced the commodities, but by the *capitalists*. The means of production, and production itself, had become in essence socialized. But they were subjected to a form of appropriation which presupposes the private production of individuals, under which, therefore, everyone owns his own product and brings it to market. The mode of production is subjected to this form of appropriation, although it abolishes the conditions upon which the latter rests.[1]

This contradiction, which gives to the new mode of production its capitalistic character, *contains the germ of the whole of the social antagonisms of today*. The greater the mastery obtained by the new mode of production over all important fields of production and in all manufacturing countries, the more it reduced individual production to an insignificant residuum, *the more clearly was brought out the incompatibility of socialized production with capitalistic appropriation*.

The first capitalists found, as we have said, alongside of other forms of labor, wage labor ready-made for them in the market. But it was exceptional, complimentary, necessary, transitory wage labor. The agricultural laborer, though, upon occasion, he hired himself out by the day, had a few acres of his own land on which he could at all events live at a pinch. The guilds were so organized that the journeyman of today became the master of tomorrow. But all this changed, as soon as the means of production became socialized and concentrated in the hands of capitalists. The means of production, as well as the product of the individual producer became more and more worthless; there was nothing left for him but to turn wage worker under the capitalist. Wage labor, aforetime the exception and accessory, now became the rule and basis of all production; aforetime complementary, it now became the sole remaining function of the worker. The wage worker for a time became a wage worker for life. The number of these permanent wage workers was further enormously increased by the breaking up of the feudal system that occurred at the same time, by the disbanding of the retainers of the feudal lords, the eviction of the peasants from their homesteads, etc. The separation was made complete between the means of production concentrated in the hands of the capitalists on the one side, and the producers, possessing nothing but their labor power, on the other. *The contradiction between socialized production and capitalistic appro-*

---

[1] It is hardly necessary in this connection to point out, that, even if the form of appropriation remains the same, the *character* of the appropriation is just as much revolutionized as production is by the changes described above. It is, of course, a very different matter whether I appropriate to myself my own product or that of another. Note in passing that wage labor, which contains the whole capitalistic mode of production in embryo, is very ancient; in a sporadic, scattered form it existed for centuries alongside of slave labor. But the embryo could duly develop into the capitalistic mode of production only when the necessary historical pre-conditions had been furnished.

priation manifiested itself as the antagonism of proletariat and bourgeoisie.

We have seen that the capitalistic mode of production thrusts its way into a society of commodity producers, of individual producers, whose social bond was the exchange of their products. But every society, based upon the production of commodities, has this peculiarity: that the producers have lost control over their own social interrelations. Each man produces for himself with such means of production as he may happen to have, and for such exchange as he may require to satisfy his remaining wants. No one knows how much of his particular article is coming on the market, nor how much of it will be wanted. No one knows whether his individual product will meet an actual demand, whether he will be able to make good his cost of production or even to sell his commodity at all. Anarchy reigns in socialized production.

But the production of commodities, like every other form of production, has its peculiar inherent laws inseparable from it; and these laws work, despite anarchy, in and through anarchy. They reveal themselves in the only persistent form of social interrelations, that is, in exchange, and here they affect the individual producers as compulsory laws of competition. They are, at first, unknown to these producers themselves, and have to be discovered by them gradually and as the result of experience. They work themselves out, therefore, independently of the producers, and in antagonism to them, as inexorable natural laws of their particular form of production. The product governs the producers.

In medieval society, especially in the earlier centuries, production was essentially directed towards satisfying the wants of the individual. It satisfied, in the main, only the wants of the producer and his family. Where relations of personal dependence existed, as in the country, it also helped to satisfy the wants of the feudal lord. In all this there was, therefore, no exchange; the products, consequently, did not assume the character of commodities. The family of the peasant produced almost everything they wanted: clothes and furniture, as well as means of subsistence. Only when it began to produce more than was sufficient to supply its own wants and the payments in kind to the feudal lord, only then did it also produce commodities. This surplus, thrown into socialized exchange and offered for sale, became commodities.

The artisans of the towns, it is true, had from the first to produce for exchange. But they, also, themselves supplied the greatest part of their own individual wants. They had gardens and plots of land. They turned their cattle out into the communal forest, which, also, yielded them timber and firing. The women spun flax, wool, and so forth. Production for the purpose of exchange, production of commodities was only in its infancy. Hence, exchange, was restricted, the market narrow, the methods of production stable; there was local exclusiveness without, local unity within; the mark in the country, in the town, the guild.

But with the extension of the production of commodities, and especially with the introduction of the capitalist mode of production, the laws of commodity production, hitherto latent, came into action more openly and with greater force. The old bonds were loosened, the old exclusive limits broken through, the producers were more and more turned into independent, isolated producers of commodities. It became apparent that the production of society at large was ruled by absence of plan, by accident, by anarchy; and this anarchy grew to greater and greater height. But the chief means by aid of which the capitalist mode of production intensified this anarchy of socialized production was the exact opposite of anarchy. It was the increasing organization of production, upon a social basis, in every individual productive establishment. By this, the old, peaceful, stable condition of things was ended. Wherever this organization of production was introduced into a branch of industry, it brooked no other method of production by its side. The field of labor became a battle ground. The great geographical discoveries, and the colonization following upon them, multiplied markets and quickened the transformation of handicraft into manufacture. The war did not simply break out between the individual producers of particular localities. The local struggles begat in their turn national conflicts, the commercial wars of the seventeenth and the eighteenth centuries.

Finally, modern industry and the opening of the world market made the struggle universal, and at the same time gave it an unheard-of virulence. Advantages in natural or artificial conditions of production now decide the existence or non-existence of individual capitalists, as well as of whole industries and countries. He that falls is remorselessly cast aside. It is the Darwinian struggle of the individual for existence transferred from nature to society with intensified violence. The conditions of existence natural to the animal appear as the final term of human development. The contradiction between socialized production and capitalistic appropriation now presents itself as *an antagonism between the organization of production in the individual workshop and the anarchy of production in society generally*.

The capitalistic mode of production moves in these two forms of the antagonism immanent to it from its very origin. It is never able to get out of that "vicious circle," which Fourier had already discovered. What Fourier could not, indeed, see in this time is: that this circle is gradually narrowing; that the movement becomes more and more a spiral, and must come to an end, like the movement of the planets, by collision with the center. It is the compelling force of anarchy in the production of society at large that more and more completely turns the great majority of men into proletarians; and it is the masses of the proletariat again who will finally put an end to anarchy in production. It is the compelling force of anarchy in social production that turns the limitless perfectibility of machinery under modern industry into a compulsory law by which every individual industrial capitalist must perfect his machinery more and more, under penalty of ruin.

But the perfecting of machinery is making human labor superfluous. If the introduction and increase of machinery means the displacement of millions of manual, by a few machine workers, improvement in machinery means the displacement of more and more of the machine workers themselves. It means, in the last instance, the production of a number of available wage workers in excess of the average needs of capital, the formation of a complete industrial reserve army, as I called it in 1845,[2] available at the times when industry is working at high pressure, to be cast out upon the street when the inevitable crash comes, a constant dead weight upon the limbs of the working class in its struggle for existence with capital, a regulator for the keeping of wages down to the low level that suits the interests of capital. Thus it comes about, to quote Marx, that machinery becomes the most powerful weapon in the war of capital against the working class; that the instruments of labor constantly tear the means of subsistence out of the hands of the laborer; that the very product of the worker is turned into an instrument for his subjugation. Thus it comes about that the economizing of the instruments of labor becomes at the same time, from the outset, the most reckless waste of labor power, and robbery based upon the normal conditions under which labor functions; that machinery, "the most powerful instrument for shortening labor time, becomes the most unfailing means for placing every moment of the laborer's time and that of his family at the disposal of the capitalist for the purpose of expanding the value of his capital." (*Capital*, p. 406, New York, 1939.) Thus it comes about that overwork of some

[2] *The Condition of the Working Class in England*, Sonnenschein and Co., p. 84.

becomes the preliminary condition for the idleness of others, and that modern industry, which hunts after new consumers over the whole world, forces the consumption of the masses at home down to a starvation minimum, and in doing thus destroys its own home market. "The law that always equilibrates the relative surplus population, or industrial reserve army, to the extent and energy of accumulation, this law rivets the laborer to capital more firmly than the wedges of Vulcan did Prometheus to the rock. It establishes an accumulation of misery, corresponding with accumulation of capital. Accumulation of wealth at one pole is, therefore, at the same time, accumulation of misery, agony of toil, slavery, ignorance, brutality, mental degradation, at the opposite pole, i.e., on the side of the class that produces *its own product in the form of capital.*" (Marx, *Capital,* p. 661, New York, 1939.) And to expect any other division of the products from the capitalistic mode of production is the same as expecting the electrodes of a battery not to decompose acidulated water, not to liberate oxygen at the positive, hydrogen at the negative pole, so long as they are connected with the battery.

We have seen that the ever-increasing perfectibility of modern machinery is, by the anarchy of social production, turned into a compulsory law that forces the individual industrial capitalist always to improve his machinery, always to increase its productive force. The bare possibility of extending the field of production is transformed for him into a similar compulsory law. The enormous expansive force of modern industry, compared with which that of gases is mere child's play, appears to us now as a *necessity* for expansion, both qualitative and quantitative, that laughs at all resistance. Such resistance is offered by consumption, by sales, by the markets for the products of modern industry. But the capacity for extension, extensive and intensive, of the markets is primarily governed by quite different laws, that work much less energetically. The extension of the markets cannot keep pace with the extension of production. The collision becomes inevitable, and as this cannot produce any real solution so long as it does not break in pieces the capitalist mode of production, the collisions become periodic. Capitalist production has begotten another "vicious circle."

As a matter of fact, since 1825, when the first general crisis broke out, the whole industrial and commercial world, production and exchange among all civilized peoples and their more or less barbaric hangers-on, are thrown out of joint about once every ten years. Commerce is at a standstill, the markets are glutted, products accumulate, as multitudinous as they are unsalable, hard cash disappears, credit vanishes, factories are closed, the mass of the workers are in want of the means of subsistence, because they have produced too much of the means of subsistence; bankruptcy follows upon bankruptcy, execution upon execution. The stagnation lasts for years; productive forces and products are wasted and destroyed wholesale, until the accumulated mass of commodities finally filter off, more or less depreciated in value, until production and exchange gradually begin to move again. Little by little the pace quickens. It becomes a trot. The industrial trot breaks into a canter, the canter in turn grows into the headlong gallop of a perfect steeplechase of industry, commercial credit and speculation, which finally, after breakneck leaps, ends where it began—in the ditch of a crisis. And so over and over again. We have now, since the year 1825, gone through this five times, and at the present moment (1877) we are going through it for the sixth time. And the character of these crises is so clearly defined that Fourier hit all of them off when he described the first as *"crise pléthorique,"* a crisis from plethora.

In these crises, the contradiction between socialized production and capitalist appropriation ends in a violent explosion. The circulation of commodities is, for the time being, stopped. Money, the means of circulation, becomes a hindrance to circulation. All the laws of production and circulation of commodities are turned upside down. The economic collision has reached its apogee. *The mode of production is in rebellion against the mode of exchange.*

The fact that the socialized organization of production within the factory has developed so far that it has become incompatible with the anarchy of production in society, which exists side by side with and dominates it, is brought home to the capitalists themselves by the violent concentration of capital that occurs during crises, through the ruin of many large, and a still greater number of small, capitalists. The whole mechanism of the capitalist mode of production breaks down under the pressure of the productive forces, its own creations. It is no longer able to turn all this mass of means of production into capital. They lie fallow, and for that very reason the industrial reserve army must also lie fallow. Means of production, means of subsistence, available laborers, all the elements of production and of general wealth, are present in abundance. But "abundance becomes the source of distress and want" (Fourier), because it is the very thing that prevents the transformation of the means of production and subsistence into capital. For in capitalistic society the means of production can only function when they have undergone a preliminary transformation into capital, into the means of exploiting human labor power. The necessity of this transformation into capital of the means of production and subsistence stands like a ghost between these and the workers. It alone prevents the coming together of the material and personal levers of production; it alone forbids the means of production to function, the workers to work and live. On the one hand, therefore, the capitalistic mode of production stands convicted of its own incapacity to further direct these productive forces. On the other, these productive forces themselves, with increasing energy, press forward to the removal of the existing contradiction, to the abolition of their quality as capital, to the *practical recognition of their character as social productive forces.*

This rebellion of the productive forces, as they grow more and more powerful, against their quality as capital, this stronger and stronger command that their social character shall be recognized, forces the capitalist class itself to treat them more and more as social productive forces, so far as this is possible under capitalist conditions. The period of industrial high pressure, with its unbounded inflation of credit, not less that the crash itself, by the collapse of great capitalist establishments, tends to bring about that form of the socialism of great masses of means of production, which we meet with in the different kinds of joint-stock companies. Many of these means of production and of distribution are, from the outset, so colossal, that, like the railroads, they exclude all other forms of capitalistic exploitation. At a further stage of evolution this form also becomes insufficient. The producers on a large scale in a particular branch of industry in a particular country unite in a "trust," a union for the purpose of regulating production. They determine the total amount to be produced, parcel it out among themselves, and thus enforce the selling price fixed beforehand. But trusts of this kind, as soon as business becomes bad, are generally liable to break up, and, on this very account, compel a yet greater concentration of association. The whole of the particular industry is turned into one gigantic joint-stock company; internal competition gives place to the internal monopoly of this one company. This has happened in 1890 with the English *alkali* production, which is now, after the fusion of 48 large works, in the hands of one company, conducted upon a single plan, and with a capital of £6,000,000.

In the trusts, freedom of competition changes into its very opposite—into monopoly; and the production without any definite plan of capitalistic society capitulates to the production upon a definite plan of the invading socialistic society. Certainly this is so far still to the benefit and advantage of the capitalists. But in this case the exploitation is so palpable that it must break down. No nation will put up with production conducted by trusts, with so barefaced an exploitation of the community by a small band of dividend mongers.

In any case, with trusts or without, the official representative of capitalist society—the state—will ultimately have to[3] undertake the direction of production. This necessity of conversion into state property is felt first in the great institutions for intercourse and communication—the post-office, the telegraphs, the railways.

If the crises demonstrate the incapacity of the bourgeoisie for managing any longer modern productive forces, the transformation of the great establishments for production and distribution into joint-stock companies, trusts and state property, show how unnecessary the bourgeoisie are for that purpose. All the social functions of the capitalist are now performed by salaried employees. The capitalist has no further social function than that of pocketing dividends, tearing off coupons, and gambling on the Stock Exchange, where the different capitalists despoil one another of their capital. At first the capitalistic mode of production forces out the workers. Now it forces out the capitalists, and reduces them, just as it reduced the workers, to the ranks of the surplus population, although not immediately into those of the industrial reserve army.

But the transformation, either into joint-stock companies and trusts, or into state ownership, does not do away with the capitalistic nature of the productive forces. In the joint-stock companies

[3] I say "have to." For only when the means of production and distribution have *actually* outgrown the form of management by joint-stock companies, and when, therefore, the taking them over by the state has become *economically* inevitable, only then—even if it is the state of today that effects this—is there an economic advance, the attainment of another step preliminary to the taking over of all productive forces by society itself. But of late, since Bismarck went in for state ownership of industrial establishments, a kind of spurious socialism has arisen, degenerating, now and again, into something of flunkeyism, that without more ado declares *all* state ownership, even of the Bismarckian sort, to be socialistic. Certainly, if the taking over by the state of the tobacco industry is socialistic, then Napoleon and Metternich must be numbered among the founders of socialism. If the Belgian state, for quite ordinary political and financial reasons, itself constructed its chief railway lines; if Bismarck, not under any economic compulsion, took over for the state the chief Prussian lines, simply to be the better able to have them in hand in case of war, to bring up the railway employees as voting cattle for the government, and especially to create for himself a new source of income independent of parliamentary votes—this was, in no sense, a socialistic measure, directly or indirectly, consciously or unconsciously. Otherwise, the Royal Maritime Company, the Royal porcelain manufacture, and even the regimental tailor of the army would also be socialistic institutions, or even, as was seriously proposed by a sly dog in Frederick William III's reign, the taking over by the state of the brothels.

and trusts this is obvious. And the modern state again, is only the organization that bourgeois society takes on in order to support the external conditions of the capitalist mode of production against the encroachments, as well of the workers as of individual capitalists. The modern state, no matter what its form, is essentially a capitalist machine, the state of the capitalists, the ideal personification of the total national capital. The more it proceeds to the taking over of productive forces, the more does it actually become the national capitalist, the more citizens does it exploit. The workers remain wage workers—proletarians. The capitalist relation is not done away with. It is rather brought to a head. But, brought to a head, it topples over. State ownership of the productive forces is not the solution of the conflict, but concealed within it are the technical conditions that form the elements of that solution.

This solution can only consist in the practical recognition of the social nature of the modern forces of production, and therefore in the harmonizing of the modes of production, appropriation and exchange with the socialized character of the means of production. And this can only come about by society openly and directly taking possession of the productive forces which have outgrown all control except that of society as a whole. The social character of the means of production and of the products today reacts against the producers, periodically disrupts all production and exchange, acts only like a law of nature working blindly, forcibly, destructively. But with the taking over by society of the productive forces, the social character of the means of production and of the products will be utilized by the producers with a perfect understanding of its nature, and instead of being a source of disturbance and periodical collapse, will become the most powerful lever of production itself.

Active social forces work exactly like natural forces; blindly, forcibly, destructively, so long as we do not understand and reckon with them. But when once we understand them, when once we grasp their action, their direction, their effects, it depends only upon ourselves to subject them more and more to our own will, and by means of them to reach our own ends. And this holds quite especially of the mighty productive forces of today. As long as we obstinately refuse to understand the nature of the character of these social means of action—and this understanding goes against the grain of the capitalist mode of production and its defenders—so long these forces are at work in spite of us, in opposition to us, so long they master us, as we have shown above in detail.

But when once their nature is understood, they can, in the hands of the producers working together, be transformed from master demons into willing servants. The difference is as that between the destructive force of electricity in the lightning of the storm, and electricity under command in the telegraph and the voltaic arc; the difference between a conflagration, and fire working in the service of man. With this recognition at last of the real nature of the productive forces of today, the social anarchy of production gives place to a social regulation of production upon a definite plan, according to the needs of the community and of each individual. Then the capitalist mode of appropriation, in which the product enslaves first the producer and then the appropriator, is replaced by the mode of appropriation of the products that is based upon the nature of the modern means of production; upon the one hand, direct social appropriation, as means to the maintenance and extension of production—on the other, direct individual appropriation, as means of subsistence and of enjoyment.

Whilst the capitalist mode of production more and more completely transforms the great majority of the population into proletarians, it creates the power which, under penalty of its own destruction, is forced to accomplish this revolution. Whilst it forces on more and more the transformation of the vast means of production, already socialized, into state property, it shows itself the way to accomplishing this revolution. *The proletariat seizes political power and turns the means of production into state property.*

But, in doing this, it abolishes itself as proletariat, abolishes all class distinctions and class antagonisms, abolishes also the state as state. Society thus far, based upon class antagonisms, had need of the state. That is, of an organization of the particular class which was *pro tempore* the exploiting class, an organization for the purpose of preventing any interference from without with the existing conditions of production, and therefore, especially, for the purpose of forcibly keeping the exploited classes in the condition of oppression corresponding with the given mode of production (slavery, serfdom, wage labor). The state was the official representative of society as a whole; the gathering of it together into a visible embodiment. But it was this only in so far as it was the state of that class which itself represented, for the time being, society as a whole; in ancient times, the state of slave-owning citizens; in the Middle Ages, the feudal lords; in our own time, the bourgeoisie. When at last it becomes the real representative of the whole of society, it renders itself unnecessary. As soon as there is no longer any social class to be held in subjection; as soon as class rule and the individual struggle for existence based upon our present anarchy in production, with the collisions and excesses arising from these, are removed, nothing more remains to be repressed, and a special repressive force, a state, is no longer necessary. The first act by virtue of which the state really constitutes itself the representative of the whole of society—the taking possession of the means of production in the name of society—this is, at the same time, its last independent act as a state. State interference in social relations becomes, in one domain after another, superfluous, and then dies out of itself, the government of persons is replaced by the administration of things, and by the conduct of processes of production. The state is not "abolished." *It dies out.* This gives the measure of the value of the phrase "a free state," both as to its justifiable use at times by agitators, and as to its ultimate scientific insufficiency; and also of the demands of the so-called anarchists for the abolition of the state out of hand.

Since the historical appearance of the capitalist mode of production, the appropriation by society of all the means of production has often been dreamed of, more or less vaguely, by individuals, as well as by sects, as the ideal of the future. But it could become possible, could become a historical necessity, only when the actual conditions for its realization were there. Like every other social advance, it becomes practicable, not by men understanding that the existence of classes is in contradiction to justice, equality, etc., not by the mere willingness to abolish these classes, but by virtue of certain new economic conditions. The separation of society into an exploiting and an exploited class, a ruling and an oppressed class, was the necessary consequence of the deficient and restricted development of production in former times. So long as the total social labor only yields a produce which but slightly exceeds that barely necessary for the existence of all; so long, therefore, as labor engages all or almost all the time of the great majority of the members of society—so long, of necessity, this society is divided into classes. Side by side with the great majority, exclusively bond slaves to labor, arises a class freed from directly productive labor, which looks after the general affairs of society, the direction of labor, state business, law, science, art, and so forth. It is, therefore, the law of division of labor that lies at the basis of the division into classes. But this does not prevent this division into classes from being carried out by means of violence and robbery, trickery and fraud. It does not prevent the ruling class, once having the upper hand, from consolidating its power at the expense of the working class, from turning their social leadership into an intensified exploitation of the masses.

But if, upon this showing, division into classes has a certain historical justification, it has this only for a given period, only under given social conditions. It was based upon the insufficiency of production. It will be swept away by the complete development of modern productive forces. And, in fact, the abolition of classes in society presupposes a degree of historical evolution, at which the existence, not simply of this or that particular ruling class, but of any ruling class at all, and, therefore, the existence of class distinction itself has become an obsolete anachronism. It presupposes, therefore, the development of production carried out to a degree at which appropriation of the means of production and of the products, and, with this, of political domination, of the monopoly of culture, and of intellectual leadership by a particular class of society, has become not only superfluous, but economically, politically, intellectually a hindrance to development.

This point is now reached. Their political and intellectual bankruptcy is scarcely any longer a secret to the bourgeoisie themselves. Their economic bankruptcy recurs regularly every ten years. In every crisis, society is suffocated beneath the weight of its own productive forces and products, which it cannot use, and stands helpless, face to face with the absurd contradiction that the producers have nothing to consume, because consumers are wanting. The expansive force of the means of production bursts the bonds that the capitalist mode of production had imposed upon them. Their deliverance from these bonds is the one precondition for an unbroken, constantly accelerated development of the productive forces, and therewith for a practically unlimited increase of production itself. Nor is this all. The socialized appropriation of the means of production does away not only with the present artificial restrictions upon production, but also with the positive waste and devastation of productive forces and products that are at the present time the inevitable concomitants of production, and that reach their height in the crises. Further, it sets free for the community at large a mass of means of production and of products, by doing away with the senseless extravagance of the ruling classes of today, and their political representatives. The possibility of securing for every member of society, by means of socialized production, an existence not only fully sufficient materially, and becoming day by day more full, but an existence guaranteeing to all the free development and exercise of their physical and mental faculties—this possibility is now for the first time here, but *it is here.*

With the seizing of the means of production by society, production of commodities is done away with, and, simultaneously, the mastery of the product over the producer. Anarchy in social production is replaced by systematic definite organization. The struggle for individual existence disappears. Then for the first time, man, in a certain sense, is finally marked off from the rest of the animal kingdom, and emerges from mere animal conditions of existence into really human ones. The whole sphere of the conditions of life which environ man, and which have hitherto ruled man, now comes under the dominion and control of man, who for the first time becomes the real, conscious lord of nature, because he has now become master of his own social organization. The laws of his own social action, hitherto standing face to face with man as laws of nature foreign to and dominating him, will then be used with full understanding, and so mastered by him. Man's own social organization, hitherto confronting him as a necessity imposed by nature and history, now becomes the result of his own free action. The extraneous objective forces that have hitherto governed history pass under the control of man himself. Only from that time will man himself, more and more consciously, make his own history—only from that time will the social causes set in movement by him have, in the main and in constantly growing measure, the results intended by him. It is the ascent of man from the kingdom of necessity to the kingdom of freedom.

Let us briefly sum up our sketch of historical evolution.

Medieval society Individual production on a small scale. Means of production adapted for individual use; hence primitive, ungainly, petty, dwarfed in action. Production for immediate consumption, either of the producer himself or of his feudal lords. Only where an excess of production over this consumption occurs is such excess offered for sale, enters into exchange. Production of commodities therefore, is only in its infancy. But already it contains within itself, in embryo, *anarchy in the production of society at large.*

Capitalist revolution Transformation of industry, at first by means of simple co-operation and manufacture. Concentration of the means of production, hitherto scattered, into great workshops. As a consequence, their transformation from individual to social means of production—a transformation which does not, on the whole, affect the form of exchange. The old forms of appropriation remain in force. The capitalist appears. In his capacity as owner of the means of production, he also appropriates the products and turns them into commodities. Production has become a *social* act. Exchange and appropriation continue to be *individual* acts, the acts of individuals. *The social product is appropriated by the individual capitalist.* Fundamental contradiction, whence arise all the contradictions in which our present day society moves, and which modern industry brings to light.

1. Severance of the producer from the means of production. Condemnation of the worker to wage labor for life. *Antagonism between the proletariat and the bourgeoisie.*

2. Growing predominance and increasing effectiveness of the laws governing the production of commodities. Unbridled competition. *Contradiction between socialized organization in the individual factory and social anarchy in production as a whole.*

3. On the one hand, perfecting of machinery, made by competition compulsory for each individual manufacturer, and complemented by a constantly growing displacement of laborers. *Industrial reserve army.* On the other hand, unlimited extension of production, also compulsory under competition, for every manufacturer. On both sides, unheard of development of productive forces, excess of supply over demand, overproduction, glutting of the markets, crises every ten years, the vicious circle: excess here, of means of production and products—excess there, of laborers, without employment and without means of existence. But these two levers of production and of social well-being are unable to work together because the capitalist form of production prevents the productive forces from working and the products from circulating, unless they are first turned into capital—which their very superabundance prevents. The contradiction has grown into an absurdity. *The mode of production rises in rebellion against the form of exchange.* The bourgeoisie are convicted of incapacity further to manage their own social productive forces.

4. Partial recognition of the social character of the productive forces forced upon the capitalists themselves. Taking over of the great institutions for production and communication, first by joint-stock companies, later on by trusts, then by the state. The bourgeoisie demonstrated to be a superfluous class. All its social functions are now performed by salaried employees.

Proletarian revolution   Solution of the contradictions. The proletariat seizes the public power, and by means of this transforms the socialized means of production, slipping from the hands of the bourgeoisie, into public property. By this act, the proletariat frees the means of production from the character of capital they have thus far borne, and gives their socialized character complete freedom to work itself out. Socialized production upon a predetermined plan becomes henceforth possible. The development of production makes the existence of different classes of society thenceforth an anachronism. In proportion as anarchy in social production vanishes, the political authority of the state dies out. Man, at last the master of his own form of social organization, becomes at the same time the lord over nature, his own master—free.

To accomplish this act of universal emancipation is the historical mission of the modern proletariat. To thoroughly comprehend the historical conditions and thus the very nature of this act, to impart to the now oppressed proletarian class a full knowledge of the conditions and of the meaning of the momentous act it is called upon to accomplish, this is the task of the theoretical expression of the proletarian movement, scientific socialism.

Civil Disobedience and Protest

Sidney Hook

Sidney Hook (1902–   ), Professor of Philosophy in New York University, has moved from ardent liberalism to a more conservative position on public affairs. Professor Hook is author and editor of many books and articles on politics, ethics, and religion.

In times of moral crisis what has been accepted as commonplace truth sometimes appears questionable and problematic. We have all been nurtured in the humanistic belief that in a democracy, citizens are free to disagree with a law but that so long as it remains in force, they have a *prima facie* obligation to obey it. The belief is justified on the ground that this procedure enables us to escape the twin evils of tyranny and anarchy. Tyranny is avoided by virtue of the freedom and power of dissent to win the uncoerced consent of the community. Anarchy is avoided by reliance on due process, the recognition that there is a right way to correct a wrong, and a wrong way to secure a right. To the extent that anything is demonstrable in human affairs, we have held that democracy as a political system is not viable if members systematically refused to obey laws whose wisdom or morality they dispute.

Nonetheless, during the past decade of tension and turmoil in American life there has developed a mass phenomenon of civil disobedience even among those who profess devotion to democratic ideals and institutions. This phenomenon has assumed a character similar to a tidal wave which has not yet reached its crest. It has swept from the field of race relations to the campuses

Reprinted by permission of the author and the publisher from *The Humanist*, Vol. XXVII, Nos. 5–6 (1967), pp. 157–159, 192–193.

of some universities, subtly altering the connotation of the term "academic." It is being systematically developed as an instrument of influencing foreign policy. It is leaving its mark on popular culture. I am told it is not only a theme of comic books but the children in our more sophisticated families no longer resort to tantrums in defying parental discipline—they go limp!

More seriously, in the wake of civil disobedience there has occasionally developed *uncivil* disobedience, sometimes as a natural psychological development, and often because of the failure of law enforcement agencies especially in the South to respect and defend legitimate expressions of social protest. The line between civil and uncivil disobedience is not only an uncertain and wavering one in practice, it has become so in theory. A recent prophet of the philosophy of the absurd in recommending civil disobedience as a form of creative disorder in a democracy cited Shay's Rebellion as an illustration. This Rebellion was uncivil to the point of bloodshed. Indeed, some of the techniques of protesting American involvement in Vietnam have departed so far from traditional ways of civil disobedience as to make it likely that they are inspired by the same confusion between civil and uncivil disobedience.

All this has made focal the perennial problems of the nature and limits of the citizen's obligation to obey the law, of the relation between the authority of conscience and the authority of the state, of the rights and duties of a democratic moral man in an immoral democratic society. The classical writings on these questions have acquired a burning relevance to the political condition of man today. I propose briefly to clarify some of these problems.

To begin with I wish to stress the point that there is no problem concerning "social protest" as such in a democracy. Our Bill of Rights was adopted not only to make protest possible but to encourage it. The political logic, the very ethos of any democracy that professes to rest, no matter how indirectly, upon freely given consent *requires* that social protest be permitted—and not only permitted but *protected* from interference by those opposed to the protest, which means protected by agencies of law enforcement.

Not social protest but *illegal* social protest constitutes our problem. It raises the question: "When, if ever, is illegal protest justified in a democratic society?" It is of the first importance to bear in mind that we are raising the question as principled democrats and humanists in a democratic society. To urge that illegal social protests, motivated by exalted ideals, are sanctified in a democratic society by precedents like the Boston Tea Party, is a lapse into political illiteracy. Such actions occurred in societies in which those affected by unjust laws had no power peacefully to change them.

Further, many actions dubbed civilly disobedient by local authorities, strictly speaking, are not such at all. An action launched in violation of a local law or ordinance, and undertaken to test it, on the ground that the law itself violates state or federal law, or launched in violation of a state law in the sincerely held belief that the state law outrages the Constitution, the supreme law of the land, is not civilly disobedient. In large measure the original sympathy with which the original sit-ins were received, especially the Freedom Rides, marches, and demonstrations that flouted local Southern laws, was due to the conviction that they were constitutionally justified, in accordance with the heritage of freedom, enshrined in the Amendments, and enjoyed in other regions of the country. Practically everything the marchers did was sanctioned by the phrase of the First Amendment which upholds "the right of the people peaceably to assemble and to petition the Government for a redress of grievances." Actions of this kind may be wise or unwise, timely or untimely, but they are not civilly disobedient.

They become civilly disobedient when they are in deliberate violation of laws that have been sustained by the highest legislative and judicial bodies of the nation, e.g., income tax laws, conscription laws, laws forbidding segregation in education, and discrimination in public accommodations and employment. Another class of examples consists of illegal social protest against local and state laws that clearly do not conflict with Federal Law.

Once we grasp the proper issue, the question is asked with deceptive clarity: "Are we under an obligation in a democratic community always to obey an unjust law?" To this question Abraham Lincoln is supposed to have made the classic answer in an eloquent address on "The Perpetuation of Our Political Institution," calling for absolute and religious obedience until the unjust law is repealed.

I said that this question is asked with deceptive clarity because Lincoln, judging by his other writings and the pragmatic cast of his basic philosophy, could never have subscribed to this absolutism or meant what he seemed literally to have said. Not only are we under no moral obligation *always* to obey unjust laws, we are under no moral obligation *always* to obey a just law. One can put it more strongly: sometimes it may be necessary in the interests of the greater good to violate a just or sensible law. A man who refused to violate a sensible traffic law if it were necessary to do so to avoid a probably fatal accident would be a moral idiot. There are other values in the world besides legality or even justice, and sometimes they may be of overriding concern and weight. Everyone can imagine some situation in which the violation of some existing law is the lesser moral evil, but this does not invalidate recognition of our obligation to obey just laws.

There is a difference between disobeying a law which one approves of in general but whose application in a specific case seems wrong, and disobeying a law in protest against the injustice of the law itself. In the latter case the disobedience is open and public; in the former, not. But if the grounds of disobedience in both cases are moral considerations, there is only a difference in degree between them. The rejection, therefore, of legal absolutism or the fetishism of legality—that one is never justified in violating any law in any circumstances—is a matter of common sense.

The implications drawn from this moral commonplace by some ritualistic liberals are clearly absurd. For they have substituted for the absolutism of law something very close to the absolutism of individual conscience. Properly rejecting the view that the law, no matter how unjust, must be obeyed in all circumstances, they have taken the view that the law is to be obeyed only when the individual deems it just or when it does not outrage his conscience. Fantastic comparisons are made between those who do not act on the dictates of their conscience and those who accepted and obeyed Hitler's laws. These comparisons completely disregard the systems of law involved, the presence of alternatives of action, the differences in the behavior commanded, in degrees of complicity of guilt, in the moral costs and personal consequences of compliance, and other relevant matters.

It is commendable to recognize the primacy of morality to law but unless we recognize the centrality of intelligence to morality, we stumble with blind self-righteousness into moral disaster. Because, Kant to the contrary notwithstanding, it is not wrong sometimes to lie to save a human life; because it is not wrong sometimes to kill in defense to save many from being killed, it does not follow that the moral principles: "Do not lie!" "Do not kill!" are invalid. When more than one valid principle bears on a problem of moral experience, the very fact of their conflict means that not all of them can hold unqualifiedly. One of them must be denied. The point is that such negation or violation entails upon us the obligation of justifying it, and moral justification is a matter of reasons, not of conscience. The burden of proof rests on the person violating the rules. Normally, we don't have to justify telling the truth. We do have to justify *not* telling the truth. Similarly, with respect to the moral obligation of a democrat who breaches his political obligation to obey the laws of a democratic community, the resort to conscience is not enough. There must always be reasonable justification.

This is all the more true because just as we can, if challenged, give powerful reasons for the moral principle of truth-telling, so we can offer logically coercive grounds for the obligation of a democrat to obey the laws of a democracy. The grounds are many and they can be amplified beyond the passing mention we give here. It is a matter of fairness, of social utility, of peace, of ordered progress, of redeeming an implicit commitment.

There is one point, however, which has a particular relevance to the claims of those who counterpose to legal absolutism the absolutism of conscience. There is the empirically observable tendency for public disobedience to law to spread from those who occupy high moral ground to those who dwell on low ground, with consequent growth of disorder and insecurity.

Conscience by itself is not the measure of high or low moral ground. This is the work of reason. Where it functions properly the democratic process permits this resort to reason. If the man of conscience loses in the court of reason, why should he assume that the decision or the law is mistaken rather than the deliverances of his conscience?

The voice of conscience may sound loud and clear. But it may conflict at times not only with the law but with another man's conscience. Every conscientious objector to a law knows that at least one man's conscience is wrong, namely, the conscience of the man who asserts that *his* conscience tells him that he must not tolerate conscientious objectors. From this if he is reasonable he should conclude that when he hears the voice of conscience, he is hearing not the voice of God, but the voice of a finite, limited man in this time and in this place, and that conscience is neither a special nor an infallible organ of apprehending moral truth, that conscience without conscientiousness, conscience which does not cap the process of critical reflective morality, is likely to be prejudice masquerading as a First Principle or a Mandate from Heaven.

The mark of an enlightened democracy is, as far as is possible with its security, to respect the religious commitment of a citizen who believes, on grounds of conscience or any other ground, that his relation to God involves duties superior to those arising from any human relation. It, therefore, exempts him from his duty as a citizen to protect his country. However, the mark of the genuine conscientious objector in a democracy is to respect the democratic process. He does not use his exemption as a political weapon to coerce where he has failed to convince or persuade. Having failed to influence national policy by rational means within the law, in the political processes open to him in a free society, he cannot justifiably try to defeat that policy by resorting to obstructive techniques outside the law and still remain a democrat.

It is one thing on grounds of conscience or religion to plead exemption from the duty of serving one's country when drafted. It is quite another to adopt harassing techniques to prevent others from volunteering or responding to the call of duty. It is one thing to oppose American involvement in Vietnam by teach-ins, petitions, electoral activity. It is quite another to attempt to stop troop trains: to take possession of the premises of draft boards where policies are not made; to urge recruits to sabotage their assignments and feign illness to win discharge. The first class of actions fall within the sphere of legitimate social protest; the second class are implicitly insurrectionary since it is directed against the authority of a democratic goverment which it seeks to overthrow not by argument and discussion but by resistance—albeit passive resistance.

Nonetheless, since we have rejected legal absolutism we must face the possibility that in protest on ethical grounds individuals may refuse to obey some law which they regard as uncommonly immoral or uncommonly foolish. If they profess to be democrats, their behavior must scrupulously respect the following conditions:

First, it must be nonviolent—peaceful not only in form but in actuality. After all, the protesters are seeking to dramatize a great evil that the community allegedly has been unable to overcome because of complacency or moral weakness. Therefore, they must avoid the guilt of imposing hardship or harm on others who in the nature of the case can hardly be responsible for the situation under protest. Passive resistance should not be utilized merely as a safer or more effective strategy than active resistance of imposing their wills on others.

Secondly, resort to civil disobedience is never morally legitimate where other methods of remedying the evil complained of are available. Existing grievance procedures should be used. No grievance procedures were available to the southern Negroes. The Courts often shared the prejudices of the community and offered no relief, not even minimal protection. But such procedures *are* available in the areas of industry and education. For example, where charges against students are being heard, such procedures may result in the dismissal of the charges, not the students. Or the faculty on appeal may decide to suspend the rules rather than the students. To jump the gun to civil disobedience in bypassing these procedures is telltale evidence that those who are calling the shots are after other game than preserving the rights of students.

Thirdly, those who resort to civil disobedience are duty bound to accept the legal sanctions and punishments imposed by the laws. Attempts to evade and escape them not only involve a betrayal of the community, but erode the moral foundations of civil disobedience itself. Socrates' argument in the *Crito* is valid only on democratic premises. The rationale of the protesters is the hope that the pain and hurt and indignity they voluntarily accept will stir their fellow citizens to compassion, open their minds to second thoughts, and move them to undertake the necessary healing action. When, however, we observe the heroics of defiance being followed by the dialectics of legal evasion, we question the sincerity of the action.

Fourth, civil disobedience is unjustified if a major moral issue is not clearly at stake. Differences about negotiable details that can easily be settled with a little patience should not be fanned into a blaze of illegal opposition.

Fifth, where intelligent men of good will and character differ on large and complex moral issues, discussion and agitation are more appropriate than civilly disobedient action. Those who feel strongly about animal rights and regard the consumption of animal flesh as foods as morally evil would have a just cause for civil disobedience if *their* freedom to obtain other food was threatened. They would have no moral right to resort to similar action to prevent their fellow citizens from consuming meat. Similarly with fluoridation.

Sixth, where civil disobedience is undertaken, there must be some rhyme and reason in the time, place, and targets selected. If one is convinced, as I am not, that the Board of Education of New York City is remiss in its policy of desegregation, what is the point of dumping garbage on bridges to produce traffic jams that seriously discomfort commuters who have not the remotest connection with educational policies in New York. Such action can only obstruct the progress of desegregation in the communities of Long Island. Gandhi, who inspired the civil disobedience movement in the twentieth century, was a better tactician than many who invoke his name but ignore his teachings. When he organized his campaign of civil disobedience against the Salt Tax, he marched with his followers to the sea to make salt. He did not hold up food trains or tie up traffic.

Finally, there is such a thing as historical timing. Democrats who resort to civil disobedience must ask themselves whether the cumulative consequences of their action may in the existing climate of opinion undermine the peace and order on which the effective exercise of other human rights depend. This is a cost which one may be willing to pay but which must be taken into the reckoning.

These observations in the eyes of some defenders of the philosophy of civil disobedience are far from persuasive. They regard them as evading the political realities. The political realities, it is asserted, do not provide meaningful channels for the legitimate expression of dissent. The "Establishment" is too powerful or indifferent to be moved. Administrations are voted into office that are not bound by their election pledges. The right to form minority parties is hampered by unconstitutional voting laws. What does even "the right of the people to present petitions for the redress of grievances" amount to if it does not carry with it the right to have those petitions paid attention to, at least to have them read, if not acted upon?

No, the opposing argument runs on. Genuine progress does not come by enactment of laws, by appeals to the good will or conscience of one's fellow citizens, but only by obstructions which interfere with the functioning of the system itself, by actions whose nuisance value is so high that the Establishment finds it easier to be decent and yield to demands than to be obdurate and oppose them. The time comes, as one student leader of the civilly disobedient Berkeley students advised, "when it is necessary for you to throw your bodies upon the wheels and gears and levers and bring the machine to a grinding halt." When one objects that such obstruction, as a principle of political action, is almost sure to produce chaos, and that it is unnecessary and undesirable in a democracy, the retort is made: "Amen, if only this were a democracy, how glad we would be to stop!"

It is characteristic of those who argue this way to define the presence or absence of the democratic process by whether or not *they* get their political way, and not by the presence or absence of democratic institutional processes. The rules of the game exist to enable them to win and if they lose that's sufficient proof the game is rigged and dishonest. The sincerity with which the position is held is no evidence whatsoever of its coherence. The right to petition does not carry with it the right to be heard, if that means influence on those to whom it is addressed. What would they do if they received incompatible petitions from two different and hostile groups of petitioning citizens? The right of petition gives one a chance to persuade, and the persuasion must rest on the power of words, on the effective appeal to emotion, sympathy, reason, and logic. Petitions are weapons of criticism, and their failure does not justify appeal to other kinds of weapons.

It is quite true that some local election laws do hamper minority groups in the organization of political parties; but there is always the right of appeal to the Courts. Even if this fails there is a possibility of influencing other political parties. It is difficult, but so long as one is free to publish and speak, it can be done. If a group is unsuccessful in moving a majority by the weapons of criticism, in a democracy it may resort to peaceful measures of obstruction, provided it is willing to accept punishment for its obstructionist behavior. But these objections are usually a preface to some form of elitism or moral snobbery which is incompatible with the very grounds given in defending the right of civil disobedience on the part of democrats in a democracy.

All of the seven considerations listed above are cautionary, not categorical. We have ruled out only two positions—blind obedience to any and all laws in a democracy, and unreflective violation of laws at the behest of individual consciences. Between these two obviously unacceptable extremes, there is a spectrum of views which shade into each other. Intelligent persons can differ on their application to specific situations. These differences will reflect different assessments of the historical mood of a culture, of the proper timing of protest and acquiescence, and of what the most desirable emphasis and direction of our teaching should be in order to extend "the blessing of liberty" as we preserve "domestic tranquility."

Without essaying the role of a prophet, here is my reading of the needs of the present. It seems to me that the Civil Rights Act of 1964 and the Voting Acts of 1965 mark a watershed in the history of social and civil protest in the U.S. Upon their enforcement a great many things we hold dear depend, especially those causes in behalf of which in the last decade so many movements of social protest were launched. We must recall that it was the emasculation of the 15th Amendment in the South which kept the Southern Negro in a state of virtual peonage. The prospect of enforcement of the new civil rights legislation is a function of many factors— most notably the law-abiding behavior of the hitherto recalcitrant elements in the southern white communities. Their *uncivil*, violent disobedience has proved unavailing. We need not fear this so much as that they will adopt the strategies and techniques of the civil disobedience itself in their opposition to long-delayed and decent legislation to make the ideals of American democracy a greater reality.

On the other hand, I think the movement of civil disobedience, as distinct from legal protest, in regions of the country in which Negroes have made slow but substantial advances are not likely to make new gains commensurate with the risks. Those risks are that what is begun as civil disobedience will be perverted by extremists into civil disobedience, and alienate large numbers who have firmly supported the cause of freedom.

One of the unintended consequences of the two World Wars is that in many ways they strengthened the position of the Negroes and all other minorities in American political life. We do not need another, a third World War, to continue the process of liberation. We can do it in peace—without war and without civil war. The Civil Rights and Voting Acts of 1964 and 1965 are far in advance of the actual situation in the country where discrimination is so rife. Our present task is to bring home and reinforce popular consciousness of the fact that those who violate their provisions are violating the highest law of the land, and that their actions are outside the law. Therefore, our goal must *now* be to build up and strengthen a mood of respect for the law, for civil obedience to laws, even by those who deem them unwise or who opposed them in the past. Our hope is that those who abide by the law may learn not only to tolerate them but, in time, as their fruits develop, to accept them. To have the positive law on the side of right and justice is to have a powerful weapon that makes for voluntary compliance—but only if the *reasonableness* of the *prima facie* obligation to obey the law is recognized.

To one observer at least, that reasonableness is being more and more disregarded in this country. The current mood is one of growing indifference to and disregard of even the reasonable legalities. The headlines from New York to California tell the story. I am not referring to the crime rate which has made frightening strides, nor to the fact that some of our metropolitan centers have become dangerous jungles. I refer to a growing mood toward law generally, something comparable to the attitude toward the Volstead Act during the Prohibition era. The mood is more diffuse today. To be lawabiding in some circles is to be "a square."

In part, the community itself has been responsible for the emergence of this mood. This is especially true in those states which have failed to abolish the *unreasonable* legalities, particularly in the fields of marriage, divorce, birth control, sex behavior, therapeutic abortion, voluntary euthanasia, and other intrusions on the right of privacy. The failure to repeal foolish laws, which makes morally upright individuals legal offenders, tends to generate skepticism and indifference toward observing the reasonable legalities.

This mood must change if the promise of recent civil rights legislation is to be realized. Respect for law today can give momentum to the liberal upswing of the political and social pendulum in American life. In a democracy we cannot make an absolute of obedience to law or to anything else except "the moral obligation to be intelligent," but more than ever we must stress that dissent and opposition—the oxygen of free society—be combined with civic obedience, and that on moral grounds it express itself as legal dissent and legal opposition.

Utopia Reaffirmed

B. F. Skinner

B. F. Skinner (1904–   ) is Professor of Psychology in Harvard. The most articulate and best-known English-speaking behaviorist, he wrote Walden Two.

In *Walden Two*[1] I described an imaginary community of about a thousand people who were living a Good Life. They enjoyed a pleasant rural setting. They worked only a few hours a day—and without being compelled to do so. Their children were cared for and educated by specialists with due regard for the lives they were going to lead. Food was good and sanitation and medical care excellent. There was plenty of leisure and many ways of enjoying it. Art, music, and literature flourished, and scientific research was encouraged. And it seemed to me that life in Walden Two was not only good but feasible—within the reach of intelligent men of goodwill who would apply principles then emerging from the scientific study of human behavior. Some readers thought I was writing with tongue in cheek, but I was actually quite serious.

To my surprise, the book was violently attacked. *Life* magazine called it a "slander on some old notions of the 'good life.' . . . Such a triumph of mortmain, or the 'dead hand,' [as] has not been envisaged since the days of Sparta . . . a slur upon a name, a corruption of an impulse." In *The Quest for Utopia*[2] Negley and Patrick agreed that sooner or later "the principle of psychological

Reprinted by permission of the author and the publisher from *The Humanist*, Vol. XXVII, No. 4 (1967), pp. 120–122, 136–137.

[1] *Walden Two* (New York: The Macmillan Company, 1948).

[2] G. Negley and J. M. Patrick, *The Quest for Utopia* (New York: Schuman, 1952).

conditioning would be made the basis of the serious construction of utopia . . . ," but found they were quite unprepared for "the shocking horror of the idea when positively presented. Of all the dictatorships espoused by utopists," they continued, "this is the most profound, and incipient dictators might well find in this utopia a guide book of political practice." And Joseph Wood Krutch soon devoted a substantial part of his *The Measure of Man* to an attack on what he called my "ignoble utopia."[3] The controversy has grown more violent and more puzzling as the years pass.

There are probably many reasons for the current revival of interest in utopian speculation. I doubt that the pattern is set when, as one psychoanalyst has suggested, "in need of and in despair for the absent breast, the infant hallucinates the fulfillment and thus postpones momentarily the overwhelming panic of prolonged frustration." It is possible that for many people a utopia serves as an alternative to the kind of political dream which is still suppressed by vestiges of McCarthyism. For some it may show dissatisfaction with our international stance; an experimental community is a sort of domestic Peace Corps. Whatever the explanation, there is no doubt of a strong tendency to scrutinize our way of life, to question its justification, and to consider alternatives.

But this is also an anti-utopian age. The modern classics—Aldous Huxley's *Brave New World*[4] and George Orwell's *Nineteen Eighty Four*[5]—describe ways of life we must be sure to avoid. George Kateb has analyzed the issue in *Utopia and Its Enemies*[6]—a title obviously based on Karl Popper's *The Open Society and Its Enemies*,[7] which was itself an early skirmish in the war against utopia. The strange thing is the violence. One of Plato's characters calls his *Republic* "a city of pigs," but never before have dreams of a better world raised such a storm. Possibly one explanation is that now, for the first time, the dreams must be taken seriously. Utopias are science fiction, and we have learned that science fiction has a way of coming true.

[3] J. W. Krutch, *The Measure of Man* (Indianapolis: The Bobbs-Merrill Co., Inc., 1953).

[4] A. Huxley, *Brave New World* (Garden City, N.Y.: Doubleday & Company, Inc., 1932).

[5] G. Orwell, *Nineteen Eighty Four* (London: Secker & Warburg, 1949).

[6] G. Kateb, *Utopia and Its Enemies* (New York: The Free Press of Glencoe, Inc., 1963).

[7] K. Popper, *The Open Society and Its Enemies* (London: Routledge & Kegan Paul Ltd., 1945).

Utopian Techniques

We can take a step toward explaining why Utopia now seems within reach by looking at some classical examples. In his *Republic* and in part of other dialogues, Plato portrayed a well-managed society patterned on the Greek city-state. He suggested features which would presumably contribute to its success, but he put his faith in a wise ruler—a philosopher-king who, as philosopher, would know what to do and, as king, would be able to do it. It is an old and a not very honorable strategy: when you do not know what should be done, assume that there is someone who does. The philosopher-king was to patch up a defective governmental design as the need might arise.

There are those—among them theologians—who argue that the next great utopian vision was the Christian heaven. St. Augustine developed the theme in his *City of God*. It was certainly a good life based on the highest authority, but important details were missing. Everyone who went to heaven was to be happy, but it was not clear just why. No one, in fact, has ever portrayed a very interesting heaven. St. Augustine's mundane version set the pattern for the monastic communities of early Christianity, but it would be hard to defend it as a good life. The monastery was a transitory state to which men turned with assurance that it was to be followed by a better life in a world to come.

Plato hoped to find the good life *sub homine*, and St. Augustine sought it *sub deo*. It remained for Thomas More to propose that it might be found *sub lege*. More was a lawyer, and history had begun to show the importance of charters, constitutions, and other agreements which men might make among themselves in order to live peacefully together. The title of his book, *Utopia*, which gave the name to this kind of speculation, has an ambiguous etymology. The Greek root of Utopia denotes a place, but the prefix means either good or nonexistent—or possibly, and cynically, both. Within a century another lawyer, Francis Bacon, had extended More's appeal to reason in his fragmentary utopia, *The New Atlantis*, in which he also looked to government and law—although he suggested that scientists might be called on as advisers. (The scientific institution he described—Solomon's House—was in fact the model on which the Royal Society was soon founded.)

But was law and order the answer? Erasmus thought not. He supported More's utopian vision, but he had reservations. Reason might contribute to the good life, but it was a mistake to overlook other things. Erasmus was amused by the fact that More's name was the Latin root for "fool," and he whimsically defended his friend by writing *The Praise of Folly*. Government, he said, is all very well, but were it not for the folly of sex no one would be born, and were it not for the folly of appetite no one would survive, to be governed.

It was not long before further doubt was cast on the necessity or sufficiency of law and order. Round-the-world voyagers returning from the South Seas brought back stories of a good life which flourished without benefit of civilization on the European pattern. Men were peaceful and happy although completely ignorant of Western morals and with little or no visible government. Diderot developed the theme in his *Supplement to the Voyage of Bougainville*—for example, in the amusing scene in which a Catholic priest and a Tahitian chief discuss sexual morality. Jean-Jacques Rousseau took a stronger line: government was not only unnecessary, it was inimical to the good life. Natural man—the noble savage— was wise and good; government corrupted him. Here were the beginnings of a philosophy of anarchy which still finds a place in utopian speculation.

(The South Seas proved that natural man was not only good but self-sufficient. Governments made men dependent upon other men, but the shipwrecked sailor, aided by the abundant resources of a tropical isle, could be master of all he surveyed. A special kind of utopian writing began to take shape when Robinson Crusoe put the solitary good life to the test. Frontier America offered many opportunities to the individual *coureur de bois,* and the theme was still strong in the middle of the nineteenth century when Henry David Thoreau built his own tropical island on the shores of Walden Pond.)

Exaggerated reports of life in the South Seas led to a rash of idyllic utopias, many of them set in the tropics. And now, for the first time, such a world seemed feasible. It is true that the Greeks dreamed of Arcadia, which was a real place, and proposals to found a utopia were occasionally made (according to Gibbon, the Emperor Gallienus was on the point of offering the philosopher Plotinus a captured city so that he might try Plato's experiment when, perhaps fortunately for Plotinus, the emperor was called away on emergencies of state), but More and Bacon were not drawing blueprints; they were simply describing societies with which contemporary life might be compared. The South Seas, however, were real, and life on that pattern could therefore be taken seriously. Etienne Cabet's *Voyage en Icarie*[8] was one of the most popular of the idyllic utopias, and Cabet actually came to America in the 1850s planning to set up Icaria on the Red River in Texas. He died in St. Louis, Missouri, but a community on the Icarian principle survived for some time in the Middle West.

It was the idyllic type of utopia which Karl Marx attacked. To portray a good life was one thing, to bring it about quite another. In this sense Marx was anti-utopian, but he had his own vision, and it was not entirely unrelated to the South Sea idyll. It was possible that human happiness might be traced not so much to the absence of government as to an abundance of goods. Nature could not always be counted upon to supply what men needed to be happy in the style of the South Seas, but man would provide for himself if he were able. A Utopia hinged on economic principles.

The notion had been developing for a long time. Goods were essential to the good life, but where were they to be found? Bacon had argued that science was power, and the technology which he advocated and which began to emerge in the seventeenth century seemed a possible answer. If men were not producing the wealth they needed to be happy, it was because they did not know how. Science would come to the rescue. The great encyclopedia of Diderot and D'Alembert was to have this effect. Many recipes, formulae, and systems for the production of wealth were trade, guild, or family secrets. Publish them and men would go busily to work.

Marx thought he saw another reason why men were not producing the wealth they needed for happiness: the means of production were being sequestered by selfish people. The good life would follow when the tools of production were made available to everyone. This was the solution emphasized in nineteenth-century utopias, exemplified in England by William Morris's *News from Nowhere*[9] and in the United States by Edward Bellamy's *Looking Backward*.[10] The doctrine that the good life will follow when each has been supplied "according to his need" is scriptural: it is St. Augustine, not St. Karl. It has remained, of course, a strong utopian theme: technology is to solve all our problems by making everyone affluent. A few years ago Mr. Khrushchev announced that before long all food, clothing, and housing in Russia would be free. The good life was just round the corner.

[8] E. Cabet, *Voyage en Icarie* (Paris: Bureau du Populaire, 1848).

[9] W. Morris, *News from Nowhere* (Boston: Roberts Brothers, 1890).

[10] E. Bellamy, *Looking Backward* (Boston: Ticknor and Company, 1888).

An irritating problem survived. Given both the skills and the means, men may still not produce wealth. Nineteenth-century theorists found it necessary to appeal to a natural compulsion to work. William Morris describes a man looking for work, not to earn money but simply to express a need. When I once asked a Russian economist why men will work when all food, clothing, and housing are free, he replied with a confident smile, "For the common good," but that is by no means certain. "To each according to his need" must be balanced by "from each according to his ability"—an assignment which has so far proved to be beyond the reach of economics. And there are other kinds of goods which physical technology has not yet been able to supply. A more comprehensive behavioral science is needed.

Behavioral Utopias

Rousseau knew that natural man would not solve all his problems, and Marx knew that economic principles would not suffice, and both took other characteristics of human behavior into account. A thoroughgoing behavioral utopia, however, was to wait for the twentieth century. The two leading figures of behavioral science in this century are Freud and Pavlov. Curiously enough, no utopian novel seems to have been written on Freudian principles. Pavlov was drawn into utopian speculation by accident. In 1917 the Russians needed the principle of the conditioned reflex to support their ideology, and they made Pavlov a national hero. If men were neither productive nor happy, it was the fault of their environments, and with the help of Pavlovian principles the Russian government would change the world and thus change men. But by the early 1930s the position had become embarrassing, as Bauer has noted.[11] The government had had its chance, and Russians were not yet conspicuously productive or happy. Pavlov went out of favor, and for twenty years Russian research on conditioned reflexes was confined to physiological processes not closely related to behavior. When the Second World War restored Russia's confidence, Pavlov returned as an intellectual hero, and

[11] R. Bauer, *The New Man in Soviet Psychology* (Cambridge: Harvard University Press, 1952).

the conditioned reflex was given another chance to build the good life.

Meanwhile, Aldous Huxley had explored the utopian implications of Pavlov's work in *Brave New World*. The book is, of course, a satire, heralding the threat rather than the promise of the conditioned reflex. There is nothing really new about conditioning, and Huxley seems to have known it. When Miranda in *The Tempest* exclaims, "Oh, brave new world that has such creatures in it," she is talking about creatures washed up on the shores of her utopian island who have come from the contemporary world.[12] For Huxley the conditioned reflex was a means of determining what the citizens of his brave new world should call good. It was important, for example, that certain kinds of workers should not be distracted by literature or nature, and babies who were destined to be workers of that sort were therefore appropriately conditioned. They were put on the floor of a laboratory near a few attractive books and bouquets. As they moved toward them and touched them, they were electrically shocked or frightened by loud noises. When they tried again, the treatment was repeated. Soon they were safe: they would never again take an interest in literature or nature. Pavlov had something to say about changing what is good about the good life because he had studied responses which have to do with what one feels. The good life which Huxley portrayed (with contempt, of course) *felt* good. It is no accident that it turned to an art form called the "feelies" and to drugs which produced or changed feelings.

The good things in life have other effects which need to be considered. One is the satisfaction of needs in the simple sense of the relief of distress. We sometimes eat to escape from the pangs of hunger and take pills to allay pain, and out of compassion we feed the hungry and heal the sick. For such purposes we design a culture which provides for each "according to his need." But satisfaction is a limited objective; we are not necessarily happy because we have everything we want. The word *sated* is related to the word *sad*. Simple abundance, whether in an affluent society, a benevolent climate, or a welfare state, is not enough. When people are supplied according to their needs, *regardless of what they are doing*, they remain inactive. The abundant life is a candy-mountain

---

[12] The title of the French translation—*Le meilleur des mondes*—makes the same point. Pangloss assures Candide that it is *this world*, in spite of its diseases, earthquakes, and famines, which is the best of all possible worlds. Nor were Huxley's economics part of any world of the future; they were early Keynesian or Rooseveltian. His psychedelic drug "soma," though it anticipated other versions, was used in a manner not unlike that of alcohol on a lost weekend.

land or Cockaigne. It is the *Schlaraffenland*—the idler's land—of Hans Sachs, and idleness is the goal only of those who have been compulsively or anxiously busy. The important thing is what people are doing at the moment they receive the things which "satisfy their needs." The things called "good" strengthen any behavior which produces them.

The rewarding effects of goods have, of course, not gone unrecognized. The philosophy of hedonism asserts that men act to achieve pleasure and avoid pain, and utilitarianism applies the principle to economics, government, and religion. But philosophies are not enough. Wages, personal affection, and imprisonment are rewards and punishments, but predictions based on them frequently go awry. We may know how much a person is paid, but we cannot thereby predict how hard he will work. We may know that a child's parents are affectionate, but we still cannot tell whether the child will conform or rebel. We may know that a government is tyrannical or benevolent, but we cannot predict whether its people will submit or revolt. To explain our failures we invent other kinds of pleasures, pains, and needs— many of them quite fanciful.

The basic principle in hedonism or utilitarianism is not wrong, it is simply not precise. It is true that men work for money and affection and to avoid the whip, and that they pursue happiness and seek relief from pain. At a comparable level of analysis it is true that water boils when heated, freezes when chilled, runs downhill, and soaks into a sponge. Both sets of facts are useful and may be important in the early stages of a science, but neither remains important for very long in either an effective technology or a precise analysis.

A further step is to learn more about the kinds of consequences which serve as rewards or punishments and to create new kinds, possibly through Pavlovian conditioning. But the important thing is not the quantity or nature of pleasures and pains, or of their sources. What we need to know is exactly what a man is *doing* when he "maximizes pleasure" or "minimizes pain"—how, in other words, so-called rewards and punishments are contingent upon his behavior. This is the field of operant conditioning (not to be confused with the conditioned reflexes of Pavlov). An experimental analysis of contingencies of reinforcement has made it possible to predict and control behavior with surprising precision in a wide variety of circumstances. The facts and principles it has uncovered are obviously relevant to the design of social systems.

The curious thing is that contingencies of reinforcement have so long been overlooked. Yet this fact is perhaps only an example of the principle of operant conditioning itself. It may be that men go straight to the things which make life good simply because they are reinforced for doing so. Food, sex, security, the approval of one's fellow men, works of art, music, and literature—these are the things men want and act to get, and therefore the things they mention when they are asked to describe a world in which they would like to live. The significant fact is that *they seldom mention what they are to do to get them.* They specify a better world simply as they wish for it, dream of it, or pray for it, giving no thought to the manner of their getting it.

It may be argued that contingencies of reinforcement become less and less important as men do less and less to get the things they want. Food, shelter, and protection from predators and enemies were once secured only through long hours of exhausting and often dangerous labor. But the invention of clothing, housing, agriculture, and weapons has changed all that, and the acts of invention have been reinforced by the change. It may eventually be unnecessary to do more than push a button (an almost effortless electronic button at that) to solve such problems. That will be little more than wishing, and contingencies can then, indeed, be ignored. But that day is not yet here, nor are all contingencies so easily disposed of. Social reinforcers, for example, are particularly hard to analyze and arrange (in part just because they have been misused in solving the simpler problem; men have avoided hard or dangerous work by getting others to work for them, just as they got some of the good things in life by stealing them). And in any case, we still have to face the problem of what men will do, and enjoy doing, when it is not necessary to do anything. We are just beginning to appreciate the significance of the problem of leisure.

In throwing fresh light on the contingencies of reinforcement under which men live, the experimental analysis of operant behavior has led to a technology of behavioral management foreshadowed by the "behavioral engineering" and the "cultural engineering" of *Walden Two*. At the time the book was written (1945) these technologies were largely fanciful, but they have now been successfully realized in a number of different kinds of "communities" such as institutions for psychotics, homes for retardates, and training schools for juvenile delinquents, not to mention standard classrooms. It is true that these communities are not composed of representative samples of the population at large, but they are not too far from communities in the utopian sense.[13]

[13] Some experiments in behavioral management are reported in R. Ulrich, T. Stachnik, and J. Mabry, *Control of Human Behavior* (Glenview, Ill.: Scott, Foresman & Company, 1966).

A community may be thought of as a pilot experiment, similar to the pilot plant in industry or the pilot experiment in science, where principles are tested on a small scale to avoid the risks of size. It is no accident that utopias have usually been isolated geographically, since border problems can then be neglected, or that they have usually implied a break with tradition (symbolized in religious communities, for example, by a ritual of rebirth), since problems raised by conflicting cultures are then minimized. A community also has a special advantage over the world at large because practices can be more easily initiated there and the effects more clearly observed. Given these helpful simplifications and the demonstrated power of a behavioral technology, a successful utopia is not too hard to imagine. Why is it feared?

Liking a Way of Life

A common objection to Walden Two (and no doubt to other utopias) goes like this: "I shouldn't like to live there. I don't mind doing the things the author is at pains to save me from doing, I don't like to do some of the things I should be expected to do, and I like to do things I could not do. Granted that life there meets many traditional specifications of the Good Life and compares favorably with existing cultures, it is still a world designed to please the author, and he is bound by his own culture, not mine. He would like to live there, of course, but he must not expect me to join him."

We "like" a way of life to the extent that we are reinforced by it. We like a world in which both natural and social reinforcers are abundant and easily achieved and in which aversive stimuli are either rare or easily avoided. Unfortunately, however, it is a fact about man's genetic endowment and the world in which he lives that immediate rewards are often offset by deferred punishments, and that punishments must often be taken for the sake of deferred rewards. To maximize net gains we must do things we do not like to do and forgo things we like. A culture cannot change these facts, but it can induce us to deal with them effectively. Indeed, this is its most important function.

It is not too often sucessful. A common practice, for example, is to extract rules from the prevailing contingencies, natural or social, and to make positive and negative reinforcers contingent upon the behavior of following them. The rule-following contingencies are often unskillfully designed, and members of a culture seldom take net consequences into account. On the contrary, they resist control of this sort. They object to what they are asked to do and either drop out of the culture—as hermits, hobos, or hippies— or remain in it while challenging its principles.

Contingencies of reinforcement which maximize net gains need to be much more effectively designed. Conditioned reinforcers can be used to bridge the gap between behavior and its remoter consequences, and supplementary reinforcers can be arranged to serve until remote reinforcers can be brought into play. An important point is that effective contingencies need to be programmed. That is, they are effective only when a person has passed through a series of intermediate contingencies. Those who have reached the terminal contingencies will be productive, creative, and happy—in a word, maximally effective. The outsider confronted with the terminal contingencies for the first time may not like them or be able to imagine liking them.

The designer must take something else into account which is still more difficult to bring to bear on the individual member. Will the culture *work?* It is a question which is clarified by the concept of a community as an experiment. A community is a thing, having a life of its own. It will survive or perish, and the designer must keep that fact in mind. The problem is that survival is often furthered by behavior which is not only not reinforced but may have punishing (even lethal) consequences. Phylogenic contingencies of survival supply examples. When a member of a herd of grazing animals spots the approach of a predator and utters a warning cry, the group is more likely to escape and survive, but the member who emits the cry calls attention to himself and may perish. Ontogenic contingencies of reinforcement work in the same way: a culture induces a hero to die for his country or a martyr for his religion.

Contingencies which promote survival are also usually badly designed. Something seems to be gained if the culture can be identified with a race, nation, or religious group, but this leads to jingoistic excesses. Contrived sanctions, positive and negative, are often spurious. The result is a different kind of dropout, who objects to taking the survival of a culture as a "value." The protest sometimes takes this form: "Why should I care whether my way of life survives or contributes to the way of life of the future?" An honest answer would seem to be, "There is no good reason, but if your culture has not convinced you that there is, so much the worse for your culture." The thoughtful person may inquire further. Why should the *culture* care whether it survives? Survival for what? How do we know that a culture is evolving in the right direction? Questions of this sort show a misunderstanding of the nature of evolution, biological or cultural. The processes of mutation and selection do not require, and may not provide, any advance plan of the state toward which they lead.

A well-designed culture is a set of contingencies of reinforcement under which members behave in ways which maintain the culture, enable it to meet emergencies, and change it in such a way that it will do these things even more effectively in the future. Personal sacrifice may be a dramatic example of the conflict of interests between the group and its members, but it is the product of a bad design. Under better contingencies behavior which strengthens the culture may be highly reinforcing. A jingoistic nationalism may be an easy way of underlining the good of a group, but the survival of a culture regarded simply as a set of practices, quite apart from those who practice them, can also be made the basis for a design. (It is significant that current discussions of survival are likely to speak of competition between ways of life rather than between nations or religions.) Here again effective contingencies must be programmed, and the terminal contingencies will not necessarily be "liked" by those who confront them for the first time.

The problem, in short, is not to design a way of life which will be liked by men *as they now are* but a way of life which will be liked by those who live it. Whether those who are not part of a culture like it may have a bearing on whether they join and therefore on the promotion of a new culture and possibly on the design of early features intended to attract outsiders or prevent the defection of new members. It has no bearing on the ultimate goodness of the design. It is nevertheless in its effects on human nature—on the genetic endowment of the species—that any environment, physical or social, is to be evaluated.

The man who insists upon judging a culture in terms of whether or not he likes it is the true immoralist. Just as he refuses to follow rules designed to maximize his own net gain because they conflict with immediate gratification, so he rejects contingencies designed to strengthen the group because they conflict with his "rights as an individual." He sets himself up as a standard of human nature, implying or insisting that the culture which produced him is the only good or natural culture. He wants the world he wants and is unwilling to ask why he wants it. He is so completely the product of his own culture that he fears the influence of any other. He resists change, like the child who said: "I'm glad I don't like broccoli because if I liked it, I'd eat a lot of it, and I hate it."

Objections to a Designed Culture

Many of those who like a given way of life may still object to it if it has been deliberately designed. Suppose one of the critics of *Walden Two* were to happen upon a small isolated community where—to repeat our first paragraph—people were working only a few hours a day and without compulsion, children were being cared for and educated by specialists with due regard for the lives they were going to lead, food was good and sanitation and medical care excellent, and art, music, literature, and science flourished. Would he not exclaim, "Here is the good life!" But then let him discover that the community was the product of an explicit design, and the spectre of the designer would spoil it all. Why?

Design implies control, and there are many reasons why we fear it. The very techniques are often objectionable, for control passes first to those who have the power to treat others aversively. The state is still identified with the power to punish, some religious agencies still claim to mediate supernatural punishments, and schoolboys are still caned. This is "control through fear," and we naturally fear it. Nonaversive techniques are available to those who can use positive reinforcement—a wealthy government can reinforce the behavior it wants instead of punishing the behavior it does not want—but the end state may still show exploitation.

The archetype of a nonexploiting controller is the benevolent dictator. We suspect him because we cannot imagine why he should control benevolently. Yet in some of the special communities we have noted, the contingencies which control the designer do not conflict with those he uses in his design. In the design of a ward in a hospital for psychotics, for example, the fact that patients will make fewer demands on the staff and yet display as much dignity and happiness as their pathology permits is enough to explain the behavior of the designer. If in a home for retarded children, aversive control is minimal and happiness and dignity therefore maximal, and if some of the children can learn enough to be able to live effectively in the world at large, these effects will be among the important reinforcers of those who design such a community. If juvenile delinquents behave well in a training school and at the same time acquire skills which will permit them to lead nondelinquent lives after they leave it, the design of such a culture can be explained. In each of these communities a way of life is designed for the good of those who live it and for the good of the designer, and the two goods do not conflict. Nevertheless, technologies of this sort are often opposed just because control is being exerted.

Democracy is an effort to solve the problem by letting the people design the contingencies under which they are to live or—to put it another way—by insisting that the designer himself live under the contingencies he designs. It is reasonable to suppose that he will not use aversive techniques if he himself will be affected by them or positive techniques which lead to exploitation if he himself will be exploited. But specialization is almost inevitable (minorities readily understand how difficult it is to keep the controller and the controllee in the same skin), and specialization implies special contingencies which are still open to suspicion.

One safeguard against exploitation is to make sure that the designer never controls; he refuses to put his design into effect himself or is forbidden to do so or—better still—dies. In *Walden Two* the protagonist, Frazier, has simply abdicated. (As an additional assurance that he exerts no current control, he was given what might be called negative charisma.) But he may still be feared. A particularly subtle kind of exploitation survives. No matter how benevolent he may be, or how far from the exercise of power, the designer gets credit for the achievements of the community, and the credit is taken from those who live in it. A ruler who discovers a better way of inducing people to behave well gets credit for an orderly society, but at the expense of those who live in it, who would be more admired if they behaved well in a disorderly society. A man who designs a better way of teaching gets credit for the benefits of improved education, but at the expense of the students, who would be more admired if they learned when badly taught or not taught at all. The industrialist who designs a better way of producing goods gets credit for increased production, but at the expense of the workers, who would get more credit for being efficient and enterprising under another system. A utopia as a completely managed culture seems to work a wholesale despoliation of this sort. Its citizens are *automatically* good, wise, and productive, and we have no reason to admire them or give them credit. Some critics have gone so far as to say that they have been robbed of their very humanity. Mr. Krutch has accused me of

dehumanizing men, and C. S. Lewis entitled a book on this theme
The Abolition of Man.

We admire people and give them credit for what they do in
order to induce them to behave in admirable ways. As I have
shown elsewhere,[14] we are particularly likely to do so when no
other kind of control is available. When alternative practices are
invented, or when the world changes so that the behavior at issue
is no longer necessary, the practice of admiration is dropped. (It
is a temporary measure, the weakness of which is suggested by the
fact that we do not admire those who are obviously behaving well
simply because they have been admired for doing so.) Admiration
often supplements aversive control (we admire those who meet
their responsibilities and hence need not be punished), and it may
indeed represent an early form of an alternative practice, but it
must eventually yield to other alternatives. As we come to understand human behavior and its role in the evolution of cultures,
and practically the contingencies which induce men to design
cultures, we must dispense with the practice of giving personal
credit. But that step is disturbing for other reasons.

Man and His Destiny

The notion of personal credit is incompatible with the hypothesis that human behavior is wholly determined by genetic and environmental forces. The hypothesis is sometimes said to imply that
man is a helpless victim, but we must not overlook the extent to
which he controls the things which control him. Man is largely
responsible for the environment in which he lives. He has changed
the physical world to minimize aversive properties and maximize
positive reinforcements, and he has constructed governmental,
religious, educational, economic, and psychotherapeutic systems
which promote satisfying personal contacts and make him more
skillful, informed, productive, and happy. He is engaged in a
gigantic exercise of self-control, as the result of which he has come
to realize more and more of his genetic potential. He has reached
a very special point in that story. He is the product of an evolu-

---

[14] B. F. Skinner, "Man," *Proceedings of the American Philosophical Society,* CVIII, No. 6 (December 1964).

tionary process in which essentially accidental changes in genetic endowment have been differentially selected by accidental features of the environment, but he has now reached the point at which he can examine that process and do something about it. He can change the course of his own evolution through selective breeding, and in the not too distant future he will quite possibly change it by changing his chromosomes. The "value-judgments" which will then be demanded are beginning to attract attention.

The point is that *we have long since reached a comparable stage in the evolution of cultures.* We produce cultural "mutations" when we invent new social practices, and we change the conditions under which they are selected when we change the environments in which men live. To refuse to do either of these things is to leave further changes in our culture to accident. But accident is the tyrant really to be feared. Adventitious arrangements of both genetic and environmental variables have brought man to his present position, but we must remember that they are responsible for its faults as well as its virtues. The very misuse of personal control to which we object so violently is the product of accidents which have made the weak subject to the strong, the dull to the sharp, the well-intentioned to the selfish. We can do better than that. By accepting the fact that human behavior is controlled —by things if not by men—we take a big step forward, for we can then stop trying to avoid control and begin to look for the most effective kinds.

Whether we like it or not, survival is the value by which we shall be judged. The culture which takes its survival into account is most likely to survive. To recognize that fact is not, unfortunately, to resolve all our difficulties. It is hard to say what kinds of human behavior will prove most valuable in a future which cannot be clearly foreseen. Nor is it easy to identify the practices which will generate the kinds of behavior needed, but here at least we have made some progress. The design of behavior to specification is the very essence of a technology derived from an experimental analysis.

The authors of the classical utopian literature proposed to achieve the good life they described in ways which are now seen to be inadequate, but the value of utopian thinking must not be underestimated. In a curious way it has always taken cultural evolution into account. It has scrutinized the sources of social practices, examined their consequences, and proposed alternatives which would presumably have more desirable consequences—and all in an experimental spirit characteristic of science.

In the long run, of course, we must dispense with utopian

simplifications, for the real test of a culture is the world at large. (The anti-utopians, of course, are talking about that world too; they would scarcely be so violent about a community of a few hundred people.) And the persistent question about that test is this: Is it to be *our* culture which survives and contributes most to the culture of the future? We can point to certain reassuring features. We enjoy the advantages which flow from the very practice of changing practice; until recently we have been perhaps unique in our disposition to try new ways of doing things. We give thought to consequences. Our practice of asking whether something works or whether something else would work better is often criticized as a crude pragmatism, but it may prove to have been an important cultural mutation. We readily change practices because we are not greatly restrained by revelation or immutable decrees, and for similar reasons we are free to pursue a science of behavior. Above all, we have recognized the need for the explicit design of a way of life.

But not all signs are propitious. The contingencies of reinforcement which shape and maintain the behavior of the cultural designer are not yet very clear. Obvious economic contingencies bring yearly improvements in automobiles, for example, but there are no comparable forces at work to improve governmental and ethical practices, education, housing, or psychotherapy. The survival of the culture has not yet been brought to bear in a very effective way on those who are engaged in government in the broadest sense.

Another danger signal is anti-utopianism itself (the clarification of which may be one of the most important contributions of utopian thinking). Anti-utopian arguments are the utopian arguments of an earlier era; that is why we call them reactionary. At one stage in the evolution of a culture, for example, aversive control may be effectively centralized in a despotic government. The appropriate philosophy or literature which supports it may outlive its usefulness without losing its power and will continue to support those who oppose any change—say, to democratic practices. Something of the same sort is now happening with respect to the doctrine of individual freedom. In undermining despotic control it is important to convince the individual that the power to govern derives from him, that he can free himself of restraining forces, that he can make a unique contribution, and so on. This is done by calling him free and responsible, admiring him for meeting his responsibilities, and punishing him for failing to do so. The supporting philosophy or literature has remained effective. It is responsible for the current anti-utopianism which insists that individual freedom is the chief goal of a culture.

A scientific analysis of human behavior and of genetic and cultural evolution leads to a different position, in which the individual is not regarded as an origin or source. He does not initiate anything. Nor, of course, is it he who survives. (The doctrine of survival after death is a source of personal reinforcers appropriate only to an earlier design.) What survives are the species (Homo sapiens) and the culture. They are "above the individual" in the sense that they are responsible for him and outlive him. Nevertheless, a species has no existence apart from its members or a culture apart from the people who engage in its practices. It is only through effects on individuals that practices are selected or designed. If by "man" we mean a member of the human species with its unique genetic endowment, its human nature, then man is still the measure of all things. But it is a measure we can use effectively only if we accept it for what it is, as this is revealed in a scientific analysis rather than in some earlier conception, no matter how convincing that conception may have been made or how effective it may have proved to be in an earlier stage of the culture.

It has been argued that it was the well-governed city-state which suggested to the Greeks that the universe itself might show law and order and that in their search for the laws which governed it they laid the foundations of modern science. The problems of government have grown more difficult, and no modern state is likely to be taken as the model of a lawful system. It is possible that science may now repay its debt and restore order to human affairs.

Index

Absolutism, ethical, 353–366
Action: causes of, 153f, 156, 164, 169f; character, 191ff, 200; choice, 185–189; creative, 194; intelligent, 205ff; intentions, 342ff; justification, 202n, 209, 211; motives for, 154, 158, 169f, 340ff; passion, 204–213; reasons, 199–213; right, 331; rules, 205–213; selfish vs. altruistic, 340ff, 414; theory of, 196–213; voluntary, 340f, 413
Action theory, 196–213
Agnosticism, 278f, 289
Alienation, 259, 262
Ambiguity: fallacies of, 92, 241ff, 354f, 372ff; in natural languages, 26; of "Social group," 362f; of "Standard," 354f; truth and, 40f
Analysis, philosophical: classical, 25f; criticized, 141f, 145, 297f; informal fallacies, 91ff; as intrinsically valuable, 28f; moral concepts, 189; nature of, 24ff, 92, 133ff; ordinary language, 27f, 184f, 188f, 240ff; reductive, 26f; religion, 260f; therapeutic, 28, 137; types, 24f
Anarchy, 405, 410, 429, 447ff, 453, 467
Argument: from analogy, 305; categorical syllogism, 71ff; causal, 214; conclusions, 61; disjunctive syllogism, 86f; explanation, 106, 111; form, 67, 84, 91; formally fallacious (invalid), 71, 76, 85f, 91; inductive, 61ff, 215, 227f; inference, 61; modus ponens form, 84f; modus tollens form, 83f, 108; nature of, 61; philosophy of, 92; premises, 61; premises, suppressed, 68; reductio ad absurdum, 108; sound, 62, 84f; valid, 61f, 73–74, 77, 84f, 89, 90, 106
Aristotle, 16, 23, 37, 67, 214
Art (see also Aesthetics), 19, 26, 260
Association of ideas, 14, 17, 34
Assumptions, 8ff, 11ff, 13, 15, 20, 23f, 112
Astronomy, 18
Atheism, 278f
Attitudes, 378ff
Augustine, Saint, 466
Austin, J. L., 29, 52f, 55
Ayer, A. J., 48f, 55

Bacon, F., 12, 23, 466
Barnard, M., 265
Barth, K., 327
Behavior: abnormal, 203–207; character, 200; conditioning, 20f, 239, 296, 464–481; explanation of, 164, 197–213; Freud on, 198-213 passim; homeostasis, 208–213; Hull, 198; McDougall, 197f; motives, 199ff, 464–481; needs, 208; rule-following, 144f, 200–213; Stagner, 210–213; Thorndike's Law of effect, 212
Being, 6, 256ff, 277, 280ff
Belief (see also Assumptions), 10ff, 18, 42, 378–385
Bellamy, E., 468
Bergson, H., 265
Berkeley, G., 243f
Black, M., 29, 55, 115
Blanshard, B., 38–39
Boyle, R., 103–104, 107

Brandt, R. B., 56
Broad, C. D., 4–12 passim, 29f
Buddhism, 276

Cabet, E., 468
Campbell, C. A., 174–196
Camus, A., 274f
Capitalism, 434–452
Carnap, R., 50, 55, 329
Causes (see also Induction): of action, 169f, 201–213, 221; Aristotle on, 214; chance, 171f, 192; choice, 187f, 191ff; empiricism, 219f; as entailment, 214f, 221ff; explanation, 107, 203–213, 220f; Heisenberg, 286; Hume, 214–218, 219–221; nature of, 9ff, 214ff, 219ff, 286f; in physics, 286ff; as reasons, 223; as regular sequence, 214–218, 219–221; Sartre, 286f; Schlick, 164ff; in speculative metaphysics, 214, 278–298; of world, 279–288 passim
Certainty (see also Knowledge, necessity, logic), 3, 122–123, 247f, 286
Certification, 316
Chance, 171f, 192, 299–306
Character, 191ff, 200
Charles, J. A. C., 103, 104, 107
Choice, 157f, 185–189, 399
Citizenship, 405
Civil disobedience, 406, 453–463
Clarification: as analysis, 25f; as conceptual orientation, 146f; as explication, 114; philosophy, 132ff
Classes: calculus of, 66–78; definitions, 43f; empty or null, 68f; inference, 63f, 67–78; social, 434–452
Cohen, M. R., 95
Colors and color words, 14f, 135, 368f
Commending, 399f
Communism, 405, 434
Compact, contract (see "Social contract")
Complement, logical, 69
Concepts, 9f, 14f, 19f, 22ff, 97–98, 142ff, 144f
Conclusions (see Argument)
Conditioning, psychological, 20f, 259, 296, 464–481
Conditions: causal, 10, 13f, 107; necessary, 34f, 43, 99, 188, 204ff, 239f; sufficient, 34f, 43, 82, 99, 188, 204ff
Confirmation, 317, 329
Connectives, logical, 79–82, 89f
Connotation: logical (see also Descriptive meaning), 33, 43, 44
Conscience, 420, 432f, 456, 457f
Constants, logical (see Connectives)
Contract (see Social contract)
Contradiction (see also Inconsistency): assertion, 308f, 378f; defined, 14f, 68; disagreement, 378f, 457; inference, 58, 60f, 68, 308f; logical possibility, 36; meaning, 308f; negation, 308f; self-contradiction, 27, 33, 59, 249, 404, 413
Contraposition, 70f
Conversion, logical, 70f
Copleston, F. C., 11, 254, 278–298

Cosmological argument (*see* God, existence proofs)
Creation, 194
Crombie, I., 316
Cultural relativism (*see* Relativism)

Danto, A. C., 29, 56, 115
Darwin, C., 121, 196, 344, 440
Death, 35, 110
Deduction (*see also* Logic), 60, 64f, 107f
Definition: connotative, 34f, 43f; color words, 14f, 135, 368f; denotative, 44f; descriptive or analytic, 19, 25, 240ff; genus and difference, 43f, 47, 63; of "good," 367ff, 388; *ignoratio elenchi*, 241ff; inference, 63, 66f; nature of, 19, 43, 368f, 388, 403; ostensive, 135f; "persuasive," 398; rules of, 45f; stipulative, 26f, 240ff
De Kruif, P., 101
Democracy, 422–433, 453–463, 477
Democritus, 121
Demonstration, 64, 102, 316 (*see also* Proof, Verification, Certification)
Denotation, 44f
Descartes, R., 126
Descriptions: and science, 100; theory of logical, 49f, 282
Descriptivist fallacy, 6f, 49
Determinism: arguments for, 13, 152ff, 165ff; "hard," 150–162; libertarianism and indeterminism, 191ff; mechanism, 150–162; no proof of, 172f; "soft," 151, 163–173, 183ff
Dewey, J., 20, 39, 101f, 360
Dialectic, 132, 134, 442ff, 438f
"Dimension of Depth," 256ff, 277
Disagreement: in attitude, 378ff; in belief, 378ff; ethical, 356ff, 378–385; language, 20; philosophical, 126ff, 140f; science, 356, 382f
Discovery, general, 148f
Dissent, 420, 453–463
Dray, W., 106, 115
Dream, percepts, 244f
Drugs, 263–277, 470
Duty (*see* Moral obligation)

Ecology, 23f
Edwards, P., 215, 236–252
Egoism (*see also* Motives, altruism), 332–341, 344, 347f, 349f, 407–421
Einstein, A., 134
Emotive theory of ethics, 27f, 48f, 378ff, 387f
Empedocles, 121
Empiricism and causes, 219ff
Engels, F., 406, 434–452
Entailment: defined, 14; implication, 61, 79, 81f; theory of causality, 214f
Epistemology (*see* Knowledge)
Equality: natural, 407ff, 422f, 426, 428
Equivocation (*see* Fallacies, informal)
Erasmus, D., 467
Eschatology (*see* Immortality)
Ethics: anthropology, 357f; Christian, 360f; comparative, 358f; defined, 331, 368f; disagreement, 356ff, 378–385; explanation, 114, 164; "is-ought" distinction, 372f; metaethics, 331; normative, 380f; politics, 405, 410; re-

form, 364, 398; relativity, 353–366; right actions, 331; science, 138, 382f; skepticism, 48f, 337, 350; "social group," 362f; standards, 354f, 404; vagueness, 138
Eucharist, 272
Events, 105f, 110f
Evolution, theory of, 4, 14, 23, 121
Ewing, A. C., 214f, 219–228
Existence, 19, 68, 69, 256ff, 279ff, 282, 283f
Existentialism, 147, 260, 255, 261, 274f
Explanation, scientific: averages, 109f; covering law theory, 105f, 164, 220; deductive-nomological, 107; events, 105ff, 110; explanandum-explanans, 106f; explication, 114; historical, 109ff, 220; homeostasis and, 208–213; Hull on, 198; justification, 202n, 209, 211; in metaphysics, 283f, 297f; needs and, 208ff; "partial" or "sketch," 111f; Peters on, 197–213; philosophical, 172f; Popper on, 198; prediction, 106f; purpose in nature, 299–306; by reasons and causes, 197–213; reductionism, 99, 109, 197; retrodiction, 107; as satisfying, 98f; in social sciences, 164; statistical-probabilistic, 107ff; unique events, 110f

Fact, 37, 38, 98, 102, 103, 216ff, 222ff, 280, 372f
Faith and knowledge, 328
Fallacies, formal (*see also* Argument, valid): affirming the consequent, 85f, 92; contraposing, E or I, 71; converting A, 71, 92; defined, 67, 91, 108f; denying the antecedent, 86; philosophy, 92
Fallacies, informal: *ad populam*, 93; accident, 93; *ad hominem*, 92; of ambiguity, 92, 94, 241ff, 254f; amphiboly, 94; appeal to ignorance, 93; authority, 93; complex question, 24, 93, 99f; composition, 94, 112, 285f; defined, 91f; "descriptivist fallacy" example, 6f, 49; division, 94; equivocation, 94, 241ff, 354f; false cause, 93; genetic, 92; hasty generalization, 93; *ignoratio elenchi*, 93, 241ff; *petitio principi* (begging question), 93; *post hoc*, 93; reification, personification, 94; of relevance, 92f
Falsifiability meaning criterion (*see also* Verifiability), 10f, 27, 307ff
Falsification (*see* Verification)
Fate, 150, 162
Feigl, H., 29, 56, 115f
Feudalism, 435, 436, 439
Fichte, J. G., 130
Flew, A., 27, 56, 116, 253, 307–310
Force, use of, 405, 416, 430, 448
Fourier, C., 441, 443
Freedom, political (*see* Liberty, Rights)
Free will: causes, 13, 201–213, 221f; constraint, restraint, 158f, 168, 170, 175; creativity, 194; criticized, 178–196; D'Holbach on, 159–162; drugs, alcohol and, 168; ignorance, 160f; introspection, 194; intuitive feeling of, 160, 194ff; Kant on, 164f; libertarianism and indeterminism, 191ff; mental illness and, 168ff, 172; Nowell-Smith on, 184f; presupposes causality, 171f; reasons, 199–213; religion, 150, 153; responsibility, 153, 182f; Schlick on, 163–173, 174–177; scientific laws, 152, 154, 175;

"self," 194f; Stevenson on, 186; utopia, 464–481

Frege, G., 54f, 65

Freud, S., 20, 111, 198–213 *passim*, 271, 344f, 469

Functions, 79f, 91

Garvin, L., 332, 336–352

Geometry, 11, 88

Glaucon, 332ff

God: concept of, 9, 307, 330; defined, 279; existence, proofs, 94, 254, 278–298, 299–306; Jesus, 326ff; knowing God, 283f, 326ff; as love object, 289ff; love of, 308f; moral law, 294; Tillich on, 255–277

"Golden Rule," 412

"Good," concept of, 19, 49, 331f, 367–377, 386–404; Moore on, 367–377

Government (*see also* State, Social contract): branches, 429ff; consent, 406, 421, 426ff, 454; dissent, 406, 420f, 453–463; dissolution of, 419ff, 431ff, 447f, 452; herd instinct and, 417f; law and decree, 430; leisure, 418, 470ff; limits of, 431ff, 462f; property, 428ff; punishment, 430; revolution, 431ff; Rousseau, 467; security, purpose of, 415f, 428, 430f; use of force, 416, 430

Group, 109, 110, 362f

Happiness, 45ff, 372f, 464–481

Hare, R. M., 28, 48f, 332, 386–404

Heaven, 317ff, 466

Hedonism (*see* Happiness)

Hegel, G. W. F., 120, 130

Heidegger, M., 50, 261

Hempel, C. G., 56, 105–113, 116

Heraclitus, 120

Hick, J., 253, 311–330

History, 109, 110–113, 112f, 220

Hitler, A., 292f, 456

Hobbes, T., 37, 109, 197, 406–421

Holbach, P., Baron D', 150–162

Homeostasis, 208–213, *passim*

Hook, S., 406, 453–463

"Horseshoe," defined, 82

Hospers, J., 30, 56, 116

Hull, C., 198

Human nature: Darwin and Freud on, 344ff; egoism, 333–335; criticized, 340ff; Hobbes on, 406ff, 418; Locke on, 406; Rousseau on, 467; Wilson, J., on, 142f

Hume, D., 27, 163, 167, 214–221 *passim*

Huxley, A., 266, 268, 465, 470

Hypothesis, scientific, 7f, 101ff, 104f, 107f, 121, 300ff, 315f, 328

Idealism, metaphysical, 39

Identity, "is" of, 374f

Ideographic studies, 110f

Ideas (*see also* Assumptions, Belief, and Concepts), 14ff, 16f, 23, 31

Images, mental, 16f, 21, 101

Immortality, 315, 319, 320, 324ff, 481

Implication, 14, 61, 79ff

Induction: deduction, 58ff, 247, 249; Edwards, P., on, 215, 236–252; Ewing on, 222ff; explanation, 107; Hume on, 215–218; inductive evidence, 237, 251f; nature of, 60ff, 90f; not just "particular to general," 64f; "principle of," 103, 237, 247; "problem of," 11, 236ff, 215; Russell on, 215, 229–235; Will, F. L., on, 249; Williams, D., on, 240

Inference (*see also* Logic), 14, 46, 59, 60, 61, 66f, 68f, 88f, 91, 108

Inference rules, 88f, 91, 108

Instinct, 32f

Intelligence, 205ff

Intension, defined, 33f

Intentions, 342f

Introspection, 16, 115, 194

Intuition and free will, 195f

James, W., 30, 39, 41, 56, 272f, 275

Jesus, 326ff, 360f

Justice, 410, 413, 415, 431, 455

Justification and explanation, 202n, 209, 211

Kant, 126, 137

Kekulé, F., 101

Knowledge: belief, 18; certainty, 61ff, 122f, 247f; conditioning, 20f; faith, 328; of God, 283f, 326ff; in lower animals, 20f; of moral values, 292f; Plato on, 26; questions about, 9; theory of, 37, 114; traditional definition of, 19

Krutch, J. W., 465, 477f

Labor, 425, 436, 437, 438ff, 441, 448, 464–481

Langer, S., 134

Language: artificial and natural languages, 26f; commending, 28, 49, 388f, 399f; conventions, 19, 51; definition, 19; descriptive, 32, 50f, 392; directive use, 50f; disagreement, 20; falsification, 307ff, 314f; ideas, 14ff, 31; informative, 32, 48f, 50f, 392; as an instrument, 21ff, 31; learning of language, 16f, 21, 390; ordinary, 28f; performative use, 52f; problem solving, 20; religious, 253f, 307–330; use and mention, 18; uses, 16f, 22ff, 48ff, 308; Wittgenstein on, 19, 27, 45, 47, 49, 390; word coinage, 14f, 22

Law, scientific, 47, 102f, 120f, 191ff: of acceleration, 103; behavioral, 113, 197ff; descriptive, not prescriptive, 164ff, 175; evidence for, 124, 236; of gases, 103f; as generalizations, 103f, 107f, 175, 220, 226, 236n; of gravity, 98, 102, 105, 107, 236–252 *passim*; history, 112f; of refraction, 103f, 105f; Schlick on, 164ff; theories, 102f

Law, statutory, 407–421, 422–433, 453f, 455, 456, 462f

Laws of nature (*see* Law, scientific, Natural law, Human nature)

Leary, T., 267n

Leibniz, G. W., 26, 138, 279f

Leisure and politics, 418, 470ff

Lewis, C. I., 57, 95, 319

Lewis, C. S., 478

Liberty, political (*see also* Rights), 411, 422–433 *passim*, 464–481

Life, meaning of, 256, 275, 278f

Linguistic recommendation (*see also* Fallacies, informal), 26, 243ff

Locke, J., 16, 17, 37, 56, 406, 422–433
Logic: contradiction, 14, 68; deductive, 59ff; entailment, 14; existence, 68f, 216ff; form in, 67; grammar, 49f, 136f; ideas, 14f; inductive, 60f; knowledge, 58; language, 14ff, 136f, 387f; metaphysics, 297f; philosophy, 14ff, 136f, 281, 297f; psychology, 65, 321f; punctuation, 87; symbolic, 79–91
Logical calculi: class of predicate, 66–78; functional, 91; sentential or propositional, 79ff
Logical positivism (or Logical empiricism), 26, 27, 55, 118, 125, 174–196, 253, 378
Love and God, 289ff, 308f

Macaulay, T. B., 337
McDougall, W., 197f
MacIntyre, A., 307
Majority, 426ff
Man (see Human nature)
Marx, K., 97, 114, 120, 271, 406, 436
Material implication, 81ff
Mathematics, 65, 96, 123
Matter, 26, 121, 272
Maxwell, G., 115f
Meaning, existential, 256ff, 275, 278f
Meaning, linguistic: connotative, 33, 43f; context, 52f; definition, 19, 43f, 135, 368f; denotative, 44f; descriptive, 19, 28, 32ff, 307ff; "emotive," 27, 48f, 378, 384f; empirical meaningfulness, 307–330; evaluative, 28, 49, 390ff; falsifiability and, 307–310, 314f; grammar and, 49f, 136f; human nature, 142f; intensional, 33f; meaning units, 18; no science of, 135; of religious utterances, 307–330; of sentences, 25f, 50f, 133; speaker's, 51ff; of terms, 19f, 43f, 135f, 282ff; theories of, 16f, 24–29, 134, 307ff; truth, 22, 32ff, 53f, 133, 307–330; use, 27f, 44f, 48f, 284, 308, 368; verifiability theory, 27, 134
Metaethics, 292f, 294, 295, 331, 353ff, 356ff, 360, 365, 367–377, 378–385, 386, 387, 388
Metaphysics: causal arguments, 214, 278–288; Copleston and Russell on, 278–298 passim; essence—accident, 272; essence and existence, 283f; explanation in, 283f; logic, 297f; method in, 146; philosophy as, 5, 131; proofs of God, 278, 306; "sufficient reason" in, 283f
Metchnikoff, I. I., 101
Mill, J. S., 26, 94, 105
Mind, 205ff, 263–277, 319ff
Moore, G. E., 45, 49, 185f, 279, 331, 367–377, 387f
Moral action, 194, 179, 296
Moral obligation, 294–298, 372f, 454ff
Moral values, 292f, 353–366, 410
More, T., 466
Morris, W., 468
Motives: for action, 154, 158, 169f, 199–203, 464–481; altruistic, 340; conscious, 199–202; Hobbes on, 409, 413; and needs, 208; prudential, 413f; selfish, 340, 413; unconscious, 202ff, 344ff
Mysticism, 263–277 passim, 288f, 290
Myths, religious

Nagel, E., 30, 56, 95, 110, 116
Naturalism, 371, 372, 374, 386ff

Natural law (Moral, political), 411ff, 416, 422, 423, 428
Necessity, 152ff, 166f, 204ff, 216f, 223ff, 280, 316
Needs, 208ff, 470
Negation, 53f, 79–81, 308f
Newton, I., 98, 102, 107, 121, 134
Nomothetic studies, 110f
Nowell-Smith, P., 56, 184f

Obligation (see Moral obligation)
Obversion, 70f
Ontological argument (see God, existence proofs)
Oppenheim, P., 106
Ortega y Gasset, J., 111

Paradoxes, 242ff, 342
Pavlov, I. P., 469ff
Peale, N. V., 261f
Peirce, C. S., 22
Perception (see also Knowledge), 243ff, 292
Performatives, 52
Person, 320ff
Peters, R. S., 197–213
Phenomenology, function of, 266
Philosophy: an activity, 2f, 136f; analytic, 8ff, 24ff, 48ff, 97, 114, 125ff, 132, 141f, 260f; certainty, 3, 122f; Copleston and Russell on, 297f; critical (see Philosophy, analytic); disagreement, 140f; as a "general science," 5f, 130f; generalization, 130f; history of, 5f, 120f, 125ff; as metaphysics, 5, 131; nature of, 1–30, 118–149; political, 405–481; progress in, 126ff, 145; as "pursuit of meaning," 132f; relation to other fields, 147f; science, 120f, 127f, 145; speculative, 4ff, 97, 114, 120ff, 130f, 214; as "synopsis" or world view, 5ff, 130f, 140f; systems of, 126f, 140f; as theory of knowledge, 131; value-oriented, 120, 131
Planning, 439–452, 464–481
Plato, 16, 26, 132, 333–335, 466
Pleasure, 45f, 210, 372, 373f, 375
Plotinus, 290, 467
Polanyi, M., 271
Popper, K., 116, 198, 200
Possibility, logical, 36, 60f
Postemotivism, 48, 386–404
Postulates, scientific, 105
Pragmatics (see also Language, use), 22
Predestination, 150
Predicate calculus (see Logical calculi)
Premises (see Argument)
Prescriptivism (see Postemotivism)
Presuppositions (see Assumptions)
Principles, 105, 404
Probability (see also Induction), 63f, 95, 107, 113, 286f
Problems (see also Questions), 20, 24f, 34, 98f, 101, 102, 136f, 142, 163f, 175, 288
Production, 434–452, 468ff
Progress, 257, 359f
Proofs (see also Demonstration, Validity, God), 88f, 316
Property, private, 410f, 415f, 424, 425f, 428ff, 434–452
Propositions (see also Statement) antecedent,

consequent, 83; calculus of, 79ff; categorical, 67f; compound, 79f; conditional, 79, 81f, 104, 314, 328; conjunctive, 79, 89f; contrafactual conditional, 82f, 104; disjunctive, 79, 81; existential, 19, 68f, 280; kinds, 79, 280; negative, 79, 80–81; quality in categorical propositions, 71; statements, sentences and, 133; terms of categorical propositions, 67; truths of reason and truths of fact, 280; universal and particular, 69

Protest, political, 431f, 433f, 453–463

Punishment, 168, 169, 180f, 430

Purpose in nature, 200f, 299–306

Pythagoreans, 121

Questions: "how," "why," 100; open, 375f; open question method, 375f; philosophical, 4, 24ff, 34, 122, 132, 136f, 142, 146, 146f, 367; religious, 255–262, 277; scientific, 4, 98, 100, 136f

Quine, W. V. O., 56, 95

Ramsey, F. P., 55

Rationalization (*see also* Egoism, Motives), 344f

Reality, 5ff, 34, 243ff

Reason, 20, 280, 411f, 429, 456ff, 465–481

Reasoning (*see also* Inference, Thinking, Logic), 65, 456ff

Reasons, 199–203, 223ff, 236f, 246, 247, 283f

Reduction, 26, 99, 109, 197, 296

Reform, 364, 398, 434–481

Relations, logic of, 91, 315

Relativism, cultural: Copleston and Russell on, 294f, 297f; defined, 355f, 366; Dewey and Westermarck on, 360; Stace on, 332, 353–366

Relativity, 19, 40ff, 353–366

Religion: analytic philosophy and, 260f; culture and, 260; drugs and, 263–277; ethics and, 279; historical, 255–262; morality and, 290–298 *passim;* nature of, 256ff, 267f, 276f; popular movements in, 261f; progress and, 257ff; religious knowledge, 298ff, 311–330; religious living, 276f; and space travel, 257f, 323; and science, 258ff; symbols in, 258f, 262; Taoism, 276; Tillich on, 255–262; and values, 279, 290–298 *passim;* Zen Buddhism, 276

Religious experience: and abnormal psychology, 271, 289, and alcohol, 266; cause of, 288–291; Copleston on, 288ff; demons, devils, etc., 289f; discipline and, 264; and drugs, 263–277; "encountering God," 326; Freud on, 271f; Huxley, J., on, 288f; James on, 272f; nature of, 256f, 267f, 276f, 288ff; and proof of God, 288–291; physiology and, 263–277; and religious living, 289ff; Russell on, 288ff; Smith, H., on, 263–277

Religious language, 253–330

Responsibility: and avoidability, 183ff; and choice, 185–189; and free will, 182–183; and heredity, 180; human *vs.* animal, 179; intuitive feeling of, 170f, 189f; moral, 164ff; and punishment, 180f; Schlick on, 169f

Revolution, 431ff, 435ff, 447ff, 450, 451f

Revelation, 326f

Right (*see* Ethics)

Rights, 405, 407–421, 422, 424, 425, 428, 429, 430, 431f, 461, 462

Romanticism, 467

Rousseau, J.-J., 467, 469

Rules, 49f, 144f, 200f

Russell, B., 7, 11, 38, 49f, 57, 64, 96, 118, 120–124, 229–235, 236–252, 254, 278–298

Ryle, G., 57, 65, 319, 330n

St. Paul, 320

Salvation, 259

Sartre, J.-P., 261, 286f

Schelling, F. W. J. von, 130

Schlick, M., 57, 118, 125–139, 150f, 163–173, 178–196 *passim,* 319

Schopenhauer, A., 139

Science: and critical (analytic) philosophy, 8ff, 13, 118f; and description, 100; and discovery, 100f; disagreement in, 356, 382f; and ethics, 138, 344ff, 357f, 372, 382ff; history of, 5f, 129f, 145f; and hypothesis, 8, 101; and man, 121f, 257ff; and method, 100f; philosophy of, 114f, 145; and religion, 257ff; and speculative philosophy, 6ff, 118, 120, 131; and theory, 102f

"Self, the" and free will, 194f

Self-interest (*see* Egoism, Motives)

Self-preservation, 408, 424, 429f, 474, 481

Sellars, W., 30, 56, 115

Sense data, 26, 243f

Sentences, 18f, 32, 50f, 79ff, 133

Shapere, D., 116

Skepticism, 123, 213–236 *passim,* 278f, 289, 337, 366

Skinner, B. F., 406, 464–481

Snell (Snellius), W., 103f, 107

Smith, Huston, 253, 263–277

Social contract, 333, 407–421, 422–433

Socialism, 405, 434–452

Society: and economics, 435; egoism, altruism and, 349f; evolution of, 434–452, 478f; and moral reform, 364; Rousseau, 467; "social group," vague and ambiguous, 362f; social planning, 439ff, 464–481; Thoreau, 406, 467; utopian, 464–481

Socrates, 129, 132, 159f, 459

Sovereignty, 406–421, 422–433

Space, 257f, 323

Speculative philosophy (*see* Philosophy)

Spencer, H., 375

Spinoza, B., 126

Stace, W., 268ff, 332, 353–366

Stagner, R., 210, 213

Standards, moral, 354f, 404

State, the civil, 405, 407–421, 422–433, 445, 446, 447ff, 456, 462, 464–481

State of nature, 407–421, 422–433

Statements: analytic, 59, 280, 308, 368; defined, 32; empirical (contingent), 33, 103, 280, 307–330 *passim,* 368; and facts, 103; Leibniz on truths of reason and truths of fact, 280; and propositions, 133; self-contradictory, 33; and sentences, 32, 133; tautologies, 308; value, 123, 368

Stevenson, C. L., 48, 186, 331f, 378–385, 398

Stipulative meanings (*see also* Linguistic recommendation), 42, 47
Strawson, P. F., 53ff, 57, 96
Subconscious (*see* Unconscious)
Substitution, rule of, 45f
Survival, 408, 424, 429f, 474, 478ff
Symbolic logic (*see* Logic)
Symbols, 26, 43, 62, 67, 72, 74f, 87, 94, 258f, 262
Syntax, and logic, 62, 94

Tarski, A., 38, 55, 57
Tautology, 27, 32, 59, 280, 308
Taylor, R., 254, 299–306
Technology, 23f, 257ff
Teleological argument (*see* God, Existence, Proof)
Terms, 19, 20ff, 66–78, 135, 282, 284, 367ff, 373f
Theology, 253, 307–330
Theoretical entities, 104f
Theory, scientific, 102f, 104, 106
Theory of knowledge (*see* Knowledge)
Thinking (*see also* Inference and Reasoning), 65
Thoreau, H. D., 406, 467
Thorndike, E. L., 212
Tillich, Paul, 253, 255–262, 277
Tools, 12, 20, 21–24, 148f, 257f
Toulmin, S., 57, 96, 103, 116
Truth: and belief, 18f, 37ff, 42; as coherence, 38f; and consensus, 288; as correspondence, 37f; indefinable, 30; and meaning, 15, 22, 32ff, 133, 136; pragmatic, 39, 41–42; redundancy, 40, 42, 53ff; "relativity" of, 40ff; as a relation, 37; semantic theory, 38, 55; theories, 36ff, 53f; and validity, 61f
Truth conditions, 34f, 55, 58, 79f, 82, 83
Truth functions, 79f
Truth tables, 82, 83, 79, 89
Type-token distinction, 21f, 32, 41, 59

Unconscious, 198–213 *passim*
Universals, 6
Universe of discourse, 72f
Urmson, J. O., 199, 395, 399
Use and mention (*see* Language)
Utilitarianism, 471f
Utopia, 406, 464–481

Vagueness, 26, 136, 138f, 362f, 395
Validity: deductive, 61f, 72f; logical, 15, 74; and logical form, 62, 67, 84, 89; of syllogisms, 72f; tested by formal proofs, 88f; tested by truth tables, 83, 88, 89f; and truth, 61f
Value terms and statements, 27f, 123, 138, 355f, 362f, 372ff, 384, 395, 398, 399
Variable, 74f, 109f
Verifiability (*see* Falsifiability), 27, 57, 133, 174–196, 311–330
Verification, 32, 33f, 36, 307–330
Vidler, A. R., 264
Vienna circle (*see also* Logical positivism), 118, 125

Waismann, F., 57
War, 409, 410, 416, 431, 423, 440, 454
Watts, A., 265
Westermarck, E., 332, 360, 365
Whitehead, A. N., 96
Williams, D., 240
Wilson, J., 57, 118f, 140–149
Wisdom, human, and philosophy, 23f, 121, 132, 139
Wisdom, J. O., 27, 30, 307
Wittgenstein, L., 19, 27, 30, 45, 47, 49, 57, 138, 390
World view (*weltanschauung*), 7, 130ff, 140f, 317f

Zaehner, R., 264, 269f
Zen Buddhism, 276